HISTORICAL DICTIONARY

The historical dictionaries present essential information on a broad range of subjects, including American and world history, art, business, cities, countries, cultures, customs, film, global conflicts, international relations, literature, music, philosophy, religion, sports, and theater. Written by experts, all contain highly informative introductory essays on the topic and detailed chronologies that, in some cases, cover vast historical time periods but still manage to heavily feature more recent events.

Brief A–Z entries describe the main people, events, politics, social issues, institutions, and policies that make the topic unique, and entries are cross-referenced for ease of browsing. Extensive bibliographies are divided into several general subject areas, providing excellent access points for students, researchers, and anyone wanting to know more. Additionally, maps, photographs, and appendixes of supplemental information aid high school and college students doing term papers or introductory research projects. In short, the historical dictionaries are the perfect starting point for anyone looking to research in these fields.

HISTORICAL DICTIONARIES OF INTERNATIONAL ORGANIZATIONS

Jon Woronoff, Series Editor

European Organizations, by Derek W. Urwin. 1994
International Tribunals, by Boleslaw Adam Boczek. 1994
Aid and Development Organizations, by Guy Arnold. 1996
United Nations Educational, Scientific and Cultural Organization (UNESCO), by Seth Spaulding and Lin Lin. 1997
Refugee and Disaster Relief Organizations, Second Edition, by Robert F. Gorman. 2000
Arab and Islamic Organizations, by Frank A. Clements. 2001
International Organizations in Sub-Saharan Africa, Second Edition, by Terry M. Mays and Mark W. DeLancey. 2002
League of Nations, by Anique H.M. van Ginneken. 2006
NATO and Other International Security Organizations, by Marco Rimanelli. 2008
International Organizations, by Michael G. Schechter. 2010
International Monetary Fund, Third Edition, by Sarah Tenney and Norman K. Humphreys. 2011
World Health Organization, Second Edition, by Kelley Lee and Jennifer Fang. 2013
Inter-American Organizations, Second Edition, by David W. Dent and Larman C. Wilson. 2014
World Bank, Second Edition, by Sarah Tenney and Anne C. Salda. 2014
International Organizations in Asia and the Pacific, Second Edition, by Derek McDougall, 2014
International Organizations in Africa and the Middle East, by Terry M. Mays, 2015
European Union, 2016 Edition, by Finn Laursen, 2015
Human Rights and Humanitarian Organizations, Third Edition, by Thomas E. Doyle, Robert F. Gorman, and Edward S. Mihalkanin, 2017
International Relations, by Peter Lamb and Fiona Robertson-Snape, 2017
United Nations, Second Edition by Jacques Fomerand. 2018
Multinational Peacekeeping, Fourth Edition, by Terry Mays. 2020
Brexit, by Finn Laursen, 2021.

Historical Dictionary of Brexit

Finn Laursen

ROWMAN & LITTLEFIELD
Lanham • Boulder • New York • London

Published by Rowman & Littlefield
An imprint of The Rowman & Littlefield Publishing Group, Inc.
4501 Forbes Boulevard, Suite 200, Lanham, Maryland 20706
www.rowman.com

6 Tinworth Street, London, SE11 5AL, United Kingdom

British Library Cataloguing in Publication Information Available

Library of Congress Cataloging-in-Publication Data

Names: Laursen, Finn, author.
Title: Historical dictionary of Brexit / Finn Laursen.
Description: Lanham : Rowman & Littlefield, [2021] | Series: Historical dictionaries of international organizations | Includes bibliographical references. | Summary: "Historical Dictionary of Brexit contains a chronology, an introduction, an extensive bibliography, and more than 300 cross-referenced entries on the terms, people, and events that shaped Brexit"—Provided by publisher.
Identifiers: LCCN 2020046503 (print) | LCCN 2020046504 (ebook) | ISBN 9781538113608 (cloth) | ISBN 9781538113615 (ebook)
Subjects: LCSH: European Union—Great Britain—Dictionaries. | Great Britain—Politics and government—2007—Dictionaries. | Great Britain—Foreign relations—1997—Dictionaries.
Classification: LCC HC240.25.G7 L375 2021 (print) | LCC HC240.25.G7 (ebook) | DDC 341.242/2094103—dc23
LC record available at https://lccn.loc.gov/2020046503
LC ebook record available at https://lccn.loc.gov/2020046504

Contents

Editor's Foreword

The story of the relations between Great Britain and the European Union is a long and complicated one. Long since it opted out of actual membership in the EU (or then European Economic Community) back in 1950, set up a rival group known as the European Free Trade Association (EFTA) in 1961, applied for EU membership in 1971 where it became an "awkward partner" for decades—although to many it seemed much longer—only to withdraw at midnight on 31 January 2020, at which time it became a fully sovereign country again, although there was much doubt within the country as to just what it would do since the membership and separation had involved so many politicians, factions, and even parties—the Conservatives, Labour, and, to make a point clearly, a Brexit party. It also sucked in all the major politicians of all parties, including Harold Macmillan, Harold Wilson, Margaret Thatcher, John Major, Boris Johnson, and countless more in the UK, as well as some abroad, like Charles de Gaulle and Jacques Delors.

Given the long saga, the cast of hundreds, thousands, or whatever, it is fairly obvious that this series would not be complete without a book on Brexit, not only to bring us up to date with what has happened but also to prepare us for what will happen. We do not know what it will be, but we can already be certain that there will be many further twists and turns and goodness knows even a second edition of this book. As a historical dictionary in our standard format, it provides a truly impressive list of acronyms and abbreviations, necessary to distinguish the players, and a rather long chronology to get a blow-by-blow view of events. But there is also the core section, namely, a dictionary with solid and extensive entries on all of the main players, the main acts of legislation, the major moves ahead, or backward, or off to the side somewhere, and much of the reasoning that went into them and seemed exceptionally important at the time until thought through again, and then altered or left as is, for now at least. And of course there is the bibliography, to fill in all the many details and help readers understand the mood of the times and the reasoning behind the various steps.

It was not easy to find a suitable author for this book, since it required a very broad view of European organizations, many of them intimately involved in the proceedings traced, insight into what was done, said, and even thought by the many players, all of whom were very deeply concerned about the outcomes, and of course the many countries on different sides of the divide at different times. We were thus very happy that the task was taken over by Finn Laursen, who we already know from the *Historical Dictionary of the European Union* a few years back and whose experience was acquired both in his home country of Denmark and in the United States and Great Britain, where he was a lecturer at the London School of Economics, 1985–1988. For several decades now he was written papers, reports, and books, listed in the bibliography, and especially presently serving as the editor-in-chief of the *Oxford Encyclopedia of European Union Politics*.

Jon Woronoff
Series editor

Acknowledgments

I want to thank Jon Woronoff, the series editor, for the invitation to write this book about Brexit, the exit of the United Kingdom (UK) from the European Union (EU).

A few years ago, I authored the *Historical Dictionary of the European Union* (2016 edition) in this series of Historical Dictionaries. So, I knew the template, which made it easier to get started on this one on Brexit. However, when I started on the project it was difficult to predict when and how it would all finish and it ended out taking longer than expected.

According to the exit article in the Lisbon Treaty, Article 50, a country deciding to leave the EU would have two years to negotiate a withdrawal agreement. Given the fact that UK Prime Minister Theresa May invoked Article 50 on 31 March 2017, Brexit was expected to happen before 31 March 2019. The original contract for this book manuscript therefore was end of June 2019. By then, however, Brexit had still not happened. It had been extended to 31 October. Another deadline passed. The new British prime minister Boris Johnson reached a slightly different agreement with the EU, after he had won a parliamentary election, which was accepted by the new Parliament. Brexit could take place on 31 January 2020.

The manuscript deadline, therefore, was extended, in the hope of eventually being able to finish the account of the saga. In the meantime, I had committed myself to other writing as well as teaching assignments, so this manuscript was finished only at the end of June 2020.

Actually, the Brexit saga did not finish on the official Brexit day, when the UK left the EU. A transition period scheduled to last till 30 December 2020 started, in which the future relations have to be negotiated, a process that may take longer than the 11 months scheduled, but which may also end without an agreement.

I want to thank Rowman & Littlefield for patience with British and EU politics, and myself.

Finn Laursen
Viborg, Denmark
June 2020

Reader's Note

Brexit—British exit from the European Union (EU)—is a story about a bilateral relationship, between a state, the United Kingdom (UK), which unites England, Scotland, Wales, and Northern Ireland in one state, and the EU, which is a union of states, which creates a political system, where there is some pooling and delegation of sovereignty in common supranational institutions, which make binding decision, that is, decisions that must be accepted by the member states and their citizens. The special kind of institutions created originally in the 1950s, according to the founding fathers of the European Communities (EC), should be able to advance the common European interest instead of the separate national interests, thereby increasing the chance of peace and economic prosperity in Europe.

The UK did not accept the philosophy behind the European integration project back in the 1950s when it all started. The UK joined the EC with delay in 1973, together with Ireland and Denmark. Some may argue that many UK politicians—and people—never fully accepted the continental European political integration philosophy. Many kept talking about the importance of UK "sovereignty," sometimes translated as being fully in control. But can any country be fully sovereign in a world where states are increasingly interdependent, sensitive, and vulnerable to the actions of other states?

For many years the UK was a difficult partner in the EC and later in the EU created by the Maastricht Treaty in 1993, which itself was very controversial in the UK.

The UK took a turn toward exit when the British voters were promised a referendum by Conservative prime minister David Cameron in 2013. In the referendum, which took place in June 2016, about 52 percent of the UK voters cast ballots in favor of "leave." Thus started the saga of negotiating a withdrawal agreement, which we try to trace in this book.

To communicate about and understand Brexit, we need to know something about EU and UK politics and political systems. Some knowledge about negotiations can be useful too. Even the media have talked about "chicken games." Most of the terms we need are well known in accounts of political processes, domestic or international. But some new concepts did emerge, like

Brexit itself, and hard vs. soft Brexit. An early UK proposal, the Chequers plan, used terms like "common rule book," "frictionless trade," and a "facilitated customs arrangement." Both these Brexit-specific terms and the more common terms used in EU and UK politics—and international politics—will be explicated in the dictionary part of this book, and the introduction will go into some detail on the UK relationship with the European integration process from the very beginning in the 1950s as well as during the negotiating process.

Brexit was about a divorce agreement. Brexit took place on 31 January 2020. The future relationship between the UK and the EU remains to be negotiated. In that sense Brexit may be followed by a post-Brexit saga.

Acronyms and Abbreviations

AA	Association Agreement
ACP	African, Caribbean, and Pacific
AFSJ	Area of Freedom, Security and Justice
ALDE	Alliance of Liberals and Democrats for Europe
ASEAN	Association of Southeast Asian Nations
Benelux	Belgium, the Netherlands, and Luxembourg
CAP	Common Agricultural Policy
CCT	Common Customs Tariff
CEECs	Central and Eastern European Countries
CET	Common External Tariff
CETA	Comprehensive Economic and Trade Agreement
CFP	Common Fisheries Policy
CFSP	Common Foreign and Security Policy
COREPER	Committee of Permanent Representatives
CSDP	Common Security and Defence Policy
CSU	Christian Social Union
DCFTA	Deep and Comprehensive Free Trade Agreement
EAEC	European Atomic Energy Community
EC	European Community or European Communities
ECB	European Central Bank
ECJ	European Court of Justice
ECOFIN	Economic and Finance Council
ECR	European Conservatives and Reformists
ECSC	European Coal and Steel Community
EDC	European Defence Community
EEA	European Economic Area
EEA	European Environment Agency
EEAS	European External Action Service
EEC	European Economic Community
EFDD	Europe of Freedom and Direct Democracy Group
EFSA	European Food Safety Authority
EFSM	European Financial Stabilization Mechanism

EFTA	European Free Trade Association
EIB	European Investment Bank
EMEA	European Medicines Agency
EMS	European Monetary System
EMSA	European Maritime Safety Agency
EMU	Economic and Monetary Union
ENP	European Neighborhood Policy
EP	European Parliament
EPAs	Economic Partnership Agreements
EPC	European Political Cooperation
EPO	European Patent Office
EPP	Group of the European People's Party (Christian Democrats)
EPU	European Political Union
ERDF	European Regional Development Fund
ERM	Exchange Rate Mechanism
ERM II	Exchange Rate Mechanism II
ESCB	European System of Central Banks
ESDI	European Security and Defence Identity
ESDP	European Security and Defence Policy
ESM	European Stability Mechanism
ESS	European Security Strategy
EU	European Union
EUISS	European Union Institute for Security Studies
EUMC	European Union Military Committee
EUMS	European Union Military Staff
EUPM	European Union Police Mission
EURATOM	European Atomic Energy Community
EUROPOL	European Police Office
FAC	Foreign Affairs Council
FDI	Foreign Direct Investment
FIFG	Financial Instrument for Fisheries Guidance
FPÖ	Austrian Freedom Party
FTA	Free Trade Area
FVO	Food and Veterinary Office
GAC	General Affairs Council
GATS	General Agreement on Trade in Services
GATT	General Agreement on Tariffs and Trade
GDP	Gross Domestic Product
GIs	Geographical Indications
GMOs	Genetically Modified Organisms
GNI	Gross National Income

GNP	Gross National Product
GREENS/EFA	Group of the Greens/European Free Alliance
GUE/NGL	European United Left/Nordic Green Left
HR/VP	High Representative/Vice President
ICS	Investment Court System
IIA	Inter-institutional Agreement
IGC	Intergovernmental Conference
IMF	International Monetary Fund
ISDS	Investor State Dispute Settlement
JHA	Justice and Home Affairs
MEP	Member of European Parliament
MFF	Multiannual Financial Framework
MFN	Most Favored Nation
NATO	North Atlantic treaty Organization
NGO	Non governmental organization
NTBs	Non-Tariff-Barriers to Trade
OECD	Organization for Economic Co-operation and Development
OEEC	Organization for European Economic Cooperation
OMC	Open Method of Coordination
OSCE	Organization for Security and Cooperation in Europe
PCA	Partnership and Cooperation Agreement
PSC	Political and Security Committee
QMV	Qualified Majority Voting
S&D	Group of the Progressive Alliance of Socialists and Democrats in the European Parliament
SBAs	Sovereign Base Areas
SEA	Single European Act
SGP	Stability and Growth Pact
SIS	Schengen Information System
SIS II	Schengen Information System II
SPD	German Socialist Party
TAC	Total Allowable Catch
TEC	Treaty Establishing the European Community
TEU	Treaty on European Union
TFEU	Treaty on the Functioning of the European Union
TRIMS	Trade-Related Aspects of Investment Measures
TRIPS	Trade-Related Aspects of Intellectual Property Rights
TSCG	Treaty on Stability, Coordination and Governance in the Economic and Monetary Union
TTIP	Transatlantic Trade and Investment Partnership

UK	United Kingdom
UKIP	United Kingdom Independence Party
UN	United Nations
UPC	Unified Patent Court
U.S.	United States
WEU	Western European Union
WIPO	World Intellectual Property Organization
WTO	World Trade Organization

Maps

EC-9: 1973: Denmark, Ireland, and the United Kingdom became members of the European Community.

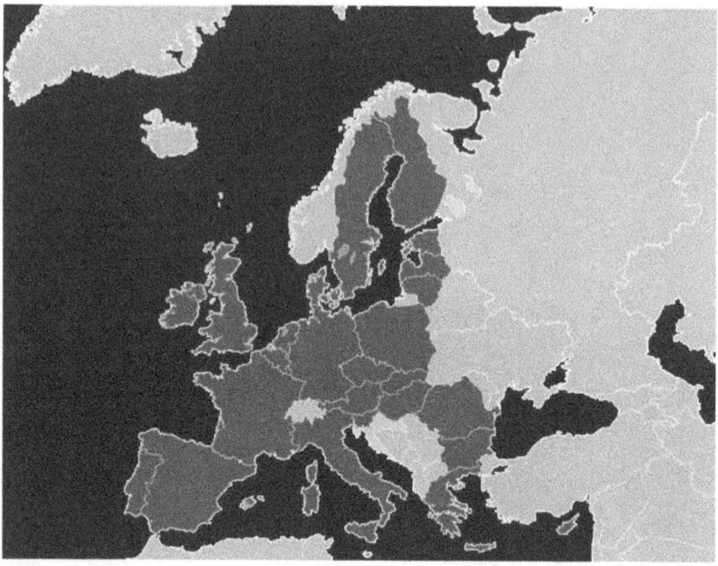

EU-28: 2013: Latest Enlargement, Croatia became member of the European Union.

EU-27 2020: EU POST-BREXIT.

The United Kingdom (UK).

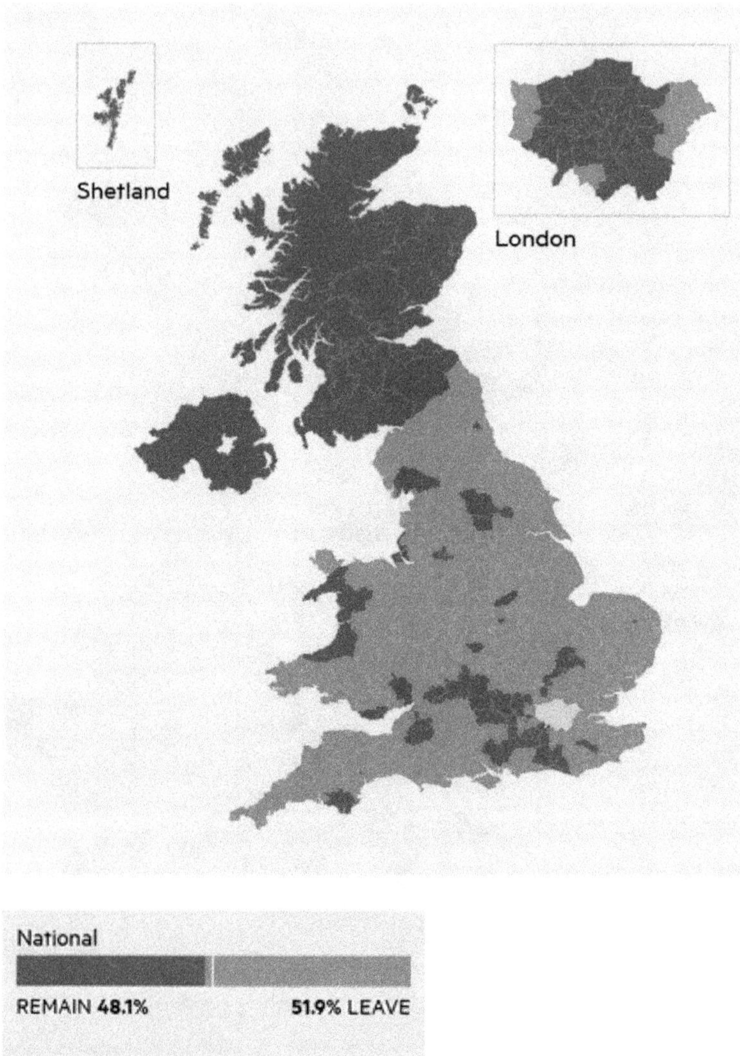

The Brexit referendum, 2016.

Solution to the Irish border issue according to Boris Johnson's Brexit deal with the EU, October 2019.

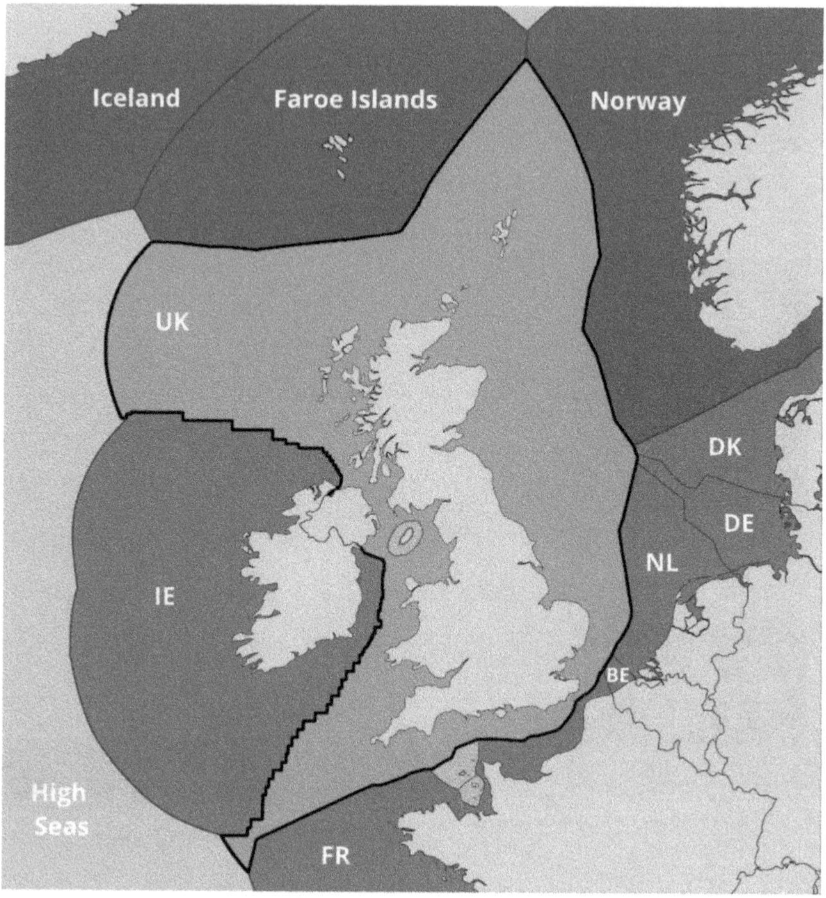

Exclusive Economic Zones of the UK and neighbouring coastal states.

Chronology

23 January 2013 Prime Minister David Cameron declares that he is in favor of an in-out referendum based on a new settlement for the UK in the EU (Bloomberg speech).

22 May 2014 The UK Independence Party (UKIP) wins 27 percent of the popular vote in the European Parliament election and gains 24 seats, out of the UK's 73 seats. The Labour Party wins 20 and the Conservatives 19 seats.

19 February 2016 David Cameron reaches an agreement with the other EU members, including a seven-year emergency brake on in-work benefits for EU citizens, indexation of child benefit payments for children living outside the UK, a possibility of forcing a debate between eurozone "ins" and "outs" about new eurozone laws, and a statement that the UK "is not committed to further political integration" and that "references to ever-closer union do not apply to the United Kingdom."

23 June 2016 UK holds referendum on EU membership with a slim majority of voters, 51.9 percent, choosing to leave the EU, while 48.1 percent vote to remain.

24 June 2016 Prime Minister David Cameron announces his resignation.

13 July 2016 Theresa May becomes UK prime minister. David Davis is appointed Secretary of State for Exiting the European Union to oversee withdrawal negotiations. Boris Johnson is appointed foreign secretary.

27 July 2016 EU Commission president Jean-Claude Juncker appoints Michel Barnier as the EU's chief Brexit negotiator.

8 September 2016 The European Parliament, which needs to accept the withdrawal agreement, appoints liberal MEP Guy Verhofstadt as its top Brexit representative.

2 October 2016 Theresa May informs the Conservative Party conference that she will trigger the EU's Article 50 by the end of March 2017, and sets out various British red lines and promises to make the UK "a fully independent, sovereign country."

3 November 2016 The UK's High Court rules that the UK government cannot trigger Article 50 without parliamentary approval, a ruling later confirmed by the Supreme Court.

3 January 2017 Sir Ivan Rogers, the UK ambassador to the EU, resigns. In a letter to his staff, he warns of the dangers of "muddled thinking" in London.
4 January 2017 Sir Tim Barrow, a career diplomat and former ambassador to Russia, is appointed as the UK's new ambassador to the EU.

17 January 2017 Prime Minister Theresa May gives her Lancaster House speech in which she sets out her government's priorities in the Brexit negotiations, including specifically leaving the EU's internal market and customs union. A no-deal would be better than a bad deal, she says.

24 January 2017 The UK's Supreme Court rejects the government's appeal in the Gina Miller case, ruling that the parliament must vote on whether Article 50 exit procedures can be triggered.

2 February 2017 The UK government publishes its Brexit White Paper, setting out its strategy for exiting the EU.

13 March 2017 The UK Parliament passes the European Union (Notification of Withdrawal) Bill, later confirmed by the Queen's "Royal Assent," giving the green light to trigger Article 50.

29 March 2017 Theresa May sends a letter to the European Council president Donald Tusk, triggering Article 50, setting 29 March 2019, as the UK's departure day.

31 March 2017 European Council president Donald Tusk publishes draft negotiation guidelines for Brexit talks for the EU27, setting out the key issues—encompassing citizens' rights, the border between Northern Ireland and the Republic of Ireland, and the financial settlement—to be discussed in the first phase of talks. Tusk reiterates that future relations and trade discussions may only begin once the key issues are resolved.

18 April 2017 Theresa May unexpectedly announces a snap general election to be held in June.

29 April 2017 EU27 leaders unanimously endorse the draft guidelines for Brexit negotiations.

22 May 2017 The European Commission publishes the negotiating directives, giving the green light for negotiations to start, confirming financial settlement, citizens' rights, and arrangements for the Irish border as key issues to be settled first.

8 June 2017 The UK holds snap general elections as Theresa May attempts to consolidate the power of the Conservative Party. She miscalculates and loses the majority in parliament, leaving her with a minority government backed by Northern Ireland's conservative Democratic Unionist Party (DUP).

19 June 2017 Brexit negotiations begin with establishing the timeline for talks, and forming negotiating groups.

17–20 July 2017 Second round of negotiations takes place in Brussels. Both sides say they are committed to the Good Friday Agreement, has secured peace and stability in Northern Ireland. Negotiators set out to compare positions on citizens' rights. Barnier urges the UK to clarify its position on the financial settlement and its plans to secure a frictionless border between Northern Ireland and the Republic of Ireland.

28–31 August 2017 During the third round of talks, further progress is made on citizens' rights, but the role of the European Court of Justice in enforcing them and the extent of the UK's financial obligations still remain outstanding key issues.

9 September 2017 The EU Commission publishes several negotiating papers, including on Northern Ireland, emphasizing that it is the UK's responsibility to propose solutions for the post-Brexit Irish border.

22 September 2017 Prime Minster Theresa May makes a speech in Florence to clarify the UK's Brexit position. She says that the UK will honor its budget commitments, and she proposes a two-year transition period.

25 September 2017 The fourth round of talks is held in Brussels a week later than planned to allow for May's Florence speech. EU negotiators hope to see a detailed commitment following May's pledges in Florence, but the UK still does not disclose details about its financial obligations. The UK offers to transpose the withdrawal agreement into UK law and ensures the UK courts can refer directly to it, but there is no agreement on the future role of the European Court of Justice.

9–12 October 2017 The fifth round of negotiations makes no progress on the key issues. No further rounds of talks are scheduled, leading Barnier to say that negotiations have reached a "deadlock."

16 October 2017 EU Commission president Jean-Claude Juncker hosts Prime Minister Theresa May for dinner, ahead of a crucial EU summit. The two agree that Brexit talks must "accelerate over the months to come."

20 October 2017 EU27 leaders agree that the Brexit talks have not made "sufficient progress" to be able to move into the next phase of negotiations.

9–10 November 2017 A new negotiating round kicks off among growing concerns about the slow pace of negotiations. EU leaders will assess the state of talks again at the meeting of the European Council set for the 14–15 December summit.

4 December 2017 British prime minister Theresa May travels to Brussels in the hope of finalizing the deal on the terms of divorce with the EU, but last-minute objections from her political allies, the Democratic Unionist Party (DUP), over the Irish border issue prevent the agreement.

8 December 2017 A deal is finally reached on the key divorce issues between the EU and the UK after DUP has agreed to a compromise text on the Irish border issue. British prime minister Theresa May and EU Commission president Jean-Claude Juncker announce the deal in the early hours of the morning in Brussels.

15 December 2017 The European Council agrees that "sufficient progress" has been achieved on the key divorce issues with the UK to move to the second phase of the negotiations.

2 March 2018 Theresa May gives more hints of compromise in a speech at Mansion House in London. The Brexit talks has seen the UK make some concessions in major policy areas including free movement, budget contributions, the role of the European Court of Justice (ECJ), trade, and fishing rights.

19 March 2018 The UK and EU publish a preliminary, incomplete draft agreement on the UK's withdrawal. The text is color-coded, with whole sections left white indicating that "no agreement has yet been found."

23 March 2018 The European Council publishes new guidelines for the continued negotiations.

6 July 2018 A UK White paper on the Future Relationship between the United Kingdom and the European Union, known as the Chequers plan, is finalized. It suggests a much softer Brexit than earlier statements had suggested, including a "common rulebook" with the EU on goods.

8 July 2018 Davis resigns as Secretary of State for Exiting the European Union because of disagreement with Theresa May's Chequers plan. Dominic Raab is appointed as his successor the following day, when Foreign Secretary Boris Johnson and other ministers also resign.

21 September 2018 EU rejects the Chequers plan. It is seen as an attempt to "cherry-pick" from EU rules. European Council president Donald Tusk says that parts of it "will not work" and risk "undermining the single market." Other EU leaders make similar criticisms. May's proposal for the Irish border is dismissed as illegal by Michel Barnier.

14 November 2018 EU and UK negotiators finally agree on the draft Withdrawal Agreement.

15 November 2018 Dominic Raab resigns as Secretary of State for Exiting the European Union because of disagreement with Theresa May's Withdrawal Agreement. Stephen Barclay is appointed as his successor the following day.

22 November 2018 The negotiators agree on the Political Declaration setting out the framework for the future EU-UK relationship.

25 November 2018 The 27 EU member states endorse the Withdrawal Agreement and the Political Declaration, which then still need the approval of the UK and European parliaments to take effect. The agreement is made possible after May adapts her Brexit plan to include a temporary all-UK customs union with the EU to resolve the controversial Irish border issue, known as "backstop."

13 December 2018 Theresa May survives a vote of confidence in her leadership of the Conservative Party. But she is forced to promise to step down before the next election, amid an angry backlash to her Brexit deal. A vote in the parliament is postponed until January because of the strength of opposition.

15 January 2019 First "meaningful vote" is held on the Withdrawal Agreement in the UK House of Commons. The UK Government is defeated by 432 votes to 202. It is the worst government parliamentary defeat in UK history.

30 January 2019 The UK Parliament gives Theresa May a mandate to go back to Brussels to seek "alternative arrangements" to the Irish backstop.

12 March 2019 Second "meaningful vote" on the Withdrawal Agreement with Theresa May's Government is lost again by 391 votes to 242. The UK's attorney general has said that a hastily revised "legally binding" deal with the EU, that the backstop is not permanent, does not guarantee that the UK can exit the backstop unilaterally.

14 March 2019 UK Government motion passes 412 to 202 to extend the Article 50 period.

20 March 2019 Theresa May requests the EU to extend the Article 50 period until 30 June 2019.

21 March 2019 The European Council offers to extend the Article 50 period until 22 May 2019 if the Withdrawal Agreement is passed by 29 March 2019 but, if not, then the UK has until 12 April 2019 to indicate a way forward. The extension is formally agreed the following day.

23 March 2019 Hundreds of thousands of pro-EU protesters march in London to demand a second referendum on the UK's membership.

29 March 2019 The original end of the Article 50 period and the original planned date for Brexit. Third vote on the Withdrawal Agreement after being separated from the Political Declaration. UK Government defeated again, this time by 344 votes to 286.

5 April 2019 Theresa May requests for a second time that the EU extend the Article 50 period until 30 June 2019.

10 April 2019 The European Council grants another extension to the Article 50 period but to 31 October 2019. However, the UK has to hold European Parliament elections in May 2019; otherwise, it has to leave on 1 June 2019.

23 May 2019 The UK takes part in elections for the European Parliament, obliged to do so as it is still an EU member.

24 May 2019 Theresa May announces that she will resign as Conservative Party leader, effective 7 June, due to being unable to pass her Brexit plans through parliament, while continuing as prime minister until a Conservative leadership contest can take place.

27 May 2019 The European Parliament election results bring victory for Nigel Farage's Brexit Party. There is a strong showing of pro-Remain parties, the Liberal Democrats, and the Greens, but May's Conservatives and the Labour Party opposition suffer great losses.

23 July 2019 Boris Johnson wins the Conservative Party leadership contest after several weeks of ballots.

24 July 2019 Boris Johnson enters Downing Street 10 as the UK's new prime minister.

19 August 2019 Johnson issues a formal plea to the EU to drop the Irish backstop from the Withdrawal Agreement. The EU refuses.

28 August 2019 The UK Parliament is prorogued (suspended) for five weeks, upon advice given to Queen Elizabeth II by Boris Johnson's government.

3 September 2019 21 rebel Conservative MPs vote against the government in protest at its Brexit strategy of driving the UK toward an exit from the EU by 31 October, with or without an agreed deal. They are expelled from the party.

5 September 2019 Johnson says that he will rather be "dead in a ditch" than ask for another Brexit extension. It is one of several such comments over the summer and early autumn, where Johnson insists that the UK will leave the EU by 31 October.

9 September 2019 The "Benn bill" becomes law, in effect preventing the UK from leaving the EU with no exit deal, without parliament's consent.

24 September 2019 The UK's Supreme Court rules unanimously that the government's suspension of parliament is unlawful. The House of Commons reopens for business.

29 September 2019 The Conservative Party conference opens with a new slogan: "Get Brexit done."

3 October 2019 The UK government sends a new Brexit plan to Brussels, including the removal of the backstop. It is widely greeted with skepticism, and rejected by the European Commission three days later.

8 October 2019 UK-EU talks all but collapse amid acrimony. EU Council president Donald Tusk accuses Johnson of playing a "stupid blame game."

10 October 2019 UK and Irish prime ministers Boris Johnson and Leo Varadkar announce a "pathway to a possible deal" as they meet in England.

17 October 2019 The UK and EU announce dramatically that they have reached a new Brexit deal, ahead of a Brussels summit. It eliminates the Irish backstop, following a compromise which sees the UK in particular make concessions over Northern Ireland, which will stay in the customs union and part of the internal market in order to avoid checks along the Irish border, but creating a kind of border in the Irish Sea.

19 October 2019 At a special Saturday sitting, British MPs withhold their approval of the deal until legislation implementing Brexit can be adopted. It means that Johnson is obliged to seek another Brexit delay from the EU. Another huge pro-EU march takes place in London.

22 October 2019 Johnson puts Brexit legislation on "pause," citing MPs' obstacles.

28 October 2019 The EU agrees to offer the UK a Brexit extension until 31 January 2020.

29 October 2019 The House of Commons approves a general election on December 12, lifting previous objections to Boris Johnson's repeated requests.

1 December 2019 Ursula von der Leyen takes office as European Commission president, replacing Jean-Claude Juncker. The new European Council president is Charles Michel, taking over from Donald Tusk.

12 December 2019 The UK's general election is won convincingly by Boris Johnson's Conservatives, who gain an 80-seat majority. But Scotland and Northern Ireland in particular register strong anti-Brexit votes.

9 January 2020 The UK House of Commons votes 330 to 231 in favor of the Withdrawal Agreement Bill.

23 January 2020 The UK's EU Withdrawal bill becomes law.

29 January 2020 The European Parliament approves the Withdrawal Agreement.

30 January 2020 The Council of the European Union concludes the Withdrawal Agreement.

31 January 2020 The UK officially leaves the EU at midnight CET (11 p.m. UK time).

1 February 2020 The UK becomes a "third country." An 11-month transition phase begins, running to 31 December 2020. Most arrangements will remain the same but both sides face a race against the clock to reach an agreement on the future EU-UK relationship. An extension of the transition period, however, is a possibility.

Introduction

THE UK AND THE START OF EUROPEAN INTEGRATION

Today's European Union (EU) started in 1950. On 9 May that year the French foreign minister Robert Schuman suggested the creation of what became the European Coal and Steel Community (ECSC) by the Treaty of Paris in 1951 (in force in 1952). It was negotiated in an Intergovernmental Conference chaired by Jean Monnet, the brain behind the Schuman Plan. The UK was invited to take part in the negotiations but turned down the invitation.[1]

The British government had doubts about the main ideas in the Schuman Plan, especially the idea of creating a supranational authority that would make binding decisions. This conflicted with British ideas of national sovereignty, especially parliamentary sovereignty. But there were also economic reasons. While France depended on import of coal from Germany, Britain was largely self-sufficient in coal and steel, and trade-wise depended much more on the Commonwealth than Europe in 1950.[2]

Another French proposal for further European integration, the Pleven Plan proposed in the autumn of 1950, which was to establish a European Defence Community (EDC), including setting up of a European Army, wasn't joined by the UK either. The plan was a response to the American request for a German contribution to the defense of the West after the start of the Korean War in June 1950. A draft treaty was negotiated by the six ECSC member states, but it was rejected by the French National Assembly in August 1954, after the death of Stalin and a cease-fire in Korea had reduced the pressures. At that point the British played an important role in getting the Brussels Treaty of 1948, a defense treaty involving the UK, France, and the Benelux countries, revised to create the Western European Union (WEU) including West Germany and Italy, which subsequently also joined NATO.

When the six countries that formed the ECSC in 1952, after the defeat of the EDC in 1954, started considering further integration in 1955, the UK government showed some interest and took part in some preliminary deliberations in the Spaak Committee set up by the Six at a meeting of foreign ministers in

Messina in 1955. Eventually the British "representative" withdrew.[3] Various committees in London had concluded that the plans for a customs union and Common Market would have serious consequences for British industry and agriculture and also negatively affect relations with the Commonwealth and the United States. Eventually the Six concluded the negotiations without Britain and created the European Economic Community (EEC) and the European Atomic Energy Community (EURATOM) by the Treaties of Rome in 1958. From that year there were thus three European Communities (EC).

Instead of EC membership the British suggested a wide free trade area (FTA) in Western Europe, and there were negotiations within the Organization for European Economic Cooperation (OEEC), which had been created in 1948 to administer the Marshal Aid from the United States to Europe. Those negotiations eventually broke down because the Six members of the EC were not seriously interested. They saw it as a way to undermine the Common Market.

As an alternative to the EC the UK then went ahead and formed the European Free Trade Association (EFTA) in 1960 together with Austria, Switzerland, Portugal, and the three Scandinavian countries: Denmark, Norway, and Sweden.[4] EFTA was sometimes referred to as the Outer Seven at the time. The situation then was that there were two economic groupings in Western Europe, the Inner Six working to establish a Common Market with a number of common policies and supranational institutions, and the Outer Seven limiting the ambitions to an FTA without common policies and only weak intergovernmental decision-making. In a way there were two different integration philosophies confronting each other: one based on supranational institutions and one based on traditional intergovernmental cooperation.[5]

THE UK SEEKS MEMBERSHIP

The UK government, however, relatively quickly decided that there were costs of exclusion from the EC, the more dynamic of the two organizations. The UK Conservative government under Harold Macmillan therefore applied for membership in 1971, and so did Denmark and Norway. Ireland, which had not joined EFTA, also applied. Various reasons are usually mentioned for the application, some economic, some political. Economic growth increased in the EC, but stagnated in the UK. British trade with Commonwealth countries was declining. And the "special relationship" with the United States did not always work the way the British expected, something the British had learned already during the Suez crisis in 1956, where the Americans turned against France and the UK.

The saga of the EC's first enlargement started. Negotiations began. There were three main problematic areas: Commonwealth, EFTA, and the EC's Common Agricultural Policy (CAP). The latter had established high guaranteed prices for the farmers, leaving it to consumers to pay prices above world market prices. The UK supported farmers through deficiency payments, which kept prices lower for consumers. In 1973 the French president General Charles de Gaulle vetoed British membership, worried about whether the UK would be an American "Trojan Horse" inside the EC. His step upset the five other EC members, but they had no alternative to accepting it.[6]

The UK applied again in 1967 under Labour Prime Minister Harold Wilson, but another veto followed from the General. It was only after General de Gaulle stepped down as French president in 1969 that the situation opened up for membership negotiations. The new French president Georges Pompidou agreed to the idea of enlargement, which was strongly supported by the five other EC members: West Germany, Italy, and the three Benelux countries—Belgium, the Netherlands, and Luxembourg. A famous summit among the Six in The Hague in December 1969 decided for "completion, enlargement and deepening," completion mostly concerning an agreement on how to finance the CAP through so-called own resources consisting of customs duties, agricultural levies, and 1 percent of the value-added tax (VAT) collected by the member states. Deepening including proposal for an Economic and Monetary Union (EMU) and some foreign policy cooperation.

The conclusions from the Hague Summit allowed accession negotiations to start in 1970 with the UK, Denmark, Norway, and Ireland. They were concluded in 1972. The Norwegian people turned down the accession agreement in a referendum. In Denmark and Ireland membership was accepted by referendums. The UK accepted membership by a parliamentary vote. The three countries joined the EC from January 1973.

During the accession negotiations, which took place while Edward Heath from the Conservative Party was prime minister in the UK, the applicants had to accept the so-called *acquis communautaire*, the achievements at the time in the form of the treaties and adopted legislation as well as decisions by the European Court of Justice (ECJ). They further had to accept the so-called *finalité politique*, not well defined, but referred to as an "ever closer union of the peoples of Europe" in the preamble of the Treaty of Rome.

Difficult issues in the accession negotiations included the CAP and the Commonwealth, budget contributions, EMU, and fisheries policy. Import of butter and lamb meat from New Zealand and cane sugar from the Caribbean, and access to fishing water in the North Sea and the Atlantic Ocean were some of the issues. On the latter point, the Six had agreed on the principle of "equal access" to waters falling under the sovereignty of the member states just prior to the start of the accession negotiations, making this a part of the *acquis communautaire*. The UK, Ireland, and Norway wanted to be allowed to reserve a wider coastal belt of water for their own fishermen. Eventually the Accession Agreement included a ten-year derogation from "equal access" in a six-mile coastal zone, to be reviewed in 1982. The six miles was extended to 12 miles in certain regions, where the local population was heavily dependent on fisheries.[7] On CAP a six-year transition period was agreed. On the budget a seven-year phasing-in was agreed.[8]

The terms of entry were debated in the House of Commons on 28 October 1971, and entry was accepted by 356 votes in favor to 244 against. The European Communities Bill was passed into law on 13 July 1972 with a majority of 17. Most Conservative MPs supported membership. The Labour Party under Harold Wilson was largely against, but divided, with a group of supporters including Roy Jenkins.[9]

The idea of membership in the EC remained controversial in the UK after 1973. In 1974 the Labour Party under Wilson won the parliamentary election and returned as prime minister. The party had promised a renegotiation of British membership and a referendum.

During the renegotiations the UK did not get everything it asked for. No major CAP reform; only a promise of a review of the pricing system. Extension of the special arrangements for sugar from Commonwealth was secured. A complex system of calculating a reduction of the British budget contribution was also agreed.[10] The results of the renegotiation were subsequently accepted by a referendum on 5 June 1975. The Labour Party campaigned in favor of a yes to continued membership despite internal divisions. The Trade Union Congress (TUC) was especially strongly against. The Conservative Party was more united in favor of yes, including the party's new leader Margaret Thatcher. The turnout was 64.5 percent, of which 67.2 percent voted yes.[11] Not a bad result, but it did not finally settle the issue of British membership.

THE UK AS AN AWKWARD PARTNER

The UK was to become what has been called an "awkward partner" in the coming years.[12] The 1970s were not an easy period for the EC. The energy crisis put pressure on the member states' economies. The idea of EMU, accepted at the Hague Summit in 1969, and turned into a plan for EMU by 1980, was stillborn. Some monetary cooperation, the European Monetary System (EMS), did start in 1979, but Britain stayed outside the Exchange Rate Mechanism (ERM), which was created. Some foreign policy cooperation known as European Political Cooperation (EPC) started as intergovernmental cooperation outside the treaty framework. Further, it was decided to start electing the European Parliament (EP) directly, which eventually happened from 1979, with a slight delay largely because of slow British acceptance. Apart from some budgetary powers introduced by the two budgetary treaties in 1970 and 1975,[13] the EP, however, remained largely advisory, until later treaty amendments in the Single European Act (SEA) in 1987 and the Treaty of Maastricht creating the European Union (EU) in 1993.[14] The budget corrective mechanism agreed during the renegotiations failed to work. So that issue stayed on the agenda.[15]

The Thatcher Years

For most of the early years of UK membership, in the 1970s, Britain had a Labour government, first under Wilson, then James Callaghan from 1976. But the May 1979 elections were won by the Conservatives and Margaret Thatcher became prime minister.

Although Thatcher had supported the yes campaign in the 1975 referendum, she was not uncritical of the EC. She remained in power until 1990. The British budget contribution quickly became an issue again. She was a liberal in the sense that she wanted to limit government intervention in the economy. She wanted deregulation. She wanted to reduce the public sector and initiated policies to do so in the UK. She took a battle with the trade union movement, which she felt had too much influence. In macroeconomic policy she was a monetarist and not a Keynesian. She wanted to control money supply to reduce inflation. In general, she was supportive of the EC, but did not want it to interfere too much in the domestic politics of the member states. Late in her political career, in a speech at the College of Europe in Bruges, Belgium, in September 1988, she famously stated, "We have not successfully rolled back the frontiers of the state in Britain, only to see them re-imposed at a European level with a European super-state exercising a new dominance from Brussels."[16]

Thatcher regularly took some battles with her colleagues in the European Council, especially about the British budget rebate that she judged to be far too insufficient. This started at the June 1979 Strasbourg European Council meeting and continued at the November Dublin European Council later that year. After getting the rebate increased, she accepted a settlement in Venice in June 1980 of £800 million a year for 1980 and 1981. But the issue reemerged. Another settlement followed at Fontainebleau in June 1984, where she accepted a rebate of 60 percent of the difference between the British VAT based payment and EC receipts.

In January 1985 Jacques Delors became president of the Commission in Brussels. The Commission now gave highest priority to completion of the internal market. One of the two British Commissioners, Lord Cockfield, was in charge of preparing a White Paper, which eventually suggested close to 300 legislative acts to complete the internal market, that is, free movement of goods, services, capital, and people, which had all been foreseen in the Treaty of Rome. Cockfield's White Paper included taxation, frontier control, and employment policy (or social policy), which upset Thatcher.[17] One of the reasons for the difficulties of getting the necessary legislation adopted was that Article 100 of the Treaty of Rome required unanimity for harmonization of national law. It was therefore suggested that a treaty reform introducing more majority voting was necessary to facilitate decision-making.

The issue of treaty reform came up at the Milan summit in June 1985, where Thatcher and her two colleagues from Denmark and Greece voted against the calling of an Intergovernmental Conference (IGC) to negotiate a treaty amendment. The IGC went ahead since it could be called by a simple majority. The outcome, the Single European Act (SEA), was accepted at the Luxembourg European Council meeting in December 1985. It introduced an Article 100a, which allowed much of the internal market legislation to be adopted by a qualified majority vote (QMV). QMV, however, did not "apply to fiscal provisions, to those relating to the free movement of persons nor to those relating to the rights and interests of employed persons" (art. 100a(2)).

The SEA did, though, include an Article 118s, which introduced QMV for "the working environment, as regards health and safety for workers." This became an entry point for some social policy legislation the coming years.

The SEA also increased the role of the European Parliament by introducing a Cooperation Procedure requiring a second reading of internal market legislation. New chapters included one on environmental policy. EPC further got a treaty base, but remained intergovernmental cooperation outside the EC treaty framework.

In the end the Thatcher government accepted the SEA. But Lord Cockfield, who, according to Thatcher, had "gone native" in Brussels, did not get a second term as commissioner.[18]

Later in the 1980s Thatcher battled against proposals to adopt a Social Charter. Eventually in December 1989 a Charter on the Fundamental Rights of Workers was adopted as a nonbinding declaration by all member states except the UK.

The final battle was about monetary policy in the EC in the run-up to the negotiations that produced the Treaty of Maastricht in 1991 (in force in 1993). But initially it was mostly a domestic battle, because the Conservative Party was deeply divided on the issue.[19]

EMU was put on the EC agenda again in 1988 when the Hannover Summit decided to establish a committee chaired by Jacques Delors and including the governors of the central banks of the member states and a couple of independent economists to consider how to move toward EMU. The Delors report published in 1989 proposed to move toward EMU in three phases. The summit meeting in Strasbourg in December decided to call an IGC to prepare the required treaty reform to establish the EMU. Thatcher was against EMU as well as British participation in the existing ERM. Some cabinet members, including Chancellor Nigel Lawson and Foreign Secretary Sir Geoffrey Howe, supported British participation in the ERM. The disagreement led to Howe's demotion and Lawson's resignation. The two successors, John Major and Douglas Hurd, forced Thatcher to accept British participation in the ERM in October 1990.

When Howe resigned, he made a devastating resignation speech that contributed to Michael Heseltine's decision to challenge Thatcher for the party leadership. Heseltine was a leading pro-European in the party. He had resigned from the cabinet in 1986. After not getting a clear victory on the first ballot in October 1990 Thatcher decided to step down. The leadership battle was subsequently won by John Major.[20]

The Maastricht Treaty Battle

As mentioned, EMU got on the agenda again in 1988, that is, before the end of the Cold War. The fall of the Berlin Wall in 1989 opened up the perspective of German reunification and potentially membership in the EC of the now soon-to-be former communist countries in Central and Eastern Europe. In early 1990 some EC leaders started to suggest that there should also be an IGC on political union, including French president François Mitterrand and German chancellor Helmut Kohl. The idea was accepted at a meeting of the European Council in June 1990. In December the two IGCs, the one on EMU and the other on political union, started meeting in parallel.

John Major was more pragmatic that Thatcher. The UK now took part in the IGCs without, however, sharing the pro-integration attitudes of most continental European member states. It became clear relatively early that the UK was not ready for EMU. In the end, therefore, the UK got an opt-out on EMU. Denmark joined the UK in the last moment and got one too.[21]

But the UK also had some problems with the direction the negotiations took in the IGC on political union, especially the proposal to include a chapter on social policy in the new treaty. In the end the UK got an opt-out on social policy too, while the other 11 member states committed themselves to develop a social policy in what became the European Union (EU) by the Treaty of Maastricht. The negotiations were completed in Maastricht in December 1991, and it was signed in Maastricht in February 1992. The treaty entered into force in 1993 when all 12 member states had ratified.

Ratification was not an easy process in the UK because of the divisions in the governing Conservative Party.[22] The process was further delayed because a majority of the Danes voted No to the treaty in June 1992. Since the Eleven did not want to reopen the negotiations, the Danish problem became a problem for the Danish politicians to sort out. After getting over the chock the main parties got together and worked out a so-called National Compromise, which expressed the Danish wish not to take part in the third phase of the EMU, when the single currency is introduced, not to be bound by European Citizenship, not to take part in European defense policy, and only take part in Justice and Home Affairs (JHA) cooperation as long as it stays intergovernmental. The Danish requests were largely accepted by the Eleven at a meeting of the European Council in December 1992 in Edinburgh. The Danish electorate then voted yes to Danish ratification of the Maastricht Treaty, as modified by the Edinburgh decisions, in a second referendum in May 1993.

John Major had presented the results from the Maastricht summit in the House of Commons in December 1991. But the debate was postponed till May 1992, but then put on hold when the Danes voted No to the treaty. The Danish No encouraged the British Eurosceptics who now requested a referendum. Getting Maastricht ratified by the British Parliament took 210 hours' debate over 23 days and consideration of more than 600 amendments.[23] On 20 May, two days after the Danish yes, it passed on the third reading in the House of Commons by 292 votes to 112. But 41 Conservatives voted against the bill and five abstained. On 20 July it was approved in the House of Lords by 142 to 29.[24]

This did not mean that Major got peace in his party. The internal war continued. Nor did he become an easy partner in the new EU. In March 1994, as the EU prepared to accept Austria, Finland, and Sweden as new members, he picked a fight with his colleagues about the definition of a QMV in the enlarged EU. The Conservative Party conducted a very negative campaign in the EP elections in June 1994. Afterward Major vetoed Belgian Jean-Luc Dehaene as Commission president after Delors, instead insisting on Jacques Santer from Luxembourg.[25]

The IGC starting in 1996 to revise the Maastricht Treaty was basically put on a backburner by the other member states feeling that the Conservative UK government would not agree to any meaningful changes but rather tried to step back on some commitments. The hope was that New Labour under Tony Blair would be more accommodating after the upcoming elections in 1997, where he was expected to win.

The Blair New Labour Party Years

In 1983 Neil Kinnock had replaced Michael Foot as Labour leader after the election defeat that year. A "modernization" of the party started. By the time of the 1987 election it had abandoned anti-Europeanism and promised to "work constructively" in Europe.[26] But it took another ten years before Labour could return to power. The party, now led by Tony Blair, won a landslide victory in May 1997.[27]

Labour promised to give Britain "a leading role" in Europe. The 1996 IGC could now finish its work, which happened in Amsterdam in June 1997, without, however, agreeing on the main institutional changes on the agenda. One positive change seen from the European perspective was that the UK now opted-in on social policy. One hope on the continent had been that the UK would now also agree to a much stronger defense policy chapter in the treaty, but the UK was not yet ready for that. The Common Foreign and Security Policy (CFSP) was improved slightly by creating the post of High Representative for CFSP and adding the so-called Petersberg tasks (humanitarian and rescue tasks, peacekeeping tasks, and tasks of combat forces in crisis management, including peacemaking) as the definition of defense policy in the treaty. The Amsterdam Treaty also incorporated the so-called Schengen *acquis*, but the UK stayed out of this cooperation aiming at abolishing border controls.

Although EMU as such was not on the Amsterdam IGC agenda it was a sensitive subject in the UK. In 1996, before the 1997 election, Blair has said that "the British people are not yet ready to accept a single European currency," and later he promised a referendum before possibly joining a single currency.

In respect to defense an important change followed in December 1998, when a bilateral Franco-British summit took place at St Malo in France. French president Jacques Chirac and Blair declared on that occasion that "the Union must have the capacity for autonomous action, backed up by credible military forces." The experiences in Kosovo seems to have been one of the causes for Blair's decision to start supporting the French position on developing an autonomous European defense policy. Subsequently in June 1999 the European Council decided to move ahead with European Security and Defence Policy (ESDP) and start preparing its own military missions.[28] These developments were also confirmed in the Treaty of Nice (signed in 2001 and in force in 2003), where a new Article 25 established a Political and Security Committee (PSC) to "monitor the international situation in the areas covered by the common foreign and security policy and contribute to the definition of policies by delivering opinions to the Council at the request of the Council or on its own initiative." Its role would further be to "exercise, under the responsibility of the Council, political control and strategic direction of crisis management operation."[29]

Labour succeeded in winning three elections, before losing to a Conservative-Liberal Democrat coalition in May 2010. Blair stayed on as Prime Minister until 2007 when Chancellor Gordon Brown took over a prime minister.[30]

During the second term of the Blair government (2001–2005) one of the main EU issues was the Constitutional Convention, 2002–2003, and the IGC that followed, 2003–2004, eventually agreeing on the so-called Constitutional Treaty. The government went into the deliberations and negotiations with a relatively positive attitude, eventually turning less enthusiastic as some government representatives, MPs, and especially MEPs were pushing in a more pro-federalist direction than Britain wanted. In May 2003, as the convention was getting close to finishing its work, Blair, in a meeting with the Convention's president, former French president Giscard d'Estaing, threatened to veto the word "federalism" in the draft treaty as well as introduction of QMV for tax and social security policies.[31] The text of the draft constitutional treaty was changed accordingly, but contrary to British wishes it did include the Charter of Fundamental Rights as a legally binding document.

Labour promised a referendum to ratify the Constitutional Treaty, as did many other member states. However, the treaty died when the French and Dutch voted no in referendums in 2005. In 2007, after a reflection period, it was replaced by the Treaty of Lisbon, which, instead of being a completely new treaty, was a reform treaty, which amended the existing treaties, and which abolished some of the "constitutionalist" language.

Despite the fact that the Treaty of Lisbon included most of the novelties of the Constitutional Treaty it was ratified by all the member states and entered into force in 2009. In the UK case the Brown government decided that it did not need a referendum to be ratified. All the other member states, except Ireland, made similar decisions. However, it took two referendums in Ireland to get it ratified.[32]

In connection with the negotiation and ratification of the treaty, the UK secured an opt-out from the Charter of Fundamental Rights, and maintained opt-outs on migration and asylum policies. The leader of the opposition, David Cameron, promised a referendum on the Treaty of Lisbon, but when he became prime minister in May 2010 the treaty had been ratified by all the 27 member states.

The Return of the Conservatives

The May 2010 election saw the creation of a coalition government of the Conservatives and the Liberal Democrats. That was the year the financial crisis really hit Europe. Although the UK was not in the eurozone some of the decisions affected the UK. The first real challenge was the "fiscal compact"—the full name of which was the Treaty on Stability, Coordination, and Governance in the Economic and Monetary Union (TSCG). The eurozone countries wanted it as an EU treaty, but the UK threatened to veto it. Eventually it was agreed to make it an intergovernmental treaty between the eurozone countries and other EU members which might want to join, but outside the EU treaty framework. It was finally signed on 2 March 2012. The UK and the Czech Republic chose not to sign.[33]

Among the two coalition partners the Liberal Democrats were more pro-European than the Conservatives which had continued their Eurosceptic line. During the election campaign the Conservative Party had said that further European integration would require a referendum. To form a government a Coalition Agreement was worked out. In it the Liberal Democrat leader Nick Clegg accepted "that no further powers should be transferred to Brussels without a referendum." Further, "We will amend the 1972 European Communities Act so that any proposed future treaty that transferred areas of power, or competences, would be subject to a referendum on that treaty—a 'referendum lock'."[34]

Whether one parliament can commit the next one may have been legally doubtful, but the "referendum lock" was a clear signal to both the other EU member states and the voters in the UK.

To implement the Coalition Agreement a European Union Bill was introduced in October 2010. It became law in July 2011. It had three key provisions.

1. A referendum would be held before there could be any further transfer of power to the EU.
2. Acts of parliament would be required before EU *passerelle* clauses could be used.
3. EU law has effect in the UK only through an act of Parliament.[35]

The European Union Bill has been interpreted as "a Boston Tea Party gesture against *creeping jurisdiction.*"[36]

THE BREXIT REFERENDUM

The defeat of the Labour Party in the 2010 election and the return of the Conservative Party as UK government, at first in a coalition with the Liberal Democrats, led to a renewed debate, not to say civil war, about European integration. The UK Independence Party (UKIP) was starting to successfully frame the debate. In 2009 it had received 16.3 percent of the votes in the European Parliament (EP) elections. In 2014 the UKIP received 27.5 percent of the vote in the EP election.[37]

On 23 January 2013, David Cameroon announced that he would negotiate a "new settlement" for Britain within the EU and put the outcome to a referendum on British EU membership if reelected in the next election.[38] This turned out to be a fatal decision. It is well known among referendum scholars that referendums are difficult to control and predict, something Danish and Irish politicians have learned a few times, and the French and Dutch governments learned to their surprise and regret in 2005. That the country with the doctrine of parliamentary sovereignty should go that way says something about pressure on old norms in British domestic politics.

Cameron's negotiations with EU27 gave some results by February 2016.[39] The Conservative Party had adopted a manifesto with some demands to the EU27 in May 2015, including demands on economic governance, sovereignty, competitiveness, and immigration. Based on that Cameron sent a letter to Donald Tusk, the president of the European Council, in November 2015. A draft proposal for an agreement followed from Tusk on 2 February 2016, and a final agreement was reached at the European Council meeting on 19 February 2016.[40]

On economic governance the agreement made it clear that non-euro countries were not responsible for bailouts and a non-eurozone country can request Council discussions on euro laws that may affect its financial stability.

On sovereignty, "ever closer union" does not apply to the UK and the UK is not committed to further political integration. A new procedure would allow 55 percent of national parliaments to block legislative proposals.

On competitiveness, all member states are "to fully implement and strengthen the internal market" and the EU will take "concrete steps towards better regulation."

On immigration, child benefits for new migrants were to be indexed to conditions in the country where the child resides. From 2020 all exported child benefits could be indexed. An emergency brake on migrant numbers in case of overriding reasons of public interest was also included.

All in all, important concessions, but the agreement fell short of what Cameron had asked for and his own party expressed disapproval afterward.[41]

The prime minister then announced that the referendum would take place on 23 June 2016. The Remain camp mostly used economic arguments, while the Leave camp talked about democratic control, money, immigration, and control of borders. Sovereignty included the role of the European Court of Justice (ECJ). Money was a question of the money Britain contributed to the

EU budget, which the Leave campaigners said could be spent better on the National Health Service (NHS). Immigration was partly a question of the many EU citizens from especially Central and Eastern European Countries (CEECs), which had arrived in the country after the 2004 and 2007 enlargements, the claim being that they took British jobs.[42]

In the end the economic arguments from the Remain camp did not resonate. The more value-oriented arguments of the Leave camp succeeded framing the issues. Bringing back control had a populist appeal.

The result of the referendum was that 51.9 percent voted leave and 48.1 percent voted remain. The turnout was 72.2 percent. If we look at the constituent parts of the UK, then it was 53.4 percent leave and 46.6 percent remain in England; 44.2 percent leave and 55.8 percent remain in Northern Ireland; 38.0 percent leave and 62.0 percent remain in Scotland; and 52.5 percent leave and 47.5 percent remain in Wales.[43] So a majority of the voters in Northern Ireland and Scotland wanted to remain in the EU, suggesting a disunited UK.

Research has shown that the two factors that mainly explained how people voted were age and education. Younger and more educated people mostly voted remain. Older and less educated people mostly voted leave.[44]

THE BREXIT NEGOTIATIONS

Following the negative referendum result Prime Minister David Cameroon resigned and was followed by the new prime minister Theresa May.

Theresa May called a snap election for 8 June 2016 in the hope of winning a larger majority to strengthen her hand in the forthcoming Brexit negotiations. The decision backfired. The Conservative Party got 318 seats, a loss of 13. It meant that the government now depended on the Northern Irish Democratic Unionist Party (DUP), which got 10 seats, a gain of two. The Labour Party got 262 seats, a gain of 30. The Scottish National Party (SNP) got 35 seats, a loss of 21. Finally, the Liberal Democrats got 12 seats, a gain of four.[45]

It was only at the Party Conference on 2 October 2016 that Theresa May started to define her position on Brexit, beyond saying that "Brexit means Brexit." By October May was committed to leaving the internal market if necessary, to abolish free movement of people, without a clear commitment. Anyway, she announced that Art. 50 would be invoked by the end of March 2018.[46]

It was in her Lancaster House speech on 17 January 2017 that the prime minster finally ruled out membership of the internal market and customs union, thus initially opting for what looked like a relatively hard Brexit.[47] This meant that the Norwegian model of the European Economic Area (EEA) was no longer an option. So, the post-Brexit solution would be some kind of free trade area (FTA). In her speech she announced 12 objectives, amounting to "one big goal of a new positive and constructive partnership between Britain and the European Union":

1. Certainty,
2. Control of our own laws,
3. Strengthen the Union (between the four nations of the United Kingdom),
4. Maintain the Common Travel Area with Ireland,
5. Control of immigration,
6. Rights for EU nationals in Britain, and British nationals in the EU,
7. Protect workers' rights,
8. Free trade with European markets,
9. New trade agreements with other countries,
10. The best place for science and innovation,
11. Cooperation in the fight against crime and terrorism, and
12. A smooth, orderly Brexit.

There was nothing about the Irish border in May's speech. In the important part on free trade with the EU she stated:

> "The agreement should allow for the freest possible trade in goods and services between Britain and the EU's member states. It should give British companies the maximum freedom to trade with and operate within European markets—and let European businesses do the same in Britain.
>
> But I want to be clear. What I am proposing cannot mean membership of the single market.
>
> European leaders have said many times that membership means accepting the '4 freedoms' of goods, capital, services and people. And being out of the EU but a member of the single market would mean complying with the EU's rules and regulations that implement those freedoms, without having a vote on what those rules and regulations are. It would mean accepting a role for the European Court of Justice that would see it still having direct legal authority in our country."

Subsequently the UK positions were further developed in a White Paper first published on 2 February 2017.[48]

It took some time, but eventually on 29 March 2017 the prime minister triggered Article 50 in the EU treaty, which stipulated a two-year period to negotiate a withdrawal agreement.[49]

On the same day the European Council issued guidelines for the negotiations.[50] The EU document mentioned some core principles, including the following: "A non-member of the Union, that does not live up to the same obligations as a member, cannot have the same rights and enjoy the same benefits as a member. In this context, the European Council welcomes the recognition by the British Government that the four freedoms of the Single Market are indivisible and that there can be no 'cherry picking'." It was also emphasized that the agreement would be a "single package," and that the EU would have a "unified position," not allowing separate negotiations between individual member states and the UK.

There would be a phased approach to the negotiations. The main purpose would be to assure an orderly withdrawal. A first phase therefore would, inter alia, look at citizens' rights and UK financial commitments while a member. However, an agreement on the future relationship "can only be finalized and concluded once the United Kingdom has become a third country." But "an overall understanding on the framework for the future relationship should be identified during the second phase of the negotiations." There might also be transitional arrangements.

The guidelines then went on to deal with the withdrawal agreement, singling out "reciprocal guarantees to safeguard the status and rights" of EU and UK citizens after the UK's withdrawal, a single financial settlement, and making sure to avoid a hard border between Northern Ireland and the Republic of Ireland, thus supporting "the goal of peace and reconciliation enshrined in the Good Friday Agreement."

Concerning the future relationship, the EU took note of the fact that the UK did "not seek to remain in the Single Market, but would like to pursue an ambitious free trade agreement." According to the EU, "any free trade agreement should be balanced, ambitious and wide-ranging." At the same time, it should not undermine the "integrity and proper functioning" of the internal market. Finally, there was a reference to the treaty's principle of "sincere cooperation," thus appealing for a unified position the 27 member states (EU27) vis-à-vis the UK.

On 5 April 2017 the European Parliament (EP) adopted a resolution on the negotiations with the UK.[51] It considered Brexit "an unprecedented and regrettable event." Continued membership of the internal market and/or the customs union would have been the optimal solution, but not possible because of UK objections to the four freedoms and the jurisdiction of the ECJ. The EP was especially concerned about the consequences for Northern Ireland and the preservation of the Good Friday Agreement "in all its parts." It made sure to remind all parties that "the withdrawal agreement can only be concluded with the consent of the European Parliament. As is also the case for any possible future agreement on relations between the European Union and the United Kingdom as well as any possible transitional arrangements."

As the negotiations started on 19 June 2017 there was a high degree of unity on the EU side, between the institutions and member states. It was more unclear what the UK actually wanted, and the Conservative Party was divided internally.

A few days after the start of the official negotiations the *Financial Times* outlined six scenarios for Brexit:[52]

1. No deal
2. Divorce-only agreement
3. Limited tariff-free deal
4. Far-ranging trade deal
5. Customs union
6. Single market.

Since the UK had ruled out customs union and single market, the main question was whether the parties could reach a far-ranging trade deal. Given the red lines, a comprehensive free trade deal would arguably be the best achievable long-term relation. No deal and divorce-only agreements would imply returning to the rules of the World Trade Organization (WTO), including tariffs and non-tariff barriers to trade (NTBs), which could be costly. Concerning Free Trade Agreements (FTAs) the EU already had several, the most far-reaching at the time being the Comprehensive Economic and Trade Agreement (CETA) with Canada. Eventually Prime Minister May decided that she wanted something more than the CETA, but less than the European Economic Area (EEA), which had Norway, Iceland, and Lichtenstein taking part in the internal market.

Phase One of the Negotiations

Negotiations started on 19 June 2017, focusing first on the three separation issues of citizens' rights, the Irish border, and a financial settlement. The chief negotiators were David Davis for the UK and Michel Barnier from the EU.[53] It was noticed in the press at the time that the EU delegation arrived with thick ring binders while the UK delegation brought no documentation. In connection with the second meeting in July 2017 Barnier expressed impatience with the UK's lack of clarity.[54]

On 22 September 2017 Prime Minister May made a speech in Florence outlining "a new era of cooperation and partnership between the UK and the EU."[55] She now mentioned Northern Ireland:

> "We have recognized from the outset there are unique issues to consider when it comes to Northern Ireland.
>
> The UK government, the Irish government and the EU as a whole have been clear that through the process of our withdrawal we will protect progress made in Northern Ireland over recent years—and the lives and livelihoods that depend on this progress.
>
> As part of this, we and the EU have committed to protecting the Belfast Agreement and the Common Travel Area and, looking ahead, we have both stated explicitly that we will not accept any physical infrastructure at the border."

On the economic partnership May still ruled out the single market and customs union. She also ruled out EEA membership, under which the UK would have "to adopt at home—automatically and in their entirety—new EU rules. Rules over which, in future, we will have little influence and no vote."

May recognized that the FTA recently negotiated with Canada was "the most advanced free trade agreement the EU has yet concluded." However, "compared with what exists between Britain and the EU today, it would nevertheless represent such a restriction on our mutual market access that it would benefit neither of our economies." No further clarification was given about the shortcomings she saw in the EU's Comprehensive and Economic Trade Agreement (CETA) with Canada.

Concerning the third issue in the first phase of the negotiations, the so-called divorce bill, May was short in her Florence speech. She was conscious that the UK departure would cause "uncertainty for the remaining member states and their taxpayers over the EU budget." She found some of the claims—from the EU side presumably—"exaggerated and unhelpful." But, "the UK will honour commitments we have made during the period of our membership."

It was also in the Florence speech that May asked for a two-year transition period after Brexit where the details of the future relationship would be negotiated.[56]

On 3 October 2017 the EP adopted a resolution on the state of play of the negotiations.[57] It reiterated the positions taken in the 5 April 2017 resolution. It supported a "time-limited transitional period" where the whole *acquis communautaire*, including the four freedoms, "under the full jurisdiction of the Court of Justice of the European Union ('CJEU')" would continue. The Parliament took note of what May had said in her Florence speech about the financial settlement, but awaited "concrete proposals from the UK Government it that regard." In general, the EP said that it was "vital that the commitments undertaken by the Prime Minister of the United Kingdom in her speech of 22 September 2017 translate into tangible changes to the United Kingdom's position and into concrete proposals accordingly."

Negotiations moved slowly through the autumn.[58] But a first agreement in principle was reached by 8 December 2017, dealing with the three separation issues singled out for the first phase.[59] The joint report that was issued consisted of 15 pages. The main points were the following:

1. Citizen's rights: the objective was to provide reciprocal protection. It dealt with various aspects, including family members, social security, health care, role of the Court of Justice of the EU (CJEU), Commission monitoring, and so on.
2. Ireland and Northern Ireland: commitments to the peace process (Good Friday agreement of 1998), UK commitment to avoid hard border. "In the absence of agreed solutions, the United Kingdom will maintain *full alignment* (emphasis added) with those rules of the Internal Market and the Customs Union which, now or in the future, support North-South cooperation . . . The United Kingdom will ensure that no new regulatory barriers develop between Northern Ireland and the rest of the United Kingdom" (known as *back-stop*). "The people of Northern Ireland who are Irish citizens will continue to enjoy rights as EU citizens, including where they reside in Northern Ireland"—detailed arrangements to be negotiated in next phase.
3. Financial settlement: complex methodology outlined. No figures mentioned.[60]

The EP responded to the Joint Report by adopting a new resolution on the play of the negotiations on 13 December 2017.[61] The Members of the European Parliament (MEPs) criticized the UK chief negotiator, David Davis, for calling "the outcome of phase 1 of the negotiations a mere statement of intent'," which risked undermining the good faith which had been built during the negotiations. Reflecting of a framework for a future EU-UK relationship the EP reiterated its position that an association agreement based on Article 217 of the Treaty of the Functioning of the European Union (TFEU) would be an appropriate framework. It was suggested that such future agreement should have four pillars: trade and economic relation, thematic cooperation, internal security, and foreign and security cooperation.

Phase Two of the Negotiations

The 8 December 2017 agreement allowed the negotiations to continue. The European Council adopted guidelines for the second phase on 15 December 2017.[62] It welcomed the Joint Report and called on the negotiators to complete the work on all withdrawal issues.

As mentioned previously the UK had suggested a transition period of around two years after withdrawal to negotiate the future relationship. The EU agreed to such transition period "covering the whole of the EU acquis, while the United Kingdom, as a third country, will no longer participate in or nominate or elect members of the EU institutions, nor participate in the decision-making of the Union bodies, offices and agencies." At the same time, the UK would participate in all EU policies during the transition period. "All existing Union regulatory, budgetary, supervisory, judiciary and enforcement instruments and structures" would continue to apply to the UK, and the UK would continue to take part in the customs union and the single market during the transition and thus also comply with the EU trade policy.

The Commission decided on 20 December 2017 to support a transition period until 31 December 2020, a little less than two years, but until the end of the multiannual Financial Framework in force at the time.

Negotiations kept moving slowly.

On 14 March 2018 the EP adopted a resolution on the framework of the future EU-UK relationship.[63] It was longer and more detailed than previous resolutions. Referring to the speeches that Prime Minister May had given on various occasions, the EP concluded that "she has not yet set out a consistent view on future EU-UK relations." In order to "avoid a cliff-edge scenario when the UK leaves the EU," transitional arrangements including the full EU *acquis* were necessary. A political declaration on the future relationship should be attached to the Withdrawal Agreement. The EP now went into quite some detailed considerations of future trade and economic relations. Based on the assumption that the UK would not accept membership of the internal market and the customs union, the EP stated, inter alia:

- A Deep and Comprehensive Free Trade Area requires a binding mechanism for convergence with the EU *acquis* and a binding role for the CJEU [Court of Justice of the European Union] in the interpretation of Union law and does not allow cherry-picking of sectors of the internal market;
- The current UK position is only compatible with a trade agreement pursuant to Article 207 TFEU   in order to get a comprehensive FTA/association agreement the UK would have to consider "its current red lines."
- Under an FTA market access for services is limited and always subject to exclusions, reservations, and exceptions.

Specifically, about services the EP now said "that leaving the internal market would lead to the UK losing both passporting rights for financial services and the possibility of opening branches in the EU subject to UK supervision." And this warning to the UK: "prudential carve-out and limitations in the cross-border provisions of financial services are a customary feature of FTAs."

Further, "with respect to food and agricultural products, access to the EU market is conditional on strict compliance with all EU law and standards, notably in the fields of food safety, GMOs, pesticides, geographical indications, animal welfare, labelling and traceability, sanity and phytosanitary standards, and human, animal and plant health."

Finally, on fisheries: "reciprocal market access for fishery products has to be negotiated as part of the future agreement, . . . access to the EU domestic market must be conditional on the access for EU vessels to the UK fishing grounds and their resources, as well as on the level of cooperation in the management of shared stocks."

On 19 March 2018, a joint UK-EU report on withdrawal was published where about 75 percent of an agreement was agreed.[64] It had six parts:

1. Common Provisions
2. Citizens' Rights
3. Separation Provisions
4. Transition
5. Financial Provisions
6. Institutional and Final Provisions

The hope now was that a final draft would be ready on 18–19 October 2018, leaving enough time for ratifications before the official leave date of 29 March 2019.

Key aspects on the transition period as outlined in the 19 March 2018 joint report were:

- The transitional period would last from Brexit day on 29 March 2019 to 31 December 2020.
- EU citizens arriving in the UK between these two dates would enjoy the same rights and guarantees as those who arrive before Brexit. The same would apply to UK expats on the continent.
- The UK would be able to negotiate, sign, and ratify its own trade deals during the transition period.
- The UK would still be party to existing EU trade deals with other countries.
- The UK's share of fishing catch would be guaranteed during transition, but the UK would effectively remain part of the Common Fisheries Policy without a direct say in its rules, until the end of 2020.

- Northern Ireland would effectively stay in parts of the single market and the customs union in the absence of other solutions to avoid a hard border with the Republic of Ireland. This so-called backstop made this part very controversial in the UK.

A few days later, on 23 March 2018, the EU published new guidelines.[65] They included the following points:

- "Balance of rights and obligations . . . ensure a level playing field."
- "The four freedoms are indivisible and there can be no 'cherry picking'."
- "The Union will preserve its autonomy as regards its decision-making."
- The European Council would work for "a balanced, ambitious and wide-ranging free trade agreement (FTA) . . . [to] be finalised and concluded once the UK is no longer a Member State."
- Trade in goods: "maintain zero tariffs and no quantitative restrictions with appropriate accompanying rules of origin."
- Appropriate customs cooperation.
- Disciplines on technical barriers to trade (TBT) and sanitary and phyto-sanitary (SPS) measures.
- Framework for voluntary regulatory cooperation.
- Trade in services: "Aim of allowing market access to provide services under host state rules, including . . . right of establishment for providers."
- Access to public procurement markets, investments, and protection of intellectual property rights, including geographical indications.

Many of these points were already dealt with in the Comprehensive Economic and Trade Agreement (CETA) with Canada, but the UK government at the time wanted more than the CETA.

Negotiations continued, but progress continued to be slow. What kind of customs arrangement could solve the Irish border problem was one of the issues.[66] Prime Minister May was caught in a two-level game with pressure in both London and Brussels.

A more concrete UK plan followed in July, namely, the so-called Checkers plan. It was agreed by the cabinet on 6 July 2018 as a relatively short document.[67] It was subsequently turned into a much more detailed 104-page-long White Paper published on 12 July.[68] The UK proposal was to establish a free trade area for goods, including agri-food. The UK and EU would maintain a "common rulebook," which meant a UK commitment to ongoing harmonization with EU rules on goods in order to provide for "frictionless trade" at the border. This meant that the UK would stay in the internal market for goods. The controversial question of the role of the ECJ was suggested solved by a joint institutional framework where UK courts would interpret the rules in the UK with due regard to EU case law and the ECJ would interpret the rules in the EU. However, the ECJ would remain the ultimate legal authority on EU rules. The White Paper introduced the concept of a "facilitated customs arrangement." It was a rather complex proposal, where the UK would apply EU tariffs and trade policy for goods intended for the EU, but its own tariffs and trade policy for goods intended for consumption in the UK. The White Paper also suggested that the UK should continue active participations in some EU agencies, such as European Aviation Safety Agency, the European Chemicals Agency, and the European Medicines Agency. Concerning services, it was confirmed that the UK would leave the internal market. This would mean that it could no longer take part in the EU's "passporting" regime. Instead the UK would seek some "equivalence" regime. Finally, the White Paper confirmed that free movement of people would come to an end. However, citizens could travel freely, without a visa, for tourism and temporary business activity.[69]

The day after the meeting at Chequers Brexit secretary David Davis resigned. He especially objected to the "common rule book" policy, which would hand "control of large swathes of our economy to the EU."[70] The following day Foreign Secretary Boris Johnson also resigned.[71]

According to one source the Chequers plan resembled the EU's association agreement with Ukraine, which is bringing Ukraine closer to the EU. David Davis preferred something more like a "Canada-style" free trade agreement.[72]

The biggest loser in the Chequers plan potentially was the London-focused financial services, depending on what new regulatory arrangement could be found. Without an agreement services would revert to WTO rules.[73]

David Davis was replaced by Dominic Raab as UK Brexit secretary. He met Michel Barnier, the EU Brexit negotiator, later that month. After the meeting Barnier said at a joint press conference that the Chequers plan would put "the integrity of our Customs Union, our Common Commercial Policy, our regulatory policy, and our fiscal revenue" at risk.[74]

After a meeting between Barnier and Raab the following month Barnier told the press that agreeing on a "backstop" on Northern Ireland that avoids a "hard border" was the last major outstanding issue to conclude the Withdrawal Agreement.[75] The moment the EU had rejected the Chequers plan with "common rulebook" and "facilitated customs arrangement" the Northern Irish border reemerged as an issue.

The two sides blamed each other for the impasse. If May tried to deal with individual EU member state leaders, she would be reminded that Barnier was the EU's chief negotiator. In an effort to deal with her two-level game problem May told the Conservative Party on 3 October, "If we don't come together, we risk ending up with no Brexit at all."[76] But Boris Johnson, her former foreign secretary, kept asking for the Chequers plan to be dropped in favor of a Canada-type deal that would not need the UK to apply EU regulations on trade.[77] This, however, would not solve the Northern Irish border problem.

The issue was becoming one of Chequers versus a Canada-style free trade agreement with one or more plusses. Both had problems with parliamentary arithmetic. The Chequers plan was opposed by the European Research Group of 60 Conservative MPs and the Democratic Unionist Party (DUP). Canada+ was opposed by the Labour Party, the Scottish National Party (SNP), and an estimated 30–40 Conservative MPs. Neither plan would get the support of at least 325 MPs in the 650-member House of Commons. The third possibility of staying in the customs union was supported by Labour, SNP, Liberal Democrats, and *Plaid Cymru* MPs, but would May survive negotiating that option?[78]

The self-imposed deadline of the end of October 2018 for the Withdrawal Agreement was not met completely. A Withdrawal Agreement and a Political Declaration were agreed between the European Commission and the UK negotiators, with some delay on 14 November, and endorsed by the European Council on 25 November 2018.[79]

The Withdrawal Agreement confirmed a 21-month transition period, called "implementation period." In this period the UK would follow EU rules without representation in the EU institutions. A possible extension of the period was foreseen. The period would be used to negotiate the future relationship between the EU and the UK.

The Agreement included the methodology for calculating the financial settlement, the "divorce bill," but no figure. The BBC mentioned that it was expected to "be at least £39bn." Later estimates reduced the figure somewhat.

Concerning citizens' rights, the EU citizens in the UK and UK citizens in EU member states would retain their residency and social security rights.

In respect to the Irish border the Withdrawal Agreement included the controversial backstop: If no agreement concerning the Irish border were to be found during the interim period there would be "a single customs territory between the Union and the United Kingdom." The UK would not be able to leave the backstop unilaterally without an agreement with the EU. Northern Ireland would follow internal market rules on movement of all products, including agricultural products. With the EU's customs code applied in Northern Ireland, Northern Irish businesses could bring goods into the Irish Republic and other parts of the internal market. The arrangement would also give UK goods tariff- and quota-free access to the remaining 27 EU member states. To ensure fair competition there were provisions on state aid, competition, taxation, and social and environmental standards.

The Withdrawal Agreement also dealt with fisheries policy. A separate agreement was to be negotiated about EU fishermen's access to UK waters: "The Union and the United Kingdom shall use their best endeavours to conclude and ratify 'an agreement' on access to waters and fishing opportunities." The agreement, presumably, would also have to deal with UK fishery products' access to the EU internal market, so there would be some basis for a deal.

In respect to laws and disputes the Withdrawal Agreement foresaw that the UK would remain under the Court of Justice of the EU (CJEU) during the transition period. The agreement further foresaw the creation of an arbitration system to deal with disputes afterward.

Finally, the agreement also included protocols on Gibraltar and the British military bases in Cyprus.[80]

In parallel with the Withdrawal Agreement the parties agreed on a Political Declaration dealing with future UK-EU relations.[81]

The Political Declaration was a nonbinding, relatively short document. It set out the framework for the future relationship in relatively general terms. It talked about "an ambitious, broad, deep and flexible partnership across trade and economic co-operation, law enforcement and criminal justice, foreign policy, security and defence and wider areas of co-operation." The future relationship would be "consistent with the Union's principles, in particular with respect to the integrity of the Single Market and the Customs Union and the indivisibility of the four freedoms." At the same time, it would also "ensure the sovereignty of the United Kingdom," whatever that meant.

Concerning trade in goods the declaration said that the relationship should be "as close as possible, with a view to facilitating the ease of legitimate trade." The parties envisaged "comprehensive arrangements that will create a free trade area, combining deep regulatory and customs cooperation, underpinned by provisions ensuring a level playing field for open and fair competition." The section on tariffs further talked about "ambitious customs arrangements that, in line with the Parties' objectives and principles . . . [would] build and improve on the single customs territory provided for in the Withdrawal Agreement which obviates the need for checks on rules of origin."

This text on customs arrangements was of course linked with the backstop. Prime Minister May managed to win support for the deal from her cabinet.[82] However, four members of the cabinet resigned, including the Brexit secretary Dominic Raab.[83] They feared that temporary customs arrangements to avoid a hard border between Northern Ireland and the Irish Republic could easily turn into a permanent customs union. In his resignation letter he stated:

> "For my part, I cannot support the proposed deal for two reasons. First, I believe that the regulatory regime proposed for Northern Ireland presents a very real threat to the integrity of the United Kingdom.
>
> Second, I cannot support the indefinite backstop arrangement, where the EU holds a veto over our ability to exit. The terms of the backstop amount to a hybrid of the EU Customs Union and Single Market obligations. No democratic nation has ever signed up to be bound by such an extensive regime, imposed externally without any democratic control over the laws to be applied, nor the ability to decide to exit the arrangement. That arrangement is now also taken as the starting point for negotiating the Future Economic Partnership. If we accept that, it will severely prejudice the second phase of negotiations against the UK."[84]

The departure of the Brexit secretary weakened the prime minister's hand vis-à-vis the Parliament.

A couple of other aspects of the Political Declaration should be mentioned. In the section on services and investment it was stated, "The Parties should conclude ambitious, comprehensive and balanced arrangements on trade in services and investment in services and non-service sectors, respecting each Party's right to regulate." Concerning market access, it stated, inter alia, "The arrangements should include provisions on market access and national treatment under host state rules for the Parties' service providers and investors, as well as address performance requirements imposed on investors." With respect to regulatory aspects, the declaration called for "a framework for voluntary regulatory cooperation." More specifically about financial services, obviously an important aspect of the future relationship, it was stated:

> Noting that both Parties will have equivalence frameworks in place that allow them to declare a third country's regulatory and supervisory regimes equivalent for relevant purposes the Parties should start assessing equivalence with respect to each other under these frameworks as soon as possible after the United Kingdom's withdrawal from the Union.

On the difficult issue of fisheries, the parties committed themselves to reach an agreement:

> While preserving regulatory autonomy, the Parties should cooperate on the development of measures for the conservation, rational management and regulation of fisheries, in a non-discriminatory manner. They will work closely with other coastal states and in international fora, including to manage shared stocks.
>
> Within the context of the overall economic partnership the Parties should establish a new fisheries agreement, *inter alia*, access to waters and quota shares.

The parties also foresaw cooperation in several other areas, including judicial cooperation, as well as foreign and defense policy cooperation.[85]

The European Council accepted the Withdrawal Agreement at a meeting on 25 November 2018. "We are leaving the EU but we are not leaving Europe," May said on the occasion. German chancellor Angela Merkel could not hide her disappointment. "It's tragic that the UK leaves the European Union," she said.[86]

INVOLUNTARY DEFECTION: THE IMPORTANCE OF DOMESTIC POLITICS

The Withdrawal Agreement reached in November 2018 now needed to be ratified on both sides. On the EU side this meant that it had to be approved by the Council of Minsters by a qualified majority vote (QMV) after receiving the European Parliament's consent (Article 50(2) TEU).

On the UK side it meant that both the House of Commons and the House of Lords should approve it. This was confirmed in the UK European Union (Withdrawal) Act 2018.[87] That Act required votes on the content of the Withdrawal Agreement and Political Declaration, something referred to as "meaningful votes."[88]

The first meaningful vote was planned for 11 December 2018, but postponed until 15 January 2019, because Prime Minister May realized she did not have the required majority in the Parliament. Her efforts to try to get some changes in the text did not succeed. Commission president Jean-Claude Juncker said that the EU was open to offer "clarifications," but he insisted that the agreement was the "best possible, the only possible" deal.[89] Prior to meeting her EU27 colleagues May had survived a no-confidence vote in the House of Commons on 13 December 2018, where no less than 117 of her MPs voted against her. Before the vote she had promised not to lead the Conservative Party into the next election.[90]

The "meaningful vote" on 15 January was lost by the government by a wide margin.[91] There were 432 no votes; only 202 voted yes. This was a major defeat;[92] 196 Conservative MPs supported the deal; 118 Conservative MPs voted against. Clearly the prime minister had serious problems getting her own party to support her. The 10 DUP MPs also voted against. The following day, however, May survived a no-confidence vote proposed by Labour leader Jeremy Corbyn, 305 votes to 325. The 118 Conservative MPs who had voted against her Withdrawal Agreement the day before swung behind her. The 10 DUP MPs now also supported her.[93]

The Parliament actively debated and voted on various proposals to try to steer the process. On 29 January 2019 they voted to reject a "no deal" and in another vote they called for the so-called backstop to be scrapped. The

Parliament also voted against an extension of Article 50 and a proposal from the Labour Party to keep the UK permanently in the EU customs union.[94]

Theresa May now said she would go to Brussels to seek a "pragmatic solution" without specifying what that could mean.[95] Days later when EU's chief negotiator Barnier met the new UK Brexit secretary Stephen Barkley he urged the UK government to endorse the idea of the UK staying permanently in the EU's customs union as also proposed by Labour leader Corbyn. But May had rejected that idea in a letter to Corbyn on 10 February 2019.[96]

Prior to a second "meaningful vote" on 12 March 2019, May claimed that she had got "legally binding" assurances from the EU that the "backstop" would not be permanent. She said that the UK government would make a "Unilateral Declaration" stating that if the "backstop comes into use and discussions on our future relationship break down . . . there would be nothing to prevent the UK instigating measures that would ultimately dis-apply the backstop."[97] These assurances did not do the trick. The second meaningful vote was another defeat for the government. There were 242 yes votes, but 391 no votes. The no votes included 75 Conservative MPs and the 10 DUP MPs.[98] Sadly for May, Attorney General Geoffrey Cox had concluded in a legal opinion that the "Joint Instrument" agreed between May and EU negotiators in Strasbourg would not allow the UK to unilaterally drop the Irish backstop. The "legal risk" of being trapped by the Irish backstop according to Cox, therefore, "remains unchanged."[99]

The following day, 13 March 2019, a government motion whether to pursue on no-deal Brexit was proposed. An amendment proposed by Caroline Spelman categorically rejecting a no-deal passed narrowly by 312 votes to 308. The amendment, however, was nonbinding.[100]

On 14 March 2019, then, given the approaching Brexit day, 29 March, the Parliament voted to extend Article 50 to 30 June by 413 to 202 votes after some amendments were rejected.[101] 30 June was the last day for the UK to avoid having to take part in the May 2019 EP elections. A first extension was granted by the EU on 21 March 2019, until 12 April, or, in the case that the MPs approved the Withdrawal Agreement, until 22 May 2019.[102]

On 27 March 2019 a series of so-called "indicative votes" took place in the House of Commons in the hope of finding a way to move forward. They included: no deal, Common Market 2.0, EFTA and EEA, customs union, Labour alternative (permanent customs union and close alignment with the single market), revocation to avoid No Deal, referendum on the Withdrawal Agreement, and Managed No Deal.[103] They were all defeated. The closest to passing was the customs union proposed by Kenneth Clarke. It received 265 yes votes, but 271 no votes.[104] The Parliament's effort to "seize control" failed.[105]

May then wanted to give the Withdrawal Agreement one more chance. But the Speaker John Bercow ruled out a third vote on the same proposal, so the Political Declaration was taken out and the vote was solely about the Withdrawal Agreement. That third "meaningful vote" took place on 29 March 2019. Third time lucky? No. The agreement was defeated with 344 no votes, receiving 286 yes votes.[106]

A new round of indicative votes followed on 1 April 2019. This time the Speaker had reduced the proposals to four: Customs Union, Common Market 2.0, confirmatory public vote, and revocation of Article 50 to avoid No Deal. Once again, the proposals all failed to get a majority. Customs Union was the closest to passing, getting 273 yes votes, but 276 no votes.[107]

Prime Minister May responded to the situation by offering cross-party talks. This was criticized by many Brexiteers, including Boris Johnson. A divided Labour Party demanded that the UK stay in a customs union and that a second referendum should remain an option. With the likelihood of a broader coalition for the Withdrawal Agreement looking slim the pressure for requesting a further extension to Article 50 increased.[108] On 4 April the House of Commons voted narrowly by 313 to 312 to seek another extension to avoid the UK crashing out on 12 April.[109] The UK quietly starting to prepare for participation in the EP elections on 23 May 2019.[110] May continued to try to reach a cross-party compromise, but she was still not willing to accept Labour's idea of staying in a customs union because it would bar the UK from negotiating its own bilateral trade agreements.

After authorization by the House of Commons on 8 April 2019, May requested an extension until 30 June 2019. On 10 April she announced that the EU27 had agreed to an extension until 1 June if the UK failed to participate in the May EP elections, otherwise until 31 October 2019.[111]

A fourth meaningful vote was now considered by May, but it was rejected by Conservative Eurosceptics and the Labour Party.[112]

On 24 May 2019 Theresa May announced that she would resign as Conservative Party leader on 7 June, but continue to serve until a new leader of the Conservative Party could be elected.[113] She was still serving when U.S. president Donald Trump visited the UK at the beginning of June. She tended her resignation as prime minister to the Queen on 24 June.

UK Participation in the European Parliament Election

Short of having accepted the Withdrawal Agreement the UK had to take part in the EP election on 23 May 2019. As predicted the big loser was the Conservative Party, and the big winner was Nigel Farage's Brexit Party. In terms of votes these were the shares of the participating parties: Brexit Party 31.6

percent, Lib Dem 20.3 percent, Labour 14.1 percent, Greens 12.1 percent, Conservative 9.1 percent, SNP 3.6, Plaid Cymru 1 percent, Change UK 3.4 percent, and UKIP 3.3 percent. In terms of seats won these were the results: Brexit Party 29, Lib Dem 16, Labour 10, Greens seven, Conservative four, SNP three, Plaid Cymru one. Compared with the previous elections in 2014 the main change was that the new Brexit Party replaced UKIP. The two biggest parties in the House of Commons both lost votes in the EP elections, while the Lib Dems and the Greens, both pro-Remain, added votes.[114]

Those elected served in the EP until Brexit finally happened on 31 January 2020.

Enter Boris Johnson: A Game of Chicken?

Subsequently, after internal debates the Conservative membership elected Boris Johnson as party leader and he became prime minister on 24 July 2019.

The list of candidates at the outset was rather long. Actively seeking no-deal were Andrea Leadsom and Esther McVey. Open to no-deal in October were Boris Johnson, Dominic Raab, and Sajid Javid. Against no-deal in October were Michael Gove, Jeremy Hunt, and Mark Harper. Finally, against no-deal at all were Rory Stewart and Matt Hancock.[115]

The new prime minister Boris Johnson entered the job with a determination to get the UK out of the EU by 31 October 2019, the deadline now agreed with the EU. He intended to try to get a better deal in Brussels. But if that turned out to be impossible, he would go for a no-deal Brexit, he said.

The two sides in the Brexit game, as we have seen, had conflicting red lines. The EU insisted on the integrity of the internal market, including the four freedoms: free movement of goods, services, capital, and people. Further, the EU had insisted that no new hard border should emerge between Northern Ireland and the Republic of Ireland. The UK insisted on leaving the customs union and the internal market, the biggest problem with the internal market being free movement of people. These red lines clashed in Northern Ireland. The so-called backstop was invented to deal with the problem. If Northern Ireland would stay in the customs union and to some extent in the internal market until a future relationship could be negotiated/invented, that would maintain the open border, but it would force the other parts of the UK to stay in the customs union too, and the UK would then not be able to negotiate its own free trade agreements with other countries.

A no-deal solution would lead to the reintroduction of WTO rules, thus tariffs, and if there was no regulatory alignment, there would also be border checks on product standards, and so on, thus leading to a hard border, which could affect the fragile peace in Northern Ireland.

Johnson set out to find another agreement with the EU than the one May had negotiated. He appeared determined to get the UK out by 31 October 2019. Was Brexit becoming a Game of Chicken? Did Johnson expect/hope that Brussels would blink first because of his commitment, come what may? Was there any chance on an agreement? It would presuppose that someone could find a way to square the circle. Or could minor changes in the backstop language get Johnson to declare victory and get the Parliament to accept it?

There were also suggestions that Johnson in reality was preparing for a parliamentary election, in the hope of getting a more amenable parliament? There was a lot of speculation in the media.

When he formed his cabinet most of the ministers in May's previous cabinet were sacked. Most of the new cabinet members had been leading figures in the Vote Leave campaign. Dominic Raab became foreign secretary and Johnson's de facto deputy. Priti Patel became home secretary, Theresa Villiers environment secretary, and Andrea Leadsom business secretary. Michael Gove got a senior post. Stephen Barclay stayed on as Brexit secretary. Dominic Cummings, the controversial strategist of Vote Leave campaign, became one of Johnson's chief advisers in 10 Downing Street.[116]

The two-level game continued. Johnson wanted to renegotiate May's Withdrawal Agreement. He focused on the backstop, which he wanted to get deleted. No way, answered Michel Barnier from Brussels. Elimination of the backstop would be unacceptable.[117] Johnson then threated to leave on 31 October, "no ifs, no buts."

The other level in the two-level game was domestic. There was no majority for a no-deal Brexit in the House of Commons. There were speculations that Johnson might call a snap election. But according to the UK's Fixed Term Parliamentary Act, short of losing a confidence vote, that would require two-thirds of MPs agreeing to an election. Johnson's first effort to deal with the parliament was to announce its prorogation on 28 August 2019, for five weeks, from 9 September until 14 October, with the approval of the Queen.[118] The idea was to limit the time available for the Parliament to deal with the issues. But the prorogation was widely criticized as undemocratic, and on 24 September the Supreme Court ruled that it was indeed unlawful.[119]

On 4 September 2019 the opposition joined by 21 Conservative rebels led by former Conservative minister Oliver Letwin seized control of the Parliament agenda to debate an anti no-deal Brexit bill proposed by backbencher Hilary Benn. Johnson failed to stop the bill blocking a no-deal Brexit, and he lost a vote on whether to hold an early election. The motion to hold an early election received 298 votes to 56, but needed 434 votes in favor. Johnson's angry response was to oust 21 MPs from the Conservative Party, including former chancellor Philip Hammond and Winston Churchill's grandson

Nicholas Soames. Also included were Kenneth Clark, Dominic Grieve, and Oliver Letwin.[120]

The so-called Benn Act also required the prime minister to send a letter to the EU asking for an Article 50 extension until 31 January 2020 if MPs had not approved a withdrawal deal or approved a no-deal Brexit by 19 October 2019.[121]

A second attempt on 9 September to call an early election also failed. It received 293 votes against 46 with 303 not voting.[122] Prior to the vote Johnson's younger brother, Education Minister Jo Johnson, had resigned.[123]

Johnson maintained that he wanted to "get Brexit done." At the beginning of October, the UK government sent a proposal to Brussels, which included the removal of the backstop, which in turn was rejected by the European Commission. Bilateral talks on 8 October collapsed, with European Council president Donald Tusk accusing Johnson of playing a "stupid blame game" Said Tusk, "At stake is the future of Europe and the UK as well as the security and interests of our people. You don't want a deal, you don't want an extension, you don't want to revoke, quo vadis?"[124]

At the brink of collapse of the negotiations were the two sides reviewing their "best alternative to no deal" (BATNA)? A no-deal would be costly to both sides, the UK and the EU. Arguably, therefore, Johnson's threat of a no-deal Brexit was not very credible.

Striking the Deal

On 10 October 2019 Johnson had a three-hour meeting with the Irish prime minister Leo Varadkar. The meeting marked a change in the rhetoric. The two leaders now said that they could see "a pathway to a possible deal." It appears that Johnson was proposing a regulatory border between Northern Ireland and Britain, initially for four years, combined with "a process of renewable democratic consent by the executive and assembly of Northern Ireland."[125]

Could the deal be done quickly so that the UK could leave on 31 October? Johnson was under parliamentary orders to seek an extension until 31 January 2020 if no deal allowed for Brexit on 31 October.[126] The signals from a meeting of the General Affairs Council on Article 50 in Luxembourg on 15 October were reasonably positive.[127]

On 17 October 2019, a UK-EU Brexit deal, which would remove the Irish backstop, was announced.[128] According to the new deal there would be no customs duties on goods brought into Northern Ireland from the other parts of the UK. However, if there was a risk that the good would be "exported" into the Irish Republic—or other parts of the EU—there would be a customs duty to pay at the point of entry into Northern Ireland. If the good would stay in Northern Ireland the importing firm would get a refund. But there would be no refund of goods that moved to the Republic of Ireland—or other parts of the EU. A joint committee would be established to deal with the practical details.[129]

That was not all. In order to avoid border checks between Northern Ireland and the Republic of Ireland the former would in effect remain in the EU's internal market and customs union, including for agricultural products. It meant that key areas of EU legislation would continue to apply in Northern Ireland. In order for this not to appear undemocratic a "democratic consent" mechanism was inserted in the Protocol on Ireland/Northern Ireland (Art. 18 in Revised Protocol). According to this mechanism the members of the Northern Ireland Assembly will decide before the fourth year of the Protocol's operation whether the provisions of the Protocol shall continue to apply. After that the assembly will decide every four years whether to continue the provisions.[130]

The remaining parts of the Withdrawal Agreement negotiated the year before by Prime Minister May stayed largely unchanged.

However, it was not only a question of striking a deal with EU27, but could Johnson get his agreement accepted in the House of Commons? On 17 October Northern Ireland's DUP announced that they could not accept Johnson's plan: "As things stand, we could not support what is being suggested on customs and consent issues, and there is a lack of clarity" on value-added tax.[131]

On 19 October Johnson tried to get the House of Commons to accept his agreement by a "meaningful vote." But the House passed an amendment proposed by Oliver Letwin, which made the acceptance depend on implementing legislation, the enactment of a Withdrawal Agreement Bill.[132] To pass the legislation would require the bill going through several stages in both the House of Commons and the House of Lords before becoming law.[133] Johnson therefore wrote to European Council president Donald Tusk on 19 October 2019, requesting an extension until 31 January 2020. Remarkably, the letter was unsigned.

On 22 October Johnson got support for the proceeding of the Withdrawal Agreement Bill by 329 votes to 299, but the MPs rejected his fast-track timetable, making it impossible to leave on 31 October.[134] Johnson had to abandon his plan to leave the EU on 31 October. Instead he planned an election. On 29 October he got the approval of the House of Commons for a general election on 12 December 2019.[135] The day before the EU had approved the extension to 31 January 2020.[136]

The election on 12 December gave Johnson an 80-seat majority, which allowed him to complete his deal with the EU. The Conservative Party won

365 seats, an increase of 66; Labour 203 seats, a loss of 42; SNP 48, a gain of 13; the Liberal Democrats 11, a loss of 10. The results were particularly bad for Labour and the Liberal Democrats.[137] Afterward Labour leader Corbyn announced that he would not lead Labour at the next election and the Liberal Democratic leader Jo Swinson, who lost her seat, stepped down. SNP, on the other hand, won an election landslide in Scotland.[138] In Northern Ireland the Democratic Unionist Party (DUP) won eight seats, a loss of two; Sinn Féin got seven seats, unchanged.

Johnson's win was welcomed by EU27.[139]

With a large parliamentary majority, the House of Commons could approve the EU Withdrawal Bill on 9 January 330 to 231 votes.[140] It got the Royal Assent on 23 January 2020.[141] The following day Commission president Ursula von der Leyen and European Council president Charles Michel signed the Withdrawal Agreement, and it was sent to the EP, which gave its consent on 29 January. The European Council formerly adopted, by written procedure, the decision on the conclusion of the Withdrawal Agreement on behalf of EU27 on 30 January.[142] The UK could leave the EU on the 31 January 2020 at midnight CET (11pm UK time).

That concluded the first part of the Brexit saga. Negotiations about the future relationship could start, optimistically scheduled to finish by the end on 2020, after the so-called transition period.

FUTURE SCENARIOS

The Brexit negotiations were focused on reaching a Withdrawal Agreement. The negotiation of the future relationship will follow afterward during an interim period where the UK will remain part of the *acquis communautaire*, the internal market in particular, without being represented in the EU institutions. But the discussion of various scenarios for the future started early on. Often the comparison was with existing arrangements of the EU with third countries, stretching from the relatively close relationship of Norway, Iceland, and Lichtenstein, known as the European Economic Area (EEA) at one end of a continuum and a relationship based on GATT/WTO rules at the other end, meaning Most-Favored-Nation (MFN) treatment, that is, the same treatment as other WTO members which do not have some free trade agreement or customs union with the EU, based on article XXIV in GATT. Among countries having a customs union with the EU we can mention Turkey, and among countries having FTAs with the EU we can mention Canada. The Theresa May government expressed the preference for something less than the Norway model but more than the Canada model.

What we know in the early days after Brexit on 31 January 2020 is what the parties agreed in the revised Political Declaration attached to the Withdrawal Agreement, on Economic Partnership, the text says, inter alia:

> The Parties agree to develop an ambitious, wide-ranging and balanced economic partnership. This partnership will be comprehensive, encompassing a Free Trade Agreement, as well as wider sectoral cooperation where it is in the mutual interest of both Parties. It will be underpinned by provisions ensuring a level playing field for open and fair competition. . . . It should facilitate trade and investment between the Parties to the extent possible, while respecting the integrity of the Union's Single Market and the Customs Union as well as the United Kingdom's internal market, and recognising the development of an independent trade policy by the United Kingdom.[143]

What that will mean in practice remains to be seen. Later the text also talks about "deep regulatory and customs cooperation." Further, "The economic partnership should through a Free Trade Agreement ensure no tariffs, fees, charges or quantitative restrictions across all sectors with appropriate and modern accompanying rules of origin, and with ambitious customs arrangements that are in line with the Parties' objectives and principles." And on regulations, "While preserving regulatory autonomy, the Parties will put in place provisions to promote regulatory approaches that are transparent, efficient, promote avoidance of unnecessary barriers to trade in goods and are compatible to the extent possible." Concerning services, the aim is cooperation toward some kind of equivalence of regulations. There should in principle be free movement of capital and payments. Concerning public procurement, the aim is to go beyond the WTO Government Procurement Agreement (GPA). Given that the UK has ruled out free movement of persons the aim should at least be visa-free travel for short-term visits. The Common Travel Area (CTA) between the UK and Ireland will continue.

On the sensitive area of fisheries policy, the Political Declaration included the following:

1. While preserving regulatory autonomy, the parties should cooperate on the development of measures for the conservation, rational management and regulation of fisheries, in a nondiscriminatory manner. They will work closely with other coastal states and in international fora, including to manage shared stocks.
2. Within the context of the overall economic partnership the parties should establish a new fisheries agreement on, inter alia, access to waters and quota shares.

3. The parties will use their best endeavors to conclude and ratify their new fisheries agreement by 1 July 2020 in order for it to be in place in time to be used for determining fishing opportunities for the first year after the transition period.

So, on the insistence of the EU the fisheries aspect of the future relationship was singled out as being so important that an agreement should be found by 1 July 2020, before the other aspects of the future relationship could be tackled.

The Political Declaration also suggested future cooperation in Foreign and Security policy areas and the Justice and Home Affairs areas. Management should take place through a Joint Committee. Independent arbitration panels should be used to settle disputes. These might refer questions of interpretation of EU law to the Court of Justice of the European Union (CJEU).

The Political Declaration also mentions that the EU will be negotiating under Article 218 TFEU concerning international agreements. It does not mention Article 217, the more specific article concerning association agreements, suggesting possibly that the ambition is somewhat reduced because of the UK positions, but Article 218 TFEU does mention association agreements among the various kinds of agreements that can be negotiated, specifically saying that an association agreement requires the consent of the EP.

Article 217 on association agreements talks about crating "privileged links," with "reciprocal rights and obligations," and "institutions designed to implement and monitor the agreement." It usually includes some kind of privileged trade or a free trade agreement and some sharing of relevant EU regulations, the so-called *acquis communautaire*. Often it will also include some political and cultural cooperation and mention respect for human rights and democratic governance.[144]

Given what we know about the positions of the two sides, the EU27 and the UK, and what they agreed on in the Political Declaration, what is the most likely outcome?[145] The UK has stated that it does not want to take part in the internal market. That rules out the Norway model, the EEA. Nor does the UK want to stay in the customs union. That rules out the Turkey model. It seems that both parties rule out the no deal option about the future relations, although the UK may continue to use it as a threat during the negotiations. If no-deal is avoided it rules out the WTO model. What then about the Swiss model? Based on a huge number of bilateral agreements it leaves Switzerland partially in the internal market and there is free movement and Switzerland takes part in the Schengen Area. Switzerland further makes a contribution to the EU budget. So that model, it seems, is excluded. Looking next at the association agreement that the Ukraine, Georgia, and Moldova have with the EU, the Deep and Comprehensive Free Trade Area (DCFTA), there are some good elements from a British perspective: control of immigration is possible, independent trade policy is possible, no obligatory contribution to the EU budget, not in the Common Agricultural Policy (CAP), nor the Common Fisheries Policy (CFP), there is tariff-free trade with the EU and access to the EU internal market for services and possibility of voluntary participation in EU programs. However, the regulatory part and partial jurisdiction of the CJEU, which put the DCFTA into the category of association agreements, are problematic from the stated British point of view. That leaves the Canada model, and other recent FTAs with other industrial countries, like the FTAs with South Korea, Singapore, and Japan. The Canada model scores well on the main UK "red lines": control of immigration, no CJEU jurisdiction, no applicability of EU regulations, possibility of independent trade policy, no budgetary contributions to the EU, and exit from the CAP and CFP. So, what is the problem with CETA? There is very limited access to the EU's internal market for services, none for financial services. The FTA with Singapore does include financial services, so the inclusion of financial services in an FTA is not excluded. However, although these FTAs create free trade for industrial goods, they certainly do not establish the "seamless and frictionless border," which May talked about in her Lancaster speech in 2017.[146] Probably the UK has given up on that requirement since then. In conclusion, a CETA+, maybe CETA++, would preferably have to deal with services, including financial services and transport services. Some mutual recognition of standards, or equivalence agreements, and facilitation and minimization of border checks could further contribute to reducing the costs of non-tariff barriers to trade (NTBs).

NOTES

1. For general historic introductions to European integration, see Marie-Thérèse Bitsch, *Histoire de la construction européenne* (Brussels: Editions Complexe, 1999); Desmond Dinan, *Europe Recast: A History of European Union* (Basingstoke and New York, NY: Palgrave Macmillan, 2004); and Wilfried Loth, *Building Europe: A History of European Unification* (Oldenbourg: De Gruyter, 2015).

2. Alex May, *Britain and Europe since 1945* (London and New York, NY: Routledge, 2013).

3. Françoise de La Serre, *La Grande-Bretagne et la Communauté européenne* (Paris: Presses Universitaires de France, 1987).

4. May, *Britain and Europe since 1945*, 31.

5. Charles Pentland, *International Theory and European Integration* (London: Faber and Faber Limited, 1973).

6. Miriam Camps, *Britain and the European Community 1955–1963* (Princeton, NJ: Princeton University Press, 1964).

7. Finn Laursen, *The Development of the EU as a Sea-Policy Actor: Fish, Ships and Navies* (Cheltenham: Edward Elgar, 2020).

8. May, *Britain and Europe since 1945*, 50.

9. Ibid., 52–53.

10. Ibid., 59–60.

11. Ibid., 62 and 111. For more extensive treatment, see Anthony King, *Britain Says Yes: The 1975 Referendum on the Common Market* (Washington, DC: American Enterprise Institute, 1977); and David Butler and Uwe Kitzinger, *The 1975 Referendum*, 2nd Edition (New York, NY: Macmillan Press, 1996).

12. Stephen George, *An Awkward Partner: Britain in the European Community* (Oxford: Oxford University Press, 2nd Edition, 1994; 3rd Edition, 1998).

13. Finn Laursen, "The Merger Treaty Creating a Single Commission and Council of the European Communities," Forthcoming in *Oxford Encyclopedia of European Union Politics* (Oxford: Oxford University Press), doi:10.1093/acrefore/9780190228637.013.1150.

14. Finn Laursen, ed., *Designing the European Union: From Paris to Lisbon* (Basingstoke: Palgrave Macmillan, 2012).

15. May, *Britain and Europe since 1945*, 63–65.

16. Margaret Thatcher, "Speech to the College of Europe ('The Bruges Speech')," https://www.margaretthatcher.org/document/107332.

17. Ibid., 72.

18. Ibid., 73.

19. Robert Wester, "The United Kingdom and European Political Union," in *The Intergovernmental Conference on Political Union*, eds. Finn Laursen and Sophie Vanhoonacker (Dordrecht: Martinus Nijhoff Publishers, 1992), 189–201.

20. May, *Britain and Europe since 1945*, 75–78.

21. Wester, "The United Kingdom and European Political Union," op. cit., 200.

22. Edward Best, "The United Kingdom and the Ratification of the Maastricht Treaty," in *The Ratification of the Maastricht Treaty*, eds. Finn Laursen and Sophie Vanhoonacker (Dordrecht: Martinus Nijhoff, 1994), 245–78.

23. May, *Britain and Europe since 1945*, 84.

24. See also Best, op. cit., 272–73.

25. May, op. cit., 86.

26. Ibid., 68–69.

27. Ibid., 87.

28. On the Amsterdam Treaty developments, see also Edward Best, "The United Kingdom: From Isolation Towards Influence?" in *The Amsterdam Treaty: National Preference Formation, Interstate Bargaining and Outcome*, ed. Finn Laursen (Odense: Odense University Press, 2002), 359–78.

29. See also Henrik Larsen, "United Kingdom: New Approach and New Influence?" in *The Treaty of Nice: Actor Preferences, Bargaining and Institutional Choice*, ed. Finn Laursen (Leiden: Martinus Nijhoff Publishers, 2006), 307–21; and Steen Rynning, "The European Security and Defence Policy: Coming of Age?" in ibid., 479–501.

30. On this period, for an overview, see especially Andrew Geddes, *Britain and the European Union* (London: Palgrave Macmillan, 2013), Chapter 4.

31. Ibid., 95.

32. For more on these developments, see Finn Laursen, ed., *The Making of the EU's Lisbon Treaty: The Role of the Member States* (Brussels: P. I. E. Peter Lang, 2012).

33. Geddes, *Britain and the European Union*, 106–10.

34. Quoted from ibid., 103.

35. For more on these points, see ibid., 105. A *passerelle* is a provision in the EU treaty that allows the Council by a unanimous vote to pass from unanimity to QMV.

36. By Professor Phillip Allott, quoted in ibid., 105.

37. Geoffrey Evans and Anand Menon, *Brexit and British Politics* (Cambridge: Polity Press, 2017), 9–10.

38. Ibid., 9. See also "Cameron Takes Gamble with In/put EU Referendum Pledge," *Euractiv*, January 23, 2013. For text of the so-called Bloomberg speech, see https://www.gov.uk/government/speeches/eu-speech-at-bloomberg.

39. "EU Reform Deal: What Cameron Wanted and What He Got," https://www.bbc.com/news/uk-politics-eu-referendum-35622105 (accessed April 4, 2019).

40. For the essential aspects of the different demands and agreements, see "David Cameron's EU Reform Deal Scorecard," https://blogs.spectator.co.uk/2016/02/david-camerons-draft-eu-deal-full-text/ (accessed April 4, 2019). For the full text of the final agreement, see conclusions from "European Council Meeting," February 18–19, 2016, http://data.consilium.europa.eu/doc/document/ST-1-2016-INIT/en/pdf.

41. Evans and Menon, op. cit., 48–49.

42. Ibid., 51–57.

43. https://www.bbc.com/news/politics/eu_referendum/results (accessed July 17, 2019).

44. Jack Glynn and Anand Menon, "Brexit," in *The British General Election of 2017*, eds. Philip Cowley and Dennis Kavanagh (Cham: Palgrave Macmillan, 2018), 21–40.

45. https://www.bbc.com/news/election/2017/results (accessed July 19, 2019).

46. Michelle Cini and Nieves Pérez-SolórzanoBorragán, "Brexit," in *European Union Politics*, 6th Edition, eds. Michelle Cini and Nieves Pérez-SolórzanoBorragán (Oxford: Oxford University Press, 2019), 410.

47. "The Government's Negotiating Objectives for Exiting the EU: PM Speech," https://www.gov.uk/government/speeches/the-governments-negotiating-objectives-for-exiting-the-eu-pm-speech (accessed August 10, 2919).

48. "The United Kingdom's Exit from and New Partnership with the European Union White Paper," February 2, 2017, https://www.gov.uk/government/publications

/the-united-kingdoms-exit-from-and-new-partnership-with-the-european-union-white-paper.

49. *The Prime Minister's Letter*, March 29, 2017, https://assets.publishing.service.gov.uk/government/uploads/system/uploads/attachment_data/file/604079/Prime_Ministers_letter_to_European_Council_President_Donald_Tusk.pdf.

50. https://www.consilium.europa.eu/en/press/press-releases/2017/04/29/euco-brexit-guidelines/.

51. "European Parliament, Resolution of April 5, 2017 on Negotiations with the United Kingdom Following its Notification that it Intends to Withdraw from the European Union (2017/2593(RSP))," http://www.europarl.europa.eu/doceo/document/TA-8-2017-0102_EN.html?redirect.

52. "Hard or Soft Brexit? The Six Scenarios for Britain," https://www.ft.com/content/52fb4998-573f-11e7-9fed-c19e2700005f (accessed July 18, 2019).

53. "Brexit Talks Start with Smiles, Focus on Tough Issues," *Euractiv*, June 19, 2017.

54. "No Solution in Sight for Brexit's Controversial Issues," *Euractiv*, July 20, 2017.

55. "PM's Florence Speech: A New Era of Cooperation and Partnership between the UK and the EU," https://www.gov.uk/government/speeches/pms-florence-speech-a-new-era-of-cooperation-and-partnership-between-the-uk-and-the-eu (Accessed August 10, 2019).

56. "May Asks for Two-Year Transition Deal after Brexit," *Euractiv*, September 22, 2017.

57. "European Parliament Resolution of October 3, 2017 on the State of Play of Negotiations with the United Kingdom (2017/2847(RSP))," http://www.europarl.europa.eu/doceo/document/TA-8-2017-0361_EN.html.

58. "Brexit Talks Resume, Slow Progress Set to Cause Delays in Roadmap," *Euractiv*, November 9, 2017.

59. "Brexit Breakthrough as Commission Says 'Sufficient Progress' Made," *Euractiv*, December 8, 2017.

60. "Joint Report from the Negotiators of the European Union and the United Kingdom Government on Progress during Phase 1 of Negotiations under Article 50 TEU on the United Kingdom's Orderly Withdrawal from the European Union," December 8, 2017, https://ec.europa.eu/commission/sites/beta-political/files/joint_report.pdf.

61. "European Parliament Resolution of December 13, 2017 on the State of Play of Negotiations with the United Kingdom (2017/2964(RSP))," http://www.europarl.europa.eu/doceo/document/TA-8-2017-0490_EN.html.

62. https://www.consilium.europa.eu/media/32236/15-euco-art50-guidelines-en.pdf. See also "Post-Brexit 'Free Trade' Talks with UK to Start in January, EU Says," *Euractiv*, December 20, 2017.

63. "European Parliament Resolution of March 14, 2018 on the Framework of the Future EU-UK Relationship," https://www.europarl.europa.eu/doceo/document/TA-8-2018-0069_EN.html.

64. "Draft Agreement on the Withdrawal of the United Kingdom of Great Britain and Northern Ireland from the European Union and the European Atomic Energy Community Highlighting the Progress Made (Coloured Version) in the Negotiation Round with the UK of March 16–19, 2018," https://ec.europa.eu/commission/sites/beta-political/files/draft_agreement_coloured.pdf.

65. https://www.consilium.europa.eu/media/33458/23-euco-art50-guidelines.pdf.

66. " 'The Clock is Ticking'—EU Warns Britain of Poor Brexit Progress," *Euractiv*, May 15, 2018.

67. "At-a-Glance: The New UK Brexit Plan Agreed at Chequers," https://www.bbc.com/news/uk-politics-44749993.

68. "The Future Relationship between the United Kingdom and the European Union," https://www.gov.uk/government/publications/the-future-relationship-between-the-united-kingdom-and-the-european-union/the-future-relationship-between-the-united-kingdom-and-the-european-union-html-version.

69. See also Chris Morris, "Brexit: What Does the Government White Paper Reveal?" https://www.bbc.com/news/uk-44807561.

70. "Brexit Minister Davis Steps Down in Big Blow to May," *Euractiv*, July 9, 2018.

71. "The Path Boris Johnson Took to Resigning as Foreign Secretary," https://www.theguardian.com/politics/2018/jul/09/boris-johnson-his-path-to-resigning-as-foreign-secretary.

72. "UK Brexit Paper Backs Ukraine-Style Association Pact," *Euractiv*, July 12, 2018.

73. "May's Brexit Blueprint Faces Backlash after Sacrificing Services," *Euractiv*, July 13, 2018.

74. "EU Rejects Britain's Key Elements of Special Customs Plan after Brexit," *Euractiv*, July 27, 2018.

75. "Brexit Talks 'Continuous', Say Negotiators as They Vow to Ramp Up Talks," *Euractiv*, July 21, 2018.

76. "Back Me or Risk Collapse of Brexit, May Warns Warring Tories," *Euractiv*, October 3, 2018.

77. "Tusk Slams UK Slurs on EU, Urges 'Canada +++' Brexit Deal," *Euractiv*, October 5, 2018.

78. "War on All Fronts as May Faces Puzzle of Brexit Rubik's Cube," *Euractiv*, October 17, 2018.

79. "Withdrawal Agreement and Political Declaration on the Future Relationship between the UK and the EU as Endorsed by Leaders at a Special Meeting of the European Council on November 25, 2018," https://www.gov.uk/government/publications/withdrawal-agreement-and-political-declaration (Accessed July 19, 2019).

80. For a summary of the Withdrawal Agreement, see: https://www.bbc.com/news/uk-46237012. See also "The 585-Page Draft Brexit Agreement in a Nutshell," *Euractiv*, November 15, 2015.

81. "Political Declaration Setting Out the Framework for the Future Relationship between the European Union and the United Kingdom," https://assets.

publishing.service.gov.uk/government/uploads/system/uploads/attachment_data/file/759021/25_November_Political_Declaration_setting_out_the_framework_for_the_future_relationship_between_the_European_Union_and_the_United_Kingdom__pdf.

82. "May Wins Narrow Cabinet Backing for Brexit Deal," *Euractiv*, November 15, 2018.

83. "UK Cabinet Chaos as May Tries to Steady the Ship," *Euractiv*, November 16, 2018.

84. "Dominic Raab Resigns as Brexit Secretary Saying Brexit Deal is 'Real Threat' to UK's Integrity," https://www.getsurrey.co.uk/news/surrey-news/dominic-raab-resigns-brexit-secretary-15418633 (accessed August 1, 2019).

85. For a summary of the Political Declaration, see "Brexit: What is in the Political Declaration," https://www.bbc.com/news/uk-politics-46303751.

86. "Sadness the Flavour of the Day as EU27 Approve Brexit Deal," *Euractiv*, November 25, 2018.

87. "European Union (Withdrawal) Act 2018," http://www.legislation.gov.uk/ukpga/2018/16/section/13/enacted/data.pdf.

88. "Brexit: What Has to Happen in the UK and EU Parliaments to Ratify Withdrawal and Future Trade Agreements," https://theconversation.com/brexit-what-has-to-happen-in-uk-and-eu-parliaments-to-ratify-withdrawal-and-future-trade-agreements-107127.

89. "Juncker Warns May: 'No Room' to Renegotiate Brexit Deal," *Euractiv*, December 11, 2018.

90. "Warm Words But No Brexit Concessions, as May Leaves Brussels Empty-Handed," *Euractiv*, December 14, 2018.

91. "Government Loses 'Meaningful Vote in the Commons'," https://www.parliament.uk/business/news/2019/parliamentary-news-2019/meaningful-vote-on-brexit-resumes-in-the-commons/.

92. "May to Face Confidence Vote after Brexit Deal Suffers Crushing Defeat," *Euractiv*, January 15, 2019.

93. "May Offers Cross-Party Brexit Talks after Surviving Confidence Vote," *Euractiv*, January 16, 2019.

94. "Tear Up Irish Backstop, MPs Tell May in New Brexit Twist," *Euractiv*, January 29, 2019.

95. "May Will Seek 'Pragmatic' Solution to Brexit Deal in Brussels," *Euractiv*, February 4, 2019.

96. " 'Something Has to Give,' Barnier Tells Brexit Britain," *Euractiv*, February 12, 2019.

97. "May Gets 'Legally Binding' Assurances on Backstop from Last-Ditch Strasbourg Trip," *Euractiv*, March 12, 2019.

98. "Government's Brexit Deal Defeated Again in 'Meaningful Vote'," https://www.parliament.uk/business/news/2019/march/key-brexit-vote-as-meaningful-vote-returns-to-the-commons/.

99. "UK Set to Demand Brexit Extension after MPs Hand Heavy Defeat to May," *Euractiv*, March 12, 2019.

100. "Spelman Amendment: Full List of How MPs Voted on Dame Caroline Spelman's Attempt to Block a No-Deal Brexit," https://inews.co.uk/news/brexit/no-deal-brexit-amendments-mps-full-list-caroline-spelman/.

101. "How Did You MP Vote on Extending Article 50?" https://www.theguardian.com/politics/ng-interactive/2019/mar/12/how-did-your-mp-vote-in-the-march-brexit-votes. See also "May to Request Brexit Delay after MPs Back Extension," *Euractiv*, March 14, 2019.

102. Institute for Government, "Article 50 Extension," https://www.instituteforgovernment.org.uk/explainers/article-50-options.

103. For description of content, see "Business for Wednesday," March 27, 2019, https://publications.parliament.uk/pa/cm201719/cmagenda/ob190327.htm#_idTextAnchor007.

104. "What's Next for Brexit? No Commons Majority in Indicative Votes," https://www.parliament.uk/business/news/2019/march/whats-next-for-brexit-house-of-commons-holds-indicative-votes/.

105. See also, "May Offer to Quit Fails to Clean the Brexit Mess," *Euractiv*, March 28, 2019.

106. "Commons Votes to Reject Government's EU Withdrawal Agreement," https://www.parliament.uk/business/news/2019/march/mps-debate-and-vote-on-the-withdrawal-agreement-with-the-european-union/.

107. "House of Commons Holds Second Round of Indicative Votes," https://www.parliament.uk/business/news/2019/april/house-of-commons-holds-second-round-of-indicative-votes/.

108. "May Offers Cross-Party Talks, Increasing Hopes of Soft Brexit," *Euractiv*, April 3, 2019.

109. "Commons Vote 313 to 312 to Seek Brexit Extension," *Euractiv*, April 4, 2019.

110. "On the Quiet, UK Prepares for 'Zombie' European Elections," *Euractiv*, April 5, 2019.

111. "Prime Minister's Statement after Article 50 Extended to October 31, 2019," https://www.parliament.uk/business/news/2019/april/prime-ministers-statement-after-article-50-extended-to-31-october-2019/.

112. "Theresa May's 'New Brexit Deal' Set for Rejection Again," *Euractiv*, May 22, 2019; "Brexit: May's Final Effort to Win Backing Falls Flat as MPs Reject 'New' Deal," https://www.theguardian.com/politics/2019/may/21/may-offers-mps-vote-on-second-referendum-in-new-brexit-deal.

113. "Theresa May Quits: UK Set for New PM by End of July," https://www.bbc.com/news/uk-politics-48395905.

114. "European Election 2019: UK Results in Maps and Charts," https://www.bbc.com/news/uk-politics-48403131.

115. "Deal or No Deal? Britain's PK Hopefuls Divided over Brexit," *Euractiv*, June 11, 2019.

116. "Johnson Purges the No Deal Non-Believers," *Euractiv*, July 25, 2019.

117. "EU Rebuffs Boris Johnson's Call to Rework Brexit Deal," *Euractiv*, July 26, 2029.

118. "Johnson Mulls Snap Election as MPs Seek to Block No-Deal Brexit," *Euractiv*, September 2, 2019.

119. Alasdair Blair, "The United Kingdom and the European Union," Forthcoming in the Oxford Research Encyclopedia of Politics (OREP).

120. "Concerned Boris Johnson Suffers Triple Commons Defeat," https://www.theguardian.com/politics/2019/sep/04/cornered-boris-johnson-suffers-triple-commons-defeat.

121. Institute for Government, "Article 50 Extension," op. cit.

122. "Brexit: Boris Johnson's Second Attempt to Trigger Election Fails," https://www.bbc.com/news/uk-politics-49630094.

123. "Johnson to Hold New Vote on Snap Election, as Brother Quits Over Brexit Strategy," *Euractiv*, September 5, 2019.

124. "Tusk Tells British PM Johnson to Stop Playing 'Stupid' Brexit Blame Game," *Euractiv*, October 8, 2019.

125. "New Brexit Hopes after Johnson and Varadkar Say 'Pathway to Deal' Exists," *Euractiv*, October 11, 2019.

126. "Britain, EU Enter Make-Or-Break Brexit Week," *Euractiv*, October 14, 2019.

127. "EU and UK on Brink of a Brexit Deal Despite Unionist Concerns," *Euractiv*, October 17, 2019.

128. "Brexit: What is in Boris Johnson's New Deal with the EU," https://www.bbc.com/news/uk-50083026 (accessed March 19, 2020). For a detailed account, see "Brexit: EU Leaders Approve Brexit Deal as Boris Johnson Looks to Parliament—As It Happened," https://www.ft.com/content/63a605e8-3180-39dd-aad0-bbfe635a3b59.

129. For the text of the revised protocol, see https://ec.europa.eu/commission/sites/beta-political/files/revised_withdrawal_agreement_including_protocol_on_ireland_and_nothern_ireland.pdf.

130. For a detailed explanation, see David Phinnemore, "Democratic Consent and the Protocol on Ireland/Northern Ireland," http://qpol.qub.ac.uk/democratic-consent-and-the-protocol-on-ireland-northern-ireland/.

131. "DUP Blocking Brexit Deal, Pound Plummets on Summit Day," *Euractiv*, October 17, 2019.

132. Institute for Government, "Article 50 Extension," op. cit.

133. See also "Explainer: As Johnson Pushes Ahead with Brexit, What Happens Now in UK's Parliament?" *Euractiv*, October 22, 2019.

134. "Johnson's Deal Secures Majority but Parliament Pushes for Ratification Delay," *Euractiv*, October 22, 2019.

135. "Johnson Demands December Election, Abandons 'Do or Die' Brexit Promise," *Euractiv*, October 24, 2019; "Johnson Gets His Election as Lawmakers Finally Agree December Poll," *Euractiv*, October 29, 2019.

136. "EU Approves Brexit 'Flextension' until 31 January," *Euractiv*, October 29, 2019.

137. "Election Results 2019: Boris Johnson Returned as PM with All Constituencies Declared," https://www.theguardian.com/politics/ng-interactive/2019/dec/12/uk-general-election-2019-full-results-live-labour-conservatives-tories.

138. https://www.bbc.com/news/election-2019-50765773. See also "Brexit Confirmed as Johnson Secures Decisive Election Win," *Euractiv*, December 13, 2019.

139. "EU Leaders Prepare for Brexit after Johnson Win," *Euractiv*, December 13, 2019.

140. "British Lawmakers Finally Approve Historic Brexit Deal," *Euractiv*, January 10, 2020.

141. https://services.parliament.uk/bills/2019-21/europeanunionwithdrawalagreement.html.

142. "Brexit: Council Adopts Decision to Conclude the Withdrawal Agreement," https://www.consilium.europa.eu/en/press/press-releases/2020/01/30/brexit-council-adopts-decision-to-conclude-the-withdrawal-agreement/.

143. https://ec.europa.eu/commission/sites/beta-political/files/revised_political_declaration.pdf.

144. Institute for Government, "UK-EU Future Relationship: Association Agreements," https://www.instituteforgovernment.org.uk/explainers/future-relationship-association-agreements.

145. For discussions of options, see for instance Institute for Government, "The Options for the UK's Trading Relationship with the EU," (June 2017), https://www.instituteforgovernment.org.uk/explainers/options-uk-trading-relationship-eu, and more detailed and recent version, "Brexit Brief: Options for the UK's Future Trade Relationship with the EU," https://www.instituteforgovernment.org.uk/sites/default/files/publications/Brexit%20Options%20A3%20November%20update.pdf.

146. Institute for Government, "Frictionless Trade? What Brexit Means for Cross-Border Trade in Goods," https://www.instituteforgovernment.org.uk/sites/default/files/publications/5704%20IFG%20-%20Frictionless%20Trade%20Web.pdf.

A

ACQUIS COMMUNAUTAIRE. *Acquis communautaire* is the French term for what has been achieved, originally by the **European Communities** (EC), later the **European Union** (EU), in terms of treaties, legislation (**regulations**, **directives**, and **decisions**), as well as decisions by the **European Court of Justice** (ECJ), now known as **Court of Justice of the European Union** (CJEU). The term is especially used in connection with enlargements, where it was established already in connection with the first **enlargement** in 1973 that the candidates must accept and implement all the *acquis*. Exceptions could be negotiated for certain transition periods. The *acquis* has, of course, grown over the years, so joining today requires a much larger legislative adaptation than in the earlier years. Later in the integration process, especially in connection with treaty reforms, some countries succeeded getting more permanent **opt-outs** from the *acquis*, including the **United Kingdom** (UK) at the time of the **Treaty of Maastricht**, where the UK got opt-outs for **Economic and Monetary Union** (EMU), and **Justice and Home Affairs** (JHA) cooperation. During the **Brexit transition period**, the UK will have to decide whether it wants to take part in some parts of the *acquis*, mostly to facilitate future trade. According to the solution to the **Irish border** in the final **withdrawal agreement** reached in October 2019, **Northern Ireland** will maintain parts of the *acquis* to avoid border controls on the border between Northern Ireland and the **Republic of Ireland**, including standards for agricultural goods, thus a regulatory differentiation between Northern Ireland and the other parts of the UK.

ACQUIS POLITIQUE. *Acquis politique* is the French term for what has been achieved in the foreign political area, first under **European Political Cooperation** (EPC) from 1970, later under the **Common Foreign and Security Policy** (CFSP) established by the **Treaty of Maastricht** in 1993. Under CFSP, there is no legislation, but various strategies have been outlined and decisions made. This foreign policy cooperation is intergovernmental and based on unanimity or **consensus**. The *acquis politique* is therefore less developed and much weaker than the ***acquis communautaire***. But candidate countries are also expected to accept the *acquis politique* to become members of the **European Union** (EU) and be willing to contribute to its further development. This was made quite clear in connection with the 1995 **enlargement**, when the formerly neutral countries of Austria, Finland, and Sweden joined the **European Union** (EU). There will most likely be a common interest in some cooperation in foreign security and defense policy areas after **Brexit**. The **United Kingdom** (UK) will continue as a member of the North Atlantic Treaty Organization (NATO).

AGRICULTURAL POLICY. *See* COMMON AGRICULTURAL POLICY (CAP).

ALIGNMENT. *See* REGULATORY ALIGNMENT.

ANOTHER REFERENDUM. Some opponents of **Brexit** have called for a second **referendum**, which the Conservative government of Prime Minister **Theresa May** rejected. The campaigners for a second referendum called their proposal a **People's Vote**. The **Labour Party** under **Jeremy Corbyn** was split but eventually moved toward support for a second referendum as some of the complex issues of Brexit became clearer. The argument against a second referendum used by **Brexiteers** was that the British people had made a clear decision in the first referendum in June 2016.

AREA OF FREEDOM, SECURITY AND JUSTICE (AFSJ). The **Treaty of Maastricht** establishing the **European Union** (EU) included **Justice and Home Affairs** (JHA) cooperation in a third intergovernmental pillar apart from the supranational Community cooperation in the first pillar. The **Treaty of Amsterdam** subsequently introduced the concept of an **Area of Freedom, Security and Justice** (AFSJ), which was to be established gradually. At first, many of the policies under JHA would be moved to the first pillar ("communitarized"), leaving **Police and Judicial Cooperation in Criminal Matters** in the third pillar. By moving asylum, **immigration**, and Judicial Cooperation in Civil Matters to the first pillar the **European Commission**'s role was enhanced, the **European Court of Justice** (ECJ) became competent to judge cases, majority voting would eventually be introduced, and the **European Parliament** (EP) would get more powers ("the **Community method**"). This process, which was started by the Treaty of Amsterdam, was foreseen in the Treaty of Maastricht. A big further step was taken by the **Treaty of Lisbon**, which abolished the pillar structure, so that all JHA now fall under the more efficient Community method. The **United Kingdom** (UK) opted out of most

JHA cooperation, but had the possibility of opting in on particular parts of this cooperation.

ARTICLE 50 TEU. Article 50 of the **Treaty on European Union** (TEU) deals with a member state's withdrawal from the **European Union** (EU). A member state that wants to withdraw must notify the **European Council**. The EU will then negotiate and conclude an agreement with the withdrawing state, "setting out the arrangements for its withdrawal, taking into account of the framework for its future relationship with the Union." Once an agreement is reached, it is concluded by the **Council of the European Union** by a **qualified majority vote** (QMV), after obtaining the consent of the **European Parliament** (EP). The article includes a two-year period after notification to reach a **Withdrawal Agreement**. Prime Minister **Theresa May** triggered Article 50 at the end of March 2017, so the **United Kingdom** (UK) was expected to leave by the end of March 2019, but an extension of the period was twice agreed while May was prime minister, and once after **Boris Johnson** became prime minister, because of problems getting the **UK Parliament** to accept the negotiated agreements. Withdrawal finally took place on 31 January 2020 after a new UK Parliament had been elected in December 2019. Notice, the withdrawal agreement does not include an agreement on the future relationship. Such relationship can be negotiated only after the leaving country has become a non-member state, referred to as a third country.

ARTICLE 218 TFEU. Article 218(3) of the **Treaty on the Functioning of the European Union** (TFEU) gives details on how the **European Union** (EU) organizes its negotiations. It includes recommendations from the **Commission**, an authorizing decision from the **Council of the European Union** and the possibility of nominating a Union negotiator.

ASSOCIATION AGREEMENTS. According to the **Treaty of Rome**'s Article 238, "The Community may conclude with a third State, a union of States or an international organization agreements establishing an association involving reciprocal rights and obligations, common action and special procedures." Therefore, an association agreement is a special kind of agreement that goes beyond a mere trade or cooperation agreement. This is still the basic definition after the **Treaty of Lisbon** has entered into force, but procedures of adopting an association agreement have changed over time. The **Single European Act** (SEA) introduced the requirement of **assent** by the **European Parliament** (EP). Until the Treaty of Lisbon unanimity was required in the **Council**, but since the Treaty of Lisbon the **Council** can normally act by a

qualified majority vote (QMV). Association agreements are negotiated by the **European Commission**, based on a **mandate** from the Council.

Since the entry into force of the Treaty of Lisbon the relevant treaty article is 217 TFEU.

Gradually the list of association agreements has become rather extensive, now including:

1. Agreements with African–Caribbean–Pacific (ACP) countries, now under the Cotonou Agreement.
2. Agreements with some European neighbors, starting with Greece and **Turkey** in the 1960s.
3. Various Euro-Mediterranean agreements, including North African and Middle Eastern states.
4. **"Europe" agreements** with Central and Eastern European Countries (CEECs) after the end of the Cold War.
5. The **European Economic Area** (EEA) Agreement with **Norway**, Iceland, and Lichtenstein.
6. Stabilization and Association Agreements (SAA) with Western Balkan states.
7. Some individual agreements, like those with Chile and South Africa.
8. Recently, association agreements have also been offered to Eastern Partnership countries (including **Ukraine**).

Association agreements usually establish an Association Council, where ministers meet, and an Association committee, where officials meet. There are special arrangements with groups of states like ACP and EEA. Often, there are also meetings of parliamentarians. Whether the future relationship between the EU and the **United Kingdom** (UK) will be based on an association agreement remains to be seen. In case of a **Hard Brexit**, there will by definition be a limited or no agreement; in case of a **Soft Brexit**, there will be an agreement, which may fall in the category of an association agreement—even if it will most likely be less comprehensive than the EEA.

B

BACKSTOP. A so-called backstop was part of the first **Withdrawal Agreement** negotiated by Prime Minister **Theresa May** and the **European Union** (EU) in 2018. It promised that the open border between **Northern Ireland** and the **Republic of Ireland** would continue after the **transition period** from the entry in force of the Withdrawal Agreement, if there was no agreement on the future relationship between the **United Kingdom** (UK) and the EU then. This transition period would have ended on 31 December 2020 had the Withdrawal Agreement been concluded by the end of March 2019. In the case of a **Hard Brexit**, it is expected that border checks that do not exist today will be reintroduced, which can have serious consequences for peace in Northern Ireland. Since May could not get the Withdrawal Agreement, which she negotiated with the EU, accepted by the **UK Parliament**, she eventually stepped down in June 2019. The new Prime Minister **Boris Johnson**, from July 2019, set out to get some changes in the Withdrawal Agreement in the negotiations with the EU, with focus on the backstop. Eventually, in October 2019, a new Withdrawal Agreement was agreed. While May's backstop would have kept the UK in the EU customs union if no agreement on the future relationship solving the problem had been reached at the end of the transition period, the Johnson agreement creates a kind of customs border in the Irish sea, requiring goods entering Northern Ireland from the other parts of the UK to pay taxes/ duties at specific "entry points" in Northern Ireland, if they are considered "at risk" of being transported to the Republic of Ireland.

BARCLAY, STEPHEN (1972–). Stephen Barclay served as Secretary of State for exiting the European Union from 15 November 2018, when he replaced **Dominic Raab**. He remained loyal to Prime Minister **Theresa May** during her battles with the **UK Parliament** and continued when **Boris Johnson** took over as prime minister. He served until **Brexit Day** on 31 January 2020.

BARNIER, MICHEL (1951–). Michel Barnier, a former French foreign minister (2004–2005) and European Commissioner for Regional Policy, 1999–2004, and for Internal Market and Services, 2010–2014, was appointed the **European Union's** (EU) chief **Brexit** negotiator in October 2016. He has negotiated with his British counterparts on the basis of **mandates** from the remaining 27 EU member states, in close cooperation with the **European Commission**. He has gained the reputation of being an effective diplomatic operator.

Michel Barnier, Chief Brexit negotiator for the EU, 2016–2019. *Source*: Courtesy of the European Union.

BENN BILL. The "Benn bill," so called after **Labour Party Member of Parliament** (MP) Hilary Benn, was adopted by the **United Kingdom (UK) Parliament** on 9 September 2019, preventing the UK from leaving the **European Union** (EU) with no exit deal, without parliament's consent. It was repealed by the UK's EU **Withdrawal Act** on 23 January 2020.

BERCOW, JOHN (1963–). John Bercow was Speaker of the **House of Commons** from 2009 to 2019. He had been a **Member of Parliament** (MP) from 2009. His period as Speaker, renewed no less than four times, included the tumultuous period in the first half of 2019, when Prime Minister **Theresa May** tried without success to get her **Withdrawal Agreement** with the **European Union** (EU) accepted by the **UK Parliament**. The position of Speaker is supposed to be nonpartisan, but he was criticized by some as being biased against **Brexit** because of some of his decisions about which proposals could be put to a vote. He announced in September 2019 that he would step down later in the autumn and did so in November 2019. In January 2020, he became part-time professor of politics at Royal Holloway, University of London.

BLAIR, TONY (1953–). Tony Blair became prime minister of the **United Kingdom** (UK) on 2 May 1997 after his **Labour Party** won the parliamentary elections. He subsequently also won the elections in 2001 and 2005. He stepped down in 2007, letting his Labour Party colleague **Gordon Brown** to take over.

European partners who had grown increasingly frustrated by the previous **John Major Conservative Party** government eagerly awaited his win in 1997. Labour's return to power after a long absence allowed the 1996 **Intergovernmental Conference** (IGC) to conclude the **Treaty of Amsterdam** negotiations, which the new government joined fully, including the **Social Policy** chapter, where the UK had got an **opt-out** at the time of the **Treaty of Maastricht** negotiations. However, the Labour government did not change UK policy in respect to **defense policy** as much as had been hoped by most partners. In December 1998, though, under influence of the deteriorating situation in Kosovo, the UK moved toward the idea of accepting an autonomous **European Union** (EU) defense policy. At a Franco-British summit in St. Malo, France, Blair and President Jacques Chirac agreed on a declaration, which called for the EU to have "capacity for autonomous action, backed up by credible military forces . . . in order to respond to international crises." This became the start of important developments in the **European Security and Defense Policy** (ESDP), later called the **Common Security and Defense Policy** (CSDP) after the entry into force of the **Treaty of Lisbon**. Initially Blair also seemed willing to take the UK into the **euro**. Eventually he promised a **referendum** on the issue, which never took place, and which would probably have had a negative outcome.

BREXIT. Brexit is the name given the British exit from the **European Union** (EU). During the financial crisis in 2010 the possible departure of Greece from the eurozone had been referred to as Grexit.

BREXIT DAY. Brexit day is 31 January 2020, the day that the **United Kingdom** (UK) officially left the **European Union** (EU).

BREXITEER. A Brexiteer is someone who supports, or supported, the **United Kingdom's** (UK) exit from the **European Union** (EU) during the 26 June 2016 UK **referendum** and afterward during the negotiations with the EU about the **Withdrawal Agreement**.

BREXIT PARTY. The Brexit Party was formed in January 2019 by some members who left the **UK Independence Party** (UKIP), including **Nigel Farage**. While the UKIP had 23 **Members of the European Parliament** (MEPs) before the split, the Brexit Party won 30 seats in the May 2019 **European Parliament** (EP) election, out of 73 seats for the **United Kingdom** (UK). These seats were occupied without taking part in any of the **Political Group in the European Parliament**, as *non-inscrit* (NI), until Brexit day on 31 January 2020. In the December 2019 general election in the UK the party decided not to stand candidates in constituencies won by the **Conservative Party** in the previous election. The party got 2 percent of the vote, winning no seats in the **House of Commons**.

BRITAIN STRONGER IN EUROPE. "Britain Stronger in Europe" was the name of the main organization campaigning for **Remain** in the **United Kingdom** (UK) **European Union** (EU) membership **referendum** debate in 2016. The rival organization was "**Vote Leave**." In September 2016, after losing the referendum, Britain Stronger in Europe became Open Britain. In April 2016 Open Britain launched the unsuccessful **People's Vote** campaign for a second EU referendum.

BROWN, GORDON (1951–). Gordon Brown is a British politician who was prime minister 2007–2010, and leader of the **Labour Party**. He replaced **Tony Blair** as prime minister and Labour Party leader. He was succeeded by Ed Miliband as Labour Party leader and **Conservative Party's David Cameron** as prime minister in 2010.

BUDGET. The total EU budget for 2019 was €165.8 billion. The so-called **Multiannual Financial Framework** (MFF) for the period 2014–2020 was €1,082.5 billion, representing 1.02 percent of the gross national income (GNI) of the 28 member states. The two biggest headings include "Smart and Inclusive Growth"—with the biggest subheading "Economic, social and territorial cohesion" (mainly **regional policy**) and the second biggest heading "Sustainable Growth: Natural resources" (mainly the **Common Agricultural Policy** [CAP]) together taking about 70 percent of the budget. Including the two biggest expenditures together with other expenditures makes it a little difficult for citizens to see exactly where the money goes.

The composition of expenditures has changed over time. The CAP has usually taken the biggest amount of money. Although it represented only 10 percent in 1965, it rose to 88 percent in 1970. It fell in relative terms to 71 percent in 1980, 51 percent in 2000, and 41.3 percent in 2011. On the other hand, expenditures to the **structural funds** have increased. In 1975, they represented about 5 percent. In 2005, they had risen to about a quarter and by 2011 more than a third. This includes money going through the European Social Fund (ESF), **the European Regional Development Fund (ERDF),** and the Cohesion Fund, the latter created by the **Treaty of Maastricht** in 1993. Although roughly 1 percent of GNI sounds like a small budget the **European Union** (EU) spending can be important to some recipients, including Greece, Spain, Portugal, and **Ireland** in the 1990s. After the Eastern **enlargements** from 2004 transfers for the CAP and structural funds are important to the new member states in Central and Eastern Europe (CEECs).

The revenue side of the budget is based on so-called own resources. Since 1970 these have included customs duties, agricultural levies, and a percentage of value-added tax (VAT). A fourth resource was added in 1988, a certain percentage of each member state's GNI. The **United Kingdom** (UK) has continuously felt that the country contributed too much to the EU budget, so a rebate was negotiated in the mid-1980s when **Margaret Thatcher** was prime minister. *See also* BUDGETARY PROCESS.

BUDGETARY PROCESS. The budget is annual, but it has to fit into the **Multiannual Financial Framework** (MFF), which is currently adopted for a seven-year period (2014–2020). Both the adoption of the MFF and the annual budget is normally politically controversial. The expenditure side is the most difficult. Who gets what? Net contributors will usually try to limit the budget. Net recipients will likely ask for more money. **Members of the European Parliament** (MEPs) may have their ideas, including pet projects they want funded.

The draft budget is proposed by the **European Commission**, which also has ideas to promote. The proposal goes to both the **Council** and **European Parliament** (EP), who jointly must adopt the budget in the end. Before getting there, they will both normally propose changes, the Council often suggesting cuts in the Commission draft, the EP more likely to be supportive of the Commission Proposal. The current procedures for the budgetary process are based in the **Treaty of Lisbon**, which has put the Council and Parliament on par as the budgetary authority in the union. The old distinction between compulsory and non-compulsory expenditure was abolished. In addition, the MFF is now mentioned in the treaty. It is adopted as a Council Regulation where the EP has the right of **consent**. Previously the MFF, or multi-annual "financial perspective" as it was called when it was introduced in 1988, was based on an Inter-Institutional Agreement (IIA), which allowed the **European Council** to strike the deal every five, seven years later. By giving the EP the right to consent on the MFF the Treaty of Lisbon contributes to making the Council and EP more equal partners in the budgetary process, thus arguably making the process more democratic. *See also* BUDGET.

C

CAMERON, DAVID (1966–). David Cameron was prime minister of the **United Kingdom** (UK) 2010–2016. He was elected a **Member of Parliament** (MP) in 2001. He became leader of the **Conservative Party** in 2005. In the 2010 general electing the Conservative Party won 306 seats, not enough to form a government on its own. After long negotiations, Cameron formed a coalition with the **Liberal Democrats**, the first coalition government in the UK since the Second World War. As other **European Union** (EU) countries, the UK had to battle the financial crisis. The EU remained controversial in the country and Cameron promised a **referendum** on continued UK membership of the EU if the Conservatives won an outright majority in the next general election. In the general election in 2015 Cameron secured a majority in the **UK Parliament** and continued as prime minister in a Conservative-only government. During the ensuing referendum campaign in 2016 he supported continued British membership of the EU. The referendum followed some negotiations with the EU where Cameron secured some concessions, which seemed not to make much of a difference during the campaign. In the agreement with the EU it was recognized that the UK was not committed to further political integration in the EU, and the other member states agreed to some limitations on in-work benefits and child benefits for migrant workers, guarantees that member states outside the eurozone would not be required to fund euro bailouts, and some lowering of the administrative burdens in the **internal market**. Cameron claimed that the agreement gave the UK a "special status" in the EU. After he lost to the **Leave campaign** he resigned as prime minister and was succeeded by **Theresa May**.

CANADA. Canada is an important country in the external relations of the **European Union** (EU), partly because of the historical relations between Canada and the **United Kingdom** (UK). Since 1972, when the first **enlargement** of the **European Community** (EC) was confirmed, there have been high-level bilateral consultations between the EC and Canada. Since 1973 Canada has had an ambassador to the EC. In 1976, Canada concluded a Framework Agreement for Commercial and Economic Cooperation with the

EC. It created what was called a "contractual link." It spoke in general terms about commercial and economic cooperation. Institutionally it created a joint cooperation committee (JCC) to "promote and keep under review the various commercial and economic co-operation activities envisaged." The JCC would normally meet at least once a year. (Interestingly, the United States [U.S.] did not get a similar contractual link with the EC at the time.) However, the outcome was modest.

During the 1980s the internal market plans in Europe rekindled Canada's interest in Europe, but the government first sought a free trade agreement (FTA) with the U.S., which eventually was to include Mexico as the North American Free Trade Area (NAFTA) in the early 1990s. During the 1990s, formal relations between Canada and the EU were expanded, but proposals for free or freer trade kept running into difficulties.

Partly under the influence of the difficulties of agreeing on further liberalization of international trade within the World Trade Organization (WTO), the Canadian government spoke out in favor of a **free trade agreement** (FTA) with the EU in 2007. A joint study published in 2008 concluded that an FTA would have important economic benefits for both sides. A summit in Prague in 2009 then decided to start negotiations of a **Comprehensive Economic and Trade Agreement** (CETA). After long and difficult negotiations, a political agreement on the sensitive areas was reached in 2013. A draft treaty text was published in September 2014. After its publication a major debate erupted about **investor state dispute settlement** (ISDS). During the negotiations agricultural products, **geographical indicators** (GIs), **intellectual property rights** (IPR), and **public procurement** were among the difficult issues. In the final CETA the ISDS was replaced by an **Investment Court System** (ICS). CETA was signed on 30 October 2016 and most parts entered into force provisionally on 21 September 2017, awaiting ratification by the EU member states for the whole agreement to enter into force. *See also* COMMON AGRICULTURAL POLICY (CAP); COMMON COMMERCIAL POLICY (CCP).

CANADA MODEL. Canada model refers to Canada's **free trade agreement** with the **European Union** (EU), the **Comprehensive Economic and Trade Agreement** (CETA). It creates free trade for industrial products and some liberalization for trade with agricultural products, in many cases based on quotas. It also includes some provisions on **services**, **intellectual property rights**, and **investment** protection. If the **United Kingdom** (UK) were to get a free trade agreement with the EU like CETA it would be free to negotiate its own trade agreements with countries other than the EU. But an FTA still requires border controls, which might affect the border between

Northern Ireland and the **Republic of Ireland**, which, presumably, the solution negotiated by **Boris Johnson** in October 2019 in the **Withdrawal Agreement** would take care of, by moving the border to the Irish Sea instead of the land border. An FTA normally include rules of origin (ROOs), which will determine whether a product can pass the border tariff free. Product standards, including food standards, may also need to be checked in some manner, before or at the border. This part pf the problem can be solved with Northern Ireland retaining pertinent EU standards by staying partly in the **internal market**.

It should be mentioned that it took about seven years to negotiate the CETA, and it is not likely that its content can be copy-pasted into a bilateral EU-UK agreement, or UK-Canada agreement for that matter.

CANADA PLUS. During the **Brexit** negotiations with the **European Union** (EU) about a divorce agreement, Prime Minister **Theresa May** would say that beyond the divorce agreement she wanted something more than the Canadian **free trade agreement**, the **Canada model**, but less than the Norwegian relationship with the EU, known as the **European Economic Area** (EEA), which includes full participation in the **internal market** of the **four freedoms**, **free movement** of goods, **services**, capital, and people. Exactly what she wanted more than the Canadian model remained somewhat vague, but it could have included more provisions to facilitate **financial services** trade.

CANADA PLUS PLUS PLUS. Some Brexiters, including **David Davis** and **Boris Johnson**, at some point talked about an improved Canada-style **free trade agreement**. Johnson put forward a "SuperCanada" plan that would abolish all tariff and quotas, cover **services** as well as goods, and ensure full **mutual recognition** of regulations and standards, and technological solutions to keep supply chains operating. He also suggested that border checks in **Ireland** could be carried out away from the border, something included in the deal he later secured with the **European Union** (EU) as prime minister in October 2019. It is somewhat unclear to what extent he still supports the other parts of that plan after he has become prime minister. We may only find out late in the game.

CHARTER OF FUNDAMENTAL RIGHTS. Article 6 of the treaties after the **Treaty of Lisbon** entered into force states, "The Union recognizes the rights, freedoms and principle set out in the Charter of Fundamental Rights of the European Union of 7 December 2000, as adopted at Strasbourg, on 12 December 2007, which shall have the same legal value as the Treaties." It took a fair amount of deliberations and negotiations to get to that point.

At the meeting of the European Council in Tampere in October 1999, it was decided that the Charter should be drafted by a so-called Convention, which would have 15 representatives from the then 15 member states, 16 **Members of the European Parliament** (MEPs), 30 members of national parliaments, and a member of the **European Commission** representing the Commission president. By September 2000, the Convention had agreed on the text of the Charter, which was subsequently adopted as a political document by the **European Council** in Nice in December 2000.

Since the Convention method was considered successful, it was used to draft the Constitutional Treaty in 2002–2003. Here it was decided to include the Charter as part of the Constitutional Treaty in view of making it legally binding. When the Constitutional Treaty was abandoned after the "no" votes in **referendums** in France and the Netherlands in 2005 it was decided not to include it in the new reform treaty that replaced the Constitutional Treaty and which subsequently became the **Treaty of Lisbon**, but instead give it the "same legal value as the Treaties."

The Charter has 54 articles and is divided into seven chapters: Dignity, Freedoms, Equality, Solidarity, **Citizens' Rights**, Justice, and General Provisions. It thus includes both classical, mostly political, rights, and the more controversial economic and social rights.

During the final negotiations of the Treaty of Lisbon, the **United Kingdom** (UK) secured a de facto opt-out from the Charter, joined by Poland. In the end, the Czech president Václav Klaus insisted on getting the same arrangement as the UK and Poland to sign the treaty. It was decided to promise that the Czech Republic will be able to be included in the UK-Polish protocol on the occasion of the next substantive reform of the treaties.

CHEQUERS PLAN. Chequers is the name of the British prime minister's country retreat. The Chequers Plan was agreed there by the **United Kingdom** (UK) cabinet on 6 July 2018. It was developed further in a **White Paper** published on 12 July 2018. The latter had chapters on economic partnership, security, cooperation, and institutional arrangements. The plan suggested a close relationship with the **European Union** (EU) based on an **association agreement**. Central to the plan was the aim of a free trade area for goods which would maintain **frictionless trade**, supported by a **common rulebook** and a new **facilitated customs arrangement**. The plan would require continued harmonization with EU rules, which could limit friction at the border between **Northern Ireland** and the **Republic of Ireland**. The plan led to the resignation of Brexit Secretary **David Davis** and Foreign Secretary **Boris Johnson**, and it was rejected by the European Union (EU). **Brexiteers** feared that the plan would tie the UK to the EU without influence on future rules. The EU dismissed it as **cherry-picking**.

CHERRY-PICKING. During the **Brexit** negotiations the **European Union** (EU) negotiators and leading EU politicians maintained that the **four freedoms** of **free movement** of goods, **services**, capital, and people of the **internal market** are indivisible. So, the **United Kingdom** (UK) could not "cherry-pick" the best aspects, like free movement of goods, but not free movement of people. Another term used was eating *à la carte*, or having one's cake and eating it too. To have the benefits of the internal market there are obligations that must be accepted.

CITIZEN'S RIGHTS. During the negotiations of the **Withdrawal Agreement** the question of the rights of **European Union** (EU) citizens in the **United Kingdom** (UK) and the rights of the UK citizens in the EU was singled out as one of the most important issues at the beginning. In the December 2017 agreement concluding the first phase of the negotiations both sides made commitments to allow these citizens to stay and maintain certain rights. The UK has introduced the concept of "**settled status**." EU citizens and their families who have lived for five years in the UK can apply for "settled status," which allows them to stay in the UK for as long as they want. Similarly, UK citizens and their families will continue to have their rights of residency in EU countries during and after the **transition period**.

CITIZENSHIP. The **Treaty of Maastricht** on a proposal by Spain introduced citizenship of the Union. "Every person holding the nationality of a Member State shall be a citizen of the Union" (Article 8). The rights conferred on the citizens are the following:

1. The right to move and reside freely within the territory of the member states,
2. The right to vote and to stand as a candidate at municipal elections in the member state in which he resides,
3. The right to vote and to stand as a candidate in elections to the **European Parliament** (EP) in the member state in which he resides,
4. The right to protection by the diplomatic or consular authorities of any member state in a third country if his home country is not represented,
5. The right to petition the EP,
6. The right to apply to the Ombudsman established at the same time.

In the Danish **referendum** on the Treaty of Maastricht, there was some confusion about the implications of Citizenship of the Union. Some Danes thought that Citizenship of the Union would replace national citizenship. One of the Danish reservations (or **opt-outs**) agreed at the meeting of the **European Council** in Edinburgh in December 1992 concerned citizenship.

Subsequently the **Treaty of Amsterdam** made it explicit that Citizenship of the Union "shall complement and not replace national citizenship" (Article 17 TEC). Needless to say, through **Brexit** British citizens lose the mentioned citizenship of the Union rights.

CLARKE, KENNETH (1940–). Kenneth Clark is a British Conservative politician. He was a **Member of Parliament** (MP) from 1970 to 2019. He had been Chancellor of the Exchequer from 1993 to 1997. From 2017 to 2019 he was the longest serving MP, giving him the title of Father of the **House of Commons**. He opposed **Brexit** from within the **Conservative Party**. On 4 September 2019 the Conservative whip was withdrawn from him and 20 other MPs (meaning not being entitled to sit as Conservatives) for voting with the Opposition on a motion. He sat the remainder of his time in the **UK Parliament** as an independent.

CLIFF EDGE. One of the various metaphors used in the **Brexit** debate was a cliff-edge Brexit, referring to a Brexit without an agreement with the **European Union** (EU), sometimes also referred to as a **hard Brexit**. In case of no agreement the trade relations between the **United Kingdom** (UK) and the EU will be based on **World Trade Organization** (WTO) rules, meaning the reintroduction of **tariffs** requiring customs checks at borders. This might lead to queues at borders between the UK and the EU, including possibly the border between **Northern Ireland** and the **Republic of Ireland**. It would also affect other policy areas, including air travel, fisheries, **financial services**, and **citizens' rights**.

CO-DECISION PROCEDURE. *See* ORDINARY LEGISLATIVE PROCEDURE.

COMMISSION. *See* EUROPEAN COMMISSION.

COMMITTEE OF PERMANENT REPRESENTATIVES (COREPER). The Committee of Permanent Representatives is usually referred to as COREPER, the French acronym. It existed from the beginning, but was only mentioned explicitly with that name in the **Merger Treaty** in 1965. The Committee is responsible for preparing the work of the **Council**, and it makes some important decisions. The Permanent Representatives represent the member states in Brussels. They are national officials at the ambassadorial level. There are actually two COREPERs: COREPER II and I. The Permanent Representatives meet in COREPER II, while their deputies meet in COREPER I. COREPER I deals mostly with social and economic issues, while COREPER II deals mostly with political, financial, and foreign policy issues. COREPER oversees the work of more than 200 Council working groups of national officials. In the process of preparing Council meetings, many decisions are actually made by COREPER if there is agreement at that level. They become "A" points on the agenda of the Council meeting, where they are adopted without discussion. "B" points on the Council agenda, on the other hand, require discussion and final decisions by the Council.

COREPER exists alongside the Special Committee for Agriculture and the Monetary Committee with sectoral responsibilities as well the **Trade Policy Committee** that originally was called the Article 113 Committee, because it was mentioned in Article 113 of the **Treaty of Rome**. It is now, after the entry into force of the **Treaty of Lisbon**, mentioned in Article 207 TFEU.

The **Treaty of Maastricht** extended the responsibilities of COREPER to include **Common Foreign and Security Policy** (CFSP) in the second pillar and **Justice and Home Affairs** (JHA) in the third pillar, but here the Political Committee that had previously dealt with **European Political Cooperation** (EPC) survived, and a so-called K4 Committee became co-responsible for JHA. (K4 was the article in the treaty that established the committee.) COREPER, however, was supposed to be *primus inter pares* to assure coordination. With the abolition of the pillar structure by the Lisbon Treaty further streamlining has taken place strengthening COREPER, and the Political Committee has become the Political and Security Committee (PSC, sometimes referred to as COPS based on its French name *Comité politique et de sécurité*). It plays an important role in CFSP as well as Common Security and Defence Policy (CSDP).

COMMON AGRICULTURAL POLICY (CAP). The Common Agricultural Policy (CAP) is one of the original policies of the **European Economic Community** (EEC) and one of the most important ones. The general principles were outlined in Article 39 of the **Treaty of Rome**:

1. to increase agricultural productivity (technical progress, rational development of production, optimum utilization of factors of production),
2. to stabilize markets,
3. to assure availability of supplies, and
4. to ensure reasonable prices for consumers.

A single internal market with common prices was to be established and there would be joint financing. The details of the original policy were worked out in tough negotiations in the early 1960s under Commissioner Sicco Mansholt. The farmers were guaranteed certain prices for their products. Import levies (a variable tariff) were used to protect the market and export subsidies were used to sell (read dump) surplus production on the world market, which tended to have lower prices than those guaranteed the farmers inside the common market.

The system of guaranteed prices was problematic. It led to surplus production, which was dumped, on the world market, which in turn created trade conflicts with trading partners. The prices were higher for the consumers than world market prices. The intensive farming was not good for the **environment**. The costs of financing the system quickly started taking by far the biggest part of the **European Community (EC) budget**.

Some smaller reforms were adopted in the 1980s, but the first major reform was forced on the EEC in connection with the Uruguay Round of trade negotiations within the **General Agreement on Tariffs and Trade** (GATT). Until the Uruguay Round agriculture had been exempt from GATT rules. Now it was on the agenda, and in order to complete the negotiations the **United States** (U.S.) and other producers of agricultural products insisted that the EEC had to reform the CAP, especially to get rid of export subsidies. This led to the first major reform, known as the McSharry reform in 1992, which included some reductions in support prices and introduction of compensatory aid (direct income support, not dependent on output, but land area), as well as early retirement schemes, and afforestation of agricultural land. Other reforms followed, especially in connection with the Eastern **enlargements** of **the European Union** (EU) to include the Central and Eastern European Countries (CEECs). Some of these had important agricultural production, so the budgetary costs were a concern. The next major reform therefore took place in 1999 as part of Agenda 2000, the package to prepare the next big enlargement.

The 1999 reform was followed by a midterm reform in 2003. From now on payments to farmers were no longer dependent on production ("decoupling"). The single farm payment depended on size of the land. To get the single farm payment the farmer had to respect 18 statutory requirements in the fields of **environment**, public health, animal and plant health, and animal welfare, and keep their land in good agricultural and environmental conditions.

Given **Brexit**, the **United Kingdom** (UK) is now leaving the CAP, but will probably have to find a national substitute.

COMMON COMMERCIAL POLICY (CCP). The Common Commercial Policy (CCP) is, like the **Common Agricultural Policy** (CAP), one of the original policies of the **European Economic Community** (EEC), and an extremely important one. The **Treaty of Rome** establishing the EEC gave a special role to the **Commission** in negotiating trade agreements with third countries as well as multilaterally in the **General Agreement on Tariffs and Trade** (GATT). Negotiations take place on the basis of a **mandate** adopted by a **qualified majority vote** (QMV) by the Council, and a special **trade policy committee** of high-level national officials oversees the negotiations. This was outlined in Article 113 of the Treaty of Rome, which, interestingly enough, did not mention the **European Parliament** (EP). At the beginning commercial policy dealt with trade in goods. The treaty specifically mentioned tariff rates, liberalization, and export policy, including anti-dumping policy.

In recent years, the definition of trade has expanded to include new issues, especially when the Uruguay Round of GATT included **services**, **trade-related aspects of intellectual property rights** (TRIPS), and **trade-related aspects of investment measures** (TRIMS). After the conclusion of the Uruguay Round the **European Court of Justice** (ECJ) concluded in a judgment in 1994 that some of these new areas were competences shared by the EEC and the member states, which meant that the agreement also had to be ratified by the latter. The following treaty reforms therefore tried to expand the European Union's (EU) definition of trade to facilitate the conclusion and ratification of future trade agreements. The **Treaty of Amsterdam** included services and intellectual property, but required unanimity in the Council as well as consultation of the EP. The **Treaty of Nice** took a step further and introduced qualified majority voting (QMV) for services and intellectual property, except for "cultural and audiovisual services, educational services, and social and human health services," where unanimity would still be required in the Council, since these areas were still considered shared competences. Finally, the Treaty of Lisbon (Article 207 TFEU) has added investments to the definition of trade policy, and it now falls under the **ordinary legislative procedure** (OLP), which means that the EP has finally become a co-legislator. It is thus the rules of the Treaty of Lisbon that will apply to a possible future EU-UK trade agreement of some kind: Council mandate, Commission as negotiator, and the EP as co-decider. *See also* COMMON CUSTOMS TARIFF (CCT); TRADE POLICY COMMITTEE.

COMMON CUSTOMS TARIFF (CCT). The **European Economic Community** (EEC) was established as a **customs union**. It meant that a common customs tariff (CCT) was to be introduced. The **Treaty of Rome** foresaw this happening over a 12-year transition period. At the same time internal tariffs and quantitative restrictions (QRs) were to be abolished. The aim was to establish an external tariff that was roughly the average of the previously existing national tariffs. The process was actually completed in 1968 faster than foreseen. Creating a customs union creates more trade internally, but may divert trade externally, depending on the level of the common tariff. The CCT has been reduced several times since the beginning in 1958 through trade liberalization rounds in the **General Agreement on Tariffs and Trade** (GATT), now part of the **World Trade Organization** (WTO). The CET is one of the instruments of the **Common Commercial Policy** (CCP). The **Withdrawal Agreement** negotiated by Prime Minister **Theresa May** in November 2018 included the **United Kingdom** (UK) remaining in the customs union to avoid border control between **Northern Ireland** and the **Republic of Ireland** until another solution could be found. The subsequent Withdrawal Agreement negotiated by Prime Minister **Boris Johnson** in October 2019 left Northern Ireland in the customs union, thus creating a de facto customs border in the Irish Sea. There will further be some **regulatory alignments** with the **internal market** standards to avoid border controls of product standards along the Irish land border.

COMMON FISHERIES POLICY (CFP). The Common Fisheries Policy (CFP) goes back to the **Treaty of Rome**, which considered fish products agricultural products (Article 38). Therefore, the general principles of **Common Agricultural Policy** (CAP) were applicable to fisheries policy. The first CFP was developed prior to the first **enlargement** in 1973, which saw Denmark, **Ireland**, and the **United Kingdom** (UK) joining, but membership rejected by **referendum** in **Norway**, where fisheries districts voted overwhelmingly against membership. The basic idea was to share the fishing waters of the member states as common Community waters, but a six-nautical-mile zone was reserved for coastal fishing. Further developments in the CFP must be seen in connection with the developments in the international law of the sea. From 1975, beginning with Iceland, a number of countries introduced 200-mile fisheries zones. The idea of a 200-mile Exclusive Economic Zone (EEZ), where living resources were reserved for the coastal states, was eventually accepted in the UN Convention on the Law of the Sea (1982). The **European Community** (EC) accepted this development in 1976 and introduced a European Community 200-mile zone, first in the North Sea and Atlantic Ocean, where the living resources would be a shared resource.

Fish stocks constitute a typical common pool problem. The individual fisherman has no incentive to limit his fishing effort. Stocks will therefore easily be overexploited. The EC as a result had to restrict access in various ways and control that the limits were respected. A system of Total Allowable Catches (TACs) was introduced, and the TACs were divided into national quotas. This was supplemented with technical measures, including net sizes, minimum sizes of fish, rules about by-catches, and so on. Gradually it got more and more complex, but overfishing kept being a problem. Various reforms of the CFP have taken place over the years but fraud in the industry remains an issue. The **European Union** (EU) has also negotiated a number of fisheries agreements with third countries, thereby making more stocks available for EU fishermen. Spain, which joined in 1986, still has a huge fishing fleet, and much of its catch comes from the South Atlantic.

Fisheries policy will be an important part of the future relations between the EU and the UK. Traditionally a number of fishermen from the other EU member states have fished in what becomes UK waters with Brexit. The EU is therefore insisting on getting an agreement concerning EU fishermen's access to UK waters before going into details with the future trade relationship. The UK fishermen, on the other hand, will have an interest in access to the EU market for fishery products.

COMMON FOREIGN AND SECURITY POLICY (CFSP). The Common Foreign and Security Policy (CFSP) became a policy of the **European Union** (EU) as the second pillar of the EU created by the **Treaty of Maastricht** in 1993. It was an improved version of the previously existing **European Political Cooperation** (EPC), the foreign policy cooperation dating back to 1970. It was established as intergovernmental cooperation without supranational decision-making procedures. Therefore, the **European Commission**, although associated with CFSP, did not play an important role. Nor was the **European Court of Justice** (ECJ) competent in the second pillar.

The objectives of CFSP were the following:

1. To safeguard the common values, fundamental interests and independence of the Union;
2. To strengthen the security of the Union and its member states in all ways;
3. To preserve peace and strengthen international security;
4. To promote international cooperation;
5. To develop and consolidate democracy and the rule of law, and respect for human rights and fundamental freedoms.

According to the Treaty of Maastricht, the foreign ministers could adopt common positions and joint actions. Common positions were part of what was termed systematic cooperation. Joint actions would be based on general guidelines from the European Council. Normally decisions would require unanimity. However, the **Council** could in an *ad hoc* fashion decide that certain decisions could be made by a **qualified majority vote** (QMV). The **European Parliament** (EP) would be consulted; the Commission would be "fully associated" with the work. It got a right of initiative shared with all member states. The Political Committee of Political Directors, which existed under EPC, was maintained. It had to monitor the international situation and implementation of agreed policies. However, the **Committee of Permanent Representatives** (COREPER) was also given a role in CFSP.

An important novelty was the inclusion of defense policy. Article J.4(1) specified, "The common foreign and security shall include all questions related to the security of the Union, including the eventual framing of a common defence policy, which might in time lead to a common defence." The rather hesitant language was due to skepticism on the part of some pro-Atlantic member states, especially the **United Kingdom** (UK). The development of the Union's defense policy was delegated to the **Western European Union** (WEU). The compromise type of language was also clear in Article J.4(4), which stated, "The policy of the Union in accordance with this article shall not prejudice the specific character of the security and defence policy of certain Member States and shall respect the obligation of certain Member States under the North Atlantic Treaty and be compatible with the common security and defence policy established within that framework." Therefore, the pro–North Atlantic Treaty Organization (pro-NATO) policy of some member states was acceptable and so was the Irish policy of neutrality.

CFSP was on the agenda of the 1996 Intergovernmental Conference (IGC) that eventually led to the **Treaty of Amsterdam**. It was an area where the treaty actually included some important innovations. It created the post of a **High Representative for the Common Foreign and Security Policy**. It was decided that the secretary general of the **Council** would fill the post. The first to do so was Javier Solana. Further, a policy planning and early warning unit was established under his responsibility, in co-operation with the Commission. The treaty also introduced something called "constructive abstention," a procedure that allowed a member state that did not want to take part in some policy to abstain and allow the other members to move ahead.

Efforts to develop CFSP, while staying within intergovernmental decision-making, continued with the **Treaty of Lisbon**. Although the treaty abolished the pillar structure, it clearly states that CFSP is subject to specific rules and procedures (Art. 24 TEU). It remains intergovernmental. The High Representative (HR) position was redefined. It became the **High Representative of the Union for Foreign Affairs and Security Policy**, and the position includes being Vice President (VP) of the Commission. The HR/VP further chairs the **Foreign Affairs Council** (FAC), and is assisted by the new **European External Action Service** (EEAS) (Art. 27 TEU). Catherine Ashton from the UK was the first to occupy the new position when the Lisbon Treaty entered into force in 2009. From November 2014, Federica Mogherini, from

Italy, occupied it, and from December 2019 it is occupied by Josep Borrell from Spain.

Because of its intergovernmental nature it should be possible to include some foreign policy cooperation with the UK post-**Brexit**.

COMMON MARKET. The term "common market" was used in the **Treaty of Rome** establishing the **European Economic Community** (EEC), and for many years the EEC was referred to as the Common Market. An important element of the Common Market was the **Customs Union**, which abolished tariffs and quantitative restrictions internally among the member states in the Common Market. Apart from **free movement** of goods, the treaty further included provisions for free movement of **services**, capital, and people. Together these have been called the **four freedoms**. They remain the central parts of what is now called the **internal market** by the treaties, and also referred to as the single market. Inside the common market the Treaty of Rome also stipulated the creation of some common policies, including especially **competition policy**, the **common agricultural policy** (CAP), and **transport policy**.

COMMON RULEBOOK. The term "common rulebook" was used in Prime Minister **Theresa May**'s so-called **Chequers plan**. It suggested the maintenance of some **European Union** (EU) regulations and product standards in the future relations between the **United Kingdom** (UK) and the EU to facilitate "frictionless trade at the border." It would not include **services**, so it was less than the full participation of **Norway** in the **European Economic Area** (EEA).

COMMON SECURITY AND DEFENCE POLICY (CSDP). Common Security and Defence Policy (CSDP) is the name used in the **Treaty of Lisbon** for what had previously been called European Security and Defence Policy (ESDP). It was the **Treaty of Maastricht** in 1992 that mentioned defense policy for the first time, but originally its development was delegated to the **Western European Union** (WEU). In June 1992 there was a meeting of the WEU in Petersberg, near Bonn, where it was decided that the organization could take care of soft security missions, defined as humanitarian and rescue tasks; peace-keeping tasks; and tasks of combat forces in crisis management, including peace-making. These became known as the **Petersberg tasks**. They did not include collective defense. On the proposal of the nonaligned members of the **European Union** (EU), Finland and Sweden in particular, the Petersberg tasks were included in the **Treaty of Amsterdam** as the definition of the EU's defense policy.

The development of an autonomous European defense policy was still controversial at the time of the Treaty of Amsterdam negotiations. The new **Labour Party** government in the **United Kingdom** (UK) had not changed the UK position as some other member states had hoped. But about a year and a half later, in December 1998, there was a Franco-British summit in Saint Malo in France, where President Jacques Chirac and Prime Minister **Tony Blair** adopted the important Saint Malo Joint Declaration, where they said that "the Union must have the capacity for autonomous action, backed up by credible military forces."

The EU followed up on the Franco-British initiative during the German Presidency in the first half of 1999, partly under impression of the deteriorating situation in Kosovo. The European Council meeting in Cologne in June started the further development of the ESDP, that is, a defense policy not depending on the WEU. The meeting of the European Council in Helsinki in December 1999 took a further implementing decisions. Quickly a set of ESDP Institutions were set up:

- **Political and Security Committee** (PSC)—political directors of Foreign Ministries;
- Military Committee of the EU (EUMC)—Chiefs of Defence of member states;
- Military Staff of the EU (EUMS)—performs early warning, strategic planning, and situation assessment.

Later a Committee for Civilian Aspects of Crisis Management was also created.

The Political and Security Committee was mentioned in the Treaty of Nice and soon afterward the WEU ceased to exist, its functions basically being taken over by the EU.

The Treaty of Lisbon has given CSDP a more prominent place than ESDP used to have. It extends the Petersberg tasks to include disarmament, post-conflict stabilization, and fight against terrorism, and it includes a mutual defense clause much like Article V in the WEU treaty. It also mentions the European Defence Agency. It allows for enhanced cooperation among a smaller group of member states and creates Permanent Structured Cooperation among the more capable member states to develop the military capability, and it is now possible to entrust a task to a group of member states.

How defense-related cooperation will develop between the EU and the UK in the future will depend on the post-**Brexit** negotiations. The UK will remain a member of NATO, and most EU member states are members of NATO.

COMMUNITY METHOD. The Community Method is the name given to the original decision-making procedures in the **European Communities** (EC) created in the 1950s. The central aspects were an exclusive right of initiative of the **European Commission**, possibilities of adopting some legislation by a **qualified majority vote** (QMV) in the **Council**, and the **European Court of Justice** (ECJ) making binding judgments. It is usually contrasted with intergovernmental cooperation where the Commission plays a minor or no role, where the Council decides by unanimity and the ECJ has no or only a very peripheral role. Even if the **Treaty of Lisbon** has now abolished the term "European Community" in the treaty the designation "Community method" will probable survive. The supranational powers given to the Commission and ECJ from the beginning arguably means that the member states have delegated a part of their sovereignty to these Community institutions, something many **United Kingdom** (UK) politicians never fully accepted. The term "sovereignty" was used in the **Brexit** debate by the **Leave campaign**, which wanted to "take back control." The role of the ECJ—now **Court of Justice of the European Union** (CJEU)—is a controversial issue in the negotiations concerning the future UK-**European Union** (EU) relations.

COMPETENCE. In the **European Union (EU)** context "competence" can be translated as legal authority. The treaties determine in what areas the EU can act. The **Treaty of Lisbon** has tried to create greater clarity by including lists of different kinds of competences. The Union has "exclusive competence" in the following areas (Article 3 TEU):

(a) **Customs union**,
(b) The establishment of the competition rules necessary for the functioning of the **internal market**,
(c) Monetary policy for the Member States whose currency is the **euro**,
(d) The conservation of marine biological resources under the **common fisheries policy**,
(e) **Common commercial policy**.

Further, the Treaty of Lisbon stipulated in Article 3(2): "The Union shall also have exclusive competence for the conclusion of an international agreement when its conclusion is provided for in a legislative act of the Union or is necessary to enable the Union to exercise its internal competence, or in so far as its conclusion may affect common rules or alter their scope."

The list of the areas where the Union has competences shared with the member states is rather long (Article 4 TEU):

(a) **Internal market**
(b) **Social policy**
(c) Economic, social, and territorial **cohesion**
(d) **Agriculture and fisheries**, excluding the conservation of marine biological resources
(e) **Environment**
(f) Consumer protection
(g) **Transport**
(h) **Trans-European networks**
(i) Energy
(j) **Area of freedom, security, and justice**
(k) Common safety concerns in public health matters

There are also areas where the Union has competence to "carry out actions to support, coordinate or supplement actions of the Member States" (Article 6 TEU):

(a) Protection and improvement of human health
(b) Industry
(c) Culture
(d) Tourism
(e) Education, vocational training, youth, and sport
(f) Civil protection
(g) Administrative cooperation

Not all competences fit in neatly. The Union also has competence to carry out activities in areas of research, technological development, and space, as well as in areas of development cooperation and humanitarian aid. There is also coordination of economic policies, where the Union can adopt measures and guidelines. This includes employment. Finally, the Union has some competence in **Common Foreign and Security Policy** (CFSP), without giving it a name.

COMPETITION POLICY. Competition policy is one of the original policies and a very important one. It is also one where the **European Commission** and the **European Court of Justice** (ECJ) have very strong powers. The Commission basically makes, implements, and enforces competition policy. It was originally based on Articles 85–94 EEC (now Art. 101–109 TFEU). It is directed against both companies and governments. The purpose is to create a level playing field and assure fair prices for the consumers. The policy prohibits:

1. Agreements between undertakings Art. 101 TFEU (ex. Art. 85 EEC)
2. Abuse of dominant position Art. 102 TFEU (ex. Art. 86 EEC)
3. Aids granted by states (some state aids are legal and some can be approved), Art. 107 TFEU (ex. Art. 92 EEC)

The original policy did not deal with mergers, but a Merger Regulation was adopted in 1989. Mergers of a certain size must be approved by European Commission.

The role of competition policy in the future relationship between the **European Union** (EU) and the **United Kingdom** (UK) will be on the agenda in the post-**Brexit** negotiations. State aid, for instance, can affect the "**level playing field**" the EU wants to maintain in trade relations. It is to be expected that competition policy will remain important in future UK-EU relations.

COMPREHENSIVE ECONOMIC AND TRADE AGREEMENT (CETA). *See* CANADA.

CONFEDERAL GROUP OF EUROPEAN UNITED LEFT–NORDIC GREEN LEFT (GUE/NLG). The Confederal Group of European United Left–Nordic Green Left is a party group in the **European Parliament** (EP) of leftish, somewhat EU skeptical, parties. After the May 2019 elections it is the seventh group in size with 41 seats.

CONSENSUS. There is consensus in a body if everybody agrees on a measure. The chair can conclude that there is consensus if nobody objects to a measure. It is thus basically the same as unanimity, but establishing unanimity requires a vote. It has been argued that there is a consensus culture in the **European Union** (EU). Despite the many voting rules the member states prefer consensus. No one likes to be outvoted, so there will often be a search for consensus instead of moving to a vote.

CONSENT PROCEDURE. The **Single European Act** (SEA) originally introduced the consent procedure in 1987, then called the assent procedure. When a treaty article specifies that a decision requires the assent/consent of the **European Parliament** (EP) it means that the EP has a right of veto. It cannot propose amendments. Originally, the two main areas of assent were **association agreements** and accession treaties. In the **Treaty of Lisbon**, it is now called the consent procedure, and its use has been extended. The **Multiannual Financial Framework** (MFF), for instance, now requires the consent of the EP to be adopted (Article 312 TFEU). The EP had to give its consent to the **Brexit Withdrawal Agreement**. *See also* ENLARGEMENT.

CONSULTATION PROCEDURE. This is the oldest of the legislative procedures in the **European Union (EU).** In the original **European Community** (EC) treaties in the 1950s this was the main procedure. The Parliamentary Assembly, as the **European Parliament** was then called, was consulted on some legislation. However, the **Council** was the sole legislator. The Council, based on a proposal from the **Commission**, made the final decision either by unanimity or by a **qualified majority vote** (QMV), depending on the article in the original treaties. The **Treaty of Lisbon** has made co-decision the **ordinary legislative procedure** (OLP), which is most commonly used. But the consultation procedure still exists as one of the so-called special legislative procedures. It is used for politically sensitive issues where the member states retain responsibility for policy making and where unanimity is applied. Examples include some aspects of **Justice and Home Affairs** (JHA) cooperation.

CONSUMER POLICY. The Treaty of Rome establishing the **European Economic Community** (EEC) did not mention consumer policy explicitly, but elements of a policy in this area started to emerge in the late 1960s and early 1970s. A Consumer Consultative Committee was established in 1973. The first treaty to mention consumer protection was the **Single European Act** (SEA). To facilitate the creation of the **internal market** the SEA introduced **qualified majority voting** (QMV) for much of the required legislation, specifying that Commission proposals concerning "health, safety, environmental protection and consumer protection" should "take as a base a high level of protection" (Article 100a(3) of SEA). The **Treaty of Maastricht** subsequently included a title on consumer protection, which, apart from internal market legislation, mentioned "specific action which supports and supplements the policy pursued by the Member States" in this area. Such action would require consultation of the European Economic and Social Committee (EESC) and could be adopted under the co-decision procedure (Article 129a).

Organizations representing consumer interests have sometimes felt that consumer policy did not get the priority it requires. The so-called mad cow disease in 1996 gave these organizations stronger arguments, and they found a strong ally in the **European Parliament** (EP).

According to the **Treaty of Lisbon**, "Consumer protection requirements shall be taken into account in defining and implementing other Union policies and activities" (Article 12 TFEU).

CONSERVATIVE PARTY. The **United Kingdom** (UK) Conservative Party is the party that has been in power during the **Brexit** negotiations, first led by Prime Minister **Theresa May** 2016–2019, and afterward by Prime Minister **Boris Johnson** from July 2019. It was the previous Conservative government under **David Cameron** that called the **referendum** on British membership, which took place in June 2016, where about 52 percent of the voters voted for leaving the EU. It was a Conservative government under Prime Minister Harold Macmillan that first applied for UK membership in the then **European Community** (EC) in 1971—subsequently to be vetoed by French president **Charles de Gaulle**—and it was Conservative Prime Minister **Edward Heath** that took the UK into the EC in 1973. It was a Conservative government under Prime Minister **Margaret Thatcher** who during the 1980s took various battles with her colleagues in the EC concerning the British **budget** contribution as well as the proposed **Social Charter**, and it was a Conservative government under **John Major** who led the UK during the **Maastricht Treaty** negotiations and ratification, securing **opt-outs** in relation to **Economic and Monetary Union** (EMU), **social policy**, and **Justice and Home Affairs** (JHA) cooperation.

CONSTITUTION OF THE UNITED KINGDOM. The **United Kingdom** (UK) constitution is not a single document the way most countries have a written constitution today. It is a system of rules adopted over the centuries supplemented with case law and political conventions. Usually the Magna Carta issued by King John of England in 1215 is mentioned as an important early document. It settled a conflict between the barons and the autocratic king, who gave all "free men" the right to justice and a fair trial. "Free men" at the time was only a small proportion of the population. The majority was unfree peasants. It also stated that no taxes could be demanded without the "general consent of the realm," meaning the leading barons and churchmen. King John similarly had a conflict with the Catholic Church, which led to his excommunication in 1209 by Pope Innocent III. He eventually surrendered his Kingdom to the over-lordship of the Pope in 1213. When King John refused to meet with the rebellious barons, they renounced their oaths of allegiance to him. They went on to capture the city of London, leaving no option for the king but negotiation. The king granted the Charter of Liberties on 15 June 1215, subsequently known as Magna Carta. The king was now subject to the law agreed with the barons.

Another important development, the Bill of Rights, followed the Glorious Revolution in 1688, where King James II was replaced by William III. It established the supremacy of **UK Parliament** over the Crown. It provided for regular meetings of Parliament, free elections to the Commons, free speech in parliamentary debates, and some basic human rights, including freedom from "cruel or unusual punishment." Further, the so-called Act of Settlement in 1701 established the principle of judicial independence.

The reason why the UK constitution is called "unwritten" is that political customs, known as conventions, are still very important. Much of the way the government works is not written into law. The way the prime minister is appointed and the fact that he or she must have the confidence of the **House of Commons** are largely based on conventions.

COOPERATION PROCEDURE. The cooperation procedure was originally introduced by the **Single European Act** (SEA). It applied to **internal market** legislation. It introduced a second reading in the **European Parliament** (EP). It did not include a conciliation committee process. After the EP's second reading, the Council could overrule its proposed amendments by a unanimous vote. After the **Treaty of Amsterdam** (in force 1999) the cooperation procedure remained in use only for a small number of provisions, primarily relating to **Economic and Monetary Union** (EMU). It has been abolished by the **Treaty of Lisbon**.

CORBYN, JEREMY (1949–). Jeremy Corbyn was the leader of the main opposition party, the **Labour Party**, during the **Brexit** negotiations. He has been a **Member of Parliament** (MP) since 1983, and was elected Labour Party leader in 2015. He took the party to the left, even advocating nationalizations. He has been critical of the **European Union** (EU) but did support continued membership of the EU in the 2016 referendum. In the 2017 general election Labour increased its share of the vote to 40 percent, translating into a net gain of 30 seats, but in the 2019 general election Labour's share of the vote fell to 32 percent and the number of seats fell by 60, leading Corbyn to say that he would not lead Labour into the next election. His positions during the Brexit debates were not always very clear, often arguing for a "softer" Brexit than the one sought by the Conservative governments. He ended up supporting a **second referendum** on the **Withdrawal Agreement** in 2019. In April 2020 **Keir Starmer** was elected as new leader of the Labour Party.

COSTA V. ENEL. *Costa v. ENEL* (1964) is a very important judgment of the **European Court of Justice** (ECJ). It established the principle of the supremacy (or **primacy**) of **European Community** (EC) law. The ECJ said, inter alia, "It follows from all these observations that the law stemming from the treaty, an independent source of law, could not, because of its special and original nature, be overridden by domestic legal provisions, however framed, without being deprived of its character as community law and without the legal basis of the community itself being called into question."

COSTS OF BREXIT. The costs of **Brexit** have been estimated by various economists and think tanks. Figures vary and depend on assumptions. An assessment carried out by the **United Kingdom** (UK) government itself, which was titled "EU Exit Analysis – Cross Whitehall Briefing" and dated January 2018, looked at three of the most plausible Brexit scenarios at the time, based on existing **European Union** (EU) arrangements. Under a comprehensive free trade agreement with the EU, UK growth would be 5 percent lower over the next 15 years compared to then current forecasts. The "no deal" scenario, which would see the UK revert to **World Trade Organization** (WTO) rules, would reduce growth by 8 percent over that period. The softest Brexit option of continued single-market access through membership of the **European Economic Area** (EEA) would, in the longer term, still lower growth by 2 percent. Most economists agree that Brexit will have economic costs. Much will depend on the future relations between the UK and the EU.

COUNCIL. *See* COUNCIL OF THE EUROPEAN UNION.

COUNCIL OF THE EUROPEAN UNION. The body often referred to as the Council of Ministers started being referred to as the Council of the **European Union** after the **Treaty of Maastricht** had created the European Union. The treaties continue simply to call it the Council. The Council is composed of "a representative of each Member State at the ministerial level." The purpose of this rule is to make sure that the representative can commit the member state. Since the **Treaty of Lisbon,** it is spelled out that the Council "jointly with the **European Parliament**, exercise legislative and budgetary functions" (Article 16 TEU). Further, it is stipulated that "the Council shall act by a qualified majority except where the Treaties provide otherwise." From 1 November 2014, a qualified majority is defined as "at least 55% of the members of the Council, comprising at least fifteen of them and representing Member States comprising at least 65% of the population of the Union." This new double majority system has replaced the more cumbersome system of weighted votes that existed before, the latest version adopted by the **Treaty of Nice**.

Originally, each of the three Communities established in the 1950s had a Council. Formally, the Merger Treaty merged them to one Council in 1965. However, the Council meets in different configurations, currently ten. The **General Affairs Council** (GAC) is supposed to have a coordinating role. The **Treaty of Lisbon** created a separate **Foreign Affairs Council** (FAC), which is chaired by the **High Representative of the Union for Foreign Affairs and Security Policy**. The Council of Economic and Finance Ministers, known as the Ecofin Council, is also very important. So is the Council of Agriculture and Fisheries Ministers. These very important configurations usually meet once a month. The other Council configurations, the **Justice and Home Affairs** Council, the Competitiveness Council, the **Environment**

Council, the **Employment, Social Policy**, Health and **Consumer** Affairs Council, the **Transport**, Telecommunications and Energy Council, and the Education, Youth and Culture Council, meet less frequently.

The Council meets in public when it legislates. This rule was introduced in 1993 after the difficulties of getting the **Treaty of Maastricht** ratified, when there was a call for more transparency. It is confirmed in the current treaty (Article 16(8) TEU). From the beginning until 1993 the Council had always met behind closed doors, a practice foreign ministers were familiar with from traditional diplomacy, but not satisfactory for a legislative body.

The **Presidency** of the Council rotates every six months among the member states, except for the Foreign Affairs Council chaired by the High Representative. The meetings are in Brussels except in April, June, and October, when they are in Luxembourg, an arrangement that goes back to the Merger Treaty in 1965, when the secretariat of the **High Authority** moved to Brussels as part of the new single **Commission**, and Luxembourg insisted on compensation.

The Council is obviously a powerful body in the EU institutional setup. Arguably, it has lost some power in recent years. First, the **European Parliament** (EP) has increasingly become a co-legislator and a joint decision maker on the **budget**. Second, the **European Council** of Heads of State or Government has also become more important. *See also* VOTING.

COUNCIL SECRETARIAT. The Council Secretariat assists the **Council**. It has a staff of more than 3,000 officials divided into eight directorates-general and a legal service. It is housed in the Justus Lipsius building across from the Berlaymont building housing the headquarters of the **European Commission**.

COURT OF JUSTICE OF THE EUROPEAN UNION (CJEU). The Court of Justice of the European Union (CJEU) used to be called **the European Court of Justice** (ECJ). It was established first for the **European Coal and Steel Community** (ECSC) in the **Treaty of Paris** in 1951, in force since 1952. When the **Treaties of Rome** in 1957, in force in 1958, created the **European Atomic Energy Community** (EAEC or EURATOM) and the **European Economic Community** (EEC), it was decided that these two new Communities would share the Court of Justice with the ECSC. This was spelled out in the Convention on Certain Institutions common to the European Communities signed in Rome at the same time as the two Treaties of Rome.

The ECJ/CJEU has played an extremely important role in the history of European integration. It helped clarify the nature of **European Community** law; it interpreted the treaty law and secondary legislation. Concerning the nature of Community law, the two most important judgments were *Van Gend en Loos* (26/62) and *Costa v. ENEL* (6/64). The two established the principles of **direct effect** and supremacy (or **primacy**) of Community law. It was also the ECJ that established the principle of mutual recognition in the Casis de Dijon case, extremely important for the **internal market**. The Court is competent to judge a number of cases:

1. Infringement (Art. 258-260 TFEU): failure of a member state to fulfill its obligations; penalty payment is a possibility
2. Judicial review (Art. 263 TFEU): review of legality of acts; private citizens can also bring actions if of direct and individual concern; act may be declared void
3. Preliminary rulings (Art. 267 TFEU): interpretation of Treaties and acts of institutions
4. Other areas include: actions for damages against EU institution (Art. 268), breach of fundamental rights by a member state (Art. 269 TFEU), and employment disputes (Art. 270 TFEU)

The Court is not competent in Common Foreign and Security Policy (CFSP), except for "reviewing the legality of decisions providing restrictive measures against natural and legal persons" (Art. 275 TFEU), so-called smart sanctions.

As the workload of the ECJ kept increasing, a Court of First Instance (CFI) was created in 1989, after the **Single European Act** (SEA) made it possible (Article 32d). It mainly took **competition policy** cases and employment disputes. It has now been renamed the General Court by the **Treaty of Lisbon**. A European Civil Service Tribunal was established in 2005 to take employment disputes. It ceased to exist in 2016, when the membership in the General Court was doubled. According to the Treaty of Lisbon the Court of Justice of the European Union (CJEU) "shall consist on one judge from each Member State" and "The General Court shall include at least one judge per Member State" (Article 19 TEU). Post-**Brexit** the CJEU has 27 members and the General Court has two members per member state, that is, 54. The two courts have their seat in Luxembourg.

CUMMINGS, DOMINIC (1971–). A leading **Brexiteer**, Dominic Cummings was Campaign Director for the **Leave campaign**, 2015–2016. Before that he had been special advisor to Education Secretary **Michael Gove** (2010–2014). He is credited with coming up with the slogan "Vote Leave, Take Control," and the false figure of £350 million a week being sent to the EU, claiming the money could be better spent on saving the National Health

Service (NHS). In 2019 he became Chief Advisor to Prime Minister **Boris Johnson**.

CUSTOMS UNION. The creation of a customs union was a central part of European economic integration at the outset. In a customs union, tariffs and quantitative restrictions are abolished and a **Common Customs Tariff** (CCT) toward third countries is set up. The customs union of the **European Economic Community** (EEC) was fully established by 1968, earlier than planned in the **Treaty of Rome**. The CCT distinguishes a customs union from a **free trade area** (FTA), where the member states keep their own external tariffs. FTAs therefore also require rules of origin to avoid that all imports go through the country with the lowest tariffs. Both customs unions and FTAs will usually leave **non-tariff barriers to trade** (NTBs), such as different product standards in national legislation. Some degree of harmonization of standards or mutual recognition will be needed to deal with these. In connection with **Brexit** Prime Minister **Teresa May**'s **Withdrawal Agreement** of 2018 would have kept the **United Kingdom** (UK) in the customs union until another solution for the **Irish border** could be found, the so-called **backstop**. The Withdrawal Agreement subsequently reached by Prime Minister **Boris Johnson** left **Northern Ireland** in the customs union—and partly in the **internal market**—to avoid the reintroduction of border controls on the border between Northern Ireland and the **Republic of Ireland**. For this reason, there will be some border control between Northern Ireland and the other constituent parts of the UK, namely, **England, Scotland,** and **Wales**. *See also* INTERNAL MARKET.

CYPRUS. Cyprus joined the **European Union** (EU) in 2004 together with eight Central and Eastern European Countries (CEECs) as well as Malta. Its membership was controversial because of the division of the island since 1974 into a Greek- and a Turkish-speaking part. Various efforts to get the island reunified have taken place, but so far without success. In April 2004, there was a dual **referendum** on a reunification plan brokered by the United Nations (UN). The Turkish Cypriots approved the plan but the Greek Cypriots rejected the plan. The membership of only the Greek-speaking part of Cyprus was then allowed, strongly supported by Greece, which could block other accessions if Cyprus was not allowed to join. The **United Kingdom** (UK) still has two military bases in Cyprus, so the **Brexit Withdrawal Agreement** has a protocol on Cyprus. It aims to protect the interests of Cypriots who live and work on the military bases, known as **Sovereign Base Areas** (SBAs). The laws applicable to those Cypriots will be the same as the laws in Cyprus.

D

DAVIS, DAVID (1948–). David Davis is a Conservative British politician. He became Secretary of State for Exiting the European Union when **Theresa May** became prime minister in July 2016. He served in that capacity until he resigned on 8 July 2018, and was succeeded by **Dominic Raab**. His resignation was followed by that of Foreign Secretary **Boris Johnson** the following day. Davis and Johnson were both critical of May's "soft Brexit" approach as exemplified by her **Chequers plan**.

DECISION. A decision in the **European Union** (EU) is a legal act. It is directed to an individual, an enterprise, or a member state. It is directly binding. It is one of three legal instruments, the two other ones being **regulations** and **directives**.

DECLARATION ON CONSENT IN NORTHERN IRELAND. The so-called **backstop** relating to the border between **Northern Ireland** and the **Republic of Ireland**, which was included in the **Withdrawal Agreement** reached between Prime Minister **Theresa May** and the **European Union** (EU) in November 2018, was taken out of the subsequent agreement reached by Prime Minister **Boris Johnson** in October 2019 and replaced by a more permanent solution to avoid border controls along the **Irish border**. Out of a certain concern for democracy the **United Kingdom** (UK) government then issued a unilateral declaration allowing the Northern Ireland Assembly to provide "consent" for certain EU regulations to continue in Northern Ireland. These regulations will have to continue for certain Northern Irish products to be able to be exported to the Republic of Ireland without border checks. The first vote will take place four years after the end of the **transition period** and then there will be a vote every four years afterward. If rejected the regulations will cease to apply after two years, which in turn presumably could lead to border control of certain products exported from Northern Ireland and the Irish Republic, if no other solution is found.

DEEP AND COMPREHENSIVE FREE TRADE AGREEMENT (DCFTA). Deep and Comprehensive Free Trade Agreement is the name given to free trade agreements offered to European Neighborhood countries in Eastern Europe. Discussions of options for the future relationship between the **European Union** (EU) and the **United Kingdom** (UK) sometimes mentions the agreement with **Ukraine**. The DCFTAs are **association agreements** that aim for eventual participation of the countries concerned in the EU's **internal market**.

DEEPENING. Deepening refers to the process of expanding the scope of **European Union** (EU) legislation and improving the institutional capacity of the Union. In connection with **enlargement** (**widening**), there are usually also proposals for deepening, in view of making sure that the enlarged union can function efficiently.

DEFENSE POLICY. *See* COMMON SECURITY AND DEFENCE POLICY (CSDP).

DE GAULLE, CHARLES (1890–1970). Charles de Gaulle, president of France from 1958 to 1969, was the leader of the French resistance during the Nazi occupation (1940–1945). After the war, he was briefly involved in French politics but withdrew in 1946. His return in 1958 was due to the problem created by the war in Algeria, which the 4th Republic had not been able to solve. His followers in French politics during the 4th Republic had been against European integration, as had the Communists on the other side of the political spectrum. When he returned to power, the **Treaties of Rome** had entered into force and France had a clear interest in developing the **Common Agricultural Policy** (CAP). At first, General de Gaulle focused on Algeria and he created the 5th Republic, with a strong Presidency that he subsequently occupied. In 1960, he proposed a Union of States, an intergovernmental union that would limit the powers of the supranational **European Communities** (EC). The so-called Fouchet negotiations, however, finished in 1962 without an agreement. In January 1963, De Gaulle vetoed **United Kingdom** (UK) membership of the Communities and entered the Elysée Treaty with Germany. He favored a European Europe—led by France. He believed that the UK was too Atlantic in orientation and might pose problems for the CAP.

He pursued his battles in Brussels against supranational Europe. In July 1965 he started the so-called Empty Chair policy in response to a **European Commission** proposal for financing the CAP with "Own Resources" and increased powers to the **European Parliament** (EP) in budgetary matters. In September, he also objected to the move to use **qualified majority voting** (QMV), which was foreseen in the treaties. Eventually, after only narrowly winning the presidential elections against François Mitterrand in December 1965 he instructed his ministers to return to the **Council** meetings. Late January 1966 the so-called **Luxembourg Compromise** was reached. In it, the six member states agreed to disagree, with France insisting that when very important interests are at stake negotiations much continue until unanimous agreement is reached. In reality, this meant that France insisted on having a veto even in matters where the treaties foresaw QMV.

De Gaulle vetoed UK membership a second time in 1967. In May 1968, student and worker demonstrations weakened his position. In 1969, after losing two **referendums**, one on local government reform and one on reform of the senate, he decided to step down. He was followed by **Georges Pompidou**, who, under pressure from the five other member states, agreed to open membership negotiations with the UK and the other applicants: Denmark, **Ireland**, and **Norway**.

DELORS, JACQUES (1925–). Jacques Delors started his career working in a bank, straight from secondary school. He got involved in trade union activities and found inspiration in Left-Catholic social doctrine. Eventually he entered politics through the Socialist Party. In 1979, he was elected to the **European Parliament** (EP), where he chaired the monetary affairs committee. When François Mitterrand became president of France in 1981 Delors became minister of finance, not necessarily committed to the Socialist Keynesian policies that Mitterrand first tried. When the French franc got under pressure in 1983 Delors was instrumental in turning French economic policy toward Europe. President Mitterrand started actively supporting more European integration. Delors became president of the following **European Commission**, from January 1985. He became one of the most active and influential Commission presidents in the history of European integration. In this connection he took a few battles with British prime minister **Margaret Thatcher**, especially about social and monetary policy. During his decade as Commission president the **Single European Act** (SEA) was negotiated, the **internal market** more or less completed, **Economic and Monetary Union** (EMU) put on the agenda again and agreed to, and the Cold War ended. Also, the **European Union** (EU) was created by the **Treaty of Maastricht**. The practice of **multi-annual financial framework** was introduced by the Delors I and II packages (1988 and 1992), economic and social cohesion became an important policy, money for the structural funds was doubled twice, and **social policy** received a boost. Further, preparation for the post-1989 **enlargements** started. At the same time, it is only fair to say that his decade ended with problems, the Treaty of Maastricht ratification crisis in 1992, crises of the **European Monetary System** (EMS), high unemployment, suggesting that the internal market had not had the promised effects, and continued discussions about a **democratic deficit**, despite several institutional reforms.

After his tenure in Brussels Jacques Delors formed a think tank, *Notre Europe*, in Paris in 1996. It remains an important institution for reflection and research.

DEMOCRATIC CONSENT. The final **Withdrawal Agreement** reached between Prime Minister **Boris Johnson** and the **European Union** (EU) in October 2019 included a "democratic consent" procedure for **Northern Ireland**. *See* DECLARATION ON CONSENT IN NORTHERN IRELAND.

DEMOCRATIC DEFICIT. Debates about the democratic nature of the **European Union** (EU) started relatively early in the process of European integration. Initially much of the debate was about the powers of the **European Parliament** (EP), and governments have responded to the debate in various treaty reforms. When "own resources" were introduced in 1970 the First Budgetary Treaty started giving the EP budgetary powers. When the **Single European Act** (SEA) introduced **qualified majority vote** (QMV) in Article 100a for much **internal market** legislation, the **cooperation procedure** giving the EP a right to propose amendments to legislation was introduced. Next step was co-decision in the **Treaty of Maastricht**, which became the **ordinary legislative procedure** (OLP) used for most legislation since the entry into force of the **Treaty of Lisbon**. Therefore, there has been a gradual empowerment of the EP. Since 1979, the EP has also been directly elected, so it can claim to have a kind of European **mandate**.

The wider public debate about the alleged democratic deficit exploded after the Danish "no" to the Treaty of Maastricht in 1992. The definition of democracy was widened to include more than just parliamentary accountability and free elections. It became a wider debate about legitimacy. Should national parliaments play a bigger role, as argued by intergovernmentalists? Should the EP elect the president of the **Commission**? Should there be more transparency, such as **Council** meetings open to the public? Should access to documents be easier? Should the treaties and decision-making processes be made simpler? Could some decisions be made closer to the people? In 1993, the three institutions the Commission, the Council, and the EP signed an agreement that aimed at making the decision-making process more transparent, including openness in legislation and freer access to documents.

The Constitutional Treaty was arguably designed to respond to these various aspects of the alleged democratic deficit. That the French and Dutch people rejected it in **referendums** in 2005 was a sad commentary on that effort. The latest in the reform process is the Treaty of Lisbon, which further empowers the EP in adoption of legislation and appointment of the Commission. It also includes stipulations about the involvement of national parliaments, which get some powers in supervising the application of the subsidiarity principle.

Most approaches to the democratic deficit have been about procedures (procedural or input legitimacy). There are those who argue that results (output legitimacy) are more important. Would the EU get more support in public opinion if it could create more economic growth and jobs? Then a bigger budget might be more useful than further institutional reforms.

DIFFERENTIATED INTEGRATION. *See* ENHANCED CO-OPERATION.

DIRECT EFFECT. Direct effect is a principle of EU law established by the **European Court of Justice** (ECJ) in the 1963 *Van Gend en Loos case.* It means that the law is directly applicable. It reaches the member states or individuals concerned. It creates rights and obligations for these. Together with primacy of EU law, it is a fundamental principle of EU law, implicit in the **European Community** (EC) treaties, but made explicit by the ECJ.

DIRECTIVE. A directive is a legal act of the **European Union** (EU). It is general and binding with regard to the results but allows the member states to choose the means to achieve the results. Much of the **internal market** legislation is based on directives. It is one of three types of binding acts, the two others being **regulations** and **decisions**.

DIVERGENCE. *See* REGULATORY DIVERGENCE.

DIVORCE BILL. Divorce Bill is the name given to the financial part of the **Withdrawal Agreement**. It was one of the three issues singled out by the **European Union** (EU) as most important issue during the first phase of the **Brexit** negotiations, together with **citizens' rights** (rights of EU citizens in the UK and UK citizens in the EU after Brexit) and the **Irish border** solution (the so-called **backstop** or some other solution to avoid border controls). The estimate of the amount to be paid by the **United Kingdom** (UK) after Brexit on 31 January 2020 was £33 billion, to be paid over a number of years. It was based on the UK's share of EU **budgets** up to the end of 2020 and include continuing liabilities such as EU civil servants' pensions.

E

ECOFIN COUNCIL. The Ecofin **Council** is the Council configuration of Economics and Finance Ministers.

ECONOMIC AND MONETARY UNION (EMU). The provisions for Economic and Monetary Union (EMU) were included in the **Treaty of Maastricht** in 1992. The **Treaty of Rome** establishing the **European Economic Community** (EEC) in 1958 had no reference to EMU. But the Hague summit in 1969 decided to study the possibilities of creating an EMU. This led to the Werner Report in 1970, named after the Luxembourg Prime and Finance Minister Pierre Werner, who chaired the group that drew up the report. The proposal was to create an EMU in three stages over a ten-year period. The plan was never realized. However, currency fluctuations through the 1970s were an incentive for monetary cooperation. In 1979 the **European Monetary System** (EMS) started. It created a European Currency Unit (ECU) as a weighted basket of EEC currencies, and a European Exchange-rate mechanism (ERM) to minimize currency fluctuations. The EMS helped reduce inflation and the number of devaluations, but some member states found that it was dominated by the German Central Bank (*Bundesbank*). This led to calls for a full-fledged EMU, especially from France and Italy. On the proposal of **Commission** president **Jacques Delors**, the **European Council** decided at the Hannover meeting in 1988 to establish a committee to examine the possibilities of creating an EMU. The so-called Delors Report, issued in 1989, led to the **Intergovernmental Conference** (IGC) on EMU, which finalized the provisions in the Treaty of Maastricht.

The Treaty of Maastricht outlined the three-stage process of establishing the EMU. To take part in the third stage, where the **European Central Bank** (ECB) is created and the single currency, subsequently called the euro, is introduced, a member state had to fulfill certain so-called convergence criteria. It was decided in 1999 that 11 member states fulfilled the criteria, so they became the first participants in the eurozone. Greece joined in 2001 with a two-year delay. In January 2002, euro notes and coins started circulating in the member states except the **United Kingdom** (UK), Denmark, and Sweden. Since then the eurozone has been enlarged to include Slovenia (2007), **Cyprus** and Malta (2008), Slovakia (2009), Estonia (2011), Latvia (2014), and Lithuania (2015).

When the financial crisis hit Europe in 2009 the eurozone came under pressure with talks about some members, in particular Greece, having to leave. A policy of austerity was imposed on the countries having unsustainable sovereign debt, especially Greece, Ireland, Italy, Spain, Portugal, and, a little later, Cyprus. This was a costly policy. Ways were found to bail out the countries that needed financial assistance, and a number of other measures were adopted during the years 2010–2014. The EMU, including the eurozone, survived, but the crisis demonstrated the structural defects of the setup, with a centralized monetary policy and a decentralized fiscal policy.

ECONOMIC PARTNERSHIP AGREEMENTS (EPAs). Economic Partnership Agreements (EPAs) form an important part of the Cotonou Agreement between the European Union (EU) and African, Caribbean and Pacific (ACP) countries. These agreements between the EU and regional groups of ACP countries are proposed to replace the previous non-reciprocal preferential trade agreements offered the ACP countries under the Lomé agreements, which were no longer compatible with the **World Trade Organization** (WTO) rules. To qualify for exemption from the WTO most-favored-nation rule they have to be **free trade areas** (FTAs) (Article XIV of GATT). Negotiations of EPAs progressed slowly because many ACPs wonder whether mutual free trade was in their interest.

EMPLOYMENT AND SOCIAL POLICY. *See* SOCIAL POLICY.

ENERGY POLICY. The first of the **European Communities** (EC), **the European Coal and Steel Community** (ECSC) dealt with one part of energy policy, coal. One of the Communities created by the **Treaties of Rome**, the **European Atomic Energy Community** (EAEC or EURATOM), dealt with another source, atomic energy. However, a general energy policy chapter was missing from the treaties until the **Treaty of Lisbon**. With references to both the **internal market** and **environmental policy** the **European Union** (EU) is to work "in a spirit of solidarity" to ensure the functioning of the energy market, ensure security of energy supply, promote energy efficiency, and promote the interconnection of energy markets. Energy policy has been a controversial sector because there are have and have-not member states. The Dutch had some natural gas. The British found a fair amount of oil in the North Sea, but overall it is an area where the EU is extremely dependent on foreign supplies, oil especially from the Middle East, and natural gas from Russia, not the most stable parts of the world as demonstrated by ongoing problems in Iraq and Syria as well as the crisis in **Ukraine**. The latter crisis has produced efforts to reduce the dependence of Russia. Investments in alternative sources of energy, preferably clean energy, are now becoming an even more important part of energy policy, not just environmental policy. The exploitation of shale gas and oil has become a big issue, and nuclear energy remains controversial in some member states.

ENHANCED COOPERATION. "Enhanced cooperation" is the term used in the **Treaty of Nice** and now the **Treaty of Lisbon**. It was introduced into the treaties by the **Treaty of Amsterdam**, where it was called closer cooperation. It is also sometimes referred to as differentiated integration. The treaties allow a smaller group of member states to go ahead and establish enhanced cooperation in policy sectors where not all member states are willing to participate. There are conditions. Such cooperation must not undermine the **internal market** or economic, social, and territorial cohesion. It cannot take place in areas of exclusive competences (e.g., trade). To proceed with enhanced cooperation the **Council** decides on a proposal from the **Commission** after getting the **consen**t of the **European Parliament** (EP). As a minimum nine states must take part. The Treaty of Lisbon extends the possibility of enhanced cooperation to the **Common Foreign and Security Policy** (CFSP), where the **High Representative of the Union for Foreign Affairs and Security Policy** has to give an opinion and the Council decides by unanimity. The EP is only informed.

Historically there has been a fair amount of closer cooperation outside the treaties. The best example is the **Schengen Area** cooperation about abolishing border controls that started between the Benelux countries (Belgium, Luxembourg, and the Netherlands), Germany, and France in the 1980s. Later other countries joined and the Schengen *acquis* was incorporated into the **European Union** (EU) by the **Treaty of Amsterdam**, where it became part of the **Area of Freedom, Security and Justice** (AFSJ). At that time, all member states except the **United Kingdom** (UK) and **Ireland** had joined. Subsequently four non-member states have also joined Schengen as associate members, namely, **Norway,** Iceland, Lichtenstein, and **Switzerland**. The UK and Ireland never joined the Schengen area.

Economic and Monetary Union (EMU) is a special case of differentiated integration, but one that is based on treaty rules from the beginning. At the time of the third stage in 1999, 11 of the 15 member states were included in the eurozone of the single currency, the euro. Post-Brexit there are 19 of the 27 member states that take part in the euro. The **United Kingdom** (UK) and

Denmark have had treaty-based **opt-outs**. The other member states are supposed to join once they fulfill the convergence criteria.

The responses to the financial crisis also saw elements of differentiated integration, partly because some measures were focused on the eurozone. However, in some cases some non-eurozone countries have joined, such as the Euro Plus Pact in 2011, where the eurozone countries were joined by Bulgaria, Denmark, Latvia, Lithuania, Poland, and Romania. The so-called Fiscal Compact Treaty in 2012 was adopted outside the EU framework because the UK and the Czech Republic did not want to take part.

Despite the heated debates about enhanced cooperation since the 1990s, when it was first included in the treaties, it has so far only been applied in a few areas, divorce law, property regimes of international couples, patents, European Public Prosecutor, and permanent structured cooperation in the areas of defense and security (PESCO). The UK joined the European Unitary Patent prior to Brexit, but none of the other cases of enhanced cooperation. *See also* INTELLECTUAL PROPERTY RIGHTS.

ENLARGEMENT. Successive enlargements have played an important role in European integration history. When Robert Schuman proposed what became the **European Coal and Steel Community (ECSC)** he stressed that the future organization would be open to other European states that might want to join. This was confirmed first in the **Treaty of Paris**, and later in the **Treaties of Rome** establishing the next two Communities. Still, the first enlargement in 1973, when the **United Kingdom** (UK), **Ireland**, and Denmark joined, was delayed because of French president **Charles de Gaulle** twice vetoing UK membership, in 1963 and 1967. The first enlargement brought membership from six to nine members, and the second enlargement in 1981 saw Greece join, followed by Spain and Portugal in 1986, taking membership to 12. There were thus 12 member states when the **Treaty of Maastricht** was negotiated in 1991, after the end of the Cold War. This was the time when formerly nonaligned or neutral countries started to apply for membership and countries formerly dominated by the Soviet Union started to express an interest in membership. The new **European Union** (EU) that emerged from Maastricht had to develop an enlargement policy. The Treaty of Maastricht in Article O confirmed that any European state may apply for membership, but did not set other conditions. A state seeking to join should apply to the **Council**, which decides unanimously after consulting the **Commission** and receiving the assent—now **consent**—from the **European Parliament** (EP). Afterward, it was decided that the next enlargement with applicant countries from the **European Free Trade Association** (EFTA) could take place based on the Treaty of Maastricht. Therefore, in the 4th enlargement in 1995 Austria, Finland, and Sweden joined, taking membership to 15. **Norway** had tried to join in the first enlargement, but a referendum in 1972 gave a negative result. Norway tried again in the 4th enlargement, but the proposal was again turned down by the Norwegian people.

The next enlargement, which would include a number of Central and Eastern European Countries (CEECs), was big and demanding. Inside the EU the view was that the EU institutions needed further reforms, which was tried with little success in the **Treaty of Amsterdam** and then with mixed results in the **Treaty of Nice**. By the time of the 5th enlargement in May 2004 an **Intergovernmental Conference (IGC)** was still considering the Constitutional Treaty, which had been drafted by the Convention on the Future of Europe (2002–2003). That the CEECs could join was only promised explicitly by the **European Council** in Copenhagen in June 1993, where the main conditions—market economy, democratic government, and sufficient administrative capacity—were outlined in the so-called Copenhagen criteria. After relatively long preparations and occasionally difficult negotiations and reforms instituted by the Agenda 2000 package, especially reforms of the **Common Agricultural Policy** (CAP) and **regional policies**, ten countries joined on 1 May 2004: **Cyprus**, Czech Republic, Estonia, Hungary, Latvia, Lithuania, Malta, Poland, Slovakia, and Slovenia. The two remaining CEECs, Bulgaria and Romania, followed on 1 January 2007. The latest country to join was Croatia, which joined on 1 July 2013.

Membership of **Turkey** has remained controversial among the member states. Turkish membership was used as a threat by the **Leave campaign** in 2016 in the UK, because of the free movement that follows membership. Turkey was accepted as a candidate country in 1999 after it put a lot of pressure on EU leaders. Negotiations stated in 2005 at the same time as with Croatia, but they have moved very slowly, and are currently not advancing.

The opposite of enlargement is of course the exit of a member state. **Brexit** in 2020 is the first case of that. Previously an autonomous part of a member state has left, namely Greenland, an autonomous part of Denmark, which left in 1985.

ENVIRONMENTAL POLICY. The treaties establishing the three **European Communities (EC)** in the 1950s did not mention environmental policy. Therefore, when the EC started developing environmental policy it had to be based on other articles in the treaties. An important step was taken by the Paris summit meeting in 1972 where the heads of state or government called for the development of an environmental policy. The **Commission** followed up with communication and action plans. Another summit the next year established some principles, namely, integration of environmental considerations into all planning and decision-making processes; the "polluter pays" principle; prevention of pollution at the source; promotion of international cooperation; establishment of appropriate levels of action (local, regional, national, Community, international); and coordination and harmonization of national programs. Rather quickly, a number of directives were adopted, on water pollution, drinking and bathing water, vehicle emissions, dangerous chemicals, waste oils, and detergents. The EC also joined some international conventions, like the Paris Convention for the Prevention of Marine Pollution from Land-based Sources in 1975, the Barcelona Convention for the Protection of the Mediterranean Sea against Pollution in 1977, and the Long-Range Trans-Boundary Air Pollution (LRT AP) Convention in 1979. In the 1980s, the **Single European Act** (SEA) gave a boost to environmental policy. It established that it should contribute to preserve, protect, and improve the quality of the environment; to contribute toward protecting human health; and to ensure a prudent and rational utilization of natural resources. It introduced the **subsidiarity** principle: the Community should act if the objectives could be attained better at the Community level than at the level of the member states (Article 130r(4)). The new environmental chapter of the SEA required unanimity in the **Council**, but environmental legislation linked to the **internal market** could be adopted by a **qualified majority vote** (QMV) under the new Article 100a.

In respect to decision-making, the **Treaty of Maastricht** took matters a step further by introducing qualified majority voting (QMV) and co-decision—now **ordinary legislative procedure** (OLP)—for environmental legislation. However, a few areas were left under unanimity: provisions primarily of a fiscal nature, measures concerning town and country planning, land use with the exception of waste management and measures of a general nature, and management of water resources; and measures significantly affecting a member state's choice between different energy sources and the general structure of its energy supply.

The EU has tried to play an international leadership role in the environmental area. It has been represented at many international conferences on the environment, including the Rio "Earth Summit" in Rio in 1992. It played a very active role on climate change from the negotiation of the Kyoto Protocol in 1997. The EU played an important role in convincing enough countries to ratify the protocol so that it could enter into force in 2004. However, the outcome of the 2009 Copenhagen summit was a big disappointment for the EU. The summit adopted a nonbinding agreement negotiated by the **United States** (U.S.) and China without EU involvement. The biggest challenge in that area for the EU is to get the U.S. and emerging economies to commit to binding reductions of CO_2 emissions. The EU had more success with the Paris Climate Change conference in 2015, where the French Presidency played an important role.

ERTA CASE. In the ERTA case (1971), the **European Court of Justice** (ECJ) made an important decision of great relevance for the **European Community's** (EC) external relations. Once the EC has an internal competence it also has an external competence. For example, once it develops an **environmental policy** it can also enter into agreements with third states concerning environmental policy. Member states cannot unilaterally enter into agreements with third countries that affect competences transferred to the union.

EURO. The euro is the name of the single currency introduced at stage three of **Economic and Monetary Union** (EMU). The **Treaty of Maastricht** had referred to the single currency as the ECU—the preexisting currency unit would become a currency in its own right. However, prior to the introduction of the single currency it was decided to change the name to euro in December 1995 and the euro currency sign was designed (€). The Greek letter epsilon (ε) and the first letter of Europe inspire it. The two crossed lines signify stability. Today the euro is legal tender in the 19 eurozone countries. But it is also used in the European micro-states: Andorra, Monaco, San Remo, and the Vatican, as well as in Montenegro and Kosovo.

The **United Kingdom** (UK) and Denmark secured **opt-outs** from euro participation when the Maastricht Treaty was negotiated. Sweden has also stayed out. Both Denmark and Sweden have held **referendums** about euro participation, in both cases with negative outcome. New members of the **European Union** (EU) are in principle expected to join the euro once they fulfill the convergence criteria.

EUROPE AGREEMENTS. Europe Agreements was the name given to **association agreements** with Central and Eastern European Countries (CEECs) after the end of the Cold War. Although the **European Union** (EU) admitted that the agreements could facilitate future membership of the CEECs, it did not offer membership in the agreements. The agreements established economic cooperation as well as foreign policy coordination and cultural exchange. They established bilateral association councils, association committees and parliamentary committees. The first Europe Agreements were signed with Poland, Hungary, and Czechoslovakia in December 1991. The one with Czechoslovakia was renegotiated as separate agreements with the Czech Republic and Slovakia after the country split into two countries in 1993. Other Europe Agreements were signed with Romania and Bulgaria in 1993; with the Baltic States, Estonia, Latvia, and Lithuania, in 1995; and lastly with Slovenia in 1996.

Since Europe Agreements were so-called mixed agreements, including areas where the EU was competent and areas where the member states were competent, they had to be ratified by both the EU as such and the member states, which was time consuming. The EU therefore entered interim agreements covering the economic areas where the EU had the competence, mainly trade. The trade part of the agreements aimed at establishing mutual free trade, with the EU liberalizing faster than the CEECs, with less generous offer for agricultural than industrial products. *See also* ENLARGEMENT.

EUROPE OF FREEDOM AND DIRECT DEMOCRACY GROUP (EFDD). The Europe of Freedom and Direct Democracy Group (EFDD) was the smallest of the seven groups in the **European Parliament** (EP) elected in May 2015. It held 50 of the 751 seats after that election. The biggest number, 24, came from the **United Kingdom Independence Party** (UKIP), led by **Nigel Farage**. It was an anti-EU group. It also had 17 members from Italy, from the *Movimento 5 Stelle*. The EFDD no longer exists. In the May 2019 EP elections Nigel Farage's new **Brexit Party** won 30 of the UK's 73 seats. They worked as non-attached members (*non-incrits*—NI) of the EP until **Brexit day** on 31 January 2020.

EUROPE OF NATIONS AND FREEDOM (ENF). The Europe of Nations and Freedom was launched in 2015 in the **European Parliament** (EP). It was the smallest group in the EP then with only 37 **Members of the European Parliament** (MEPs). It was a right-wing Eurosceptic group. The French *Rassemblement National*, with 17 MEPs, was the largest national group. It took the name **Identity and Democracy** (ID) in the 2019 EP election, where it gained 76 seats and became the fifth group in size.

EUROPEAN ATOMIC ENERGY COMMUNITY (EAEC OR EURATOM). The European Atomic Energy Community (EAEC or EURATOM) was established by one of the two **Treaties of Rome** signed in 1957 and in force from 1958. The EURATOM treaty established a separate **Commission** as well as **Council** of Ministers. The **European Parliament** (EP) and **European Court of Justice** (ECJ) were shared between the three Communities from the beginning. The Merger Treaty adopted in 1965 and in force from 1967 created one European Commission and one Council for the three Communities. The EURATOM still exists as a separate organization.

EURATOM's work today is focused on nuclear safety and research. **Brexit** has also meant the **United Kingdom** (UK) withdrawing from EURATOM, despite its separate identity. Some cooperation may be expected in the future. Nuclear power accounted for 21 percent of the UK's energy supply in 2015. EURATOM has cooperation agreements with eight countries that account for 71 percent of the world's uranium production. Further, UK hospitals rely on supply of isotopes used in nuclear medicine from reactors in France, Belgium, and the Netherlands.

EUROPEAN CENTRAL BANK (ECB). The European Central Bank (ECB), located in Frankfurt, Germany, is responsible for monetary policy of the countries that have adopted the single currency, the **euro**. It started operating on 1 June 1998, seven months before the start of stage three of **Economic and Monetary Union** (EMU). It took over from the European Monetary Institute (EMI), which operated during most of stage two. The policy objectives and institutional setup were outlined in the **Treaty of Maastricht** in 1992. The ECB is politically independent and charged with assuring price stability. Inflation rates are supposed to be kept lower than but close to 2 percent. The **United Kingdom** (UK) secured an opt-out from EMU at the time of the Maastricht Treaty. Joining the euro has been discussed but never found much popular support.

EUROPEAN COAL AND STEEL COMMUNITY (ECSC). The European Coal and Steel Community (ECSC) was established by the **Treaty of Paris**, signed in 1951 and in force in 1952. The treaty was agreed for a 50-year period, so it expired in 2002. It was the outcome of the **Schuman Declaration**, by French foreign minister Robert Schuman on 9 May 1950. The Treaty of Paris was negotiated by an **Intergovernmental Conference** (IGC) in Paris, chaired by **Jean Monnet**, who had thought out the plan and suggested it to Robert Schuman. France was joined by five other European countries—the Federal Republic of Germany, Italy and the Benelux countries, Belgium, the Netherlands, and Luxembourg—in this first **European Community** (EC). It pooled the coal and steel production of the six member states and created a common market for these. It included important competition rules, allowing the ECSC to break up cartels and monopolies. It established a supranational executive, the **High Authority**, a supranational court, the **European Court of Justice** (ECJ), a **Council** of Ministers, known at the time as the Special Council as well as a Parliamentary Assembly, known as the Common Assembly. The High Authority was merged with the Commissions of the EURATOM and EEC in 1967 to form one **European**

Commission. The Common Assembly later became the **European Parliament** (EP). The **United Kingdom** (UK) showed no interest in joining the ECSC when it was formed.

EUROPEAN COMMISSION. The two Communities established by the **Treaties of Rome**—the **European Atomic Energy Community** (EAEC or EURATOM) and the **European Economic Community** (EEC)—established an "executive" called the Commission. In the Merger Treaty of 1965, in force from 1967, the two were merged with the **High Authority** of the European Coal and Steel Community (ECSC) to form a single Commission for the three European Communities (EC).

While the Commission of EURATOM had five members, the Commission of the EEC had nine: two from France, Germany, and Italy, and one from the Netherlands, Belgium, and Luxembourg respectively. In the case of the High Authority the governments nominated eight members. These in turn elected a 9th member. The new single Commission in 1967 had 14 members in a transition period until 1970, when it was reduced to nine. At the time of the first enlargement in 1973 it was enlarged to 13 members, the **United Kingdom** (UK) nominating two and Denmark and **Ireland** each one. Subsequent enlargements increased the size further. Spain got to nominate two, when the country joined in 1986. The other countries joining—Greece (1981); Portugal (1986); Austria, Finland, and Sweden (1995)—each got to nominate one. As the big enlargement with Central and Eastern European Countries (CEECs) got on the agenda in the 1990s there were calls for a reduction in the size of the Commission, including reducing the number to fewer than the number of member states. The smaller member states opposed this, so it became a controversial issue. The **Treaty of Amsterdam** negotiations did not find a solution. The **Treaty of Nice** included a protocol, saying that the number would be reduced to one per member state on 1 January 2005 and reduced further to less than the one per member state once the union gets its 27th member. The **Council** would decide by unanimity how many. Eventually the **Treaty of Lisbon** decided that the number should be two-thirds of the number of member states from 1 Novembers 2014, "unless the **European Council** acting unanimously, decides to alter this number" (Article 17(5) TEU). In order to assist Ireland in getting a yes vote in the second **referendum** on the Treaty of Lisbon it was indeed decided to keep one Commissioner per member state, so EU28 had 28 Commissioners, and after **Brexit** there are 27 Commissioners.

The Commissioners actually do not represent the member states. They are expected to promote the general interest of the union and be completely independent. They may not seek or take instructions from any government. Still the member states feel that they are represented in an indirect way by someone who knows the country well. In addition, the smaller states have often seen the Commission as a safeguard against the formation of a "directorate" of the large states.

Originally, the Commission was appointed for four years. Since the Treaty of Maastricht, it has been five years in order to align it with that of the **European Parliament** (EP). The role of president of the Commission has been strengthened somewhat in recent years. He lays down guidelines and decides the internal organization. As something new in the Treaty of Lisbon, the member states shall take into account the results of the previous EP election when they propose a candidate. The treaty then says that the candidate shall be "elected" by the EP. The president-elect will, together with the Council, adopt the list of proposed members of the Commission. Following that, "The President, the **High Representative of the Union for Foreign Affairs and Security Policy** and the other members of the Commission shall be subject as a body to a vote of consent by the European Parliament" (Article 17(7) TEU).

In 1994, the EP started the practice of hearings in the process of vetting Commission candidates. The Commission, which is a collegiate body, has the right of initiative. Most legislation requires a proposal from the Commission before the Council and EP can adopt legislation. This way the Commission is both an agenda setter and gatekeeper. The Commission has a mix of responsibilities, proposing legislation, proposing the budget and implementing it, administering policies, and making specific decision, for instance, in competition policy. It also negotiates agreements with third countries and represents the EU externally in economic policy matters. Each Commissioner has a portfolio of responsibilities that can cut across the more than 30 directorates-general. Today the Commission employs about 30,000 officials. The Commission meets weekly, usually on Wednesday. Decisions can be made by a simple majority, but are usually by consensus. The Commissioners and their *cabinets* are in the Berlaymont building, but most of the policy staff is spread out in Brussels in 70 different buildings, and some staff is in Luxembourg.

EUROPEAN COMMUNITY/EUROPEAN COMMUNITIES (EC). Historically the three Communities established by the **Treaty of Paris** and **Treaties of Rome** were often referred to as the European Communities (EC) in plural, sometimes in the singular, especially after the Merger Treaty created a single **European Commission** and a single **Council** in 1965, in force in 1967. The **European Coal and Steel Community** (ECSC) ceased to exist in

2002. The **European Atomic Energy Community** (EAEC or EURATOM) still exists as a separate organization from the **European Union** (EU). In connection with **Brexit** the **United Kingdom** (UK) has also left EURATOM.

The **Treaty of Maastricht** changed the name of the **European Economic Community** (EEC) to simply the European Community, which became the first pillar of the **European Union** (EU). The **Treaty of Lisbon** has now abolished the name as it abolished the pillar structure of the Union. So, summarizing, the EC can refer to the European Communities pre-Maastricht as well as the first pillar of the Treaty of Maastricht. That part of the treaty was referred to as the Treaty establishing the European Community (TEC). It has now, since the entry into force of the Treaty of Lisbon, become the Treaty on the Functioning of the European Union (TFEU).

EUROPEAN COMMUNITY/UNION LAW. The kind of law established by the **European Communities** (EC) in the 1950s was referred to as European Community law. It includes the primary law of the treaties and the secondary law of the legislation adopted by the EC institutions, **regulations**, **directives**, and **decisions**, as well as the judgments of the **European Court of Justice** (ECJ), now **Court of Justice of the European Union** (CJEU). At the outset, there could be doubt about the exact nature of this law, but the ECJ played an important role in clarifying that the law had **primacy** over national law and **direct effect**. This makes Community law much stronger than traditional international law. It is in many ways more like federal law. It is binding on the member states as well as individuals and legal entities, including companies. In addition, strong institutions are established to make sure the law is implemented.

Since the **Treaty of Lisbon** abolished the term "European Community" we have to talk about European Union (EU) law. However, the decisive Court decisions about the nature of this law still apply. The strength of EU law was disliked by anti-EU groups in the **United Kingdom** (UK), and contributed to **Brexit**.

EUROPEAN CONSERVATIVES AND REFORMISTS (ECR). The European Conservatives and Reformists (ECR) was the third largest group in the **European Parliament** (EP) after the May 2014 elections, with 70 of 751 seats. The largest number of members of the group came from the **United Kingdom** (UK) with 20, followed by Poland with 19 members of the group. The number of ECR seats in the EP elected in May 2019 was reduced to 62, with the **Brexit Party** taking most UK seats, and the UK **Conservative Party** only securing 4 seats, which were subsequently vacated on **Brexit day**, 31 January 2020.

EUROPEAN COUNCIL. The European Council was created in 1974 on a proposal from the French president Valéry Giscard d'Estaing. It is the meeting of heads of state or government, sometimes called the summit. The **Single European Act** (SEA) first mentioned it explicitly in the treaties in 1986, and the **Treaty of Lisbon** has made it a formal institution. Ministers of Foreign Affairs assisted the Heads of State or Government until the Treaty of Lisbon. From the beginning the president of the Commission has also been invited to attend the meetings. Until the Treaty of Lisbon, the meetings of the European Council would be chaired by rotating presidency, but since the entry into force of the Treaty of Lisbon there has been a permanent elected president, first Herman van Rompuy (Belgium) from 2009, and then Donald Tusk (Poland) from 2014 until 2019. From 1 December 2019 the post is filled by Charles Michel from Belgium. Nowadays the **High Representative of the Union for Foreign Affairs and Security Policy** also takes part in the meetings. On the other hand, foreign ministers will only take part in maximum one meeting per year.

The first summit took place in Paris in February 1961 to discuss President **Charles de Gaulle**'s plan for an intergovernmental political union, and there was a second meeting on this in July in Bonn. However, when the Fouchet negotiations about De Gaulle's union broke down. Summits, or conferences of the heads of state or government as they were called then, went out of fashion for some years. The Hague Summit in December 1969 resumed the practice. De Gaulle's successor, President Georges Pompidou, agreed to the first **enlargement**, including the **United Kingdom** (UK), whose membership had been vetoed by General de Gaulle.

Over time the European Council has become more important. According to the current treaty, "The European Council shall provide the Union with the necessary impetus and shall define the general political directions and priorities thereof" (Article 15 TEU). It does not legislate. That role is left for the **Council** and **European Parliament** (EP). However, the European Council can adopt some Legal Acts, usually by unanimity, and some appointments can be made by a **qualified majority vote** (QMV).

Problems that cannot be solved at the level of the Council sometimes end up on the agenda of the European Council. Officially, the European Council now meets twice every six months, but sometimes more often. It met very often during the eurozone debt crisis, sometimes limiting the participation to the members of the eurozone. Also, the European Council concludes **Intergovernmental Conferences** (IGC) negotiating a new treaty.

At the European Council meeting in Nice in December 2000 it was decided that future meetings normally would take place in Brussels, which is now the case. The General Secretariat of the Council assists the European Council. The **Committee of Permanent Representatives** (COREPER) and the

General Affairs Council (GAC) prepare meetings. Conclusions are issued from the meetings.

Heads of state and government of the EU member states meet in Brussels for the October 2019 European Council. *Source*: Courtesy of the European Union.

EUROPEAN COURT OF JUSTICE (ECJ). See COURT OF JUSTICE OF THE EUROPEAN UNION (CJEU).

EUROPEAN ECONOMIC AREA (EEA). The European Economic Area (EEA) was created after the end of the Cold War as an alternative to membership for members of the **European Free Trade Association** (EFTA), on the proposal from **Commission** president **Jacques Delors** in 1989. Negotiations, which started in June 1990, produced a draft treaty by 1991. This first draft had to be renegotiated because of a judgment from the **European Court of Justice** (ECJ) in December 1991 that went against the judicial system set up by the treaty. The revised proposal was ratified by all EFTA countries except Switzerland, where the people rejected it in a **referendum** in December 1992. The EEA created an arrangement where the adhering EFTA countries have free access to the **internal market**. Therefore, they take part in free movement of goods, services, capital, and people. They have taken over nearly all the ***acquis communautaire*** in those areas. Excluded from the agreement are **Common Commercial Policy** (CCP) (the EEA is a **free trade area**, not a **customs union**), **Common Foreign and Security Policy** (CFSP), **Justice and Home Affairs** (JHA), **Common Agricultural Policy** (CAP), and **Common Fisheries Policy** (CFP). It has created common institutions, but the EFTA members have to accept or reject the EU legislation, which is adopted without their presence. The common institutions are an EEA Council, an EEA Joint Committee, and an EEA Joint Parliamentary Assembly. Through these institutions, the EFTA countries can try to influence decisions through consultations and exchange of information. The EFTA side had to establish an EFTA Surveillance Authority and an EFTA Court, playing comparable roles on their side to the **Commission** and ECJ on the EU side in monitoring and assuring implementation. The EEA entered into force in 1994 but already the next year three EFTA countries joined the **European Union** (EU) as full members, namely, Austria, Finland, and Sweden. It leaves **Norway,** Iceland, and Lichtenstein as the EFTA members of the EEA. Norway tried to join the EU in 1995, but the Norwegian people rejected the accession treaty in a **referendum** in 1994.

The EEA has been mentioned as a possible option for the future relationship between the EU and the **United Kingdom** (UK). But already Prime Minister **Theresa May** ruled this option out because of the relatively close relationship it creates. Especially the free movement of people was rejected by the UK government.

EUROPEAN ECONOMIC COMMUNITY (EEC). One of the two Treaties of Rome, signed on 25 March 1957, created the European Economic Community (EEC). It entered into force on 1 January 1958. The main objectives of the EEC were to create a **customs union** and a **common market** as well as develop some common economic policies. The treaty in particular mentioned **Common Commercial Policy** (CCP), **Competition Policy**, **Transport Policy**, and **Common Agricultural Policy** (CAP). Macroeconomic coordination was also foreseen. The **Treaty of Maastricht** integrated the EEC in the **European Union** (EU) as the first pillar and renamed it **European Community** (EC) in 1993. When the **Treaty of Lisbon** abolished the pillar structure on the Union it did away with the European Community name in 2009. The EC part of the treaty became the **Treaty on the Functioning of the European Union (TFEU)**.

Seen in a historical perspective the EEC was by far the most important of the original three Communities and the **common market**, now called **internal market** by the treaties, has remained very important, next to the **Economic and Monetary Union** (EMU) introduced by the Treaty of Maastricht. The original policy areas singled out in the Treaty of Rome expanded over time through successive treaty reforms and interpretations by the **European Court of Justice** (ECJ) to include most economic policies. Successive treaty reforms also changed the original institutions, although the four central institutions created by the Treaty of Rome—the **Commission,** the **Council**, the Assembly, soon to be called the **European Parliament**

(EP), and the Court—have all remained important. Arguably, the EP was the main institutional winner in successive reforms. However, the intergovernmental part, where representatives of the member governments meet, was also strengthened by the formalization of the **European Council** and addition of intergovernmental pillars in the Treaty of Maastricht, **Common Foreign and Security Policy** (CFSP) and **Justice and Home Affairs** (JHA) cooperation. Even after the abolition of the pillar structure by the Treaty of Lisbon, CFSP stays intergovernmental cooperation. *See also* COMMUNITY METHOD.

EUROPEAN EXTERNAL ACTION SERVICE (EEAS). The European External Action Service (EEAS) was one on the main innovations in the **Treaty of Lisbon**. It was set up to strengthen the **European Union** (EU) as an international actor. The idea was first put forward during the Convention on the Future of Europe, which drafted the Treaty establishing a Constitution for Europe. When that treaty failed to be ratified, the EEAS was included in the Treaty of Lisbon. The EEAS was set up during the year 2010 after the entry into force of the Treaty of Lisbon on 1 December 2009. By this time, Catherine Ashton had become the **High Representative of the Union for Foreign Affairs and Security Policy**. Therefore, she was in charge of the setting up of the EEAS. The staff came partly from the **European Commission** and partly from the **Council Secretariat** as well as some seconded officials from member state foreign ministries. During the process of establishing the EEAS the **European Parliament** (EP) used its budgetary powers to influence some decisions, including staff regulations.

All "external action" activities are supposed to fall under the EEAS, including external economic relations, development cooperation, **Common Foreign and Security Policy** (CFSP), and **Common Security and Defence Policy** (CSDP). The EEAS, for instance, has taken over the responsibility for what used to be Commission delegations in third countries, now EU delegations. However, the Commission keeps playing an important role in the economic areas, still having Commissioners dealing with trade, development, and neighborhood policy. Therefore, the EU as an international actor still faces coordination problems. The High Representative chairs the meetings of the **Foreign Affairs Council** (FAC), but when the Council deals with trade policy it is chaired by the rotating **Presidency of the Council of the European Union**.

EUROPEAN FREE TRADE ASSOCIATION (EFTA). The European Free Trade Association (EFTA) was established through the Stockholm Convention in 1960 by countries that were not ready to join the newly founded

European Economic Community (EEC). The group included the **United Kingdom** (UK); the Scandinavian countries Denmark, Norway, and Sweden; as well as Austria, **Switzerland**, and Portugal, known as the "Outer Seven" in contrast to the "Inner Six" of the EEC. EFTA was limited to a **free trade area** (FTA) for industrial goods, and it created no supranational institutions. It followed an attempt by the UK to create a broader FTA among the members of the Organization for European Economic Cooperation (OEEC), which failed. Finland became an associate member in 1961 and a full member in 1986. Iceland joined in 1970. Lichtenstein joined in 1991. However, the UK and Denmark left in 1973, Portugal followed in 1986, and then Austria, Sweden, and Finland left in 1995, leaving Iceland, Norway, Switzerland, and Lichtenstein as the current members of EFTA. After the defection of the UK and Denmark in 1973, the remaining EFTA countries negotiated free trade area agreements with the EEC. Today's EFTA countries, except Switzerland, take part in the **European Economic Area** (EEA) through which two quasi-supranational EFTA institutions have been created: the EFTA Surveillance Authority and the EFTA Court. Through the EEA the three EFTA members take part in the **internal market**, including the **four freedoms**: free movement of goods, services, capital, and people. The UK has ruled out joining EFTA and/or the EEA after **Brexit**.

EUROPEAN MONETARY SYSTEM (EMS). The European Monetary System (EMS) was established in January 1979. It had been proposed by Commission president Roy Jenkins in October 1977. The decision to establish it was made by the **European Council** in Brussels in December 1978, with strong support from French president Valéry Giscard d'Estaing and German chancellor Helmut Schmidt.

The purpose of the EMS was to contribute to monetary stability in the **European Community** (EC). The EMS established an Exchange Rate Mechanism (ERM), which linked national currencies to an artificial currency composed of a basket of national currencies, the European Currency Unit (ECU). The ECU was backed up by national interventions as well as interventions from a European Monetary Cooperation Fund (EMCF). All member states joined the EMS in 1979, but not all joined the ERM. The **United Kingdom** (UK) joined only in October 1990 and left in September 1992. Greece joined only in March 1998 in order to qualify for euro participation. Sweden never took part in the ERM. The EMS ceased to exist in 1999 at the start of the third stage of **Economic and Monetary Union** (EMU). The ERM survived as Exchange Rate Mechanism II (ERM II) through which states not taking part in the euro could link their currency to the euro, which Denmark has done, but the UK never did.

EUROPEAN PARLIAMENT (EP). The history of the European Parliament (EP) goes back to the Common Assembly created for the **European Coal and Steel Community** (ECSC) in 1952. Subsequently an Assembly was also created by the **Treaties of Rome** for each of the following two Communities, the **European Atomic Energy Community** (EAEC or EURATOM) and the **European Economic Community** (EEC), in 1958. However, it was decided through the Convention on Certain Institutions Common to the **European Communities** (EC) at the time that there would be one Assembly common to the three Communities. This assembly was first called the European Parliamentary Assembly. In 1962, it decided to call itself the European Parliament (EP), a name that was confirmed by the **Single European Act** (SEA) in 1986.

Until direct elections starting in 1979, the members of the Assembly/Parliament were nominated by national parliaments from among their own members. The Common Assembly of the ECSC had 78 members: 18 from France, Italy, and Germany; 10 from Belgium and the Netherlands; and 4 from Luxembourg. The single assembly for the three Communities in 1958 had 142 members. Since then the number of **members of the European Parliament** (MEPs) has increased with each **enlargement**. The **Treaty of Lisbon** limited the number to 751 from the May 2014 elections. Germany will have the maximum number of 96 MEPs. The minimum number of six MEPs will go to the smallest member states: Cyprus, Estonia, Luxembourg, and Malta. The term is now five years.

Direct elections were foreseen in the three founding treaties. However, it was only the Paris summit in December 1974 which decided that direct elections should be arranged in the future. The **Council** adopted a European Elections Act in September 1976. Direct elections scheduled for 1978 eventually had to be postponed by a year because of delays in getting the enabling legislation adopted in the **United Kingdom** (UK). The first direct elections took place 7–10 June 1979. The European Elections Act had set the number of MEPs at 410. The community-wide turnout was 62 percent, with great national variation. In Belgium, where it is compulsory to vote, the turnout was 91 percent. The lowest turnout was in the UK with 32 percent.

The new Parliament started showing muscles soon. For the first time it rejected the Community **budget** the first year. In 1982 it brought an action in the **European Court of Justice** (ECJ) against the Council for failure to act in developing the common transport policy. It was also the first directly elected EP that adopted the Draft Treaty establishing the European Union in 1984, under the leadership of Italian federalist MEP Altiero Spinelli.

The EP started out as an advisory body in the 1950s. It could force the Commission to retire by a motion of no confidence, a power it still has. Beyond that, it started getting budgetary powers through the two Budgetary

Treaties in 1970 and 1975. In 1980, the ECJ decided that the Council had to wait for the opinion from the EP where the treaties gave the EP the right to be consulted (the "isoglucose" case). Therefore, the EP could at least delay legislation, which might give the Council an interest in negotiating. The Single European Act (SEA) then introduced the so-called **cooperation procedure** giving the EP a second reading of some legislation, especially **internal market** legislation. If the EP adopted an amendment at the second reading and it was accepted by the **Commission**, the Council could reject it only by unanimity. The SEA also introduced the assent, now **consent**, procedure, where the EP can veto some legislation, at the time applied for **association agreements** and accession treaties. The next step in the empowerment of the EP was the introduction of the co-decision procedure (article 189B procedure) by the Treaty of Maastricht. Since then its application has been expanded by the subsequent treaties, to become the "**ordinary legislative procedure**" (OLP) in the Treaty of Lisbon. The Treaty of Lisbon has also put the EP on par with the Council in adopting the annual budget.

The EP elects a president for two and a half years at the beginning and midway in the five-year term. In recent periods the two largest party groups, the **Group of the European Peoples Party (Christian Democrats)** (EPP) and the Socialist Group, the **Group of the Progressive Alliance of Socialists and Democrats in the European Parliament** (S&D), have sometimes agreed to share the post.

The EP works mostly through its 20 or so committees. The committees draft reports, which are debated and voted on in the plenary, which normally meets in Strasbourg. The committees normally meet in Brussels. Part of the secretariat is based in Luxembourg. These costly arrangements go back to the adoption of the Merger Treaty in 1965.

The role of the EP in appointing the Commission has been strengthened by recent treaty changes. It now "elects" the Commission president, but on a proposal from the **European Council**. *See also* POLITICAL GROUPS IN THE EUROPEAN PARLIAMENT.

EUROPEAN POLICE OFFICE (EUROPOL). The European Police Office (EUROPOL) is based on a Convention signed by **European Union** (EU) member states in 1996. It entered into force in 1998 and EUROPOL established its headquarters in The Hague, the Netherlands. It is the EU's law enforcement agency. It works closely with law enforcement agencies in the member states and in other non-EU partner countries in the fight against serious international crime and terrorism. Its staff has increased in recent years, now reaching about 1300. When the **United Kingdom** (UK) chose to opt out from the **Area of Freedom, Security and Justice** (AFSJ) in 2014, it chose to remain in Europol, but **Brexit** included leaving Europol, and the future relationship remains to be negotiated. *See also* AREA OF FREEDOM, SECURITY AND JUSTICE (EFSJ); JUSTICE AND HOME AFFAIRS (JHA); POLICE AND JUDICIAL COOPERATION IN CRIMINAL MATTERS.

EUROPEAN POLITICAL COMMUNITY (EPC). The European Political Community (EPC) was proposed in connection with the negotiations of the Treaty establishing a **European Defence Community** (EDC). The idea behind the EPC was to create more political accountability for the EDC, which would have established a European Army, if it had been fully ratified. Article 38 in the EDC treaty foresaw a future "federal or confederal structure," which would bring the **European Coal and Steel Community** (ECSC) and the EDC together. The Italian prime minister Alcide de Gasperi had proposed Article 38. When the French National Assembly rejected the EDC treaty in 1954, the EPC also died.

EUROPEAN POLITICAL COOPERATION (EPC). European Political Cooperation (EPC) was foreign policy cooperation among the member states of the **European Communities** (EC), but outside the Community treaty framework. It started in 1970, based on the so-called Davignon Report (or Luxembourg Report). It was only given a treaty basis in the **Single European Act** (SEA) in 1986, as an arrangement among the "high contracting parties." It was intergovernmental cooperation involving the foreign ministers and foreign ministries. At the beginning, it did not even establish a secretariat. Foreign ministers initially would meet twice a year in the form of a "Conference of Foreign Ministers meeting in Political Cooperation," and the political directors of the foreign ministries formed a Political Committee, which first met four times a year.

The EPC developed slowly, based on additional reports, first the Copenhagen Report in 1973, which increased the number of meetings and established regular exchange of encrypted messages known as *Correspondance européenne* (COREU). A system of working groups was also formalized. The London Report in 1981 created the Troika, of the current, former, and next presidency to provide more continuity. A small secretariat started to emerge in the **Council secretariat** in Brussels. The SEA codified these developments in 1986, but also went a little further. It said that the **Commission** was "fully associated" and the **European Parliament** (EP) "closely associated" with EPC and the states could now also "coordinate their positions more closely on the political and economic aspects of security" (Article 30(6) SEA). However, **defense policy** was still taboo.

The **Treaty of Maastricht** upgraded EPC to **Common Foreign and Security Policy** (CFSP), which became the second pillar of the **European Union** (EU) in 1993. *See also* COMMON SECURITY AND DEFENCE POLICY (CSDP).

EUROPEAN REGIONAL DEVELOPMENT FUND (ERDF). The European Regional Development Fund (ERDF) was established in connection with the first **enlargement** of the **European Communities** (EC) in 1973. Since the financing of the **Common Agricultural Policy** (CAP) disadvantaged the **United Kingdom** (UK) the government insisted on the creation of this fund, much supported by Italy. The energy crisis in 1973 delayed the start until 1975 and less money was made available than the UK had requested. Since then **regional policy** has become much more important in the EU. For some years, it was especially **Ireland**, Greece, Spain, and Portugal that benefited from financial assistance. After the 2004 and 2007 enlargements the biggest recipients are the Central and Eastern European Countries (CEECs). The ERDF is one of the so-called structural funds that support the EU's **regional policies**.

EUROPEAN RESEARCH GROUP (ERG). The European Research Group is a right-wing group of **United Kingdom** (UK) Conservative **Members of the Parliament** (MPs). The group has focused on the UK's withdrawal from the EU. Members were actively involved in the **Leave campaign** in 2016 and have called for the UK to leave the **internal market**—ruling out staying in the **European Economic Area** (EEA)—as well as the **customs union**, thus contributing to making the Irish border problem very difficult to solve.

EUROPEAN SECURITY AND DEFENCE POLICY (ESDP). *See* COMMON SECURITY AND DEFENCE POLICY (CSDP).

EUROPEAN UNION (EU). The European Union (EU) was created by the **Treaty of Maastricht**, signed in 1992 and in force from 1993. The EU had a three-pillar structure, with the **European Community** (EC) in the first pillar, **Common Foreign and Security Policy** (CFSP) in the second pillar, and **Justice and Home Affairs** (JHA) cooperation in the third pillar. The reason for the pillar structure was that it allowed for different decision-making rules. The first pillar had supranational decision-making, with strong powers given to the **European Commission** and the **European Court of Justice** (ECJ) and possibilities of **qualified majority voting** (QMV) in the **Council**. These decision rules constitute the so-called **Community method**. The two other pillars were intergovernmental, with limited powers for the European Commission and exclusion of the ECJ, and normally decisions requiring unanimity in the Council.

The Treaty of Maastricht foresaw the possibility of moving parts of JHA from the third to the first pillar, a process that was started by the **Treaty of Amsterdam**, signed in 1997 and in force in 1999. The **Treaty of Lisbon**, which abolished the pillar structure, completed the process and all JHA was "communitarized"; that is, it now falls under supranational decision-making. CFSP, however, remained intergovernmental cooperation despite the abolition of the pillar structure.

Michel Barnier, Chief Negotiator (2015–2019), Jean-Claude Juncker, President of the Commission (2014–2019), and Donald Tusk, President of the European Council (2014–2019). *Source*: Courtesy of the European Union.

EUROPEAN UNION MILITARY COMMITTEE (EUMC). *See* COMMON SECURITY AND DEFENCE POLICY (CSDP).

EUROPEAN UNION MILITARY STAFF (EUMS). *See* COMMON SECURITY AND DEFENCE POLICY (CSDP).

EUROPEAN UNITED LEFT/NORDIC GREEN LEFT (GUE/NGL). The European United Left/Nordic Green Left (GUE/NGL) was the fifth group in size in the **European Parliament** (EP) among the seven groups after the May 2014 elections. It the occupied 52 of the 751 seats. The biggest number come from **Spain** with 11, followed by **Germany** with eight and **Greece** with six members of the EP (MEPs) in this group. In the May 2019 elections, the group secured 41 seats and is the seventh group in size.

EUROSCEPTIC. A Eurosceptic is a person who is critical of the **European Union** (EU) and European integration. Some Eurosceptics advocate their countries' exit from the EU; others seek reform from inside, arguing that the EU is too centralized and interferes too much in national life.

EUROSCEPTICISM. Euroscepticism refers to attitudes critical of the **European Union** (EU) and European integration. Sometime a distinction is made between hard and soft Euroscepticism. Political parties or part groups representing hard Euroscepticism include the **UK Independence Party** (UKIP) and the **Europe of Freedom and Direct Democracy** in the **European Parliament**. Examples of soft Euroscepticism include the **European Conservatives and Reformists** group on the right and **European United Left–Nordic Green Left** on the left side in the European Parliament. The battle about the **Maastricht Treaty** was a factor contributing to Euroscepticism in the **United Kingdom** (UK) and the formation of UKIP. There has been an increase in Euroscepticism in recent years. National Eurosceptic parties include Poland's Law and Justice (PiS) party and Hungary's *Fidesz* party. So do Five Star Movement (M5S) in Italy, *Alternative für Deutschland* in Germany and *Podemos* in Spain. The **referendum** debates about the Constitutional Treaty in France and the Netherlands in 2005 may have contributed to Euroscepticism in those two countries. Later the financial crisis and immigration crisis also contributed to Euroscepticism in many EU member states. **Brexit**, however, has shown the difficulties and potential costs of exit, so general popular support for the EU has increased in most member states recently, and populists such as France's Marine le Pen, Italy's Mateo Salvini, and the Netherlands' Geert Wilders no longer support the exit of their respective countries.

EXTERNAL ACTION. "External Action" is a new term used in the **Treaty of Lisbon**. It includes external economic relations, including trade, development cooperation, humanitarian aid, as well as **Common Foreign and Security Policy** (CFSP), and **Common Security and Defence Policy** (CSDP). It follows the abolition of the pillar structure, originally created by **Treaty of Maastricht**. The idea was to bring more coherence among the different parts of "external action," but the treaty retained special provisions for CFSP and CSDP, which remain intergovernmental, while the most important part of external economic relations, the **Common Commercial Policy** (CCP), is an exclusive competence of the Union falling under the so-called **Community method.** The **Treaty of Lisbon** does give the whole Union legal personality, not just the first pillar, the European Community (EC), as previously. *See also* EUROPEAN EXTERNAL ACTION SERVICE (EEAS).

F

FACILITATED CUSTOMS ARRANGEMENT (FCA). The **United Kingdom**'s (UK) so-called **Chequers plan** published as a **White Paper** in July 2018 included a so-called Facilitated Customs Arrangement (FCA). The basic idea was to charge goods coming into the UK with destination in the **European Union** (EU) the EU customs duties while goods remaining in the UK would pay the UK customs duty, which might be different from the EU duty after **Brexit** and UK non-participation in the EU customs union. The implementation of the FCA would have required technology to identify the final destination of the goods in question. The hope was also that the border controls between **Northern Ireland** and the **Republic of Ireland** could be avoided that way. The purpose was to create trade that is "as frictionless as possible."

FARAGE, NIGEL (1964–). Nigel Farage is a British politician who was a **Member of the European Parliament** (MEP) from 1999 to 31 January 2020. In the **European Parliament** (EP) he was president of the **Europe of Freedom and Direct Democracy** from 2004 until 1 July 2019. While never succeeding in becoming a **member of the UK Parliament** (MP), he was actively involved in forming and running **the United Kingdom Independence Party** (UKIP), from 2006 to 2018, on and off. He had been a founder member from 1993. It was the UKIP that pressured Prime Minister **David Cameron** to promise a **referendum** on British membership of the **European Union** (EU) if he were to get a majority in the following election, which took place in 2015. The fateful referendum then took place in 2016. During the referendum campaign the UKIP campaigned for **Leave**. Given the delay and eventually failure in getting Prime Minister **Theresa May**'s **Withdrawal Agreement** accepted by the UK Parliament the UK ended up having to take part in the EP elections in May 2019. On 23 May 2019 the **Brexit Party** founded the year before won 29 seats in the EP, making it the biggest single party in the EP. The Brexit Party MEPs worked as *non-incrits* (NI)—not members of a party group—until they had to leave on **Brexit day**, 31 January 2020. During his period in the EP Farage succeeded having several nasty exchanges with other MEPs, who distanced themselves from his nationalistic rhetoric.

FEDERALISM. Federalism denotes a multilayered system of government, where there is a central government as well as local governments each with a degree of autonomy. Usually that autonomy is guaranteed through a constitution. Federalism differs from confederalism. In a federation the federal level can take decisions without the unanimous consent of the participating units. In a confederation, decisions at the highest level normally require unanimity. The **United States** (U.S.) was a confederation under the Articles of Confederation. It became a federation (or federal state) when the constitution worked out at the Philadelphia Convention in 1787 entered into force in 1789.

The **European Union** (EU) has elements of both federalism and confederalism. The autonomous powers given by the treaties to the **European Commission** and **European Court of Justice** (ECJ) as well as the acceptance of **qualified majority voting** (QMV) in the **Council** and direct elections of the **European Parliament** (EP), which has now become a co-legislator, can all be seen as federal elements. However, there are still some areas where the member states dominate and unanimity is required, especially **Common Foreign and Security Policy** (CFSP) and **Common Security and Defence Policy** (CSDP). For this reason, scholars have often concluded that the EU is *sui generis*, one of a kind. It does not fit neatly into our established categories.

The founding fathers of the **European Communities** (EC) in the 1950s were all inspired by federalist ideas, but the strategy chosen was one of gradualism, as seen clearly in the **Schuman Declaration** of 9 May 1950. In it, French foreign minister Robert Schuman said that Europe would not be created in one day. It would go through concrete steps that would create solidarity among the member states. Since it was Jean Monnet who inspired the Schuman Declaration, this approach is sometimes referred to as the **Monnet** method. Because the idea of gradually creating solidarity also was inspired by functionalist theories of international cooperation scholars have referred to the theory behind the European integration process as neo-functionalism, the "neo" part being the creation of supranational institutions as distinguished from intergovernmental institutions.

Not all EU political leaders have been inspired by federalist ideas. Some could even be considered anti-federalists, including French president **Charles de Gaulle** in the 1960s and **United Kingdom** (UK) prime minister **Margaret Thatcher** in the 1980s. Today we might call them **Eurosceptics**. Efforts to put a reference to a federal goal into the **Treaty of Maastricht** failed because of British opposition. A similar effort in the Convention on the Future of

Europe had the same fate. However, slowly, despite the opposition, which include voters saying no to new treaties, like the Danes in 1992 and the French and Dutch in 2005, it is possible to argue that the EU moves toward more federalism. The rejected Treaty establishing a Constitution for Europe was rescued by the **Treaty of Lisbon**. Arguably, the eurozone crisis has led to more, not less, integration with new steps toward Fiscal Union, Banking Union, and so on. Federalism, the famous F-word, as the British popular press baptized federalism, has a certain logic to it because of interdependence among the member states require joint decision-making. But, the opposition to this process increased in the UK while **David Cameron** was prime minister. Getting the EU leaders to agree that the famous formulation in the EU treaties' "ever closer union" did not apply to the UK was not enough for him to win the **Brexit** referendum in 2016.

FINANCIAL SERVICES. Financial services are included in **free moment** of **services** in the **European Union**'s **internal market**. *See also* PASSPORTING.

FINALITÉ POLITIQUE. The French term *finalité politique* refers to the end goal of European integration, which has been debated from the beginning in the 1950s until today. The **Treaty of Paris** establishing the **European Coal and Steel Community** (ECSC) in 1951, referred to "establishing an economic community, the basis for a broader and deeper community among peoples long divided by bloody conflicts" (Preamble, ECSC Treaty). The **Treaty of Rome** establishing the **European Economic Community** (EEC) said that the member states were "determined to lay the foundations of an ever closer union among the peoples of Europe" (Preamble, EEC Treaty). By the time of the negotiations leading to the **Treaty of Maastricht**, some of the less integrationist countries criticized even that formulation. Eventually the **Intergovernmental Conference** (IGC) agreed upon this formulation: "This Treaty marks a new stage in the process of creating an ever closer union among the peoples of Europe, in which decisions are taken as closely as possible to the citizen" (Article A, Treaty of Maastricht). This formulation survived in the **Treaty of Lisbon**, which added "in accordance with the principle of **subsidiarity**" (Preamble, TEU). If subsidiarity was well defined it would help, but in reality, it means different things to different people: some want the **European Union** (EU) to make more decisions and some want the EU to make fewer decisions. This tension always exists in federal or quasi-federal systems.

FISHERIES. *See* COMMON FISHERIES POLICY (CFP).

FOREIGN AFFAIRS COUNCIL (FAC). Since the entry into force of the **Treaty of Lisbon**, the Foreign Affairs Council (FAC) is the forum where foreign ministers meet to discuss and decide on **Common Foreign and Security Policy** (CFSP) issues. The **High Representative of the Union for Foreign Affairs and Security Policy** chairs the Foreign Affairs Council. Foreign ministers also meet under another formation of the Council, the **General Affairs Council** (GAC), which has a broader coordinating role, and which is chaired by the foreign minister from the country having the rotating **Presidency of the Council**.

FOREIGN AND SECURITY POLICY. *See* COMMON FOREIGN AND SECURITY POLICY (CFSP).

FOREIGN DIRECT INVESTMENTS (FDI). *See* INVESTMENTS.

FOSTER, ARLENE (1970–). Arlene Foster is a Northern Irish politician. She has been a member of the **Northern Ireland** Assembly (MLA) since 2003. She has served as the leader of the **Democratic Unionist Party** (DUP) since 2015. She was First Minister of Northern Ireland from 2016 to 2017 and again occupies that position since January 2020. When **Theresa May**'s snap election in 2017 resulted in a hung parliament it led to negotiations between May and the DUP, which had won ten parliamentary seats in the **UK Parliament**. Negotiations started on 9 June, and the final agreement was signed and published on 26 June 2017. The DUP promised to support the **Conservative Party** minority government on all important votes for the duration of the parliament. In exchange the DUP secured an extra £1 billion of funding for Northern Ireland, money to be spent on health, infrastructure, and education especially. In the end the DUP supported neither May's **Withdrawal Agreement** in 2018 nor the one negotiated by **Boris Johnson** in 2019. The December 2019 general election in the UK saw the party's representation in London reduced to eight seats. Johnson, in any case, won enough seats to form a majority government without depending on DUP votes.

FOUR FREEDOMS. The **Treaty of Rome** establishing the **European Economic Community** (EEC) was based on **four freedoms**, **free movement** of goods, **services**, capital, and people. It established a **customs union**, a **common market**, and some common policies. Free movement of goods was dealt with in greatest detail (Title I of the treaty). Inside the customs union, **tariffs** and quantitative restrictions were to be abolished. This could still leave **non-tariff barriers to trade (NTBs)**. These were to be reduced through harmonization of national legislation, which, however, required unanimity in the **Council** (Article 100 EEC). The three other freedoms were dealt with in Title III of the treaty, which made a distinction between workers and self-employed persons, the latter having a right of establishment. The completion of the common market, or **internal market** as it was later renamed in the **Single European Act** (SEA), moved forward with uneven speed. It took renewed efforts in the 1980s, with the **Commission**'s 1992 program and treaty reforms in the SEA to speed up the completion of the internal market by the agreed deadline of 1992. The SEA introduced **qualified majority voting (QMV)** for much of the required legislation to complete the internal market, which made it easier to adopt the required legislation. The free movement of people within the internal market was a major contributing factor to the "no" vote in the **Brexit referendum** in 2016.

FOX, LIAM (1961–). Liam Fox is a **Eurosceptic** British politician. He served briefly as Secretary of Defense under Prime Minister **David Cameron**, 2010–2011. After the **Brexit referendum** in 2016 Prime Minister **Theresa May** appointed him Secretary of State for International trade. He lost the position in July 2019 when Prime Minister **Boris Johnson** made a cabinet reshuffle.

FREE MOVEMENT. The **European Union**'s (EU) **internal market** is based on free movement of goods, services, capital, and people (the **four freedoms**). In the **United Kingdom**'s (UK) relationship with the EU especially the free movement of people became an issue. After the EU enlargement to include many Central and Eastern European Countries (CEECs) in 2004 and 2007, many citizens from the new member states moved to the UK to find work. A feeling emerged that these "foreigners" were taking British jobs and this was exploited by populist politicians, including the so-called **Brexiteers**. This problem is one of the reasons that the **Theresa May** and **Boris Johnson** governments have ruled out UK participation in the internal market in the future. The country wants to be fully in control of immigration. Interestingly enough the UK could have asked for an extended transition period for free movement of people after the enlargements with the CEECs, but chose not to do so.

FREE TRADE AGREEMENT (FTA). A Free Trade Agreement/Area (FTA) abolishes tariffs and quantitative restrictions to trade between the countries taking part in it. However, the participation states will remain responsible for setting tariffs and other forms of trade protection towards third countries. In Europe, the **European Free Trade Association** (EFTA) remains a good example. It was set up in 1960 to create free trade for industrial products between the **United Kingdom** (UK), Denmark, Norway, Sweden, Austria, **Switzerland**, and Portugal. It was an alternative to the **European Economic Community** (EEC), which established a **customs union** and a **common market**. A customs union goes a step further than an FTA by introducing a **common external tariff** (CET). Normally a customs union will also lead to a **common commercial policy** (CCP). A common market further includes free movement of **services**, capital, and people. Because of the different external tariffs in an FTA it must establish rules of origin so that goods from third countries do no enter through the country with lowest tariffs.

FTAs and customs unions discriminate against third countries. The rules of the **General Agreement on Tariffs and Trade** (GATT), now part of the **World Trade Organization** (WTO), require both FTAs and customs unions to include "substantially all" trade in goods to be exempt from the **most-favored nation** (MFN) principle.

FRICTIONLESS TRADE. Frictionless trade, mentioned in Prime Minister Theresa's **Chequers plan**, means that goods can pass borders without checks and other time-consuming procedures. It is more than "free trade." **Tariffs** must be abolished, but there must also be regulatory alignment to abolish **non-tariff barriers** (NTBs) to trade. In reality, to achieve frictionless trade there must also be free movement of **services** (like transport), labor (like the truck driver transporting the goods), and capital (so that the exporter can get paid), so the Chequers plan would not have achieved that by focusing on goods. The **internal market** of the **European Union** (EU) endeavors to create frictionless trade through the **four freedoms**. Frictionless trade contributes to what is referred to as a "**level playing field**," but to achieve a level playing field there must also be some common **competition policy**. By leaving the EU's customs union and internal market it is to be expected that there will be trade frictions between the **United Kingdom** (UK) and the EU in the future.

G

GENERAL AFFAIRS COUNCIL (GAC). The General Affairs Council (GAC) is a formation of the **Council** where foreign ministers or ministers of European affairs meet. The GAC is chaired by the minister from the country holding the six-month rotating **presidency**. It has a coordinating function. Until the **Treaty of Lisbon**, it also dealt with foreign affairs, but the Lisbon Treaty has introduced a **Foreign Affairs Council** (FAC), which is chaired by the **High Representative of the Union for Foreign Affairs and Security Policy**. Issues falling under the **Common Foreign and Security Policy** (CFSP) are discussed and decided upon in the FAC.

GENERAL AGREEMENT ON TARIFFS AND TRADE (GATT). The General Agreement on Tariffs and Trade (GATT) goes back to 1947. It established certain rules for trade among the contracting parties, including the **most-favored nation** (MFN) principle, which requires equal treatment of all contracting parties. So, if a trade advantage was negotiated with one contracting party it should be extended to the other parties. Exempt from the MFN rule were **customs union** and **free trade areas** (FTAs). It also included the principle of **national treatment**, which means that foreign products could not be taxed differently from domestic products. An important contribution from GATT was the gradual reduction of **tariffs** through rounds of trade policy negotiations. The Uruguay Round, 1986–1994, reduced tariffs for goods and for the first time dealt with **services** and **intellectual property rights**, and it established the **World Trade Organization** (WTO), of which GATT is a part. The WTO also included a much-strengthened dispute settlement system.

The **European Commission** represents the **European Union** (EU) in GATT and now also other WTO bodies and negotiations. This is an important part of the **Common Commercial Policy** (CCP) going back to the **Treaty of Rome** establishing the **European Economic Community** (EEC).

GENERAL AGREEMENT ON TRADE IN SERVICES (GATS). The General Agreement on Trade in Services (GATS) was one of the outcomes of the Uruguay Round. It entered into force in 1995. It extended the multilateral trade system under the **World Trade Organization** (WTO) to the **service** sectors. *See also* COMMON COMMERCIAL POLICY (CCP)

GENERAL COURT. The General Court is the new name of the Court of First Instance (CFI) created after the adoption of the **Single European Act** (SEA). Like the **European Court of Justice** (ECJ)—now **Court of Justice of the European Union** (CJEU)—it has its seat in Luxembourg. It hears cases concerning judicial review, infringement, compensation for damage, and employment cases between EU institutions and staff. It now has two judges from each member state. They are appointed for a renewable term of six years. Their judgments can in some cases be appealed to the ECJ.

GEOGRAPHICAL INDICATIONS (GIs). The **European Union** (EU) has defined a geographical indication as "a distinctive sign used to identify a product as originating in the territory of a particular country, region or locality where its quality, reputation or other characteristic is linked to its geographical origin." The EU has taken a lead both internally among the EU members and internationally to protect geographical indications (GIs). This is obviously important to producers, but can also be an advantage to the consumers, so they know what they are buying. Examples often mentioned are Cognac, Roquefort cheese, Sherry, Parmigiano Reggiano, Parma hams, and Tuscany olives. Internationally GIs fall under the **Trade-Related Aspects of Intellectual Property Rights** (TRIPS) agreement under the **World Trade Organization** (WTO). In recent years the EU has pursued the protection of GIs in bilateral trade agreements, such as the EU-Korea Free Trade agreement, the EU-Singapore Free Trade Agreement, the Trade Agreement between the EU and Columbia and Peru, and the Comprehensive Association Agreement between the EU and Central America. The recently concluded **Comprehensive Economic and Trade Agreement** (CETA) with Canada protects more than 140 GIs, including Grana Padano, Roquefort, Elia Kalamatas Olives and Aceto balsamico di Modena. Five cheeses—Asiago, Gorgonzola, Feta, Fontina, and Munster—required difficult negotiations. GIs were a difficult agenda point for the **Transatlantic Trade and Investments Partnership** (TTIP) negotiations with the **United States** (U.S.), negotiations that were terminated when Donald Trump became President of the U.S.

GLOBALIZATION. "Globalization" is the term used to describe the growing interdependence between nations because of increased international trade and cultural exchanges. It makes nations sensitive and vulnerable to what happens elsewhere in the world. It has created a complex network of global supply chains that have contributed to economic growth. Some scholars have seen **Brexit** as a response to globalization.

GIBRALTAR. Gibraltar is a British territory with a special status. Since 2004 it was allowed to take part in **European Parliament** (EP) elections. In the British **Brexit referendum** in 2916 more than 95 percent of the votes were cast in favor of **Remain**. Geographically placed at the southern tip of Spain that **European Union** (EU) member state has a special interest in its future relationship with Gibraltar. The **Withdrawal Agreement** has a protocol on Gibraltar. A special committee with only representatives from Spain and the **United Kingdom** (UK) will be created to deal with Gibraltar-EU matters such as free movement of people and border control. Gibraltar, like the UK, was never part of **Schengen.**

GOOD FRIDAY AGREEMENT. The Good Friday agreement, also called the Belfast Agreement, was reached on 10 April 1998 after more than two years of talks. It followed about 30 years of conflict between Unionists, who wanted **Northern Ireland** to remain part of the **United Kingdom** (UK), and Nationalists, who wanted Northern Ireland to become part of the **Republic of Ireland**. The two main parties to the agreement were the Ulster Unionist Party (UUP) led by David Trimble and the Social Democratic and Labour Party led by John Hume. The two leaders won the 1998 Nobel Peace Prize. The American politician George Mitchell played an important role in the negotiations, and the agreement was signed, among others, by British prime minister **Tony Blair** and Irish prime minister Bertie Ahern. The agreement aimed to get the two warring sides to work together in the Northern Ireland Assembly, which was given powers previously exercised in London, a process known as devolution. The agreement did not work perfectly, and it broke down in January 2017. Since then Northern Ireland has not had a functioning government. If **Brexit** leads to a hard border between Northern Ireland and the Republic of Ireland there is fear that the conflict may become violent again. The solution found in Prime Minister **Boris Johnson's Withdrawal Agreement** is to keep Northern Ireland in the **European Union** (EU) **customs union**, and partly in the **internal market**, and introducing some border checks between Northern Ireland and the rest of the UK.

GOVE, MICHAEL (1967–). Michael Gove is a Conservative British politician who has been a **Member of Parliament** (MP) since 2005. He held a couple of positions in the **David Cameron** cabinet between 2010 and 2016. He was a leading spokesperson of the Vote **Leave campaign** in 2016. He became Secretary of State for Environment, Food and Rural Affairs in the second **Theresa May** cabinet in June 2017 and served until July 2019. When **Boris Johnson** then became prime minister, he appointed Gove chancellor of the Duchy of Lancaster with responsibilities that included preparations for a no-deal Brexit. In February 2020 he became Minister for the Cabinet Office.

GREEN PARTY OF ENGLAND AND WALES. The Green Party of England and Wales is one of three Green political parties in the **United Kingdom** (UK), the two other ones being the Scottish Green Party and the Green Party in Northern Ireland. The latter two separated amicably from the former in 1990. The Green Party supports the UK staying in the **European Union** (EU). They have one **Member of Parliament** (MP) in London after the December 2019 election. They won seven seats in the **European Parliament** (EP) election in May 2019, which were vacated on **Brexit day**, 31 January 2020.

GREENLAND. Greenland was a Danish colony until 1953, when it became an integral part of the Kingdom of Denmark. As such it joined the **European Communities** (EC) together with the European part of the kingdom in 1973. In 1979 Greenland was granted home rule—somewhat similar to what the Faroe Islands had—which opened the possibility of holding a **referendum** about continued membership of the EC. Such referendum took place in 1982, where a majority voted in favor of leaving the EC. A treaty to that effect was agreed in 1984. It took effect in 1985. Greenland then became one of the EC's overseas countries and territories (OCTs). Apart from the OCT association there is also a Fisheries Partnership Agreement with the **European Union** (EU) and Greenland receives financial aid from the EU, partly through the structural funds and partly in exchange for access to fishing waters for fishermen from EU countries. Trade dependency with the EU is very high. *See also* COMMON FISHERIES POLICY (CFP).

GROUP OF THE ALLIANCE OF LIBERALS AND DEMOCRATS FOR EUROPE (ALDE). The Alliance of Liberals and Democrats for Europe (ALDE) used to be the third largest group in the **European Parliament** (EP), but after the May 2014 elections, it was number four in size, having been overtaken by the **European Conservatives and Reformists** (ECR) with 70 seats. It held 67 of the 751 seats. In the May 2019 election ALDE was joined by French president Emmanuel Macron's La République en Marche (LREM) party and was renamed **Renew Europe**. It gained 108 seats and became the third biggest group. *See also* EUROPEAN PARLIAMENT (EP); POLITICAL GROUPS IN THE EUROPEAN PARLIAMENT.

GROUP OF THE EUROPEAN PEOPLE'S PARTY (CHRISTIAN DEMOCRATS) (EPP). The Group of the European People's Party (Christian Democrats) (EPP) is currently the largest political group in the **European Parliament** (EP). It occupied 221 of the 751 seats after the May 2014 elections. The biggest number of these came from Germany, namely, 34, followed by Poland with 23, France with 20, and Italy with 17. In the May 2019 elections, the EPP won 182 seats, but remained the biggest group despite the losses. Germany won 29 seats, Poland 17, and Romania 14. It is a right-of-center group with inspiration from Catholic social doctrine. Due to its size, it is very influential in the legislative process.

GROUP OF THE GREENS/EUROPEAN FREE ALLIANCE (GREENS/EFA). The Greens/European Free Alliance (Greens/EFA) was the sixth in size among the seven groups in the **European Parliament** (EP) after the May 2014 elections. It had 50 **Members of the EP** (MEPs). The biggest number came from Germany with 13, followed by France and the **United Kingdom** (UK) with six each. It increased its number of seats to 74 in the May 2019 elections, becoming the 4th group in size. Germany elected the largest group with 25 MEPs, followed by France with 12 Green MEPs. The UK elected 12, which stepped down on **Brexit day**, 31 January 2020.

GROUP OF THE PROGRESSIVE ALLIANCE OF SOCIALISTS AND DEMOCRATS IN THE EUROPEAN PARLIAMENT (S&D). The Group of the Progressive Alliance of Socialists and Democrats in the European Parliament (S&D) is currently the second-largest group in the **European Parliament** (EP). It occupied 191 of the 751 seats after the May 2014 elections. The biggest number of these came from Italy, namely, 31, followed by Germany with 27, the **United Kingdom** (UK) with 20, and Romania with 16. In the May 2019 elections, the party group won 154 seats, the biggest national groups being Spain 20, Italy 19, Germany 16, and Romania 10. The UK also won 10 seats, a huge loss compared with 2014. They were subsequently vacated on **Brexit day**, 31 January 2020. In the legislative process, it has often worked with the **Group of the European People's Party** (EPP). Together the two groups can dominate the proceedings. It is noticeable, however, that both European People's Party (EPP) and S&D lost seats in 2019, partly to the Greens, partly to EU skeptical groups.

H

THE HAGUE SUMMIT. The Hague Summit on 1–2 December 1969 was a very important event in the history of European integration. It was at this meeting that the Heads of State or Government of the **European Communities** (EC) decided to open for accession negotiations with the **United Kingdom** (UK) and other applicants, Denmark, **Ireland**, and **Norway**. The slogan of the meeting was "completion, **enlargement** and **deepening**." Completion was mostly about the financing of the **Common Agricultural Policy** (CAP) with "own resources." Deepening was about further steps in the integration process, first a proposal to move toward **Economic and Monetary Union** (EMU) over a ten-year period, and starting foreign policy cooperation. The meeting became possible after the French president **Charles de Gaulle** had stepped down that year and Georges Pompidou had become president. Another key person at the summit was the new German chancellor Willy Brandt. The **Commission** was invited to take part in the discussions the second day.

HARD BORDER. Hard border refers to a border with various checks. It would be the outcome of a **hard Brexit**. Even a **free trade agreement**, which abolishes tariffs, will require checks, if it does not also include a high degree of **regulatory alignment**.

HARD BREXIT. In a hard Brexit the **United Kingdom** (UK) cuts the main formal ties with the **European Union** (EU). The opposite is a **soft Brexit**, where the UK continues to have close formal ties with the EU. The main ties that **Brexiteers** have wanted to cut are **free movement** of people, the need to pay money to the EU as a member, and the fact that EU law overrides UK law. So those that favor a hard Brexit want a maximum degree of independence from the EU. When **Theresa May** decided to rule out membership on the **internal market** (the **Norwegian model**) and the **customs union** (the **Turkish model**) she had decided for a relatively hard Brexit, but her **Chequers plan** in July 2018 had elements of a softer Brexit. To some people a hard Brexit means leaving the EU without an agreement.

HARMONIZATION. Provision for harmonizing national law was originally in Article 100 of the **Treaty of Rome** establishing the **European Economic Community (EEC)**. It required unanimity in the **Council**. The treaty used the term "approximation." The reason for efforts to harmonize national law was to avoid different product standards and regulations creating **non-tariff-barriers (NTBs)** to trade within the **common market**. The **Single European Act** (SEA) in 1987 introduced **qualified majority voting** (QMV) for much of this harmonization, thereby helping to speed up the completion on the **internal market**. QMV, however, did not apply to "fiscal provisions, to those relating to the free movement of persons nor to those relating to the rights and interests of employed persons" (Article 100A of SEA). After the entry into force of the **Treaty of Lisbon** in 2009, the rules for approximation of laws can be found in Article 114 and 115 TFEU. The **ordinary legislative procedure** (OLP) is now used. The same exceptions as in the SEA still apply.

HEATH, EDWARD (1916–2005). Edward Heath, who had been elected as a Conservative British **Member of Parliament** (MP) in 1950, was strongly in favor of British membership of the **European Communities** (EC). In his maiden speech in 1950, he advocated British membership of the **European Coal and Steel Community** (ECSC). When Prime Minister Harold Macmillan applied for British membership in 1961, he made Edward Heath the chief British negotiator. French president **Charles de Gaulle** vetoed this first effort in January 1963. The Conservatives lost the election in 1964 to the **Labour Party**. De Gaulle also blocked a second application from the **United Kingdom** (UK) in 1967. By the time of the elections in 1970, Heath had become the leader of the **Conservative Party** and the party won the elections. Prior to the elections, **The Hague summit** in December 1969 had opened up the possibility of EC membership, and Heath got along well with the new French president **Georges Pompidou**. The breakthrough in accession negotiations took place at a meeting between the two leaders in May 1971. Heath could sign the accession treaty on 22 January 1972 in Brussels. He then succeeded getting the treaty ratified by a divided Parliament, where a breakout group of Labour MPs led by **Roy Jenkins** helped secure passage of the bill. The UK joined on 1 January 1973.

Heath then lost an election in February 1974 to the Labour Party. Four months later, he lost a party leadership contest to **Margaret Thatcher**. When Prime Minister **Harold Wilson** went through a "renegotiation" process with his EC partners and called a **referendum** in June 1975 both Heath and Thatcher supported a "yes" vote for continued British membership of the EC.

HIGH AUTHORITY. The High Authority was the name of the supranational "executive" established by the **European Coal and Steel Community** (ECSC) in 1952. The first to occupy the presidency of the High Authority was **Jean Monnet**, one of the founding fathers of European integration. The High Authority was deliberately set up with strong powers and was based on the idea that it should represent the common European interest, not the separate national interests. The Merger Treaty, creating a single Commission for the three Communities, merged the High Authority with the **Commission** of the **European Economic Community** (EEC) and the Commission of the **European Atomic Energy Community** (EAEC or EURATOM) in 1967.

HIGH REPRESENTATIVE FOR THE COMMON FOREIGN AND SECURITY POLICY. The position of High Representative for Common Foreign and Security Policy (CFSP) was introduced by the **Treaty of Amsterdam**, which entered into force in 1999. The treaty assigned the job to the Secretary General of the **Council**. The first—and last—to hold the job was Javier Solana from Spain, former secretary general of the North Atlantic Treaty Organization (NATO). He occupied the job until the entry into force of the **Treaty of Lisbon** in December 2009, when the job was redefined and renamed **High Representative of the Union for Foreign Affairs and Security Policy**. It was during Solana's tenure that a European Security Strategy (ESS) was worked out and presented in December 2003, setting priorities and listing the main threats to European security, including terrorism. Solana is generally considered to have done a very good job, especially considering the limitations of the position.

HIGH REPRESENTATIVE OF THE UNION FOR FOREIGN AFFAIRS AND SECURITY POLICY. The current High Representative (HR) position is based on the **Treaty of Lisbon,** which created a so-called double-hatted position. The current HR is also a vice president (VP) of the **Commission** and a member of the **Foreign Affairs Council** (FAC), which she or he chairs. The idea was to create more coherence between the work of the Commission and the **Council**, which had been kept rather separate in the past. The HR/VP is also in charge of the new **European External Action Service** (EEAS), established in 2010. The joining together of the external economic relation (traditionally a Commission prerogative) and CFSP (traditionally a member state prerogative) is not complete, however. The Commission still has Commissioners and Directorate Generals dealing with trade, development, and neighborhood policy. Therefore, the work of the EEAS is very much focused on **Common Foreign and Security Policy** (CFSP) and **Common Security**

and Defence Policy (CSDP). However, the former Commission delegations now all fall under the EEAS.

The first to hold the new HR position was Lady Catherine Ashton, a British **Labour Party** politician, who was a surprise choice in 2009. She had briefly been Commissioner for Trade, where she replaced Peter Mandelson in 2008. However, given the policy of having different nationalities, political affiliations, and gender represented among the top positions, by being woman and Labour Party member, she fitted in after the appointment of **Herman van Rompuy** from **Belgium** (Flemish Christian Democrat) as president of the **European Council** in 2009. The next HR/VP from 1 November 2014 to December 2019 was **Federica Mogherini** from Italy, also belonging to the Socialist political group. Since December 2019 the post is filled by **Josep Borrell** from Spain, also a socialist, previously Foreign Minister of Spain. *See also* COMMON FOREIGN AND SECURITY POLICY.

HOUSE OF COMMONS. The House of Commons is the lower chamber of the bicameral **United Kingdom** (UK) Parliament. *See also* PARLIAMENT OF THE UNITED KINGDOM.

HOUSE OF LORDS. The House of Lords is the upper chamber of the bicameral **United Kingdom** (UK) Parliament. *See also* PARLIAMENT OF THE UNITED KINGDOM.

HUMAN RIGHTS. *See* CHARTER OF FUNDAMENTAL RIGHTS;

HUNT, JEREMY (1966–). Jeremy Hunt is a British Conservative politician. He has been a **Member of Parliament** (MP) since 2005. He served as Secretary of State for Foreign and Commonwealth Affairs from 9 July 2018, when **Boris Johnson** resigned from the post. He was a candidate for the leadership in the **Conservative Party** when **Theresa May** resigned in 2019. He stepped down as foreign secretary on 24 July 2019, when Boris Johnson became prime minister, but he promised to support Johnson, who had offered him another job, which he did not accept.

I

IDENTITY AND DEMOCRACY. The Identity and Democracy party group in the **European Parliament** (EP) replaced **Europe of Nations and Freedom** in the May 2019 elections. It gained 73 seats and is the fifth largest group. It is a right-wing euro-skeptical party, including the Italian *Lega* party, the French *Rassemblement National* (RN), and the German *Alternative für Deutschland* (AfD).

IMMIGRATION POLICY. Immigration policy was included in the **Treaty of Maastricht** under **Justice and Home Affairs** (JHA) cooperation in the **European Union's** (EU) third intergovernmental pillar. The **Treaty of Amsterdam** (in force in 1999) subsequently moved it to the first supranational pillar. The 1999 meeting of the **European Council** in Tampere, Finland, gave a push toward a common immigration policy, but efforts are hampered by the wish of governments to stay in control because immigration is politically sensitive in the member states. Some countries receive more immigrants, including **asylum** seekers and illegal immigrants, than others, which creates a burden-sharing problem. To what extent should illegal immigrants be returned to their home countries or the countries they transited through? Part of immigration policy is cooperation with third countries about the return of illegal immigrants. On the other hand, the EU needs highly qualified immigrants given the demographic trends in the Union. Internally in the EU there is **free movement** of people, one of the **four freedoms**. It was mainly this part of immigration that became a political issue in the **United Kingdom** (UK) after the EU **enlargements** in 2004 and 2007 brought many immigrants from the Central and Eastern European Countries (CEECs) to the UK.

INTELLECTUAL PROPERTY RIGHTS (IPRs). Intellectual property (IP) refers to creations of the mind. National and international law seek to protect intellectual property rights (IPRs). Examples are copyrights, patents, industrial design rights, and trademarks. International cooperation about IPRs takes place through the World Intellectual Property Organization (WIPO).

Since its creation after the Uruguay Round the **World Trade Organization** (WTO) includes an agreement on **Trade-Related Aspects of Intellectual Property Rights** (TRIPS). Many countries, especially some developing countries, are not good at protecting IPRs. Counterfeiting and piracy are still widespread. For this reason, the **European Union** (EU) is also insisting on getting provisions on IPRs into various agreements with third countries, including lately bilateral **free trade agreements** (FTAs) with a number of counties. National law still mainly protects IPRs, but the EU has established an Office for Harmonization in the Internal Market (OHIM) for the registration of trademarks and design and established a European Patent Office (EPO). There is also work to create a so-called unitary patent, which should be valid in the participating EU member states. Part of the proposal is the creation of a Unified Patent Court (UPC). It has been created under **enhanced cooperation**. The agreement was signed by 24 member states on 19 February 2013. Denmark held a referendum on participation in the Unified Patent Court on 25 May 2014, which was accepted by a 62.47 percent yes vote. The agreement must be ratified by 13 states, including France, Germany, and the **United Kingdom** (UK), before it can enter into force. The UK actually ratified the agreement on 26 April 2018. But after Brexit the **Boris Johnson** government let it be known in February 2020 that the UK will not seek involvement in the UPC system. The other EU27 countries, except Spain and Poland, have now signed up to the UPC system. *See also* ENHANCED COOPERATION.

INTERGOVERNMENTAL CONFERENCE (IGC). An Intergovernmental Conference (IGC) is a special meeting of the member state governments of the **European Union** (EU). It was foreseen in the founding treaties of the **European Communities** (EC), as a means to change the treaties. In the early treaty reforms, the 1965 Merger Treaty and the 1970 and 1975 Budgetary Treaties, the IGC was a short meeting at the end of the process, where the foreign ministers would sign the new draft treaty, which had previously been negotiated by the **Council** of Ministers and the **Committee of Permanent Representatives** (COREPER). However, from the negotiations of the **Single European Act** (SEA) in 1985, the IGC became the negotiating forum. It continued playing that role when the next treaties were negotiated: **Treaty of Maastricht** in 1991, **Treaty of Amsterdam** in 1996–1997, and **Treaty of Nice** in 2000, in reality becoming a kind of constitutional convention. Dissatisfaction with the way the Treaty of Nice was negotiated in 2000 led to the next treaty reform being prepared by a so-called convention, where there were representatives from national parliaments and the **European**

Parliament (EP) together with government representatives. This Convention on the Future of Europe (2002–2003) drafted a Treaty establishing a Constitution for Europe (sometimes called Constitutional Treaty). However, as legally required, the convention was followed by an IGC (2003–2004), which eventually adopted the draft Constitutional Treaty in slightly modified form. This treaty, however, failed to be ratified fully, because it was rejected in **referendums** in France and the Netherlands in 2005. This had the member states change strategy, so the subsequent treaty, the **Treaty of Lisbon**, was negotiated by the member states in a rather secretive way. The process did conclude with an IGC during the Portuguese Presidency in the second half of 2007, but most of the contents of the new treaty had been agreed during the German Presidency during the first part of the year.

The Treaty of Lisbon includes two procedures for changing the treaties in the future. There is an "ordinary revision procedure," which combines a convention and an IGC, and there is a "simplified revision procedure," which makes it possible for a unanimous **European Council** to change the articles in the **Treaty on the Functioning of the European Union** (TFEU) without calling either a convention or an IGC. This simplified procedure was applied in December 2009 to amend Article 136 TFEU to give a treaty base to the European Stability Mechanism (ESM), one of the responses to the financial crisis.

INTERGOVERNMENTALISM. Cooperation and integration efforts in Europe since the Second World War have applied both intergovernmentalism and supranationalism. The **European Communities** (EC), established in the 1950s, created institutions to which the states had delegated real power or sovereignty, especially the **Commission** and the **European Court of Justice** (ECJ). In addition, some decisions in the **Council** of Ministers could be taken by a qualified majority vote (QMV). These arrangements are referred to as supranationalism. However, a number of European institutions, including the Council of Europe, were based on intergovernmental cooperation. This meant that there was no delegation of sovereignty. The states remained in full control. Decisions would be made in committees and councils of government representatives, normally by unanimous agreement. The **European Union** (EU) as it developed has included elements of both supranationalism and intergovernmentalism. French president **Charles de Gaulle** favored intergovernmentalism as shown by his Fouchet Plan as well as his "empty chair policy" in 1965. The summit meetings of heads of state or government, formalized as the **European Council** in 1974, is also an intergovernmental element in the institutional setup. Further, the **Treaty of Maastricht** establishing the EU created two intergovernmental pillars, **Common Foreign and**

Security Policy (CFSP) as the second pillar, and **Justice and Home Affairs** (JHA) cooperation as the third pillar. In these two pillars decisions required unanimity. The Commission and ECJ played only a minor role or no role at all. However, the **Treaty of Amsterdam** started a process of moving parts of JHA cooperation (including immigration and asylum policy) to the first supranational pillar of the Union, leaving **Police and Judicial Cooperation in Criminal Matters** in a slimmer intergovernmental third pillar. This process continued with the **Treaty of Lisbon**, which formally abolished the pillar structure. However, the treaty has maintained intergovernmental procedures for CFSP. Usually supranationalism is considered a more efficient form of decision-making than intergovernmentalism. Supranationalism in the original European Communities was one of the reasons why the **United Kingdom** (UK) did not join the process from the beginning, and, arguably, the UK never fully accepted the philosophy behind supranationalism, as shown by the "taking back control" slogan during the **Brexit referendum** campaign in 2016.

INTERNAL MARKET. What was called common market in the **Treaty of Rome** creating the **European Economic Community** (EEC) has been called internal market in the treaties since the **Single European Act** (SEA) in 1987. It is also sometimes called the single market. It is arguably the most central and important part of the European integration project. It creates **free movement** of goods, **services**, capital, and people among the member states, also referred to as the **four freedoms**. In the Brexit negotiations with the United Kingdom an important question has been whether the UK should stay partly or even completely in the internal market. Through the **European Economic Area** (EEA) **Norway**, Iceland, and Lichtenstein take part in the internal market. According to the **Withdrawal Agreement** concluded by Prime Minister **Boris Johnson** with the **European Union** (EU) in October 2019, Northern Ireland will partly remain in the internal market as well as the **customs union** with the EU. *See also* COMMON MARKET.

INVESTMENTS. The **Treaty of Lisbon** for the first time included foreign direct investments (FDI) as a competence of the **European Union** (EU) under the **Common Commercial Policy** (CCP) (Art. 207 TFEU). This has allowed the EU to include FDI in bilateral trade agreements with third countries, for instance, the **Comprehensive Economic and Trade Agreement (CETA)** with **Canada**. The treaty, however, did not include other forms of investments than FDI. For this reason, it was concluded that CETA was a mixed agreement that also required ratification by the member states. Because of demonstrations against the **Investor State Dispute Settlement** (ISDS) system in the draft CETA it was changed to an **Investment Court System** (ICS) in the last moment. The EU has also been working on an investment agreement with **China** since 2013. *See also* CANADA; INVESTMENT COURT SYSTEM (ICS); INVESTOR STATE DISPUTE SETTLEMENT (ISDS).

INVESTMENT COURT SYSTEM (ICS). An Investment Court System (ICS) replaced the **Investor State Dispute Settlement** (ISDS) system originally included in the **Comprehensive Economic and Trade Agreement** (CETA) with Canada before its signature in October 2016. Subsequently ICS was included in agreements with Singapore, Mexico, and Vietnam. An Opinion by the **Court of Justice of the European Union** (CJEU) on 30 April 2019 found the ICS consistent with the **European Union** (EU) treaties. The main features of the ICS are (1) it is a permanent court and (2) it is made up of a Tribunal of First Instance and an Appeal Tribunal. Contrary to ISDS it is not based on temporary ad hoc tribunals. It will be composed of professional and independent adjudicators and will work transparently, including public hearings and documents, which will be available to nongovernmental organizations (NGOs), trade unions, and citizens' representatives, who will also be able to intervene in the proceedings.

INVESTOR STATE DISPUTE SETTLEMENT (ISDS). Provisions for Investor State Dispute Settlement (ISDS) have been included in many international trade agreements, including some of the latest bilateral **free trade agreements** (FTAs) concluded by **the European Union** (EU). It allows an investor in a foreign country to initiate proceedings against the government if changed legislation affects the company in a negative way. Therefore, the purpose is to protect investors from discrimination or expropriation. However, there is increasingly a widespread feeling that many multinational companies have exploited imprecise definitions of expropriation to claim compensation. The number of ISDS cases has increased sharply since the mid-1990s. Suddenly, when free trade critical groups discovered that ISDS was on the agenda of the **Transatlantic Trade and Investment Partnership** (TTIP) negotiations with the **United States** (U.S.) it became very controversial. There were calls for scrapping it from the negotiations as well as from the **Comprehensive Economic and Trade Agreement (CETA)** with **Canada**.

IRELAND. When the **United Kingdom** (UK) applied for membership in the **European Communities** (EC) in 1961 Ireland followed (as did Denmark and **Norway**). When French president **Charles de Gaulle** vetoed British membership in 1963, the Irish application was put on hold. When de Gaulle stepped down as president in 1969 the possibility of **enlargement** opened up. Ireland successfully negotiated an accession treaty, which was ratified by a **referendum** on 10 May 1972, where an overwhelming majority of 83.1 percent of the electorate voted "yes." Ireland became a member of the EC together with the UK and Denmark from 1 January, 1973.

Ireland is the member country that has used most referendums. When the **Single European Act** (SEA) included a title on **European Political Cooperation** (EPC), giving it a treaty basis, the Irish Supreme Court ruled that it was incompatible with the country's constitution. The ratification of the SEA therefore required a change in the constitution, which in turn required a referendum. The referendum on 26 May 1987 gave a majority of 69.9 percent, allowing Ireland to ratify the SEA. The following new treaty, the **Treaty of Maastricht**, was ratified by a referendum on 18 June 1992 with a 69.1 percent "yes" vote, and the next treaty, the **Treaty of Amsterdam** was ratified by referendum on 22 May 1998, with a 61.7 percent "yes" vote. The two next treaties, however, were first rejected by the Irish people, but then accepted in a second referendum in each case. The **Treaty of Nice** was first rejected by a 53.9 percent "no" majority on 7 June 2001. After some clarifications and stronger government involvement in promoting the treaty it was accepted by a 62.9 percent majority on 10 October 2002. Similarly, the **Treaty of Lisbon** was first rejected by a 53.4 percent "no" vote on 12 June 2008, but subsequently accepted in a second referendum by a 67.1 percent "yes" majority. Clarification mainly dealt with Ireland's policy of neutrality. However, in the case of the **Treaty of Lisbon** it included a promise that each member state would continue to nominate a commissioner.

Ireland has benefited substantially from financial assistance from the **European Union** (EU) through the **structural funds** and experienced very high growth for a number of years. It very successfully attracted investments from abroad. As the country became richer, it received less money from the structural funds. In 2009, Ireland became a net contributor to the EU.

Ireland was hit hard by the financial crisis in 2008. A housing bobble burst and several banks needed government bailouts. This in turn created a huge sovereign debt. In 2010, Ireland requested financial assistance from the European Financial Stability Facility (EFSF) and the International Monetary Fund (IMF). By 2014, Ireland had largely pulled out of the crisis. Ireland officially exited the bailout in December 2013. By late 2014 economic growth in Ireland was one of the highest in the EU. *See also* IRISH BORDER; REPUBLIC OF IRELAND.

Michel Barnier, Chief negotiator for the EU, Leo Varadcar, Irish Prime Minister, Donald Tusk, President of the European Council, and Jean-Claude Juncker, President of the European Commission. *Source*: Courtesy of the European Union.

IRISH BORDER. The border between Northern Ireland and the Republic of Ireland became one of the main issues in the **Brexit** negotiations. Both sides wanted to avoid that the border becomes a **hard border** with customs and security checks. But the two sides had great difficulties to agree on how to reach such result. If the **United Kingdom** (UK) were to stay in the **European Union** (EU) **customs union** that could contribute to solving the problem, then the UK would not be free to negotiate its own bilateral trade agreements with third countries. The **Withdrawal Agreement** reached by Prime Minister **Theresa May** with the EU in November 2018 included a so-called **backstop**, according to which the UK would stay in the customs union until a permanent solution for the border issue would be found. That solution was not accepted by the **UK Parliament**. Instead Prime Minister **Boris Johnson** negotiated an agreement in October 2019 that had **Northern Ireland** stay in the EU customs union, thus creating a kind of border in the Irish sea. There will further be some **regulatory alignment** for goods produced in Northern Ireland intended for export to Ireland, to avoid border checks between the north and the south of the island.

J

JENKINS, ROY (1920–2003). Roy Jenkins was elected a **Labour Party Member of Parliament** (MP) in 1948 in the **United Kingdom** (UK). In 1965, he was appointed Home Secretary in the first **Harold Wilson** government and two years later, he became Chancellor of the Exchequer. The Wilson government lost the election in 1970 to the **Conservative Party** under **Edward Heath**, whose government negotiated the British accession to the European Communities (EC) in 1973. Jenkins defied the official Labour Party line and supported the application to join the EC. When Wilson formed his second government in 1974 Jenkins again became Home Secretary. After Wilson's renegotiation of British membership Jenkins became a leading figure in the campaign for a "yes" vote in the **referendum** in June 1975.

Jenkins was President of the **European Commission**, 1977–1981. He succeeded, against opposition from French president Valéry Giscard d'Estaing, in securing the decision that the Commission president should represent the EC at the meetings of the Group of Seven (G7) leading industrialized countries. It was also Jenkins who revived the idea of increased monetary cooperation, in the form of a new **European Monetary System** (EMS). He proposed it in a speech at the European University Institute in Florence in 1977. He did not seek reappointment in 1981 when **Margaret Thatcher** had become prime minister of the UK. He returned to British politics and was an MP during the years 1982–1987. Afterward he was chancellor of Oxford University until his death.

JOHNSON, BORIS (1964–). Boris Johnson was a leading spokesperson for the **Leave campaign** in the 2016 **referendum**. He held various Cabinet positions. He became prime minister and leader of the **Conservative Party** in July 2019 when **Theresa May** stepped down after failing to get the **UK Parliament's** support for the **Withdrawal Agreement** she had negotiated with the **European Union** (EU). He had been Foreign Secretary from 2016 to 2018, stepping down because of disagreement with May's **Brexit** plan, known as the **Chequers plan**, in July 2018. Previously he had worked as a journalist and been Mayor of London from 2008 to 2016. After becoming prime minister, he set out to try to negotiate another Withdrawal Agreement with the EU. His proposal was to drop the so-called Irish **backstop**, which had been agreed to avoid the introduction of border controls between **Northern Ireland** and the **Republic of Ireland**. The EU, however, would not drop the backstop without an alternative solution. Johnson was up against a 31 October 2019 deadline for Brexit, which he did not want to extend. He tried to prorogue the Parliament and expelled some difficult party members. Eventually, in October, after a meeting between Johnson and Irish prime minister **Leo Varadkar** the basis for a different approach to the **Irish border** issue was found. On 17 October 2019 the **United Kingdom** (UK) and EU could announce the new deal. This, however, was too late for getting the implementing legislation through before the deadline of 31 October, so on 28 October the EU offered an extension until 31 January 2020. Johnson used the extended period to call an election on 12 December 2019, which gave him an 80-seat majority. After getting the new agreement accepted by both the **European Parliament** (EP) and the **UK Parliament** the UK left the EU on the 31st of January 2020. While Theresa May's backstop involved keeping the UK in the EU customs union with some **regulatory alignment** until a solution to the Irish border problem could be found, the Johnson backstop meant a de facto border in the Irish Sea leading to some border checks of goods from the other parts of the UK when entering Northern Ireland. If found to be "at risk" of being "exported" to the Republic of Ireland duties and taxes would have to be paid. Further, with this solution, too, there would be some regulatory alignment in Northern Ireland so that goods, including agricultural goods, could be exported from Northern Ireland to the Irish Republic without border checks.

Borris Johnson, UK Prime Minister (2019-) and Jean-Claude Juncker, President of the European Commission (2014–2019). *Source*: Courtesy of the European Union.

JOINT COMMITTEE. A panel that will supervise the implementation of the **Withdrawal Agreement**. It will have an equal number of **United Kingdom** (UK) and **European Union** (EU) representatives.

JUNCKER, JEAN-CLAUDE (1954–). Jean-Claude Juncker was prime minister of Luxembourg from 1995 to 2013. From 1989 to 2009, he was also Luxembourg's finance minister. This included the period of the negotiations of the **Treaty of Maastricht**, where he played an important role in the **Economic and Monetary Union** (EMU) part of the negotiations. He was the first permanent president of the Eurogroup of finance ministers from the eurozone countries from 2005 to 2013. In the elections to the **European Parliament** (EP) in May 2014, the main party groups proposed a candidate for president of the **European Commission**, known in the media with the German name *Spitzenkandidat.* Juncker was the candidate for the **European People's Party** (EPP). Since the EPP won most seats in the elections, most members of the EP expected him to be nominated by the **European Council**. After some hesitation, the European Council nominated him on 27 June for the position with a vote where only British prime minister **David Cameron** and Hungarian prime minister Viktor Orbán voted against. His program included ten points: A new boost for jobs, growth and **investment**; a connected digital single market; a resilient energy union with forward-looking climate change policy; a deeper and fairer **internal market** with strengthened industrial base; a deeper and fairer **economic and monetary union**; a reasonable and balanced **free trade agreement** with the U.S.; an area of justice and fundamental rights based on mutual trust; a new policy on migration; a stronger global actor; and a union of democratic change. On 15 July, Juncker presented his program to the EP. After debate, he was elected by the EP to the position of Commission President with 422 votes in favor and 250 votes against. After the appointment of **Donald Tusk** as president of the European Council and **Federica Mogherini** as **High Representative of the Union for Foreign Affairs and Security Policy** on 30 August 2014, Juncker could start putting his Commission together. Mogherini as High Representative was also a vice president of the Commission. His biggest challenge was gender balance since most member states nominated men. The new Commission took office from 1 November 2014. Eight of the 28 commissioners were women. His personal *Cabinet* had about 30 members, of whom nearly two-thirds were women. Juncker's tenure expired on 30 November 2019, when he was succeeded by **Ursula von der Leyen**. UK prime minister **Theresa May**'s negotiation of the **Withdrawal Agreement**, which she was unable to get accepted by the **UK Parliament**, took place during Jean-Claude's tenure as Commission president. UK prime minister **Boris Johnson**'s subsequent agreement was finally adopted after Ursula von der Leyen had taken over as president of the Commission.

Jean-Claude Juncker, President of the European Commission (2014–2019). *Source*: Courtesy of the European Union.

JUSTICE AND HOME AFFAIRS (JHA). Justice and Home Affairs (JHA) cooperation was included in the **Treaty of Maastricht** as the third pillar. It included **asylum policy**, border control, and **immigration policy**, combating drug addiction, combating fraud, judicial cooperation in civil matters, judicial cooperation in criminal matters, customs cooperation, and police cooperation. The Council could adopt joint positions, joint actions, and draw up conventions. The **Treaty of Amsterdam** moved JHA except **Police and Judicial Cooperation in Criminal Matters** to the first pillar. A new title established an **Area of Freedom, Security and Justice** (AFSJ), which included visas, asylum, immigration, and other policies related to the **free movement** of persons. (Visa policy had actually been in the first pillar already in the Treaty of Maastricht.) In these areas, the institutions could adopt "measures," using regulations, directives, and decisions. Measures would require unanimity in a five-year transition period. Afterward the **Council** could decide by unanimity which measures could be adopted by a **qualified majority vote** (QMV). During the interim period the right of initiative was shared between the member states and the **Commission**. After the five years, the Commission would get the exclusive right of initiative that was normal in the first pillar. From the beginning, the **European Court of Justice** (ECJ) got jurisdiction to interpret legislation. The Treaty of Amsterdam also incorporated the **Schengen *acquis***, the rules and regulations adopted under the Schengen Agreement (1985) and Schengen Implementing Convention (1990).

The Tampere meeting of the European Council in 1999 adopted a five-year program listing future action. The terrorist attack of 11 September 2001 gave new impetus to JHA cooperation. The Hague and Stockholm programs followed up the Tampere program in 2004 and 2009.

The **Treaty of Lisbon**, by abolishing the pillar structure of the Union, has included all JHA under basically the same decision rules, the **Community method**. There is Commission initiative, majority voting in the Council—with exceptions, including passports and family law—ECJ jurisdiction, and **European Parliament** (EP) co-decision (the **ordinary legislative method**), but also including emergency breaks and possibilities of **enhanced cooperation**. The change is most radical for Police and Judicial Cooperation in Criminal Matters.

The **United Kingdom** (UK), **Ireland,** and Denmark have had **opt-outs** or special arrangements in the area of JHA.

K

KINNOCK, NEIL. Neil Kinnock is a British **Labour Party** politician. He was a **Member of Parliament** (MP) from 1970 to 1995. He was the leader of the party and leader of the opposition, 1983–1992. He left the **UK Parliament** in 1995 to become a European Commissioner in the Jacques Santer Commission. He was a vice president of the **Commission** under Romano Prodi, 1999–2004. He entered the **House of Lords** in 2005. He has strongly opposed **Brexit**.

L

LABOUR PARTY. The British Labour Party has for many years been either the governing party or the official opposition. It was the official opposition during the **Brexit** period, including the **referendum** in 2016 and the **Withdrawal Agreement** negotiations, 2017–2019, under Conservative prime ministers **Theresa May** and **Boris Johnson**. **Jeremy Corbyn** led the Labour Party 2015–2020. The party's attitude toward European integration has varied over the years from relatively pro-integration under **Neil Kinnock**, 1983–1992, and **Tony Blair**, 1997–2007, to relatively EU skeptical under Corbyn. Arguably Corbyn's Eurosceptical attitude and often relatively unclear positions on Brexit contributed to making it difficult to get an agreement through the **UK Parliament**.

LANCASTER SPEECH. United Kingdom (UK) prime minister **Theresa May** made the so-called Lancaster Speech at Lancaster House in London on 17 January 2017 in London. She presented her "Plan for Britain." In it she listed 12 key priorities. (1) Certainty, (2) Control of our own laws, (3) Strengthen the Union, (4) Maintain the Common Travel Area with **Ireland**, (5) Control of **immigration**, (6) Rights for EU nationals in Britain, and British nationals in the **European Union** (EU), (7) Protect workers' rights, (8) Free trade with European markets, (9) New trade agreements with other countries, (10) The best place for science and innovation, (11) Cooperation in the fight against crime and terrorism, (12) A smooth, orderly **Brexit**. It was followed up with a **White Paper** on "The United Kingdom's exit and new partnership with the European Union" on 2 February 2017.

LEAVE CAMPAIGN. The **United Kingdom** (UK) campaign to leave the **European Union** (EU) was led by the organization "Vote Leave," which was formed in October 2015. It included politicians from most parties, with a majority from the **Conservative Party**. This last group included **Dominic Cummings**, **Michael Gove**, and **Boris Johnson**, among the more well-known ones. The rival organization was "**Britain Stronger in Europe**."

LEGAL PERSONALITY. At the outset of European integration, the three **European Communities** (EC)—the **European Coal and Steel Community** (ECSC), the **European Economic Community** (EEC), and the **European Atomic Energy Community** (EAEC or EURATOM)—all had "legal personality." The EEC treaty, for instance, stated in Article 219, that the EEC "shall have legal personality." This gave the Communities the right to conclude agreements, both within the member states and with third countries and international organizations. When the **Treaty of Maastricht** created the three-pillar European Union (EU), only the European Community in the first pillar had legal personality, although the treaty did not say so explicitly. **Common Foreign and Security Policy** (CFSP) in the second or **Justice and Home Affairs** (JHA) in the third pillar did not have legal personality. The **Treaty of Amsterdam** added an Article J14 that allowed for international agreements under CFSP and an Article K10 that did the same for JHA. Such agreements would require unanimity in the Council. The situation changed and was made clearer with the **Treaty of Lisbon**, where the pillar structure was abolished. Now the whole Union has legal personality. This is stated clearly in Article 47 TEU.

LEVEL PLAYING FIELD. Level playing field refers to fair rules of **competition**. Arguably the **European Union**'s internal market is the most developed example of a level playing field. The EU sees the creation of a level playing field in the future trade agreement with the **United Kingdom** (UK) as very important. It especially includes concerns about workers' rights, competition and state aid policy, taxation, and social and **environmental** protection. This concern was singled out at the beginning in 2017 in the EU's guidelines for the **Brexit** negotiations. *See also* FRICTIONLESS TRADE.

LIBERAL DEMOCRATS. The Liberal Democrats (Lib Dems) is a British political party. It is a social-liberal pro-European party. It supported **Remain** in the **Brexit referendum** in 2016. Due to the first-past-the-post electoral system in the **United Kingdom** (UK) it tends to be relatively underrepresented in relation to the number of votes it receives. For this reason, the party supports proportional representation. After the December 2019 elections the party has 11 **Members of Parliament** (MEPs). It has five Members of the **Scottish Parliament** and one of the **Welsh Parliament**. In the **European Parliament** (EP) the party took part in the **Group of the Alliance of Liberals and Democrats for Europe** (ALDE). In the EP election in May 2019 the party won 16 seats, which were vacated on **Brexit day**, 31 January 2020.

LIBERAL INTERGOVERNMENTALISM. Liberal intergovernmentalism is a conceptual framework for analyzing and explaining European integration mainly developed by American political scientist Andrew Moravcsik. It is suggested that we need to understand national preferences, which are based on demands from societal groups, and then study the interstate bargaining process, which produces the substantive outcomes. An important part is institutional choice, where it is argued that the member states in the **European Union** (EU) chose to "pool and delegate" sovereignty to European institutions to create "credible commitments." It is argued that the member states are very much in charge. They make the most important decisions. Moravcsik's major work is *The Choice for Europe* (Cornell University Press, 1998). Liberal intergovernmentalism is a rational theory, which puts emphasis on economic factors determining national preferences and power in interstate negotiations. Power depends on "asymmetrical interdependence." Those who need an agreement most will be the weakest.

LUXEMBOURG COMPROMISE. The Luxembourg Compromise is the name given to a gentlemen's agreement reached in Luxembourg in January 1965 to finish France's empty chair policy because of disagreement about the use of **qualified majority voting** (QMV) and so-called "own resources" for the **European Community** (EC) **budget**, largely a question of how to finance the **Common Agricultural Policy** (CAP). Associated with these issues were also the powers of the **European Parliament** (EP). The Five members other than France wanted to apply the provisions of the treaties, but France insisted that there should be unanimity if important national interests were at stake. In reality, it meant that unanimity remained the practice in the following years. Arguably, the Luxembourg Compromise slowed down the integration process the following years because of this unanimity requirement. The Luxembourg Compromise started being ignored from the 1980s when **Presidencies** of the Council began to call for votes even if some country claimed important national interests. This largely coincided with the **Single European Act** (SEA), which introduced QMV for much harmonization of national legislation to help speed up the completion of the **internal market** (New Article 100A), but the treaty already had some provisions for QMV in certain areas, for instance, the **Common Commercial Policy** (CCP) and the CAP.

M

MALTHOUSE COMPROMISE. The Malthouse compromise emerged toward the end of January 2019. It had been prepared by both "Remainers," including Nicky Morgan MP, and "**Brexiteers**" such as **Jacob Rees-Mogg** and Steve Baker MP, partly inspired by a plan put forward by the Northern Irish **Democratic Unionist Party** (DUP). It was named after the Housing Minister Kit Malthouse. According to media reports it had a Part A and Part B, which together formed a Plan C for Brexit, at a time where it seemed that it would be difficult for Prime Minister **Theresa May** to get the **Withdrawal Agreement** she had negotiated with the **European Union** (EU) accepted by the **United Kingdom (UK) Parliament**. The first part, borrowed largely from a DUP proposal, aimed for a replacement of the **backstop** with an acceptable indefinite solution. Instead of staying temporarily in the **customs union** the compromise included a **free trade agreement**, **mutual recognition** of standards, some customs facilitation, and promise not to place border infrastructure. The proposal also called for a longer transition period. The customs facilitation would rely on technological solutions away from the Irish border. Plan B dealt with the situation where the backstop could not be renegotiated. The UK would unilaterally guarantee EU **citizens' rights**, but offered a reduced financial deal as well as a "standstill" trade agreement (no tariffs, no quotas, no new barriers) during an extended implementation period. Plan B has also been seen as a **managed no deal**. The EU did not like the proposal. They did not want to reopen the Withdrawal Agreement and dismissed the idea of a technological solution.

MANAGED NO DEAL. The idea of a managed no deal is focused on using the transition, or implementation, period to prepare for a situation where there is no common agreement on the future relationship at the end of the **transitions period** set for the end of 2020, but possibly extended.

MANDATE. A mandate authorizes somebody to do something. In the **European Union** (EU) the **Commission** often negotiates based on a mandate from the **Council**, that is, the member states. In the **Brexit** negotiations a chief negotiator was appointed specifically for the Brexit negotiations, namely, **Michel Barnier**. Similarly, the **United Kingdom** (UK) negotiators had a mandate based on instructions from the UK government.

MACMILLAN, HAROLD (1894–1986). Harold Macmillan, British Conservative politician, was prime minister from 1957 to 1963. It was during his tenure that the **United Kingdom** (UK) first applied for membership in the **European Communities** (EC). French president **Charles de Gaulle** vetoed this first application on 29 January 1963. Macmillan retired from politics in October 1963. It was left to Prime Minister **Edward Heath** to take the UK into the EC in 1973.

MAJOR, JOHN (1943–). John Major, Conservative British politician, replaced **Margaret Thatcher** as prime minister on 28 November 1990 in the run-up to the **Treaty of Maastricht** negotiations. As Chancellor of the Exchequer, he had brought the British pound into the Exchange Rate Mechanism (ERM) of the **European Monetary System** (EMS), so he was expected to be more pro-integration than Margaret Thatcher. However, he largely continued her policies, given the domestic constraints. In the Treaty of Maastricht negotiations, he insisted on removing the references to **federalism**. The **United Kingdom** (UK) did not accept the **social policy** chapter and got an **opt-out**. Similarly, the UK got an opt-out from the third stage of **Economic and Monetary Union** (EMU), when the single currency would be introduced. Nor would the UK take part fully in **Justice and Home Affairs** (JHA) cooperation. In 1994, Major vetoed the appointment of Belgian prime minister Jean-Luc Dehaene as **Commission** president because he was too much of a federalist. John Major's party lost the parliamentary elections to the **Labour Party** in 1997 and was replaced as prime minister by **Tony Blair** on 2 May 1997. He retired from politics in 2001.

MAY, THERESA (1956–). Theresa May became British prime minister after the resignation of **David Cameron** in the wake of the **Brexit referendum** in June 2016. She had served as Home Secretary 2010–2016 and had been a **Member of Parliament** (MP) since 1997. Although she had supported the **Remain** side in the referendum, she appointed many leading **Brexiteers** to her cabinet, including **Boris Johnson** as Foreign Secretary, **David Davis** as Brexit Secretary, and **Liam Fox** as International Trade Secretary. On 18 April 2017 she announced that she would seek to hold an early general election on 8 June (she needed a two-thirds majority in the **UK Parliament** to call the election, which she got). She had hoped that the election would give her a larger majority in the Parliament, but the result of the elections was a hung parliament, which required her to make a deal with the Northern Irish **Democratic Unionist Party** (DUP). The deal included £1 billion extra public funding for **Northern Ireland**. Her weakened support in the Parliament was to become an important reason for her problems getting an agreement with the **European Union** (EU) accepted. Her **Chequers plan** in July 2018 led to resignations, including Brexit Secretary David Davis, who was replaced by **Dominic Raab**. After an agreement was finally reached with the **European Union** (EU) in November 2018, Dominic Raab resigned and was in turn replaced by **Stephen Barclay**. A vote scheduled for December 2018 was postponed till January 2019. The first **meaningful vote** on the agreement took place on 15 January 2019. The government was defeated by 432 votes to 202, the largest majority against a UK government in history. Another prime minister might have resigned in such a situation, but May continued stubbornly. After securing some concessions from the EU (a joint interpretative instrument, inter alia, mentioning work on alternative arrangements for the backstop) a second meaningful vote led to a second defeat on 12 March, 242 votes in favor and 391 against. Finally, a third meaningful vote took place on 29 March, where the political declaration had been removed from the package. This time the main part of the deal was defeated by 286 in favor and 344 against. The **Labour Party** leader Corbyn called for her resignation, and after some internal politics in the Conservative Party Theresa May announced on 24 May that she would resign as party leader on 7 June. She resigned on 24 July after the party had agreed on Boris Johnson as her replacement as party leader and prime minister.

Teresa May, UK Prime Minister (2016–2019), and Jean-Claude Juncker, President of the European Council (2014–2019). *Source*: Courtesy of the European Union.

MEANINGFUL VOTE. At the outset it was a little unclear what role the **United Kingdom (UK) Parliament** would have in connection with the **Withdrawal Agreement** with the **European Union** (EU). A promise was given in October 2016 that the Parliament would have a vote. To get a clarification, negotiations took place with a group of pro-EU Conservative MPs, led by Dominic Grieve, which led to Section 13 of the Withdrawal Bill, which gave the Parliament a "meaningful vote" on the agreement. It set out four conditions: (1) The documents and an associated statement have been published. (2) "The negotiated Withdrawal Agreement and the framework for the future relationship have been approved by a resolution of the House of Commons on a motion moved by a minister of the Crown." (3) A subsequent debate has taken place in the House of Lords, and (4) Parliament has passed legislation to implement the Withdrawal Agreement. This gave the Parliament a strong role, indeed a decisive role, in the ratification of the Withdrawal Agreement.

While **Theresa May** was prime minister there were three meaningful votes in the Parliament in which she failed to get support for her deal: 18 January 2019: Parliament vote against 432–202; 12 March 2019: Parliament voted against 391–242; and 29 March: Parliament rejected the Withdrawal Agreement without the Political Declaration 344–286. Eventually Prime Minister **Boris Johnson** used a different approach to do away with the need for a meaningful vote, namely, implementing legislation in the form of the **Withdrawal Agreement Act**, which passed on 20 December 2019 at second reading by 358–234. This happened after the 12 December 2019 General Election, which had given Johnson a large majority in the Parliament. This legislation received Royal assent on 23 January 2020, and the UK could leave the **European Union** (EU) on 31 January 2020.

MEMBER OF EUROPEAN PARLIAMENT (MEP). Members of the **European Parliament** (EP) are usually referred to as MEPs.

MEMBER OF PARLIAMENT (MP). Members of the **United Kingdom (UK) Parliament**, especially House of Commons, are usually referred to as MPs. But MPs can also refer to members of other national parliaments.

MERKEL, ANGELA (1954–). Angela Merkel has been chancellor of Germany since 2005. She was the leader of the center-right Christian Democratic Union (CDU) from 2000 to 2018. Thanks to Germany's weight in the world and the **European Union** (EU) and her own political skills she has become one of the most influential women in the EU and the world. Although born in Hamburg she grew up in East Germany where her father was a Lutheran clergyman. She obtained a doctorate in quantum chemistry in 1986. She entered politics after the reunification of Germany in 1990. As a member of the **European Council** she has been very influential in EU decision-making, including the financial and **immigration** crises. In connection with **Brexit** she has spoken out against a no-deal scenario but not interfered with the **Commission**'s handling of the negotiations led by **Michel Barnier**.

MICHEL, CHARLES (1975–). Charles Michel is a Belgian politician. He became president of the **European Council** on 1 December 2019, taking over that position from **Donald Tusk**. He was prime minister of Belgium from 2014 to 2019.

MOGHERINI, FEDERICA (1973–). Federica Mogherini was appointed to become the **European Union's** (EU) **High Representative of the Union for Foreign Affairs and Security Policy** to replace Catherine Ashton from 1 November 2014. She had been foreign minister of Italy since February 2014. In the EU context, she counted as a socialist, representing Italy's Democratic Party. Her relatively short governmental experience was one of the shortcomings pointed out in the run-up to the appointment, and some saw her as relatively accommodating toward Russia, which led to opposition to her appointment initially from Central and Eastern Countries (CEECs). However, with gender, political affiliation, and geography being among the factors that counted in the nomination of the new top officials she fitted in. **Donald Tusk**, a center-right politician from Poland, was appointed as the new president of the **European Council** at the same time, so from now on the CEECs were also represented at the top. **Jean-Claude Juncker**, Christian Democrat from Luxembourg, had previously been elected as the next president of the **European Commission**. She was strongly supported for the job by Prime Minister Matteo Renzi, whose party had a landslide victory in the Italian elections to the **European Parliament** (EP) in May 2014. She was followed by **Josep Borrell** from Spain, another socialist, from 1 December 2019.

MONNET, JEAN (1888–1979). Jean Monnet is arguably the most important person among the Founding Fathers of the **European Union** (EU). He thought out the strategy behind the **Schuman Declaration** in 1950, proposed it to a politician who could deliver, Robert Schuman, and helped implement it as chairman of the **intergovernmental conference** (IGC) that drafted the **Treaty of Paris** which established the first European Community, the **European Coal and Steel Community** (ECSC) from 1952. Further, he was the first president of the ECSC's **High Authority**, the independent executive set up to drive the process.

Monnet was a self-taught man. He learned by doing. He left school when he was 16 years old and started working for his family's cognac company, traveling widely in France and **Canada**, to sell cognac. During both the First and Second World Wars, he worked to coordinate the efforts of the Allies, in London and in the **United States** (U.S.). In 1919, at the age of 31, he became deputy secretary general of the League of Nations where the intergovernmental decision-making soon left him disillusioned, so he left in 1923 and returned to business, rescued the family company, worked in finance in the U.S., and was a consultant in Sweden and China. After the Second World War Monnet was asked to head the French *Commissariat general au Plan,* which set investment targets and made funds available to basic industries. He concluded that reindustrialization of Germany was inevitable. He saw a French interest in working together with Germany to mutual advantage, making sure, inter alia, that coal and iron ore were available in both countries. There was also the problem of avoiding the cartelization of coal and steel industries in the Ruhr district in Germany. These problems could be solved by joint action at the international level. Monnet further believed that a special kind of institutions were required. Common institutions should make binding law. The institutions should be independent. He did not believe in intergovernmental cooperation where a "no" from one state could stop progress. In other words, institutions should be supranational. At the same time, he was pragmatic. It was a question of finding workable solutions to real problems. A federal arrangement was the goal. However, it had to be achieved gradually by concrete steps that would create solidarity among the participating countries. These ideas are all very visible in the Schuman Declaration of 9 May 1950.

After the defeat in 1954 of the **European Defence Community** (EDC) treaty, which Monnet also had inspired, he stepped down as President of the **High Authority**. He created the Action Committee for the United States of Europe (ACUSE), where he brought together representatives from political parties and interest groups, in an effort to lobby for further integration.

MOST-FAVORED NATION (MFN). Most-favored nation (MFN) treatment is one of the most central concepts in the **General Agreement on Tariffs and Trade** (GATT), which is now part of the **World Trade Organization** (WTO). It requires a member of the WTO to extend tariff reductions negotiated with another WTO member to all WTO members, except for **free trade agreements** (FTAs) and **customs unions**.

MULTIANNUAL FINANCIAL FRAMEWORK (MFF). The practice of adopting a Multiannual Financial Framework (MFF) goes back to the first

Jacques Delors plan (Delors I, 1988–1992) adopted in 1988, and the second Delors plan (Delors II, 1993–1999). The next one was part of Agenda 2000 (2000–2006). Then followed an MFF for 2007–2013, and then the current MFF, 2014–2020. Prior to Delors I there were nearly annual battles about the **budget**. The MFF, which is itself controversial and require difficult negotiations, has made the annual budget negotiations easier, because the MFF gives certain parameters. The **Treaty of Lisbon** has made the MFF a legally binding act. It is adopted as a **Council regulation** with the **consent** of the **European Parliament** (EP).

MUTUAL RECOGNITION. Mutual recognition has become an important principle in the **internal market.** The **European Court of Justice** (ECJ) in the famous 1979 *Casis de Dijon Case* first established the principle. When there is mutual recognition a product produced legally and sold legally in one member state can also be sold in another member state. This way different national product standards do not become **non-tariff barriers** (NTBs) to trade. Therefore, the French liquor Casis de Dijon can be sold in Germany even if it did not have the alcohol content expected in liquor by German law. This principle reduces the need for establishing common European standards and facilitates trade. Questions of mutual recognition are increasingly also getting on the international trade agenda, and can be expected to become an issue in the negotiations about the future relationship between the **European Union** (EU) and the **United Kingdom** (UK).

N

NATIONAL TREATMENT. National treatment is an important principle in international trade law. Article 3 of the **General Agreement on Tariffs and Trade** (GATT) requires that imports be treated no less favorably than the same or similar domestically produced goods once they have passed customs. Article 17 of the **General Agreement on Trade in Services** (GATS) deals with national treatment for services, and Article 3 of the **Trade-Related Aspects of Intellectual Property Rights** (TRIPS) deals with national treatment of intellectual property protection.

NEO-FUNCTIONALISM. Neo-functionalism was the integration theory developed in the 1950s especially by American political scientists Ernst Haas and Leon Lindberg, starting with Haas' *The Uniting of Europe* (1958). A central concept was that of spillover, suggesting that there are certain built-in forces once integration gets started. Supranational institutions were also considered important. When French president **Charles de Gaulle** was able to put brakes on integration in the 1960s scholars wondered what happened with spillover. Lindberg and Stuart Scheingold then developed the theory to include other factors, such as leadership, bargaining exchanges, and actor socialization. Neo-functionalism dominated the early years but went out of fashion in the 1970s when the energy crisis and the first **enlargement** had negative effects for European integration. The theoretical debate resumed in the 1980s when the **Single European Act** (SEA) gave integration a new momentum. Although at first **liberal intergovernmentalism** became the center of the debate, a number of other theories were offered by various scholars. Among these, historical institutionalism resembles neo-functionalism in many ways.

NO-BREXIT SCENARIO. In the no-Brexit scenario the **United Kingdom** (UK) decides to stay in the **European Union** (EU), either by Parliamentary vote or a second **referendum**. Given that **Brexit** took place on 31 January 2020 this scenario is now excluded.

NO-DEAL SCENARIO. In a no-deal scenario the **United Kingdom** (UK) leaves without a **withdrawal agreement** or an agreement on future relations at the end of the **transition period**. After **Brexit** on 31 January 2020 the question is whether the UK will reach an agreement with the **European Union** (EU) on future relations before the end of the transition period initially set at the end of 2020, but which can be extended. Without an agreement, trade relations will revert to the rules of the **World Trade Organization** (WTO). This will include **tariffs** and border controls. High tariffs may include 36 percent for dairy products, 16 percent for cereals, 10 percent for motor vehicles, and 9 percent for meat.

NON-TARIFF BARRIERS TO TRADE (NTBs). As the **European Economic Community** (EEC) set out to create a **customs union**, it abolished tariffs and quantitative restrictions among the member states. However, a number of non-tariff barriers to trade remained in the form of product standards and various domestic regulations. The **internal market** program of the 1980s was very much about getting rid of NTBs. Today NTBs are also on the international trade agenda. As international trade negotiations have reduced tariffs, NTBs are becoming relatively more important and costly for international trade. Some of the **European Union's** (EU) recent bilateral trade negotiations, including with South Korea, **Canada,** and Japan, include efforts to reduce NTBs. NTBs will also be an issue in future relations between the **United Kingdom** (UK) and the EU. *See also* COMMON COMMERCIAL POLICY (CCP); WORLD TRADE ORGANIZATION (WTO).

NORTHERN IRELAND. Northern Ireland is a constituent part of the **United Kingdom** (UK), together with **England**, **Scotland,** and **Wales**. Before 1920 the whole of **Ireland** was part of the United Kingdom (UK), but then the main southern part of the island became independent as the **Republic of Ireland**. The history of Northern Ireland has been marked by sectarian violence led by the Irish Republican Army (IRA), which was fighting for a united Ireland. In 1969 the IRA split into the Official IRA and the Provisional IRA, the former rejecting violence, the latter continuing as an armed force until 2005, when it announced that the military campaign was over. Apart from IRA the main political groups are the **Democratic Unionist Party** (DUP), formed in 1971 by Ian Paisley, a Protestant preacher; the **Social Democratic and Labour Party** (SDLP), working for reunification through democratic means; and **Sinn Féin**, working for a united Ireland free from British rule and British presence. Between 1968 and 1998 sectarian violence, called "The Troubles," led to more than 3,500 deaths. On 10 April 1998 the parties reached the Belfast Agreement, also known as the

Good Friday Agreement, which restored self-government in the form of a 108-member Assembly, the Northern Ireland Assembly, and a power-sharing government. It was reduced in size to 90 members in 2017 in connection with an election, where the DUP won 28 seats and Sinn Féin 27 seats. In January 2020 the Northern Irish legislators formed a government for the first time since 2017 with Arlene Foster as First Minister. The previous government had collapsed in 2017. The UK **Withdrawal Agreement** reached in 2019 by Prime Minister **Boris Johnson** with the **European Union** (EU) included a unilateral UK declaration on "**Democratic consent** in Northern Ireland." The Northern Ireland Assembly will vote every four years whether certain parts of the Withdrawal Agreement shall continue to apply in Northern Ireland, starting four years after the **transition period**.

NORWAY. Norway is a relatively young nation, having had a union with Sweden from 1814 to 1905, and previously from 1523 been ruled by Danish kings. After the Second World War, it joined the North Atlantic Treaty Organization (NATO) and the Council of Europe in 1949. In 1960, it became a member of the **European Free Trade Association** (EFTA). When the **United Kingdom** (UK) decided to seek membership of the **European Community** (EC) in 1961 Norway decided to follow the British lead. However, **enlargement** was blocked by French president **Charles de Gaulle**, first in 1963 and again in 1967. Eventually membership negotiations started after **George Pompidou** had become president of France, replacing Charles de Gaulle. The accession treaty that was negotiated was put to a **referendum** in September 1972, where a majority of Norwegian voters rejected membership by a 53.6 percent "No" vote. Membership was replaced by a **free trade agreement** (FTA) with the EC, and Norway remained an EFTA member. The EC's **internal market** plan in the 1980s led to negotiations between EFTA countries and the EC about the creation of a **European Economic Area** (EEA), which would give EFTA countries access to the EU's internal market, short of membership in the EC. However, as the Cold War ended, the formerly neutral EFTA countries, Austria, Finland, Sweden, and **Switzerland**, decided to apply for EC membership. Therefore, Norway applied again in November 1992. After conclusion of another accession treaty, the Norwegian people again voted "no" to EU membership in March 1994. The EEA had entered into force that year with all EFTA countries except Switzerland, where it had been rejected in a referendum in 1992. It also meant that the Swiss application for EC membership was put on hold. From 1 January 1995 Austria, Finland, and Sweden joined the EU, and Norway was left in the EEA together with Iceland and Lichtenstein as well as in EFTA, where Switzerland remained a member. In the referendums the capital city Oslo voted "yes" to membership, but most of the country voted "no." The **Common Fisheries Policy** (CFP) and the **Common Agricultural Policy** (CAP) were among the issues. Partly because of important offshore oil and natural gas resources, Norway has had impressive economic growth in recent years, becoming one of the richest countries in the world in per capita terms. While not in the EU Norway does take part in the **Schengen agreement** since 1996 (as does Iceland), because of a preexisting Nordic Passport Union.

NORWAY MODEL. The Norway model refers to the agreement that **Norway** has with the **European Union** (EU). It gives Norway as well as Iceland and Lichtenstein access to the **internal market**, which means **free movement** of goods, **services**, capital, and people, via the so-called **European Economic Area** (EEA). It also includes some cooperation in other policy areas, but it does not include the **Common Commercial Policy** (CCP), **Common Agricultural Policy** (CAP), or **Common Fisheries Policy** (CFP). So, Norway, which is also a member of the **European Free Trade Association** (EFTA), can freely negotiate trade agreements with other countries. There is cooperation during the process of preparing new policies, but Norway is not present when the **Council** and **European Parliament** (EP) make final decisions. It gives some economic benefits, but arguably the lack of direct participation in decision-making can have political costs.

O

OPEN METHOD OF COORDINATION (OMC). The Open Method of Coordination (OMC) is sometimes used by the member states of the **European Union** (EU) where they cannot or are not ready to use the so-called **Community method**. OMC is about comparing best practices in specific policy areas, for instance, employment. Goals are set. Reports are prepared. Discussion take place. The hope is that there will be a learning process where member states improve their policies in areas where they still have competence. OMC has been the main method used in the Lisbon Strategy and now Europe 2020. The results have not been impressive. Some member states, for instance, have had problems adopting the structural reforms, including labor market reforms that could contribute to growth and job creation.

OPT-OUT. The general policy in the **European Union** (EU) is that all member states must take part in the ***acquis communautaire***, at best getting some transition period when they join. However, a few members have succeeded getting opt-outs, that is, not taking part in certain policies, usually in connection with treaty negotiations where all members can block a new treaty. Opt-outs usually take the form of protocols to the treaty. The practice mostly started with the **Treaty of Maastricht**, where the **United Kingdom** (UK) and Denmark got formal, de jure opt-outs from the third phase of **Economic and Monetary Union** (EMU), which meant that they were not obliged to take part in the single currency, the euro. Legally speaking Sweden does not have a similar opt-out, but after a negative **referendum** concerning Swedish participation in the euro in September 2003 the country has a de facto opt-out. The second policy area with opt-outs is **Justice and Home Affairs** (JHA), where the UK, **Ireland**, and Denmark got opt-outs in the Treaty of Maastricht. As long as JHA cooperation was intergovernmental Denmark could take part. Once it became supranational the opt-out would take effect. When parts of JHA, asylum, **immigration**, and judicial cooperation in civil matters, were moved from the EU's third pillar to the first pillar by the **Treaty of Amsterdam** Denmark could not take part in these policies. With the abolishment of the EU's pillar structure by the **Treaty of Lisbon** all JHA has become "communautarized," so Denmark cannot take part in police and judicial cooperation in criminal matters. However, the Treaty of Lisbon opens the way for Denmark to adopt an opt-in arrangement in the future, much like the arrangement the UK and Ireland have. A referendum on such opt-in took place on 3 December 2015, where the Danes voted no to an opt-in arrangement, which would have included Denmark opting into 22 existing regulations, including the **European Police Office (Europol)**, the latter considered most important.

At Maastricht, the UK also got an opt-out from the **Social Policy** chapter introduced by the new treaty. The treaty had two protocols, one where the UK was given the opt-out, and another one where the 11 other members committed themselves to develop a European social policy. At the time of the **Treaty of Amsterdam** in 1997 the new **Labour Party** government of **Tony Blair** ended this opt-out.

ORDINARY LEGISLATIVE PROCEDURE (OLP). The ordinary legislative procedure is the name given in the **Treaty of Lisbon** to what used to be called co-decision. It was originally introduced by the **Treaty of Maastricht**, mostly for **internal market** legislation. (It was then referred to as Article 189b procedure.) Its application has been extended to new policy areas since then, until the Treaty of Lisbon, where it becomes the most common procedure. Under this procedure, the **Council** of Ministers and the **European Parliament** (EP) are on par in the legislative process. They both have to agree before the legislation in question can be adopted. If the two side have problems agreeing, a conciliation committee can be established, with equal representation from both sides.

OSBORNE, GEORGE (1971–). George Osborne served as Chancellor of the Exchequer under Prime Minister **David Cameron** from 2010 to 2016. He was a **Member of Parliament** (MP) from 2001 to 3 May 2017. In the run-up to the **Brexit referendum** in 2016 he supported the Remain position of Cameron. When **Theresa May** became prime minister after Cameron's defeat in the referendum and resignation, she sacked Osborn, who became a backbencher until he stepped down at the 2017 general election. He then became editor of the *London Evening Standard.*

P

PARLIAMENT OF THE UNITED KINGDOM. The United Kingdom (UK) Parliament is a bicameral legislature consisting of the **House of Commons** and the **House of Lords**. The House of Commons has 650 **Members of Parliament** (MPs) elected directly by the UK public. They consider and propose new laws. They can scrutinize government policies by asking questions either in the Commons Chamber or in Committees. The House of Lords is independent from but complements the work of the elected House of Commons. It has about 800 members, among which there are 90 hereditary peers, the remaining members being appointed by the monarch on the advice of the prime minister or House of Lords appointments commission. The House of Lords scrutinizes bills that have been approved by the House of Commons. It can delay bills and force the Commons to reconsider a bill, but it cannot normally prevent bills from becoming laws.

PARTNERSHIP AND COOPERATION AGREEMENTS (PCAs). Since the end of the Cold War and the collapse of the Soviet Union the **European Union** (EU) has concluded ten Partnership and Cooperation Agreements (PCAs) with Russia and the following countries in Eastern Europe, the Southern Caucuses, and Central Asia: Armenia, Azerbaijan, Georgia, Kazakhstan, the Kyrgyz Republic, Moldova, **Ukraine**, Uzbekistan, and Tajikistan. The aim of these PCAs is to provide for political dialogue, support for strengthening democracy, and development of economies, including transition to market economy and encouragement of trade and investment. The countries in Eastern Europe and the Southern Caucuses are now (since 2004) also supported through the European Neighborhood Policy (ENP), namely, Armenia, Azerbaijan, Georgia, Moldova, and Ukraine.

***PASSERELLE* CLAUSE.** A *passerelle* clause is a clause in the treaties that allows the **European Council** or the **Council** of Ministers to change the decision-making in a more integrationist direction by replacing unanimity with **qualified majority voting** (QMV) or by introducing co-decision—now **ordinary legislative procedure** (OLP)—with the **European Parliament** (EP) without going through the normal treaty reform procedures. The use of a *passerelle* clause always requires unanimity and possibly the approval of the EP. There have been specific *passerelle* clauses since the **Treaty of Maastricht** in a number of policy areas, including **Common Foreign and Security Policy** (CFSP), the **Multiannual Financial Framework** (MFF), **social** and employment **policy**, and **Justice and Home Affairs** (JHA). These are areas where the member states have hesitated to move to QMV or co-decision, but wanted to leave open the possibility at a later stage. The Treaty of Lisbon has introduced a general, "horizontal" *passerelle* clause (Art. 48(7) TEU) allowing the European Council by unanimity to move to OLP and QMV where that method does not currently apply. It will need the **consent** of the EP and the move can be blocked by a national parliament if it objects within six months of being notified.

PETERSBERG TASKS. The **Treaty of Maastricht**, which included defense policy in the **Common Security and Defense Policy** (CFSP), delegated the development of the European defense policy to the **Western European Union** (WEU). At a **Council** of Ministers meeting of the WEU at Petersberg outside Bonn in Germany in June 1992 it was decided that military units from the WEU member states could be employed for

1. humanitarian and rescue tasks,
2. peacekeeping tasks, and
3. Tasks of combat forces in crisis management, including peacemaking.

These Petersberg Tasks were subsequently mentioned explicitly in the **Treaty of Amsterdam** as defining the EU's defense policy on suggestion of Finland and Sweden. By implication the EU's defense policy dealt with soft security issues, not collective defense, which remained the prerogative of the North Atlantic Treaty Organization (NATO). However, in 1999, after the Franco-British summit in **Saint Malo** in December 1998, the EU decided to develop an autonomous defense policy, the **European Security and Defense Policy** (ESDP). This made the WEU superfluous. This development was partly confirmed by the **Treaty of Nice**, and the latest **Treaty of Lisbon** has a more detailed section on what is now called the **Common Security and Defense Policy** (CSDP). The scope of the Petersberg tasks has been extended to include joint disarmament operations, military advice and assistance tasks, conflict prevention, and post-conflict stabilization. Beyond that, the Treaty of Lisbon also included a mutual defense clause.

PASSPORTING. Passporting is the foundation of the **European Union** (EU) **internal market** for **financial services**. Banks and financial services companies in the EU and the **European Economic Area** (EEA) can operate freely in the internal market. There is a single rulebook for financial services, not available for firms based outside the EU and EEA. Actually, there are nine different passports, each covering a different sort of financial service, such as core banking services (lending and deposit taking), market services (sales and trading), asset management, payments services, and electronic money services. Each of these passports is based on a particular EU directive or regulation. These passports are not available to third-country firms, which means a disadvantage for British banks and other financial service firms after **Brexit**, depending on which solution may be found in the negotiations about the future relationship between the EU and the **United Kingdom** (UK) after the end of the **transition period**. Short of the UK deciding to take part in the EEA, which seems unlikely, the best would probably be some agreement concerning "equivalence" of standards.

PHASED APPROACH. When the **Brexit** negotiations started with the **United Kingdom** (UK) the **European Union** (EU) insisted on a phased approach in the guidelines adopted by the **European Council** on 29 April 2017. The first phase, expected to be from June to December 2017, would deal with withdrawal issues, where three issues were singled out: the exit or **divorce bill** (financial settlement), **citizens' rights,** and the **Irish border**. The second phase, originally expected to last from January to June 2018, would deal with other issues of the **Withdrawal Agreement**, including also discussions about the future relationship as required by **Article 50 TEU**, but which could only be finalized after the UK had become a third country. The third phase, the **transition period**, would follow after Brexit, and the early idea was that it would last from 31 March 2019 to the end on 2020. Since Prime Minister **Theresa May** did not succeed in getting the Withdrawal Agreement she concluded in November 2018 accepted in time, extensions followed, first till 22 May 2019, then till 31 October 2019, and finally till 31 January 2020. It was left to the new prime minster **Boris Johnson**, to negotiate another Withdrawal Agreement in October 2019, which was accepted by a new Parliament after a general election on 10 December 2019 so that Brexit could take place on 31 January 2020. This meant a much-reduced transition period till the end of 2020, but with the possibility of an extension by either 12 or 24 months. Such extension has to take place before 1 July 2020.

PILLARS. The **European Union** (EU) created by the **Treaty of Maastricht** in 1992 had three pillars: the **European Community** (EC), the **Common**

Foreign and Security Policy (CFSP), and **Justice and Home Affairs** (JHA) cooperation. The reason for the pillar structure was a differentiation in decision-making rules in the three pillars. The first pillar used the so-called **Community method**, under which the **Commission** usually had an exclusive right of initiative, many decisions in the **Council** of Ministers could be taken by a **qualified majority vote** (QMV), and the **European Court of Justice** (ECJ) had jurisdiction to judge cases and make binding decisions. The second and third pillars, on the other hand, were intergovernmental. The member states were the dominating actors and decisions normally required unanimity. The Commission played a more marginal role, and the ECJ was largely excluded. The **Treaty of Lisbon** has now abolished the pillar structure. The three pillars are merged into one single structure, but with CFSP retaining intergovernmental decision-making procedures. Therefore, the merging of the pillars had greatest effect for JHA, where the Community method is now applied, even if the term "European Community" is no longer used in the treaty.

PLAID CYMRU–the Party of Wales. Plaid Cymru–the Party of Wales is a social-democratic Welsh political party, which advocates Welsh independence from the **United Kingdom** (UK) but supports Wales staying in the **European Union** (EU). It holds 4 of the 40 Welsh seats in the **UK Parliament** and 10 of 60 seats in the **Welsh Parliament**. It won one seat in the **European Parliament** (EP) election in May 2019, which was vacated on **Brexit day**, 31 January 2020.

POLITICAL DECLARATION. The political declaration is a nonbinding document attached to the **Withdrawal Agreement**. It seeks to set out a framework for the future relationship between the **European Union** (EU) and the **United Kingdom** (UK). A first version was included with the agreement reached by **Theresa May** in November 2018, and a revised document was included with the agreement **Boris Johnson** reached with the EU in October 2019. When the UK government published the October 2019 agreement it stated that it had the "ambition to conclude an ambitious, broad, deep and flexible partnership across trade and economic cooperation with the EU, with a free trade agreement with the EU at its core, alongside agreements on security and other areas of cooperation."

POLICE AND JUDICIAL COOPERATION IN CRIMINAL MATTERS. Police and Judicial Cooperation in Criminal Matters was the part of **Justice and Home Affairs** (JHA) cooperation, which stayed in the third pillar of the **European Union** (EU) when the other areas started to be moved to the first pillar under the **Community method** by the **Treaty of Amsterdam** in 1999. Police and Judicial Cooperation in Criminal Matters stayed as intergovernmental cooperation at the time because it was considered too sensitive for supranational decision-making. However, by the time of the **Treaty of Lisbon**, 10 years later, it was moved under the Community method in connection with the abolition of the pillar structure. *See also* EUROPOL.

POLITICAL AND SECURITY COMMITTEE (PSC). The Political and Security Committee (PSC) is a committee of member state officials at the ambassadorial level dealing with the **Common Foreign and Security Policy** (CFSP), including the **Common Security and Defence Policy** (CSDP). It is based in Brussels and meets twice weekly. It replaced the previously existing Political Committee, which had met less frequently, after the development of the **European Security and Defense Policy** (ESDP) was decided in 1999. The Helsinki meeting of the **European Council** in December that year established it as an interim body. It was the made permanent at the Nice European Council in December 2000 and formalized by a **Council** decision in 2001. Since the establishment of the **European External Action Service** (EEAS) in 2010, an EEAS official appointed by the **High Representative of the Union for Foreign Affairs and Security Policy** has chaired it. The PSC gives guidance to and receives advice from the European Union Military Committee (EUMC), the Committee for Civilian Aspects of Crisis Management (CIVCOM), and the European Union Institute for Security Studies (EUISS). It drafts opinions for the **Foreign Affairs Council** (FAC), which are passed to the Council via the **Committee of Permanent Representatives** II (COREPER II). The Foreign Affairs Council is chaired by the High Representative of the Union for Foreign Affairs and Security Policy, who might in a crisis situation chair the PSC.

POLITICAL GROUPS IN THE EUROPEAN PARLIAMENT. The **Members of the European Parliament** (MEPs) do not sit alphabetically or in national groups but in political groups organized by political affiliation. The number of groups and their names have changed regularly in the past. Some MEPs do not belong to a political group. They are known as non-attached members, or the French term *non-inscrits* (NI). Since there are various political and financial advantages in forming a group very few members remain non-attached. To form a group 25 members are required and they must represent at least one quarter of the member states, currently seven.

After the 2014 elections, there were these seven political groups in the EP:

1. **Group of the European People's Party** (Christian Democrats) (EPP)
2. **Group of the Progressive Alliance of Socialists and Democrats** in the European Parliament (S&D)
3. **Group of the Alliance of Liberals and Democrats for Europe** (ALDE)
4. **European Conservatives and Reformists** Group (ECR)

5. **Confederal Group of the European United Left–Nordic Green Left** (GUE/NGL)
6. **Group of the Greens/European Free Alliance** (Greens/EFA)
7. **Europe of Freedom and Direct Democracy** (EFDD)

After the 2014 election the MEPs from the French anti-EU *Front National* were in the NI group, since the other groups found them too extreme. The members of the other main anti-EU group, the **United Kingdom Independence Party** (UKIP), were in the EFDD.

Since the **United Kingdom** (UK) had not concluded its **Withdrawal Agreement** in time, it had to take part in the May 2019 elections. The newly formed **Brexit Party** took 31.6 percent of the British vote and won 29 seats, followed by the **Liberal Democrats**, 16 seats, **Labour Party** 10 seats, **Greens** 7 seats, **Conservatives** 4 seats, **Scottish National Party** (SNP) 3 seats and **Plaid Cymru** 1 seat. These 70 seats were vacated on **Brexit day**, 31 January 2020

After Brexit the number of MEPs was reduced to 705 Members in the following groups:

1. Group of the European Peoples Party (EPP), 187 MEPs
2. Group of the Progressive Alliance of Socialists and Democrats in the European Parliament (S&D), 147 MEPs
3. **Renew Europe Group**, 98 MEPs
4. **Identity and Democracy** (ID), 76 MEPs
5. Group of the Greens/European Free Alliance (Greens/EFA), 67 MEPs
6. European Conservatives and Reformists (ECR), 61 MEPs
7. Confederal Group of the United Left–Nordic Green Left (GUE/NGL), 39 MEPs

There were further 29 *non-inscrits* as of 28 February 2020. The Renew Europe Group is the previous ALDE joined by French president Macron's La *République en marche*. Identity and Democracy is a new version of Europe of Nations and Freedom formed in 2015.

According to the **Lisbon Treaty** the EP shall not exceed 750 members plus the president, that is, 751 MEPs. As mentioned, the number of MEPs was reduced to 705 by February 2020, indicating that not all British seats were redistributed to the remaining 27 member states. Of the 73 UK seats 27 were redistributed. The 46 will be kept in reserve for potential future enlargements. The redistribution meant that France and Spain got five more seats, Italy and the Netherlands three, **Ireland** two, and the following countries each got one more seat: Poland, Romania, Sweden, Austria, Denmark, Slovakia, Finland,

Croatia, and Estonia. The EPP and the S&D have normally been the two biggest groups. If they agree, they can dominate the work of the EP. *See also* EUROPEAN PARLIAMENT.

POMPIDOU, GEORGES (1911–1974). Georges Pompidou was president of France from 1969, when President **Charles de Gaulle** resigned, until his death of cancer in office in 1974. He had been prime minister under de Gaulle from 1962 to 1968. While he was president, The **Hague summit** took place in December 1969. He consented to opening accession negotiations with the applicant countries, the **United Kingdom** (UK), Ireland, Denmark, and **Norway**. The summit also decided about the financing of the **Common Agricultural Policy** (CAP), to establish **European Political Cooperation** (EPC) and move toward **Economic and Monetary Union** (EMU), which led to the Werner Plan, which, however, was not implemented at the time.

PRELIMINARY RULING. European Union (EU) law is applied not only by European courts but also by national courts. If these are unsure of the interpretation of Union law, they can ask the **European Court of Justice** (ECJ), now **Court of Justice of the European Union** (CJEU), for a preliminary ruling on the Union law applicable to a specific case. After the preliminary ruling, the national court will decide on the specific case. The purpose of this system of preliminary rulings is to ensure that Union law is interpreted and applied in a uniform manner in the member states. Some of the most important decisions by the ECJ have been preliminary rulings, including the **primacy** of Union law and its **direct effect**.

PRESIDENCY OF THE COUNCIL OF THE EUROPEAN UNION. The presidency of the **Council** of Ministers rotates every six months among the member states. The presidency chairs meetings of the different Council configurations except the **Foreign Affairs Council** (FAC), which, since the entry into force of the **Treaty of Lisbon**, is chaired by the **High Representative of the Union for Foreign Affairs and Security Policy**. The presidency used also to chair meetings of the **European Council**, but since the entry into force of the Treaty of Lisbon, these meetings are chaired by the elected president of the European Council. For many years the presidency rotated in alphabetic order of the member state in its national language. However, in 1998 an order was agreed where there was an effort to have one of the larger member states among each three consecutive presidencies, known as the Troika at the time. This system had to be given up in 2004 at the time of the big **enlargement** because there were too few big member states in relation to the smaller ones.

The new agreed order takes account of diversity and geographical balance, and the Troika has now become the Trio presidency.

PRIMACY. The primacy or supremacy of **European Community** law, now Union law, was implicit in the founding treaties, but not stated explicitly. Together with **direct effect**, it is a fundamental principle of **European Union** (EU) law. It has been established in judgments by the **European Court of Justice** (ECJ), especially the ***Costa v. ENEL*** case (Case 6/64). In this case, the ECJ said that the treaties had established a legal system, which has become an integral part of the legal system of the member states. A subsequent national law incompatible with Union law cannot prevail. Union law has permanently limited the sovereign rights of the member states.

PROTOCOL ON GIBRALTAR. The **Withdrawal Agreement** between the **European Union** (EU) and the **United Kingdom** (UK) includes a protocol facilitating close cooperation between Spain and the UK in respect to Gibraltar. It has provisions on **citizens' rights** and administrative cooperation between appropriate authorities in several policy areas. *See also* GIBRALTAR.

PROTOCOL ON SOVEREIGN BASE AREAS IN CYPRUS. The **Withdrawal Agreement** between the **European Union** (EU) and the **United Kingdom** (UK) includes a protocol on the Sovereign Base Areas (SBA) in Cyprus that will protect the interests of Cypriots who live and work in the SBAs after **Brexit**. *See also* CYPRUS.

PUBLIC HEALTH. Since the **Treaty of Maastricht**, the **European Union** (EU) treaties have had an article on public health (now Art. 168 TFEU). EU action is this area shall complement national policies. Basically, the area remains a national responsibility. However, the EU is encouraging cooperation between member states in the health area as well as cooperation with third states. The purpose is to assure a high level of human health protection. Apart from adopting various measures setting standards, the EU can adopt incentive measures to protect and improve human health, especially to combat major cross-border health scourges.

PUBLIC PROCUREMENT. Public procurement has been liberalized in the **European Union's** (EU) **internal market**. Projects of a certain size, in monetary terms, must be advertised. There can be no discrimination. Any EU company can bid for public work contracts in any EU country. The purpose is to create **competition** and the best prices to the benefit of consumers and taxpayers. The results from the Uruguay Round included a Government Procurement Agreement (GPA). It was revised in 2012 and entered into force in April 2014. It is a so-called plurilateral agreement. Currently there are 20 parties to the GPA, and some other countries are negotiating accession. Many of the EU's bilateral **free trade agreements** include public procurement chapters, for instance, those with Chile, Mexico, Switzerland, and CARIFORUM (the Caribbean Cotonou countries). Public procurement, however, remains a difficult issue in international trade policy. Many governments, especially local ones, like to be able to offer work contracts to local companies, with the risk of course of creating a cozy relationship between officials and businesses prone to corruption. Public procurement, for instance, was a difficult issue in the negotiations with **Canada** about the **Comprehensive Economic and Trade Agreement** (CETA). In the end, Canada agreed to open public procurement not only on the federal level but also at the provincial and, to a large extent, city levels. It is to be expected that a future trade agreement between the EU and the **United Kingdom** (UK) will have provisions on public procurement.

Q

QUALIFIED MAJORITY VOTE (QMV). The **European Communities** (EC) established in the 1950s included provisions for some kind of majority voting. In the case of the **European Coal and Steel Community** (ECSC) it was sometimes based on coal and steel production. However, the **European Economic Community** (EEC) and the **European Atomic Energy Community** (EAEC or EURATOM) attributed a certain number of votes to each member state, the bigger ones getting more votes than the smaller ones. Among the six member states in 1958 the three big member states France, Germany, and Italy each got four votes; Belgium and the Netherlands each got two votes; and Luxembourg got one vote. That added up to 17 votes in the **Council** of Ministers, and the **Treaties of Rome** set a **qualified majority vote** (QMV) at 12 votes, when the Council voted on a proposal from the **Commission**, representing the Community interest. A blocking minority would require six votes (two large member states or one large plus Belgium or the Netherlands). This weighting of votes was changed at the time of the first **enlargement** in 1973. From now on, the four big states, including the **United Kingdom** (UK), each had ten votes, Belgium and the Netherlands each five, Denmark and Ireland three, and Luxembourg two. That added up to 58 votes, and the QMV was set at 41 votes. A blocking minority would require 18 votes. The following enlargements fitted the new members into that scheme. In 1981, Greece got five votes; in 1986, Portugal got five and Spain eight votes. In EC12 in 1986, there were then 76 votes. The QMV was set at 54 votes, and a blocking minority was 23. At the time of the 1995 enlargement, Austria and Sweden each got four votes and Finland got three. It meant 87 votes. The QMV was set at 62, meaning a blocking minority of 26. This decision was controversial. It led to the so-called Ioannina compromise, giving a minority of countries certain guarantees. Facing a future large enlargement after the end of the Cold War the bigger member states started to question the existing weighting of the votes. A big enlargement with many relatively small states would tip the balance in favor of the smaller states if the weights were not adjusted, since the existing weights meant that the smaller states were relatively overrepresented. Efforts were made to make such readjustment in the negotiations leading to the **Treaty of Amsterdam** in 1997, but failed. The **Treaty of Nice**, after long and difficult negotiations, changed the weighting. When the bargaining finished the bigger member states had 29 votes, Poland and Spain 27, and then the votes were graduated down to four for Luxembourg (and three for future member Malta). The total in the **European Union** (EU) of 27 members (EU27) after enlargement would be 345 votes, with a QMV set at 255, implying a blocking minority of 91. The member states, however, remained unhappy about this solution and decided to go for yet another reform, which first led to the negotiations of the Draft Treaty establishing a Constitution for Europe, and when it failed to be ratified, it was replaced by the **Treaty of Lisbon**, which has introduced a double majority system. From 1 November 2014, the QMV requires a majority of at least 55 percent of the member states representing at least 65 percent of the EU population. This too was controversial. The get Poland to agree a new version of the Ioannina compromise was included in the treaty. *See also* VOTING.

R

RAAB, DOMINIC (1974–). Dominic Raab is a Conservative British politician. He served as Secretary of State for Exiting the **European Union** (EU) from 8 July 2018, when he replaced **David Davis**, until 15 November 2018, when he was replaced by **Stephen Barclay**. When **Boris Johnson** became prime minister in July 2019 Dominic Raab became Secretary of State for Foreign and Commonwealth Affairs as well as First Secretary of State.

Dominic Raab, UK Minister for Brexit (2018), and Michel Barnier, EU Chief Negotiator (2016–2019). *Source*: Courtesy of the European Union.

REES-MOGG, JACOB (1969–). Jacob Rees-Mogg is a Conservative British politician. He has been a **Member of the Parliament** (MP) since 2010. He supported an electoral pact between the **Conservative Party** and the **UK Independence Party** (UKIP), and campaigned for the **Leave** side in the 2016 **referendum**. He joined the Eurosceptic **European Research Group** (ERG) and became its chairman in 2018. He supported **Boris Johnson** in the 2019 leadership contest in the party and was afterward appointed as Leader of the **House of Commons**, a position different from Speaker of the House. He is quite controversial and seen by many as a reactionary upper-class person.

REFERENDUM. A referendum is a general vote by all the people of a country for a decision on a specific question. Referendums have increasingly been used by some **European Union** (EU) member states, especially to authorize ratification of new treaties, as well as applicant countries to ratify accession treaties. The founding treaties in the 1950s were all ratified by the six participating states by parliamentary authorization. The first referendum was in France in 1972 to authorize the first **enlargement** in 1973. Three of the four applicants for membership in 1972—Denmark, **Ireland,** and **Norway**—held referendums, with positive outcome in the former two, but the Norwegian people voted "no" to membership. The **United Kingdom** (UK) did not have a referendum in 1972 before joining the **European Community** (EC) in 1973. But membership was controversial. In June 1975 the UK held a referendum on continued membership of the EC, after a so-called renegotiation by the **Labour Party** government led by **Harold Wilson**. Membership was confirmed on that occasion.

Ireland is the member state with most referendums. It requires a referendum if a new treaty affects the Irish constitution. Ireland therefore has had referendums on all major treaty reforms: the **Single European Act** (SEA), the **Treaty of Maastricht**, the **Treaty of Amsterdam**, the **Treaty of Nice**, and the **Treaty of Lisbon**. In the case of the Treaties of Nice and Lisbon the Irish first voted "no," and it took second referendums after some clarifications to get "yes" votes. In the Danish case, transfer of sovereignty requires either a 5/6th majority in the Danish Parliament or a confirming referendum. Referendums took place on the SEA, and the Treaties of Maastricht and Amsterdam. In the case of the Treaty of Maastricht the first one in June 1992 was negative: a second one in May 1993, after some **opt-outs**, was positive. The three countries that joined in 1995—Austria, Finland, and Sweden—held referendums with positive outcome. In **Norway** the people rejected membership a second time in 1994. Among the ten countries joining the EU in 2004 all except **Cyprus** held referendums. Bulgaria and Romania joining in 2007 held no referendums. Denmark and Sweden also held referendums about joining the euro in 2000 and 2003 respectively, in both cases with negative outcome. In addition, it was referendums in 2005 in France and the Netherlands that derailed the Draft treaty establishing a Constitution for Europe. Spain and Luxembourg held referendums on the Constitution with positive outcomes.

The use of referendums is controversial. Some see it as the most democratic way of making important decisions. However, researchers have noticed that people do not always vote about the issue they are supposed to vote about. In addition, some of these issues are very complex. Therefore, some people argue that such decisions are better left to elected politicians who have time to study the issues carefully before making the decisions. They see representative democracy as better than direct democracy.

The latest EU referendums include an Irish one on the Treaty on Stability, Coordination and Governance in the Economic and Monetary Union (the Fiscal Compact Treaty) in 2012 and a Danish one on the Unified Patent Court in 2014. Both had positive outcome. But in 2015 the Danes voted no to an opt-in arrangement in **Justice and Home Affairs** (JHA) in December 2015.

The latest use of a referendum relating to the EU was the **Brexit** referendum on 23 June 2016 where about 52 percent of the British electorate voted for leaving the EU, probably the most consequential referendum in the history of European integration, even if the French and Dutch referendums in 2005 rejecting the Constitutional Convention were also rather important events. But Brexit was the first case of a member state withdrawing from the EC/EU, although **Greenland**, a part of Denmark, left in 1985 after a referendum in 1982 gave a majority for such step.

REGIONAL POLICY. The **European Community** (EC) gradually developed a regional policy. It got a boost at the time of the first **enlargement**. The **European Regional Development Fund** (ERDF) was created in 1975. A further boost followed with the Mediterranean enlargements in the 1980s. The **Single European Act** (SEA) in 1986, at the time of Spanish and Portuguese memberships, added the concept of "economic and social cohesion." The so-called Delors I plan in 1988 doubled the funding for the structural funds, that is, Social, Agricultural and Regional funds. The **Treaty of Maastricht** added a Cohesion Fund specifically to assist Greece, Spain, Portugal, and Greece.

REGULATION. A regulation is a legal act which has general application and which is binding in its entirety and directly applicable in all member states (Art. 288 TFEU). It can thus be compared with a federal law. The **European Union** (EU) also adopts **directives**. They are binding as to the results to be achieved, but leave it up to the member states how to achieve those results. Finally, the EU adopts **decisions**, which are binding on those to whom they are addressed.

REGULATORY ALIGNMENT. Regulatory alignment refers to the degree to which some of the **European Union** (EU) and **United Kingdom** (UK) rules governing trade and services will be the same or similar in the future. According to the UK **Chequers plan** there would be full regulatory alignment for goods but not **services**, through a **common rulebook**. The opposite is **regulatory divergence**. *See also ACQUIS COMMUNITAIRE.*

REGULATORY DIVERGENCE. After **Brexit** the **United Kingdom** (UK) will leave the **European Union** (EU) **internal market**. The country will therefore be able to develop its own regulations. These will create regulatory divergence, which can affect trade in the future. How much divergence we will see in the future will of course depend on how much the British lawmakers will want to make their own standards and regulations different from EU standards. Obviously regulatory divergence can have some advantages, creating possibilities of adjusting to local tastes, but in a globalized and interdependent world it will also have costs. *See also ACQUIS COMMUNITAIRE.*

REMAIN CAMPAIGN. Several groups campaigned for the **United Kingdom** (UK) to remain in the European Union (EU) during the **referendum** campaign in 2016, including **Britain Stronger in Europe**. Another organization was Centre for British Influence Through Europe, including Kenneth Clarke (Conservative) and Peter Mandelson (Labour). The European Movement also campaigned for remain, as well as political party–based groups, such as Labour In for Britain and Conservatives In.

REPUBLIC OF IRELAND. Republic of Ireland is the full name of **Ireland**. Although this member state of the **European Union** (EU) is normally just called Ireland, it sometimes becomes necessary to use the full name to distinguish it from **Northern Ireland**, which is a constituent part of the **United Kingdom** (UK). *See also* IRISH BORDER.

RESEARCH AND DEVELOPMENT (R&D). Research and Development (R&D) became a preoccupation of the **European Community** (EC) in the 1980s, when there was a feeling that the EC could not compete with the **United States** (U.S.), Japan, and some other leading industrialized countries. A number of research programs were started: ESPRIT for information technology, and BRITE for industrial materials. French president François Mitterrand initiated an intergovernmental program, Eureka. In 1984, the separate EU programs were brought together in a "multiannual framework program." In addition, "research and technological development" was now included explicitly in the **Single European Act** (SEA) in 1987 as well as subsequent treaties. The framework program approach was successful and funding for research has increased substantially since 1984.

RESTE À LIQUIDER. The sum of the UK's financial commitments at the time of **Brexit**, based on the UK's share of the EU **budgets** up to the end of 2020 and continuing liabilities such as EU civil servants' pensions. Also known as the **divorce bill** or financial settlement.

S

SAINT-MALO DECLARATION. The Saint-Malo Declarations was adopted by a Franco-British summit at Saint-Malo in December 1998. In this declaration, the British prime minister **Tony Blair** and French president Jacques Chirac called for the development of an autonomous European defense policy, including military forces. With other **European Union** (EU) member states agreeing at meetings of the **European Council** in June and December 1999, this was an important event in the development of the **Common Security and Defence Policy** (CSDP).

SCHENGEN AREA/*AQUIS*. The Schengen Agreement was concluded by five of the then ten member states of the **European Community** (EC) in 1985, namely, France, Germany, and the three Benelux countries. They met in Schengen in Luxembourg at the border of France and Germany. The agreement started the gradual abolition of border controls at their common frontiers. It was followed up with the Schengen Implementing Convention in 1990. It created the Schengen Information System (SIS), a common database that allows national authorities to exchange information about individuals. The convention entered into effect in 1995. The membership of Schengen grew with Italy joining in 1990 and Austria in 1995. In the meantime, the **Treaty of Maastricht** had added **Justice and Home Affairs (JHA)** cooperation, including many of the issues on the Schengen agenda. At the time of the **Treaty of Amsterdam**, it was decided to incorporate the Schengen *acquis* into the treaty. The **United Kingdom** (UK) and **Ireland** got **opt-outs**, but also got an opt-in possibility, allowing them to joins specific parts of the cooperation. Both joined the SIS and its successors. Greece joined Schengen in 2000, and Denmark, Finland, and Sweden joined in 2001. At the same time, **Norway** and Iceland became associate members, to avoid breaking up the preexisting Nordic Passport Union. **Switzerland** got the same status in 2008 after a national **referendum**. All the states that joined the **European Union** (EU) in 2004, except **Cyprus,** have joined Schengen. The latest to join the EU, Bulgaria and Romania in 2007 and Croatia in 2013 have not yet joined Schengen. Because the Schengen cooperation has abolished border controls between the participating countries, they have strengthened controls at the common external border. This includes the introduction of a common visa for third-country nationals who still require a visa. Because of **Brexit** the UK has now left the parts of JHA that it had opted into.

SCHUMAN DECLARATION. French foreign minister Robert Schuman made the famous declaration bearing his name on 9 May 1950. He proposed to pool French and German steel and coal production and create a supranational institution called the **High Authority** open to other European countries. This was to be a gradual process: "Europe will not be made all at once, or according to a single plan. It will be built through concrete achievements which first create a de facto solidarity. The coming together of the nations of Europe requires the elimination of the age-old opposition of France and Germany." The proposed organization would make war between France and Germany "not merely unthinkable, but materially impossible." The organization would make binding decisions and it would lead to "the realization of the first concrete foundation of a European federation indispensable for the preservation of peace." The declaration also stressed the economic advantages: The High Authority would assist the modernization of production, and the supply of coal and steel would be available "on identical terms to the French and German markets, as well as to the markets of other member countries." Schuman had talked about supranational union of Europe before 1950, but **Jean Monnet**, who contributed to the drafting of the declaration, inspired the concrete plan in 1950. *See also* EUROPEAN COAL AND STEEL COMMUNITY (ECSC).

SCOTTISH NATIONAL PARTY (SNP). The Scottish National Party is the largest political party in **Scotland**. It works for an independent Scotland. Its current leader is **Nicola Sturgeon**. As of December 2019, it has 47 **Members of Parliament** in London (MPs) out of 59, and 61 Members of the Scottish Parliament (MSPs) out of 129. During the 2016 **Brexit referendum** the party supported **Remain**. In the May 2019 **European Parliament** (EP) election, the party won three seats, half of the Scottish seats. They were vacated on **Brexit day**, 31 January 2020.

SCOTTISH PARLIAMENT. *See* SCOTLAND.

SCOTLAND. Scotland is one of the four constituent parts of the **United Kingdom** (UK) together with **England**, **Wales**, and **Northern Ireland**. It existed as a sovereign state until 1707 when it became a part of the new Kingdom of Great Britain. In 1997 a **Scottish Parliament** was established through devolution. It is a unicameral legislature with 129 members. The head of the Scottish government is the First Minister of Scotland. Scotland is represented in the **UK Parliament** by 59 **members of parliament** (MPs). In September 2014 there was a **referendum** on Scottish independence, where 55 percent of the electorate voted no to independence. In the UK referendum on **European Union** (EU) membership a majority of 62 percent of Scottish voters favored **Remain**, with 38 percent voting **Leave**.

SETTLED STATUS. European Union (EU) citizens and their families who have stayed in the **United Kingdom** (UK) for five years can apply for "settled status," which will allow them to stay in the UK for as long as they want.

SINGLE EUROPEAN ACT (SEA). The Single European Act (SEA) in 1986 was the first major reform of the **European Community** (EC) treaties. The main purpose was to speed up the completion of the **internal market**. The EC had relatively quickly established a **customs union**, which abolished tariffs and quantitative restrictions on trade between the member states. However, the necessary harmonization of national legislation, establishing common European product standards, turned out to be slow because of the unanimity requirement (Art. 100 EEC). The SEA introduced a new Article 100A, which included the use of **qualified majority voting** (QMV) for much of the required harmonization, the exemptions being fiscal provisions, **free movement** of persons, and rights and interests of employed persons. The SEA set the aim of progressively establishing the internal market by 31 December 1992, and defined the internal market as "an area without internal frontiers in which the free movement of goods, persons, **services** and capital is ensured." Importantly the SEA also introduced QMV for "the working environment, as regards health and safety of workers" (Art. 118A). Other novelties were chapters on economic and social cohesion, research and technological development, and **environmental policy**. Economic and social cohesion eventually meant more money for **regional policy** through the structural funds. The SEA also increased the role of the **European Parliament** (EP) by introducing the **cooperation procedure** for internal market legislations, and the assent procedure for **association agreements** and accession treaties. Further, a separate title in the SEA included provisions on "European Co-operation in the sphere of foreign policy," which gave **European Political Cooperation** (EPC) a treaty basis. The SEA was the first treaty reform where most of the negotiations took place in an **Intergovernmental Conference** (IGC). Considered a minor reform by many observers at the time it contributed to giving European integration a new momentum in the second part of the 1980s. *See also* FOUR FREEDOMS; NON-TARIFF BARRIERS TO TRADE.

SINGLE MARKET. "Single Market" is another term for what the **Treaty of Rome** establishing the **European Economic Community** (EEC) called a "**common market**" and which later treaties, from the **Single European Act** (SEA) in 1987 and onward, have referred to as the "internal market." Iceland, Lichtenstein, and **Norway** take part in the internal market through the **European Economic Area** (EEA) agreement. To assure the free movement of goods, services, capital, and people inside the internal market several common rules and standards apply. *See also* FOUR FREEDOMS; INTERNAL MARKET.

SOCIAL CHARTER. The Council of Europe adopted a European Social Charter in 1961, but legally it was not as binding as the 1950 European Convention on Human Rights. The **European Community's** (EC) Social Charter, with the full name of the Charter on the Fundamental Rights of Workers, was adopted as a nonbinding declaration in December 1989 by all member states except the **United Kingdom** (UK). **Commission** president **Jacques Delors**, who saw it as a complement to the **internal market**, spearheaded the charter. The scope of the charter was broad, covering **freedom of movement**, living and working conditions, vocational training, health and safety, special measures for young people, the elderly, and the disabled, and the right to information, consultation, and participation in the workplace. The Commission followed up with a "Social Action Program" and efforts were made to include it in the **Treaty of Maastricht**. **Margaret Thatcher's** successor **John Major** did not accept that, so the UK got an **opt-out** in the form of a protocol to the Treaty of Maastricht, but the 11 other member states moved ahead, including the introduction of **qualified majority voting** (QMV) for aspects of social policy. In 1997, the new **Labour Party** government under **Tony Blair** rescinded the opt-out and joined the EU's social policy. When the **Charter of Fundamental Rights** was negotiated and adopted as a political document in 2000 the Social Charter was incorporated. The **Treaty of Lisbon** has now made that Charter of Fundamental Rights legally binding since its entry into force in December 2009.

SOCIAL POLICY. Social policy has been part of the European integration process since the beginning in the 1950s. The **Treaty of Rome** establishing the **European Economic Community** (EEC) actually gave a rather broad definition of the social field: employment, labor law and working conditions, basic and advanced vocational training, social security, prevention of occupational accidents and diseases, occupational hygiene, and the right of association, and collective bargaining between employers and workers (Art. 118

EEC). The **Commission** was to promote member state cooperation in these fields. The member states also agreed to promote improved working conditions and an improved standard of living for workers (Art. 117 EEC). The EEC treaty further established the European Social Fund (ESF). These provisions, however, did not produce a lot of activity for many years. During the second part of the 1980s the **Jacques Delors Commission** promoted social policy to complement the **internal market** but came up against opposition from **United Kingdom** (UK) prime minister **Margaret Thatcher**, who did not want the EC involved in social policy. A **Social Charter** was adopted in the form of a declaration in 1989. A chapter proposed in the **Treaty of Maastricht** ran into difficulties. **John Major**, who had replaced Margaret Thatcher as prime minister of the UK, continued to oppose EU social policy. In the end, the UK was offered an **opt-out** and the 11 remaining members added a protocol to the treaty where they committed themselves to further developments in the social policy area. In 1997, the new **Labour Party** government under **Tony Blair** acceded to the EU's social policy at the time of the **Treaty of Amsterdam**, which also included a new chapter on employment policy, where the union was mandated to contribute to a high level of employment. The EU can adopt incentive measures, but these measures cannot include harmonization of national laws and regulations, so it is a relatively weak chapter.

Today, according to the **Treaty of Lisbon**, social policy is split up in two groups. The **ordinary legislative procedure** (OLP) applies to many areas, but the following issues, considered more sensitive, require unanimity in the **Council**: social security and social protection of the workers, protection of workers where their employment contract is terminated, representation and collective defense of the interests of workers and employers, and conditions of employment for third-country nationals legally residing in Union territory. Further, the **European Parliament** (EP) only needs to be consulted for those areas, leaving the member states very much in control (Art. 153 TFEU). *See also* SOCIAL CHARTER.

SOFT BREXIT. A soft Brexit means a Brexit that leaves the **United Kingdom** (UK) close to the **European Union** (EU) in the future, possibly by staying in the **internal market** through a future relation resembling the **European Economic Area** (EEA), also referred to as the **Norway model**. The **Theresa May** and **Boris Johnson** governments ruled out such a close relationship. A less soft Brexit could be something like the EU's **Free Trade Agreement** with **Canada**, the **Comprehensive Economic and Trade Agreement** (CETA). How hard Brexit becomes will depend on negotiations of the future relationship during the **transition period**.

STARMER, KEIR (1962–). Keir Starmer is the new leader of the **Labour Party** after **Jeremy Corbyn** stepped down in early 2020 after the party's defeat in the UK election in December 2019. He had previously been Labour's **Brexit** spokesperson.

STRUCTURAL FUNDS. A number of funds give financial aid to the less developed regions of the **European Union** (EU). They are collectively referred to as Structural Funds. The oldest is the **European Social Fund** (ESF) established by the **Treaty of Rome** with the purpose of improving employment opportunities of workers through vocational training and promotion of mobility. In connection with the first **enlargement**, the **European Regional Development Fund** (ERDF) was created in 1975 to provide assistance for productive investment and infrastructure in the regions, including in the **United Kingdom** (UK). **The Single European Act** (SEA) in 1986 introduced the concept of "economic and social cohesion" and in 1988, as part of the so-called **Jacques Delors** I package; money for the structural funds was doubled. The **Treaty of Maastricht** created a Cohesion Fund, set up specifically to assist Greece, Spain, Portugal, and **Ireland**, and **the European Council** meeting in Edinburgh in December 1992 once again doubled the money available for the structural funds. The three main structural funds—the ESF, the ERDF, and the Cohesion Fund—received €347 billion during the seven-year multiannual financial framework (MFF) for 2007–2013. For the current MFF 2014–2020, the subheading "Economic, social and territorial cohesion" will receive up to about €325 billion out of a total of €960 billion, about a third. Direct payments to farmers will take about 29 percent.

STURGEON, NICOLA (1970–). Nicola Sturgeon is a Scottish politician. Since November 2014 she has been leader of the **Scottish National Party** (SNP) and First Minister of **Scotland**. As First Minister she chairs the Scottish Cabinet. During the **Brexit** process Sturgeon has threated a second **referendum** on Scottish independence.

SUBSIDIARITY. Subsidiarity is a principle of law in the **European Union** (EU). Although arguably implicit in the founding treaties in the 1950s, it was first mentioned as a principle for **environmental policy** in the **Single European Act** (SEA). It stated that "the Community shall take action relating to the environment to the extent to which the objectives . . . can better be attained at Community level than at the level of the individual Member States" (Art. 130 R, SEA). From the **Treaty of Maastricht**, the principle is mentioned explicitly by name. The new Article 3b stated, "In areas which do not fall within its exclusive competence, the Community shall take action, in accordance with the principle of subsidiarity, only if and in so far as the objectives of the proposed action cannot be sufficiently achieved by the Member States and can therefore, by reason of the scale or effects of the proposed action, be better achieved by the Community." What this means in practice can often be difficult to decide. Although the **European Court of Justice** (ECJ) can in principle be asked to judge whether an action is justified by the subsidiarity principle, many would say that in the end it is a political question. After the Treaty of Maastricht ratification crisis in 1992 there were efforts to clarify the principle further, but with mixed results. The **Treaty of Lisbon** has therefore decided to introduce a political check on subsidiarity, giving a special role to national parliaments. A certain number of national parliaments can now issue a "yellow card," which will require the **Commission** to take a second look at a proposal, or an "orange card," which will make it more difficult for the **Council** or **European Parliament** (EP) to adopt the proposal.

SUPRANATIONALISM. Supranationalism refers to institutional arrangements where there are autonomous institutions above the nation-states that can make binding decisions. Supranational institutions constitute an important aspect of the **European Union** (EU), where the **European Commission** represents the common interests, has a right of initiative, and can make some independent decisions, especially in the area of **competition policy**. The **Council** of Ministers can make some decisions by a **qualified majority vote** (QMV), thus overriding individual vetoes. Further, the **European Court of Justice** (ECJ), now **Court of Justice of the European Union** (CJEU), makes binding decisions. The use of supranational institutions started with the **European Communities** (EC) in the 1950s, and is sometimes referred to as the **Community method**. The alternative to supranationalism is **intergovernmentalism**. The EU also includes intergovernmental cooperation, especially in **Common Foreign and Security Policy** (CFSP) and **Common Security and Defence Policy** (CSDP). In intergovernmental cooperation, the member states remain the dominant actors. Normally decisions require unanimity. The European Commission plays a lesser role, and the Court is largely excluded. **Justice and Home Affairs** (JHA) also started as intergovernmental cooperation in the Treaty of Maastricht. Part of it was moved under the Community method by the **Treaty of Amsterdam** and the rest in the Treaty of Lisbon. The Council (of Ministers) and **European Council**—of Heads of State or Government—are the intergovernmental elements in the institutional setup.

SUPREMACY. *See* COSTA V. ENEL; EUROPEAN COURT OF JUSTICE (ECJ); PRIMACY

SWINSON, JO (1980–). Jo Swinson was leader of the pro–**European Union** (EU) **Liberal Democrats** briefly in 2019. She was a **Member of Parliament** (MP), 2005–2015, and again 2017–2019. She lost her seat in the December 2019 general election.

SWISS MODEL. Swiss model refers to the current relations **Switzerland** has with the **European Union** (EU), which include a number of bilateral agreements covering several aspects of the relations. These agreements have established a high degree of free movement between Switzerland and the EU. On a few points the model is less far reaching than the **European Economic Area** (EEA).

SWITZERLAND. Switzerland has a long tradition of neutrality, which succeeded in keeping the country out of some of Europe's major wars. It joined the **European Free Trade Association** (EFTA) in 1970, and got a **free trade agreement** (FTA) with the **European Community** (EC) in 1973 when the **United Kingdom** (UK) and Denmark left EFTA to join the EC. Participation in the **European Economic Area** (EEA) was rejected in a **referendum** in December 1992, so the membership application Switzerland had sent to the EC in May 1992 was put on hold. Instead, Switzerland has negotiated a number of bilateral agreements with the **European Union** (EU) adding up to something like the EEA, and Switzerland has also become an associate member of **Schengen** agreement. Although a relatively small country Switzerland is one of the EU's main trading partners. The Brexit debates has included references to a **Swiss model**, but it falls short on some of the UK's red lines, like no **free movement** and no contribution to the EU **budget**. There are limits on free movement of **services** between Switzerland and the EU and **financial services** are not covered.

T

TARIFF. A tariff is a tax on import or export between states. Since the **European Union** (EU) is a **customs union** it can be compared with a state. There have been efforts withing the **General Agreement on Tariffs and Trade** (GATT), now part of the **World Trade Organization** (WTO), to reduce tariffs. An important principle in GATT/WTO is the **Most Favored Nation** (MFN) treatment, which means that a WTO member negotiating tariff reduction with another member state must extend those reductions to other WTO member states. States can, however, abolish tariffs by creating a **free trade area** (FTA) or customs union, in which case MFN does not apply. If the **United Kingdom** (UK) does not negotiate a future FTA with the EU it must revert to its WTO tariffs in trade with the EU, for instance, those currently applicable with the **United States** (U.S.) or Australia. Traditionally states have had two reasons for introducing tariffs: revenue and protection. By making import more expensive a tariff can protect a domestic industry, which may be good for that industry but have costs for consumers.

TARIFF-FREE TRADE. Trade free of tariffs can be achieved through a **free trade agreement** (FTA) or **customs union**. The latter solution has been ruled out by the **United Kingdom** (UK) as a long-term solution for the UK's future relations with the EU, because that would exclude the UK from negotiating its own FTAs, possibly with the **United States** (U.S.) and other important trading partners. But an FTA would allow the UK to negotiate FTAs with other trading partners.

TAXATION. Taxation basically remains a member state competence in the **European Union** (EU). Harmonization of tax rates within the EU has mostly concerned indirect taxes that can affect the working of the **internal market**. Value-added tax (VAT) was adopted as the standard sales tax in the EU in the 1960s and 1970s, and a certain part of the VAT became one of the "own resources" of the EU's **budget**. Since taxation legislation requires unanimity in the **Council** of Ministers, it has been difficult to harmonize the rate. It was only in 1992 that the ECOFIN Council agreed that member states could have one standard rate and two reduced rates. The minimum standard rate would be 15 percent, and reduced rates would be minimum five percent. An informal maximum rate for the standard rate was set at 25 percent. Some minimum rates of excise duties for alcohol, tobacco, cigarettes, and mineral oil have also been adopted. If rates diverge too much there will be an increase in border trade, such as Danes crossing the border to Germany to buy cheaper beer and wine, for instance. Therefore, market forces can force governments to change their rates. Another area of taxation where diverging national rates can be problematic is corporate taxation, where countries setting low rates may be blamed for unfair competition in efforts to attract **foreign direct investments** (FDI). **Ireland** and **Cyprus** have rates of 12.5 percent, Germany and France above 30 percent. However, the unanimity requirement makes it difficult to harmonize these rates.

TERRORISM. The fight against terrorism among the member states of the **European Community** (EC) started as informal cooperation in 1975 through the Trevi Group of high-level officials from justice and interior ministries. The **Treaty of Maastricht** formalized it as part of **Justice and Home Affairs** (JHA) cooperation in 1993. Since the **Treaty of Amsterdam** in 1999, the EU has worked to establish an **Area of Freedom, Security and Justice** (AFSJ). What was initially intergovernmental cooperation has now become supranational cooperation after the entry into force of the **Treaty of Lisbon** in 2009. Important parts are the **Schengen** cooperation about external borders, and the police cooperation that takes place through EUROPOL forms part of the AFSJ. The 9/11 attack against the **United States** (U.S.) was an incentive for increased international cooperation against terrorism, and in Europe the 11 March 2005 attack in Madrid and 7 July 2005 attack in London increased the pressure for more intra-EU cooperation in the fight against terrorism. On 30 November 2005, the **European Union** (EU) adopted a counterterrorism strategy based on four objectives: prevention, protection, pursuit, and response. A detailed action plan has been adopted dealing with various aspects of the strategy: police cooperation, border control, visas, money laundering and financing of terrorism, European arrest warrant (EAW), and so on. In an effort to deal with the root causes of terrorism, the EU promotes democracy, dialogue, and good governance.

THATCHER, MARGARET (1925–2013). Margaret Thatcher became a member of the British Parliament in 1959. She was education secretary in the **Edward Heath** government, which took the **United Kingdom** (UK) into the **European Community** (EC) in 1973. The Heath government was defeated in the general election in 1974. In 1975, Thatcher stood against Heath in the leadership election and won. She campaigned in favor of a "yes" vote in the referendum that year on the **Labour Party** government's renegotiation of British membership. In May 1979, the **Conservative Party** returned to office under her leadership. She quickly started a fight with her European colleagues about the British contribution to the annual Community **budget**, which was solved only at the summit meeting at Fontainebleau in June 1984, where the UK got an annual budget rebate. Although in favor of the **internal market** she voted against the calling of an **Intergovernmental Conference** (IGC) to reform the treaties in June 1985, but subsequently the UK did take part in the IGC, which negotiated the **Single European Act** (SEA), which led to an increased use of **qualified majority voting** (QMV) in the **Council** of Ministers. Like the French president General **Charles de Gaulle** Margaret Thatcher favored intergovernmental cooperation, not strong supranational institutions. She also opposed **Economic and Monetary Union** (EMU), the next big issue on the agenda after the SEA. Her increasingly strident attitude toward further integration, also including the **Social Charter** adopted in 1989 by her colleagues without her support, created internal disagreements in her cabinet, including the Chancellor of the Exchequer, Nigel Lawson, and the Foreign Secretary, Geoffrey Howe. Lawson resigned in October 1989 because of disagreement on British participation in the European Exchange Rate Mechanism (ERM). Some domestic issue also contributed to her increasing unpopularity. In December 1989, she was challenged in the annual contest for party leadership. She survived, but was increasingly isolated among EC leaders as decisions were made in December 1989 to call an IGC on EMU and later in June 1990 a second IGC on Political Union, which in the end produced the **Treaty of Maastricht**. On 1 November 1990, Howe resigned as deputy prime minister and former defense secretary Michael Heseltine decided to stand as a candidate for party leadership. On 22 November, Thatcher announced her resignation. In the following leadership contest, Chancellor **John Major** won and became prime minister a few days before the start of the two IGCs in Rome on 14 December 1990. Thatcher was elevated to the **House of Lords** in June 1992 from where she opposed the ratification of the Treaty of Maastricht, contributing to what became something like a civil war in the Conservative Party.

TRADE AND COOPERATION AGREEMENT (TCA). The **European Union** (EU) can negotiate trade agreements with third countries. As long as they only include what the treaties define as part of the **Common Commercial Policy** (CCP) the EU as such can conclude the agreement. But if an agreement with a third country includes more than CCP, such as political dialogue and financial assistance, then it becomes a mixed agreement and it also has to be ratified by the member states. One such agreement is a Trade and Cooperation Agreement (TCA). The first agreements offered to the Central and Eastern European Countries (CEECs) after the end of the Cold War were TCAs. Relatively soon these countries were offered **association agreements** known as **Europe Agreements**, which took relations a step further by including common institutions.

TRADE POLICY. See COMMON COMMERCIAL POLICY (CCP).

TRADE POLICY COMMITTEE. The Trade Policy Committee is a committee of senior national officials who oversee and contribute to the making of the **European Union's** (EU) **Common Commercial Policy** (CCP). It was originally created by Article 113 in the **Treaty of Rome** establishing the **European Economic Community** (EEC) in 1958, thus originally known as the Article 113 Committee. As the **Treaty of Amsterdam** changed the article numbers the committee became the Article 133 Committee, but since the **Treaty of Lisbon** entered into force it has become the Trade Policy Committee. Its role is now outlined in Article 207 TFEU. Trade policy falls under the **Foreign Affairs Council** (FAC). There is no special Council configuration of trade ministers. This contributes to the Trade Policy Committee's special role. It assists in working out mandates for trade policy negotiations by the **Commission**, and the Commission has to consult with it during the negotiations. The national trade directors meet once a month and their deputies the three weeks in between. The committee has also established expert working groups dealing with matters such as **services**, textiles, and steel.

TRADE-RELATED ASPECTS OF INTELLECTUAL PROPERTY RIGHTS (TRIPS). The **Uruguay Round** results included an Agreement on Trade-Related Aspects of Intellectual Property Rights (TRIPS). *See also* COMMON COMMERCIAL POLICY (CCP); INTELLECTUAL PROPERTY RIGHTS (IPRs); WORLD TRADE ORGANIZATION (WTO).

TRANSATLANTIC TRADE AND INVESTMENT PARTNERSHIP (TTIP). The Transatlantic Trade and Investment Partnership (TTIP) was the name of a **free trade agreement** (FTA) being negotiated between the Obama administration and the **European Union** (EU) from 2013. As is common for FTAs, the TTIP faced opposition from affected non-competitive business interests and some nongovernmental organizations (NGOs). When Donald Trump became president of the United States (U.S.) in January 2017 the TTIP was put on hold. *See also* COMMON COMMERCIAL POLICY.

TRANSITION PERIOD. Transition period in connection with **Brexit** refers to a period of time after withdrawal, originally expected to be 29 March 2019, until 31 December 2020, that is, 21 months. According to the **withdrawal agreement** negotiated by Prime Minister **Boris Johnson** in October 2019 it runs from 31 January 2020, when Brexit took place, to 31 December 2020, that is, 11 months, if it isn't extended. During the transition period the **United Kingdom** (UK) will take part in **European Union** (EU) policies but not be represented in EU institutions. It also allows time for negotiations of the details of the new future relationship. This will allow businesses and others to prepare for the moment when the new post-Brexit rules between the UK and the EU begin. **Free movement** will continue during the transition period, as the EU wanted. The UK will be able to strike its own trade deals—although they will not enter into force before the end of the transition period. Negotiation of trade agreements normally takes a long time, so it is possible that the transition period will be extended.

TRANSPORT POLICY. The **Treaty of Paris** establishing the **European Coal and Steel Community** (ECSC) in 1952 included a short section on transport policy, and there were some efforts in the early years to improve rail links. The **Treaty of Rome** establishing the **European Economic Community** (EEC) included a more detailed section on transport policy, even introducing **qualified majority voting** (QMV) for rail, road, and inland waterways. Progress, however, was slow for two reasons: transport patterns and interests diverged among the member states and thanks to the **Luxembourg Compromise** in 1966, a "veto culture" had developed. In 1982, the **European Parliament** (EP) initiated a case before the **European Court of Justice** (ECJ) against the Council for its failure to act (Art. 175 EEC, now Art. 265 TFEU). The ECJ ruled in 1985 that the Council had failed to act (Case 13/83). Transport became an important part of the **Commission**'s White Paper on Completing the **Internal Market**, and the extension of QMV to the internal market by the **Single European Act** (SEA) helped overcome the Luxembourg Compromise. The use of QMV allowed for important progress toward a common transport policy the following years, including also sea and air transport. The internal market program largely succeeded in liberalizing the transport sector, including *cabotage*, that is, transport within member states. Common legislation has also dealt with safety and **environmental** aspects of transport as well as passengers' rights.

TREATY. A treaty is a formal agreement entered by states or international organizations under international law. The **European Union** (EU) is based on treaties and various reforms of those treaties, and the EU itself has entered into treaties with third countries (non-member states) and international organizations. Some international treaties are called conventions, like the United Nations Convention on the Law of the Sea, of which the EU is a contracting party.

TREATY OF AMSTERDAM. The Treaty of Amsterdam was the first reform treaty after the **Treaty of Maastricht,** which had established the **European Union** (EU) in 1993. The negotiations of the Treaty of Amsterdam started already in 1996 and finished in June 1997. It entered into force in 1999 after having been ratified by the then 15 member states. The treaty moved parts of the third pillar, **Justice and Home Affairs** (JHA)—namely, asylum, **immigration**, and other policies related to **free movement** of persons)—to the first **European Community** (EC) pillar, which meant a move from intergovernmental cooperation to supranational cooperation after a five-year transition period. **Police and Judicial Cooperation in Criminal Matters** remained in a slimmer third pillar. The so-called **Schengen** *acquis*, the existing legislation adopted by most member states in view of abolishing internal border controls, was incorporated by the treaty, with the **United Kingdom** (UK) and **Ireland** opting out, both retaining border controls except between them. These provisions in the Treaty of Amsterdam were contributions to the progressive establishment of an **Area of Freedom, Security and Justice** (AFSJ). The second pillar of the Union, **Common Foreign and Security Policy** (CFSP), also went through some reforms, including the creation of a Policy and Early Warning unit in the **Council Secretariat** and the creation of the new post as **High Representative of CFSP**, which was filled by Javier Solana in 1999. The treaty further included an explicit mentioning of the so-called **Petersberg Tasks** (soft security, not including collective defense) as the basic definition of the EU's **defense policy**. The treaty similarly included a new chapter on employment policy and the UK opted in on **social policy** (where the country had got an opt-out at the time of the **Treaty of Maastricht**). Efforts to reform the institutions in view of future enlargements failed. They became the main agenda points for the next reforms, the **Treaty of Nice** and the **Treaty of Lisbon**.

TREATY OF LISBON. The Treaty of Lisbon is the latest major reform of the **European Union** (EU) treaties. It followed the non-ratification of the Treaty Establishing a Constitution for Europe (commonly called the Constitutional Treaty). After the rejection of the Constitutional Treaty by **referendums** in France and the Netherlands in 2005 the EU first went through a reflection pause. But eventually the decision was to rescue as much as possible from the Constitutional Treaty in a reform treaty, which would abolish state-like symbols and not be a completely new treaty but reform of existing treaties, the way treaty reform used to take place. A very detailed mandate for an **Intergovernmental Conference** (IGC) was agreed in June 2007 during the German **Presidency**. It allowed for the working out a new treaty during the second part of 2007 under the Portuguese Presidency. It was signed in Lisbon on 13 December 2007. While roughly half the member states held or had planned a referendum on the Constitutional Treaty only **Ireland** held a referendum on the Treaty of Lisbon. Since the first referendum in 2008 was negative, it required a second referendum in 2009. After some clarifications and promises to Ireland, the second referendum on 2 October 2009 was positive and the treaty could enter into force on 1 December 2009. The Treaty of Lisbon creates the framework for the current EU in two parts: the **Treaty on European Union** (TEU) and the **Treaty on the Functioning of the European Union** (TFEU). It abolishes the pillar structure established by the **Treaty of Maastricht**. This has the greatest implications for **Justice and Home Affairs** (JHA), which now all fall under supranational cooperation. The **Common Foreign and Security Policy** (CFSP) is subject to specific rules and procedures, which are intergovernmental in nature. Efforts to improve CFSP took place by making the **High Representative of the Union for Foreign Affairs and Security Policy** a vice president of the **Commission** and Chair of the **Foreign Affairs Council** (FAC) as well as establishing a **European External Action Service** (EEAS). The newly named **Common Security and Defence Policy** (CSDP) now includes a mutual defense clause and the Petersberg tasks are extended to include disarmament, post-conflict stabilization, and fight against terrorism. The **Common Commercial Policy** (CCP) is expanded to include **foreign direct investments** (FDI). Apart from the renamed and redefined High Representative post, the treaty also has introduced the post of an elected president of the **European Council** (elected for two and a half years, renewable once). **Qualified majority voting** (QMV) in the Council is extended to several new policies, and co-decision between the **Council** and the **European Parliament** (EP) becomes the **ordinary legislative procedure** (Article 294 TFEU). A new definition of QMV was found, namely, at least 55 percent of the member states comprising at least 65 percent of the population of the Union. These changes were adopted in view of improving the Union's efficiency and legitimacy.

TREATY OF MAASTRICHT. The Treaty of Maastricht creating the **European Union** (EU) was a major treaty reform. It outlined the three stages toward **Economic and Monetary Union** (EMU), added new policy areas and procedures, and reinforced foreign policy cooperation in the form of a second pillar on **Common Foreign and Security Policy** (CFSP) and created a third pillar formalizing **Justice and Home Affairs** (JHA) cooperation in a third pillar. It was decided to have an **Intergovernmental Conference** (IGC) on EMU in December 1989 and another one on Political Union in June 1990. A relatively detailed plan for EMU was worked out by a committee under the chairmanship of **Jacques Delors** in 1988 before the end of the Cold War, but the decision to have a second IGC on Political Union followed after the end of the Cold War. The treaty foresaw three stages toward EMU. It included convergence criteria, such as low government deficit and government debt, as conditions of taking part in the third stage when the European Central Bank (ECB) would be established and the single currency created. New policy chapters included education, culture, public health, consumer protection, trans-European networks (TENs), industry, development cooperation, and among the 11 member states other than the **United Kingdom** (UK): **social policy** (the UK opted out at the time). Some existing policy chapters, such as **environment** and social and economic cohesion, were improved. The treaty introduced the **co-decision** procedure requiring the **Council** and **European Parliament** (EP) to agree on some legislation, and strengthened the EP in other ways. The use of **qualified majority voting** (QMV) in the Council was extended. The treaty referred to the **subsidiarity** principle and introduced **citizenship** of the Union. The CFSP for the first time included a defense policy, although its implementation was at first delegated to the **Western European Union** (WEU), which agreed on the **Petersberg Tasks** in June 1992. JHA in the third pillar included: asylum policy, rules governing the crossing of the external borders**, immigration policy** and policy regarding nationals of third countries, combating drug addiction, combating fraud on an international scale, **judicial cooperation in civil matters**, **police and judicial co-operation in criminal matters**, and customs cooperation.

The treaty was largely negotiated in the two IGCs during 1991 and was signed in Maastricht on 7 February 1992. The Danes then rejected it in a **referendum** in June 1992, only to accept it in a second referendum in May 1993, after securing four **opt-outs** or reservations. Denmark does not take part in the third stage of EMU, European citizenship, European defense policy and JHA, when it moves from intergovernmental to supranational cooperation (as started with the **Treaty of Amsterdam** and was completed by the **Treaty of Lisbon**). The UK also got an opt-out from the third stage of EMU as well as social policy. The treaty entered into force on 1 November 1993.

TREATY OF NICE. The Treaty of Nice mainly dealt with the so-called Amsterdam leftovers, that is, institutional changes that the member states were unable to agree on in 1997, when they adopted the **Treaty of**

Amsterdam. These were re-weighting of votes in the **Council**, increased use of **qualified majority voting** (QMV) in the Council, and size and composition of the **Commission**. After long and difficult negotiations, the voting weights in the Council were changed. The bigger member states had their votes increased relatively more than the smaller member states. The use of QMV was extended to new policy areas, but less so than expected. There was no final agreement on the Commission. In a protocol to the treaty, it was stipulated that from 1 January 2005 there should be one Commissioner per member state. But from the moment that enough countries joined to reach 27member states there should be fewer Commissioners than the number of member states. How many would be decided by the Council by unanimity. There should be a rotation system based on equality. Due to the unsatisfactory conclusions of the Treaty of Nice negotiations the same issues were on the agendas, first of the Constitutional Treaty and then the **Treaty of Lisbon**. The outcome was a new voting system, so-called double majority, at least 55 percent of the member states representing at least 65 percent of the EU population. QMV became the norm. There also was an agreement to limit the size of the Commission to two-thirds of the number of members, the latter provision in reality not implemented due to a promise to **Ireland** prior to Ireland's second **referendum** of the Treaty of Lisbon. Ireland also went through two referendums on the Treaty of Nice.

TREATY OF PARIS. The Treaty of Paris established the **European Coal and Steel Community** (ECSC). It was signed on 11 April 1951, and it entered into force on 22 July 1952. The process that led to the treaty was started by the **Schuman Declaration** on 9 May 1950. In it, the French foreign minister Robert Schuman, inspired by **Jean Monnet**, suggested the pooling of the coal and steel industry of France and Germany and other European countries that might want to participate as well as the creation of a European authority, which would make binding decisions for the coal and steel industry. West Germany, led by Chancellor Konrad Adenauer, quickly accepted the invitation and so did Italy and the three Benelux countries: Belgium, the Netherlands, and Luxembourg. Negotiations started already on 20 June in Paris under the chairmanship of Jean Monnet. The treaty created a **common market** for coal and steel and set up a common **competition** (anti-trust) policy. It created a supranational authority, the **High Authority** (precursor of today's **European Commission**), as well as a so-called Special Council of Ministers (today's **Council**), a Common Assembly (today's **European Parliament** [EP]) and a Court, commonly called the **European Court of Justice** (ECJ), which remains a very important EU institution today. It also established a Consultative Committee. It introduced majority voting in the

Council, based on coal and steel production in the member states. The treaty expired after 50 years in 2002.

TREATY/TREATIES OF ROME. The two Treaties of Rome established the **European Economic Community** (EEC) and the **European Atomic Energy Community** (EAEC or EURATOM) in 1958. They were the outcome of decisions taken at the Messina Conference of foreign ministers in 1955 and prepared by a committee chaired by Paul-Henri Spaak, 1955–1956, and then negotiated through an **Intergovernmental Conference** (IGC) also chaired by Spaak, 1956–1957. The treaties were signed in Rome on 25 March 1957 and entered into force on 1 January 1958. Given the existence of the **European Coal and Steel Community** (ECSC) established by the **Treaty of Paris** (signed in 1951 and in force from 1952), there were then three **European Communities** (EC) from 1958. They shared two of the main institutions from the beginning, the **European Court of Justice** (ECJ) and Parliamentary Assembly (later called **European Parliament** [EP]), but had separate **Councils** of Ministers and "executives," the **High Authority** in the case of the ECSC and **Commissions** in the case of the EEC and EURATOM. These were merged in the so-called Merger Treaty in 1965, in force since 1967. Among the two Treaties of Rome the EEC treaty must be seen as the most important. (For this reason, the Treaty of Rome will usually refer to the EEC treaty.) It outlined steps toward a **customs union** and a **common market**, creating **free movement** for goods, **services**, capital, and persons (the **four freedoms**) and had sections on common policies for trade, **competition**, agriculture, and transport as well as coordination of macroeconomic policies and approximation of national legislation. The treaties, especially the EEC treaty, went through several reforms in the following years. In reformed version, the EEC treaty now constitutes the **Treaty on the Functioning of the European Union** (TFEU), which is the detailed part of the **Treaty of Lisbon**, in force since 2009. The EURATOM still exists as a separate organization. Through **Brexit** the **United Kingdom** (UK) has left both the EU and EURATOM.

TREATY ON EUROPEAN UNION (TEU). The Treaty on European Union (TEU) was the original name of the **Treaty of Maastricht**, which created the **European Union** (EU), but that treaty included much from earlier Community treaties in the first pillar, called the **European Community** (EC). Today TEU refers to the first general part of the **Treaty of Lisbon**, while the second part detailing the specific policies is called the **Treaty on the Functioning of the European Union** (TFEU). The Treaty of Lisbon has abolished the term "European Community."

TREATY ON STABILITY, COORDINATION AND GOVERNANCE IN THE ECONOMIC AND MONETARY UNION (TSCG). The Treaty on Stability, Coordination and Governance in the Economic and Monetary Union (TSCG), more commonly known as the Fiscal Compact or Fiscal Stability Treaty, was one of the responses to the financial and eurozone debt crisis. It involved all eurozone members and the other **European Union** (EU) member states, except the **United Kingdom** (UK) and the Czech Republic. It was signed on 2 March 2012. Due to British opposition, the treaty was not adopted as an EU treaty, but an intergovernmental treaty outside the EU framework. It entered into force on 1 January 2013 after ratification by 12 of the 17 eurozone countries at the time. **Ireland** needed a referendum to authorize ratification. A successful referendum took plane on 31 May 2012, with a 60.3 percent "yes" vote. Countries had an incentive to ratify, because only countries that ratified will have access to the permanent bail-out fund, the European Stability Mechanism (ESM). The treaty builds on the budgetary rules outlined in the Stability and Growth Pact (SGP).

TREATY ON THE FUNCTIONING OF THE EUROPEAN UNION (TFEU). *See* LISBON TREATY; TREATY ON EUROPEAN UNION.

TURKEY. Turkey became a member of the Council of Europe in 1949 and the North Atlantic Treaty Organization (NATO) in 1952. In 1963, it got an **association agreement** with the **European Community** (EC), which mentioned the possibility of future membership and included financial assistance. This agreement was frozen during the years of military rule in the country, 1980–1983. Turkey then applied for membership in the EC in 1987, but the opinion of the **European Commission** published in 1989 was negative. The Commission mentioned the country's size, poverty, high birth rate, and economic instability as well as lack of respect for human rights as problems, but it did see Turkey as potentially eligible for membership. A **customs** union between the European Union (EU) and Turkey was established in 1996. As Central and Eastern European Countries (CEECs) were pressing for and being promised membership, Turkey put pressure on the EU to be included in the list of candidates. Finally, in 1999 Turkey was recognized as a candidate. Start of negotiations was made conditional on progress on the Copenhagen criteria for membership agreed by the **European Council** in 1993. After going through various reforms in the early 2000s negotiations with Turkey started in 2005, but they have moved very slowly. In reality, there is much opposition to Turkish membership in some EU countries, especially France, Germany, and Austria. The fact that a divided **Cyprus** was admitted as EU member in 2004 has also complicated the issue. Turkey does not recognize the Cypriot government as the legitimate government of the whole island and is not willing to open its ports and airports to Cypriot traffic. Since Turkey may overtake Germany in terms of population in a few years and it remains relatively poor, despite economic progress, it will have relatively large budget implications for the EU to take Turkey in. On the other hand, there are important strategic arguments in favor of Turkish membership, the country already being an important NATO country and bordering conflict-ridden Middle East countries. For this reason, the **United States** (U.S.) has been putting pressure on the EU to admit Turkey as a member. Much will depend on the developments in Turkey after the election of Recep Tayyip Erdogan as president on 10 August 2014. Erdogan's presidency has made membership look unlikely for many years. Turkish membership was used as a threat by the **Leave campaign** during the 2016 **United Kingdom** (UK) referendum about British membership in the EU.

TURKISH MODEL. The Turkish model in the **Brexit** context refers to the **United Kingdom** (UK) staying in a customs union with the **European Union** (EU). It would solve the **Irish border** issue. But the biggest drawback seen from the British point of view is that it would not allow for an independent trade policy.

TUSK, DONALD (1957–). On 30 August 2014, the **European Council** selected Donald Tusk to become the next president of the **European Council** after Herman van Rompuy, who had held the position since 2009, when the **Treaty of Lisbon** entered into force. Tusk had been Poland's center-right prime minister from the Civic Platform party, since 2007. Educated as an historian he was known as a clever politician who had taken Poland well through the economic and financial crisis. His main shortcoming for the job initially was poor English and no knowledge of French. He did speak German though. There were various concerns in the 2014 decisions about the next top positions, as there had been previously, including in 2009. It has become a norm that those appointed for the top positions must represent different political groupings as well as different groups of countries. In the case of Tusk, his appointment was linked with the appointment of the new **High Representative of the Union for Foreign Affairs and Security Policy**, where the choice fell on **Federica Mogherini**, Italy's socialist foreign minister since February 2014, to replace Catherine Ashton. Previously **Jean-Claude Juncker**, a Christian Democrat from Luxembourg, had been elected to be president of the **European Commission**, replacing José Manuel Barroso. Donald Tusk has been actively involved in the **Brexit** negotiations, coordinating the positions of the 27 remaining member states (EU27), occasionally criticizing the

British for their inability to agree domestically. Donald Tusk's term as president of the European Council expired on 30 November 2019, when he was replaced by **Charles Michel** of Belgium.

Donald Tusk, president of the European Council (2014–2019). *Source*: Courtesy of the European Union.

U

UKRAINE. The 2004 **enlargement** of the **European Union** (EU) made Ukraine one of the EU's direct neighbors to the east. Since the country became independent at the time of the Soviet Union's collapse in 1991, the country has been split between a pro-EU part in the west and a pro-Russia part in the east. Ukraine signed a **Partnership and Cooperation Agreement** (PCA) in 1994, which went into effect in 1998. Political dialogue and financial assistance through the Technical Assistance for the Commonwealth of Independent States (TACIS) were important parts of the PCA. Currently relations fall under the European Neighbourhood Policy (ENP) as well as the more recent Eastern Partnership. In 2012, a more comprehensive **association agreement** between the EU and Ukraine was initialed, but the EU made the signing conditional on political improvements in Ukraine, where, among other things, former prime minister Yulia Tymoshenko had been imprisoned. At the same time, the Ukraine government was under pressure from Russia, which was tempting Ukraine with a **customs union**, which would also include Belarus and Kazakhstan. The association agreement with the EU was scheduled to be signed at a summit in Vilnius on 28–29 November 2013. President Viktor Yanukovych did attend the meeting, but did not sign. This sparked widespread protests in Ukraine. The protest eventually led to the ousting of the Yanukovych government in February 2014. A new interim government signed the political provisions of the association agreement on 21 March 2014, but the trade provisions were temporarily set aside until after the presidential elections on 25 May 2014. The new president Petro Poroshenko signed the economic part of the agreement on 27 June 2014. However, a joint meeting between the EU, Russia, and Ukraine on 12 September 2014 decided to postpone implementation till 31 December 2015. The economic part, the **Deep and Comprehensive Free Trade Agreement** (DCFTA), is to create free trade over a ten-year period between the EU and Ukraine; Ukraine is expected to go through economic and judicial reforms leading to convergence with EU standards and policies. The February 2014 revolution sparked by the issue of the Association Agreement with the EU has effectively split the country. First, the Crimea seceded with Russian support, considered as

Russian annexation by some; next pro-Russian forces have taken control of the eastern parts of Ukraine, especially the Luhansk and Donetsk regions, leading to war with the government in Kyiv. The EU has condemned the Russian actions and imposed sanctions against Russia. The DCFTA has also been mentioned in the debates about the future relationship between the EU and the **United Kingdom** (UK), but being designed for an eastern neighbor which has to go through economic and political transitions toward EU standards it is not an obvious choice. *See also* UKRAINIAN OPTION.

UKRAINIAN OPTION. It refers to **Deep and Comprehensive Free Trade Agreement** (DCFTA) between the **European Union** (EU) and Ukraine. In includes moving toward free trade as well as improved movement of **services** and capital, including some **regulatory alignment**, but not **free movement** of people. Migrating workers will require work permits. The DCFTA goes further on services than the EU's **free trade agreement** with **Canada**, the **Comprehensive and Economic Trade Agreement** (CETA).

ULSTER UNIONIST PARTY. The Ulster Unionist Party is a conservative party that supports the union with the **United Kingdom** (UK). It governed Northern Ireland 1921–1972. Today it is the fourth-largest party in Northern Ireland, after the **Democratic Unionist Party** (DUP), **Sinn Féin**, and the **Social Democratic and Labour Party** (SDLP). The party's leader from 1995 to 2005 was David Trimble, who supported the **Good Friday Agreement** (or Belfast Agreement), but the party was split between pro- and anti-agreement factions.

UNITED KINGDOM (UK). The United Kingdom (UK) did not join the European integration process at the beginning despite being invited. Relations with colonies and former colonies in the Commonwealth were politically and economically important. So were the transatlantic relations with the **United States** (U.S.). There were further ideological differences between the continental approach of creating supranational institutions and going beyond free trade by developing various common policies. Instead, the UK took the initiative to create the **European Free Trade Association** (EFTA) in 1960 together with Austria, Denmark, Norway, Portugal, Sweden, and **Switzerland**. EFTA was an intergovernmental organization creating a **free trade area** (FTA), but no **customs union**, common **trade policy**, or common **agricultural policy**. However, the UK realized quickly that EFTA was no match for the **European Economic Community** (EEC) created in 1957 (in force in 1958). In 1961, the UK applied for membership. In 1963, however French president **Charles de Gaulle** vetoed UK membership, and when the

UK applied a second time in 1967 de Gaulle again vetoed UK membership. It was only after de Gaulle stepped down in 1969 and his successor **Georges Pompidou** became president of France that the door was opened for UK membership. The UK joined in 1973 together with Denmark and **Ireland**. Since then the country was often a difficult member, approaching integration and cooperation with an intergovernmentalist free-trade-area philosophy that was less than what the founding member states usually aimed for. When **Margaret Thatcher** became prime minister of the UK in 1979, she battled her partners on **budget** issues, which were settled with a British rebate in 1984. She opposed calling the **Intergovernmental Conference** (IGC), which negotiated the **Single European Act** (SEA) in 1986, despite favoring the **internal market** plan. Later she opposed UK participation in **Economic and Monetary Union** (EMU), which contributed to her downfall just prior to the start of the negotiations, which led to the **Treaty of Maastricht** in 1992. **John Major**, who took over, secured the UK an **opt-out** from the third stage of the single currency, the **euro**, created in 1999, as well as an opt-out from EU **social policy**, which Thatcher had also opposed. Nor did the UK take part in the **Schengen** cooperation about border control and visas. The UK, however, did join the EU's social policy under the new **Labour Party Tony Blair** government in 1997.

Although UK membership was accepted in a **referendum** in 1975 after a renegotiation of membership conditions by the **Harold Wilson** Labour Party government, public opinion polls have continued to show low support for European integration. In 2012, Conservative prime minister **David Cameron** decided against UK participation in the **Treaty on Stability, Coordination and Governance in the Economic and Monetary Union (TSCG)**, commonly known as the Fiscal Compact or Fiscal Stability Treaty. In 2013 he promised a referendum on continued UK membership if he were to win a majority in the next election. **The United Kingdom Independence Party** (UKIP) did very well in the **European Parliament** (EP) elections in May 2014. On 7 May 2015 Cameron was reelected prime minister with a majority in the **House of Commons**. He negotiated an agreement with the EU which accepted some limitations in UK membership. The agreement was reached in February 2016, and on that basis the **Brexit referendum** took place on 23 June 2016, where about 52 percent of the British electorate voted to **Leave**.

UNITED KINGDOM INDEPENDENCE PARTY (UKIP). The history of the United Kingdom Independence Party (UKIP) goes back to 1991 when Alan Sked at the London School of Economics formed the Anti-Federalist League, which in 1993 became the UKIP. The start was influenced by Prime Minister **Margaret Thatcher**'s battles with her European colleagues and also her famous Bruges speech in 1988. The huge debate about the **Treaty of Maastricht** was a contributing factor. The party is a **Eurosceptic**, right-wing party. In 1997 a faction led by **Nigel Farage** ousted Sked. Farage became the leader of UKIP in 2006 and started exploiting concerns for **immigration**, following the big **European Union** (EU) **enlargement** in 2004, where the **United Kingdom** (UK) chose not to ask for a transition period for **free movement** of people from the Central and Eastern European Countries (CEECs) that joined. It was in the period 2013–2016 that the UKIP became an influential force. It did well in local elections in 2013 and especially in the **European Parliament** (EP) elections in 2014, when the party won 27 percent of the votes and 24 of the UK's 73 seats. In the 2015 general election they received 12.6 percent of the votes, which, however, because of the British electoral system gave only one seat in the **House of Commons**. It was the election where Prime Minister **David Cameron** had promised a **referendum** if he gained a majority. The **Conservative Party** won 331 seats, a gain of 35, which gave David Cameron a majority. During the referendum campaign in 2016 UKIP and Farage actively campaigned for Leave. By the time of the EP elections in May 2019 Farage had left UKIP and formed the **Brexit Party**, which took 30.5 percent of the votes and 29 seats, while UKIP got only 3.2 percent of the votes and no seats. The UK **Members of the European Parliament** (MEPs) elected on that occasion had to step down when the UK left the EU on 31 January 2020.

UNITED KINGDOM (UK) PARLIAMENT. The UK Parliament is a bicameral legislature consisting of the lower house, the **House of Commons**, and the upper house, the **House of Lords**. *See also* PARLIAMENT OF THE UNITED KINGDOM.

UNITED STATES (U.S.). The United States (U.S.) has traditionally been the **European Union's** (EU) largest trading partner, and there are important flows of **foreign direct investments** (FDI) both ways between the U.S. and the EU. This has created a high degree of interdependence between the two sides of the Atlantic Ocean. Since 1949, the U.S. has also been the leading country in the North Atlantic Treaty Organization (NATO), which provided security for Western Europe during the Cold War.

US-EU trade relations have gone through a number of disputes since the early 1960s. An early dispute was the famous Chicken War, 1963–1964. A more recent conflict was the one concerning European subsidies to Airbus, 1986–1992. A dispute about hormones in beef has been running since 1987, with **World Trade Organization** (WTO) dispute settlement decisions siding with the U.S. (and **Canada**). Sometimes, the U.S. threatened to use Section 301 of the U.S. Trade Act, which allowed the U.S. to use unilateral action outside the **General Agreement on Tariffs and Trade** (GATT) in response to perceived unfair trade practice. In some cases, GATT/WTO panels have contributed to the settlement of trade disputes. A long-running conflict about bananas was eventually solved in 2001, with the EU losing the WTO cases, which found the EU's preferential treatment of bananas from the African, Caribbean, and Pacific (ACP) countries in violation of the GATT.

During the 1990s, there were several efforts to institutionalize EU–U.S. relations. In 1990, the EU and the U.S. agreed on a Transatlantic Declaration (TAD). It was complemented with a New Transatlantic Agenda (NTA) signed in Madrid in December 1995. The NTA itself was formulated in very general terms, mentioning four areas of co-operation: peace and democracy, global challenges, world trade, and bridges across the Atlantic. The section on "contributing to the expansion of world trade and closer economic relations" referred to strengthening the multilateral trading system, implementing the Uruguay Round results, and completing unfinished business—in particular telecommunications and maritime services.

Discussions about a more formalized relationship between the EU and the U.S. have had relatively limited results for many years. Proposals for transatlantic free trade have come up against protectionist forces on both sides as well as a feeling that transatlantic relations should not undermine the multilateral system. The EU–U.S. summit in London in May 1998 adopted a joint statement on a Transatlantic Economic Partnership (TEP), the purpose of which was to intensify and extend cooperation in the fields of trade and investment. In 2007, a Transatlantic Economic Council (TEC) was created to accelerate government-to-government cooperation with the aim of advancing transatlantic economic integration. Finally, in 2013 the EU and the U.S. started negotiations concerning the **Transatlantic Trade and Investment Partnership** (TTIP). Both sides exhibited more determination this time than on earlier occasions. The agenda of the TTIP negotiations was broad, including market access (tariffs, rules of origin, trade defense measures, **services**, **investments**, and **public procurement**) and regulatory issues and **non-tariff barriers**, the latter being behind-the-borders obstacles to trade, including products standards, health, safety, and consumer and **environmental** protection. These issues mobilized a lot of interest groups and nongovernmental organizations (NGOs). When Donald Trump became U.S. president in January 2017 the TTIP negotiations were put on hold and trade relation deteriorated, with Trump on several occasions threatening retaliations against the EU.

V

VAN GEND EN LOOS. *Van Gend en Loos* is one of the most important judgments of the **European Court of Justice** (ECJ). It established the principle of **direct effect** in 1963. It was a preliminary ruling case requested by a Dutch court. A Dutch company initiated the case when the Dutch government imposed a new tariff on a product it imported. The ECJ ruled the tariff illegal because the **European Community** (EC) was going through a transition period toward a **customs union** and that no new tariffs could be introduced. The judgment also included an important clarification: EC law had direct effect, giving individuals, companies, and governments certain rights and responsibilities.

VARADKAR, LEO (1979–). Leo Varadkar is an Irish politician. He held various ministerial positions before becoming Taoiseach (prime minister) in June 2017. He is a member of the Fine Gael party. He is openly gay and of Indian heritage. Due to the special importance of the border between the **Republic of Ireland** and **Northern Ireland** in the **Brexit** negotiations he became an influential politician among the remaining 27 EU member states. He has opposed the return of a **hard border** between the Irish Republic and Northern Ireland and was involved in negotiating the final **withdrawal agreement** with United Kingdom (UK) Prime Minister **Boris Johnson** in October 2019.

Leo Varadkar, Irish prime minister since June 2017. *Source*: Courtesy of the European Union.

VERHOFSTADT, GUY (1953–). Guy Verhofstadt is a Flemish liberal politician. He was prime minister of Belgium at the time of the Laeken meeting of the European Council in 1991 when it was decided to convene the Convention on the Future of Europe. He is a convinced federalist. He has been a **Member of the European Parliament** (MEP) since 2009 as a member of the **Alliance of Liberals and Democrats for Europe (ALDE)** and the leader of the ALDE until 2019. At the **European Parliament** (EP) elections in May 2014 he was the candidate for the **Commission** presidency for his party group, one of the so-called *Spitzenkandidaten*. He was the EP's **Brexit** Coordinator and Chair of its Brexit Steering Group from September 2016 until **Brexit day**, 31 January 2020. He is an outspoken pro-European, who has also written several books.

VISA POLICY. Visa policy, although a part of **Justice and Home Affairs** (JHA), was already included under the first pillar in the **Treaty of Maastricht** (Article 100c), and not in the third pillar. As border controls within the **internal market** are abolished, a common visa policy is needed. Since border controls have been abolished through the **Schengen** cooperation it is within that cooperation that a common visa policy has been established, not including the **United Kingdom** (UK) and **Ireland**, which have had **opt-outs** from the Schengen cooperation, but including **Norway**, Iceland, and **Switzerland**, which have association agreements with Schengen. A list of which countries require a Schengen visa has been established as well as procedures for acquiring such a visa by citizens from third countries.

VON DER LEYEN, URSULA (1958–). Ursula von der Leyen is a German politician. She became president of the **European Commission** on 1 December 2019, taking over that position from **Jean-Claude Juncker**. She had previously served as Minister of Defense in **Angela Merkel**'s government in Germany from 2013 to 2019. She was not one of the *Spitzenkandidaten* nominated by the political groups in the **European Parliament** (EP), but won as a compromise candidate, partly because President Macron of France actively wanted a woman for the job, and she did belong to the **European People's' Party** (EPP), which reemerged as the biggest group in the EP after the May 2019 EP elections. By the time she took over the Commission Presidency the **Withdrawal Agreement** between the EU and UK had been agreed, but she can be expected to play an important role in the negotiations about the future relationship between the **European Union** (EU) and the **United Kingdom** (UK).

President of the European Commission, Ursula von der Leyen (2019-) and President of the European Council, Charles Michel (2019-) signing the Brexit agreement, January 24, 2020. *Source*: Courtesy of the European Union.

VOTING. Voting in the **Council** of Ministers has been a controversial issue on a number of occasions, and it has been on the agenda in connection with **enlargements** and treaty reforms. From the beginning the treaties included some kind of weighted voting, giving the larger member states more votes than the smaller ones, and the treaties have defined a **qualified majority vote** (QMV), which in turn implied a certain size of a blocking minority. The issue of which policies should fall under QMV or unanimity has also been controversial. The **Treaty of Lisbon** abolished the weighted votes established by the previous treaties. Since 1 November 2014, a new double majority has been introduced: at least 55 percent of the member states, representing at least 65 percent of the Union's population.

W

WALES. Wales is one of the constituent parts of the **United Kingdom** (UK) together with **England**, **Scotland,** and **Northern Ireland**. Both English and Welsh are official languages in Wales. A referendum in 1997 showed a majority of the Welsh people supporting some kind of self-government. This led to the creation of a devolved parliament, the National Assembly for Wales, in 1999. It has 60 members. Wales is represented by 40 **Members of Parliament** (MPs) in the **House of Commons**. At the latest general election in December 2019 the **Labour Party** won 22 seats, the **Conservative Party** won 14, and **Plaid Cymru** won four seats. Plaid Cymru (the Party of Wales) supports independence for Wales.

WELSH PARLIAMENT. The Welsh assembly has been renamed Senedd Cymru/Welsh Parliament in May 2020. *See also* WALES.

WESTERN EUROPEAN UNION (WEU). The Western European Union (WEU) dates back to the Brussels Treaty on Economic, Social and Cultural Collaboration and Collective Self-Defence of 17 March 1948. The treaty included a mutual defense clause between the signatories: Belgium, France, Luxembourg, the Netherlands, and the **United Kingdom** (UK). As a defense organization, the North Atlantic Treaty Organization (NATO) soon overtook it in 1949. However, in October 1954 the Brussels treaty was amended by the Paris Agreements, which established the WEU, including the original signatories as well as West Germany and Italy as members. This happened after the **European Defence Community** (EDC) treaty failed to be ratified by the French National Assembly in August 1954. The EDC would have included Germany. Now the WEU became an alternative option, but more importantly, it allowed Germany to become a member of NATO in May 1955. During the years prior to UK membership of the **European Community** (EC) in 1973, the WEU was also a forum for UK-EC consultations. Although largely dormant for many years the WEU was reactivated in 1984 as a forum for European defense policy discussions and cooperation at a time when there were disagreements within NATO about policies toward the Soviet Union.

After the negotiation of the **Treaty of Maastricht**, which included defense policy in the second pillar on **Common Foreign and Security Policy** (CFSP), the WEU was designated as the defense arm of the EU. The WEU decided at a meeting at Petersberg outside Bonn that the WEU could deal with humanitarian, peacekeeping, peacemaking, and crisis management missions on behalf of the EU (the so-called **Petersberg tasks**). However, in 1999 the EU decided to develop an autonomous defense policy, which was confirmed in the **Treaty of Nice**, so the WEU became largely superfluous. The Petersberg tasks had previously been included in the EU treaties by the **Treaty of Amsterdam**. When the **Treaty of Lisbon** included a mutual defense clause there were no real functions left for the WEU. It officially ceased to exist on 30 June 2011.

WEYAND, SABINE (1964–). Sabine Weyand is a German **European Union** (EU) senior official. She has been deputy chief negotiator of **Brexit** from October 2016, working closely with **Michel Barnier**, the chief negotiator. Previously she was also involved in trade negotiations with **Canada** and the **United States** (U.S.). From June 2019 she has been the **European Union** (EU) director-general for trade.

WHITE PAPER. A white paper is a report where a government outlines an issue, possibly arguing for some new policy, to inform the citizens, white originally indicating that it was a public document. The **European Union** (EU) has also issued some white papers, the best known being the White Paper on the Completion of the **Internal Market** issued in June 1995. The **United Kingdom**'s (UK) so-called **Chequers plan** was published as a white paper on the future relationship between the United Kingdom and the European Union on 6 July 2018. A green paper, on the other hand, will usually present various ideas and options in view of creating a public debate.

WIDENING. "Widening" is a term used for **enlargement** of the European Union (EU), often contrasted with **deepening**. In reality, the two processes have often been linked. Widening has led to new policies or changes in policies as well as institutional changes to improve the functioning of a larger union.

WILSON, HAROLD (1916–1995). Harold Wilson was a British **Labour Party** politician. The Labour Party was in opposition when the **United Kingdom** (UK) joined the **European Community** (EC) in 1973 under the leadership of **Edward Heath's Conservative Party** government. However, the Labour Party won the next election in 1974 on promising a renegotiation of the British membership terms. Wilson became a **Member of Parliament** (MEP) in 1945 and served until 1983. He was prime minister from 1964 to 1970, and again from 1974 to 1976. After the renegotiation, a **referendum** was held about continued British membership of the EC. More than 60 percent of those voting voted for continued British membership.

WITHDRAWAL AGREEMENT. If a member state of the European Union (EU) decides that it wants to withdraw from the EU it has to negotiate an agreement with the remaining member states setting out the terms of the departure. According to the treaty's Article 50 TEU it is expected to be done in a two-year period. In the case of **Brexit**, it ended up taking longer because Prime Minister **Theresa May**, who negotiated such agreement with the EU's remaining 27 member states (EU27), could not get it accepted in the **UK Parliament**. It took another prime minister, **Boris Johnson**, some changes in the agreement, and a parliamentary election (in December 2019) before the revised agreement could finally be agreed and ratified by both sides in January 2020. Among other things, it dealt with the financial settlement (**divorce bill**) and **citizens' rights** after Brexit, but the most controversial part of the agreement was the solution to assure that there would be no **hard border** between **Northern Ireland** and the **Republic of Ireland** after Brexit. The first version of the Withdrawal Agreement negotiated by May in November 2018 included a so-called **backstop** basically requiring the **United Kingdom** (UK) to stay in the EU's **customs union** until another solution to the border issue could be found. It was replaced by a different, and in principle permanent, solution, in the agreement reached by Johnson in October 2019. Here the solution is that Northern Ireland stays in the EU's customs union and partly in the internal market for goods, including agricultural goods.

WITHDRAWAL BILL/ACT. For the **UK Parliament** to ratify the **Withdrawal Agreement** negotiated with the **European Union** (EU) a Withdrawal Bill was prepared. The House of Commons passed the bill late in January 2020, so it became a Withdrawal Act, allowing the **United Kingdom** (UK) to withdraw from the EU on 31 January 2020.

WORLD TRADE ORGANIZATION (WTO). The World Trade Organization (WTO) was the new organization created by the Uruguay Round of the **General Agreement on Tariffs and Trade** (GATT) in 1995. The WTO includes the GATT as well as the new **General Agreement on Trade in Services** (GATS) and the Agreement on **Trade Related Aspects of Intellectual Property Rights** (TRIPS). The WTO also created a stronger dispute settlement system. Both the **European Union** (EU) and the now 27 member states are members of the WTO. The **Commission** negotiates on behalf of the EU based on a **mandate** from the **Council**. During negotiations, it consults regularly with the **Trade Policy Committee**, a working group of the Council composed of national officials. It also regularly informs the **European Parliament** (EP) of key WTO issues and progress in international negotiations. The highest decision-making body of the WTO is the Ministerial Conference, which meets at least every two years. The Trade Commissioner represents the EU in the Ministerial Conference. The Commission also represents the EU in the WTO General Council, which meets regularly in different configurations, including as the Dispute Settlement Body. The latest trade policy round of negotiations, the Doha Development Round, started in 2001. It has so far not produced major results. The increased number of members in the WTO has augmented the diversity of interests. As of July 2016, the WTO has 164 members. Especially major emerging countries have not been willing to go as far in liberalizing trade as the industrialized countries, including the EU, have wanted. This is one of the factors that have increased the interests in bilateral trade agreements instead of the multilateral agreements within the WTO. *See also* COMMON COMMERCIAL POLICY (CCP); INTELLECTUAL PROPERTY RIGHTS (IPR).

WTO RULES. Members of the **World Trade Organization** (WTO) are expected to follow various agreed rules, including agreed levels of **tariffs** on goods. If two members of the WTO negotiate lower tariffs, they are normally expected to extend those reductions to the other members of the WTO, known as the **Most-Favored-Nation** principle. There are two exceptions from MFN: **customs unions** and **free trade areas** (FTA). In a customs union the members abolish tariffs between themselves, but create a common external tariff. The **European Union** (EU) is a customs union. In an FTA the participating countries abolish tariffs among themselves, but they retain their own external tariffs. The **European Free Trade Area** (EFTA) is an example. The current EFTA members are Iceland, Lichtenstein, **Norway**, and **Switzerland**. The EU has negotiated FTAs with several countries, especially developing countries and neighbors in Europe, but in recent years also with leading industrialized countries, including South Korea, **Canada**, and Japan. Countries that do not have FTAs with the EU, including China, the **United States** (U.S.), and Australia, have to follow WTO rules in trade with the EU, including pay tariffs for their goods to enter the EU market. If the **United Kingdom** (UK) does not reach an agreement on future relations with the EU after the **transition period**, UK products will have to pay tariffs to enter the EU market based on WTO rules.

Appendix A

Articles 50 TEU and 218(3) TFEU

ARTICLE 50

1. Any Member State may decide to withdraw from the Union in accordance with its own constitutional requirements.
2. A Member State which decides to withdraw shall notify the European Council of its intention. In the light of the guidelines provided by the European Council, the Union shall negotiate and conclude an agreement with that State, setting out the arrangements for its withdrawal, taking account of the framework for its future relationship with the Union. That agreement shall be negotiated in accordance with Article 218(3) of the Treaty on the Functioning of the European Union. It shall be concluded on behalf of the Union by the Council, acting by a qualified majority, after obtaining the consent of the European Parliament.
3. The Treaties shall cease to apply to the State in question from the date of entry into force of the withdrawal agreement or, failing that, two years after the notification referred to in paragraph 2, unless the European Council, in agreement with the Member State concerned, unanimously decides to extend this period.
4. For the purposes of paragraphs 2 and 3, the member of the European Council or of the Council representing the withdrawing Member State shall not participate in the discussions of the European Council or Council or in decisions concerning it.
5. A qualified majority shall be defined in accordance with Article 238(3) (b) of the Treaty on the Functioning of the European Union.
6. If a State which has withdrawn from the Union asks to rejoin, its request shall be subject to the procedure referred to in Article 49.

ARTICLE 218(3) TFEU

3. The Commission, or the High Representative of the Union for Foreign Affairs and Security Policy where the agreement envisaged relates

exclusively or principally to the common foreign and security policy, shall submit recommendations to the Council, which shall adopt a decision authorising the opening of negotiations and, depending on the subject of the agreement envisaged, nominating the Union negotiator or the head of the Union's negotiating team.

Appendix B

Excerpts from Theresa May's Lancaster House Speech, 17 January 2017

THE GOVERNMENT'S NEGOTIATING OBJECTIVES FOR EXITING THE EU: PM SPEECH

(....)

OBJECTIVES AND AMBITIONS

So today I want to outline our objectives for the negotiation ahead. Twelve objectives that amount to one big goal: a new, positive and constructive partnership between Britain and the European Union.

And as we negotiate that partnership, we will be driven by some simple principles: we will provide as much certainty and clarity as we can at every stage. And we will take this opportunity to make Britain stronger, to make Britain fairer, and to build a more Global Britain too.

CERTAINTY AND CLARITY

1. Certainty

The first objective is crucial. We will provide certainty wherever we can.

We are about to enter a negotiation. That means there will be give and take. There will have to be compromises. It will require imagination on both sides. And not everybody will be able to know everything at every stage.

But I recognise how important it is to provide business, the public sector, and everybody with as much certainty as possible as we move through the process.

So where we can offer that certainty, we will do so.

That is why last year we acted quickly to give clarity about farm payments and university funding. And it is why, as we repeal the European Communities Act, we will convert the 'acquis'—the body of existing EU law—into British law.

This will give the country maximum certainty as we leave the EU. The same rules and laws will apply on the day after Brexit as they did before. And it will be for the British Parliament to decide on any changes to that law after full scrutiny and proper Parliamentary debate.

And when it comes to Parliament, there is one other way in which I would like to provide certainty. I can confirm today that the Government will put the final deal that is agreed between the UK and the EU to a vote in both Houses of Parliament, before it comes into force.

A STRONGER BRITAIN

Our second guiding principle is to build a stronger Britain.

2. Control of our own laws

That means taking control of our own affairs, as those who voted in their millions to leave the European Union demanded we must.

So we will take back control of our laws and bring an end to the jurisdiction of the European Court of Justice in Britain. Leaving the European Union will mean that our laws will be made in Westminster, Edinburgh, Cardiff and Belfast. And those laws will be interpreted by judges not in Luxembourg but in courts across this country.

Because we will not have truly left the European Union if we are not in control of our own laws.

3. Strengthen the Union

A stronger Britain demands that we do something else—strengthen the precious union between the 4 nations of the United Kingdom.

At this momentous time, it is more important than ever that we face the future together, united by what makes us strong: the bonds that unite us as a people, and our shared interest in the UK being an open, successful trading nation in the future.

And I hope that same spirit of unity will apply in Northern Ireland in particular over the coming months in the Assembly elections, and the main parties there will work together to re-establish a partnership government as soon as possible.

Foreign affairs are of course the responsibility of the UK government, and in dealing with them we act in the interests of all parts of the United Kingdom. As prime minister, I take that responsibility seriously.

I have also been determined from the start that the devolved administrations should be fully engaged in this process.

That is why the government has set up a Joint Ministerial Committee on EU Negotiations, so ministers from each of the UK's devolved administrations can contribute to the process of planning for our departure from the European Union.

We have already received a paper from the Scottish government, and look forward to receiving a paper from the Welsh government shortly. Both papers will be considered as part of this important process. We won't agree on everything, but I look forward to working with the administrations in Scotland, Wales and Northern Ireland to deliver a Brexit that works for the whole of the United Kingdom.

Part of that will mean working very carefully to ensure that—as powers are repatriated from Brussels back to Britain—the right powers are returned to Westminster, and the right powers are passed to the devolved administrations of Scotland, Wales and Northern Ireland.

As we do so, our guiding principle must be to ensure that—as we leave the European Union—no new barriers to living and doing business within our own Union are created,

That means maintaining the necessary common standards and frameworks for our own domestic market, empowering the UK as an open, trading nation to strike the best trade deals around the world, and protecting the common resources of our islands.

And as we do this, I should equally be clear that no decisions currently taken by the devolved administrations will be removed from them.

4. Maintain the Common Travel Area with Ireland

We cannot forget that, as we leave, the United Kingdom will share a land border with the EU, and maintaining that Common Travel Area with the Republic of Ireland will be an important priority for the UK in the talks ahead. There has been a Common Travel Area between the UK and the Republic of Ireland for many years.

Indeed, it was formed before either of our 2 countries were members of the European Union. And the family ties and bonds of affection that unite our 2 countries mean that there will always be a special relationship between us.

So we will work to deliver a practical solution that allows the maintenance of the Common Travel Area with the Republic, while protecting the integrity of the United Kingdom's immigration system.

Nobody wants to return to the borders of the past, so we will make it a priority to deliver a practical solution as soon as we can.

A FAIRER BRITAIN

The third principle is to build a fairer Britain. That means ensuring it is fair to everyone who lives and works in this country.

5. Control of immigration

And that is why we will ensure we can control immigration to Britain from Europe.

We will continue to attract the brightest and the best to work or study in Britain—indeed openness to international talent must remain one of this country's most distinctive assets—but that process must be managed properly so that our immigration system serves the national interest.

So we will get control of the number of people coming to Britain from the EU.

Because while controlled immigration can bring great benefits—filling skills shortages, delivering public services, making British businesses the world-beaters they often are—when the numbers get too high, public support for the system falters.

In the last decade or so, we have seen record levels of net migration in Britain, and that sheer volume has put pressure on public services, like schools, stretched our infrastructure, especially housing, and put a downward pressure on wages for working class people. As home secretary for 6 years, I know that you cannot control immigration overall when there is free movement to Britain from Europe.

Britain is an open and tolerant country. We will always want immigration, especially high-skilled immigration, we will always want immigration from Europe, and we will always welcome individual migrants as friends. But the message from the public before and during the referendum campaign was clear: Brexit must mean control of the number of people who come to Britain from Europe. And that is what we will deliver.

6. Rights for EU nationals in Britain, and British nationals in the EU

Fairness demands that we deal with another issue as soon as possible too. We want to guarantee the rights of EU citizens who are already living in Britain, and the rights of British nationals in other member states, as early as we can.

I have told other EU leaders that we could give people the certainty they want straight away, and reach such a deal now.

Many of them favour such an agreement—1 or 2 others do not—but I want everyone to know that it remains an important priority for Britain—and for many other member states—to resolve this challenge as soon as possible. Because it is the right and fair thing to do.

7. Protect workers' rights

And a fairer Britain is a country that protects and enhances the rights people have at work. That is why, as we translate the body of European law into our domestic regulations, we will ensure that workers' rights are fully protected and maintained.

Indeed, under my leadership, not only will the government protect the rights of workers set out in European legislation, we will build on them. Because under this government, we will make sure legal protection for workers keeps pace with the changing labour market—and that the voices of workers are heard by the boards of publicly-listed companies for the first time.

A TRULY GLOBAL BRITAIN

But the great prize for this country—the opportunity ahead—is to use this moment to build a truly Global Britain. A country that reaches out to old friends and new allies alike. A great, global, trading nation. And one of the firmest advocates for free trade anywhere in the world.

8. Free trade with European markets

That starts with our close friends and neighbours in Europe. So as a priority, we will pursue a bold and ambitious free trade agreement with the European Union.

This agreement should allow for the freest possible trade in goods and services between Britain and the EU's member states. It should give British companies the maximum freedom to trade with and operate within European markets—and let European businesses do the same in Britain.

But I want to be clear. What I am proposing cannot mean membership of the single market.

European leaders have said many times that membership means accepting the '4 freedoms' of goods, capital, services and people. And being out of the EU but a member of the single market would mean complying with the EU's rules and regulations that implement those freedoms, without having a vote on what those rules and regulations are. It would mean accepting a role for the European Court of Justice that would see it still having direct legal authority in our country.

It would to all intents and purposes mean not leaving the EU at all.

And that is why both sides in the referendum campaign made it clear that a vote to leave the EU would be a vote to leave the single market.

So we do not seek membership of the single market. Instead we seek the greatest possible access to it through a new, comprehensive, bold and ambitious free trade agreement.

That agreement may take in elements of current single market arrangements in certain areas—on the export of cars and lorries for example, or the freedom to provide financial services across national borders—as it makes no sense to start again from scratch when Britain and the remaining Member States have adhered to the same rules for so many years.

But I respect the position taken by European leaders who have been clear about their position, just as I am clear about mine. So an important part of the new strategic partnership we seek with the EU will be the pursuit of the greatest possible access to the single market, on a fully reciprocal basis, through a comprehensive free trade agreement.

And because we will no longer be members of the single market, we will not be required to contribute huge sums to the EU budget. There may be some specific European programmes in which we might want to participate. If so, and this will be for us to decide, it is reasonable that we should make an appropriate contribution. But the principle is clear: the days of Britain making vast contributions to the European Union every year will end.

9. New trade agreements with other countries

But it is not just trade with the EU we should be interested in. A Global Britain must be free to strike trade agreements with countries from outside the European Union too.

Because important though our trade with the EU is and will remain, it is clear that the UK needs to increase significantly its trade with the fastest growing export markets in the world.

Since joining the EU, trade as a percentage of GDP has broadly stagnated in the UK. That is why it is time for Britain to get out into the world and rediscover its role as a great, global, trading nation.

This is such a priority for me that when I became Prime Minister I established, for the first time, a Department for International Trade, led by Liam Fox.

We want to get out into the wider world, to trade and do business all around the globe. Countries including China, Brazil, and the Gulf States have already expressed their interest in striking trade deals with us. We have started discussions on future trade ties with countries like Australia, New Zealand and India. And President-Elect Trump has said Britain is not "at the back of the queue" for a trade deal with the United States, the world's biggest economy, but front of the line.

I know my emphasis on striking trade agreements with countries outside Europe has led to questions about whether Britain seeks to remain a member of the EU's Customs Union. And it is true that full Customs Union membership prevents us from negotiating our own comprehensive trade deals.

Now, I want Britain to be able to negotiate its own trade agreements. But I also want tariff-free trade with Europe and cross-border trade there to be as frictionless as possible.

That means I do not want Britain to be part of the Common Commercial Policy and I do not want us to be bound by the Common External Tariff. These are the elements of the Customs Union that prevent us from striking our own comprehensive trade agreements with other countries. But I do want us to have a customs agreement with the EU.

Whether that means we must reach a completely new customs agreement, become an associate member of the Customs Union in some way, or remain a signatory to some elements of it, I hold no preconceived position. I have an open mind on how we do it. It is not the means that matter, but the ends.

And those ends are clear: I want to remove as many barriers to trade as possible. And I want Britain to be free to establish our own tariff schedules at the World Trade Organisation, meaning we can reach new trade agreements not just with the European Union but with old friends and new allies from outside Europe too.

10. The best place for science and innovation

A Global Britain must also be a country that looks to the future. That means being one of the best places in the world for science and innovation.

One of our great strengths as a nation is the breadth and depth of our academic and scientific communities, backed up by some of the world's best universities. And we have a proud history of leading and supporting cutting-edge research and innovation.

So we will also welcome agreement to continue to collaborate with our European partners on major science, research, and technology initiatives.

From space exploration to clean energy to medical technologies, Britain will remain at the forefront of collective endeavours to better understand, and make better, the world in which we live.

11. Co-operation in the fight against crime and terrorism

And a Global Britain will continue to co-operate with its European partners in important areas such as crime, terrorism and foreign affairs.

All of us in Europe face the challenge of cross-border crime, a deadly terrorist threat, and the dangers presented by hostile states. All of us share interests and values in common, values we want to see projected around the world.

With the threats to our common security becoming more serious, our response cannot be to co-operate with one another less, but to work together more. I therefore want our future relationship with the European Union to include practical arrangements on matters of law enforcement and the sharing of intelligence material with our EU allies.

I am proud of the role Britain has played and will continue to play in promoting Europe's security. Britain has led Europe on the measures needed to keep our continent secure—whether it is implementing sanctions against Russia following its action in Crimea, working for peace and stability in the Balkans, or securing Europe's external border. We will continue to work closely with our European allies in foreign and defence policy even as we leave the EU itself.

A PHASED APPROACH

12. A smooth, orderly Brexit

These are our objectives for the negotiation ahead—objectives that will help to realise our ambition of shaping that stronger, fairer, Global Britain that we want to see.

They are the basis for a new, strong, constructive partnership with the European Union—a partnership of friends and allies, of interests and values. A partnership for a strong EU and a strong UK.

But there is one further objective we are setting. For as I have said before—it is in no one's interests for there to be a cliff-edge for business or a threat to stability, as we change from our existing relationship to a new partnership with the EU.

By this, I do not mean that we will seek some form of unlimited transitional status, in which we find ourselves stuck forever in some kind of permanent political purgatory. That would not be good for Britain, but nor do I believe it would be good for the EU.

Instead, I want us to have reached an agreement about our future partnership by the time the 2-year Article 50 process has concluded. From that point onwards, we believe a phased process of implementation, in which both Britain and the EU institutions and member states prepare for the new arrangements that will exist between us will be in our mutual self-interest. This will give businesses enough time to plan and prepare for those new arrangements.

This might be about our immigration controls, customs systems or the way in which we co-operate on criminal justice matters. Or it might be about the future legal and regulatory framework for financial services. For each issue, the time we need to phase-in the new arrangements may differ. Some might be introduced very quickly, some might take longer. And the interim arrangements we rely upon are likely to be a matter of negotiation.

But the purpose is clear: we will seek to avoid a disruptive cliff-edge, and we will do everything we can to phase in the new arrangements we require as Britain and the EU move towards our new partnership.

(....)

Appendix C

Prime Minister Theresa May's Letter to European Council President Donald Tusk Triggering Article 50

Published 29 March 2017

On 23 June last year, the people of the United Kingdom voted to leave the European Union. As I have said before, that decision was no rejection of the values we share as fellow Europeans. Nor was it an attempt to do harm to the European Union or any of the remaining member states. On the contrary, the United Kingdom wants the European Union to succeed and prosper. Instead, the referendum was a vote to restore, as we see it, our national self-determination. We are leaving the European Union, but we are not leaving Europe—and we want to remain committed partners and allies to our friends across the continent.

Earlier this month, the United Kingdom Parliament confirmed the result of the referendum by voting with clear and convincing majorities in both of its Houses for the European Union (Notification of Withdrawal) Bill. The Bill was passed by Parliament on 13 March and it received Royal Assent from Her Majesty The Queen and became an Act of Parliament on 16 March.

Today, therefore, I am writing to give effect to the democratic decision of the people of the United Kingdom. I hereby notify the European Council in accordance with Article 50(2) of the Treaty on European Union of the United Kingdom's intention to withdraw from the European Union. In addition, in accordance with the same Article 50(2) as applied by Article 106a of the Treaty Establishing the European Atomic Energy Community, I hereby notify the European Council of the United Kingdom's intention to withdraw from the European Atomic Energy Community. References in this letter to the European Union should therefore be taken to include a reference to the European Atomic Energy Community.

This letter sets out the approach of Her Majesty's Government to the discussions we will have about the United Kingdom's departure from the European Union and about the deep and special partnership we hope to enjoy—as your closest friend and neighbour—with the European Union once we leave. We believe that these objectives are in the interests not only of the United Kingdom but of the European Union and the wider world too.

It is in the best interests of both the United Kingdom and the European Union that we should use the forthcoming process to deliver these objectives in a fair and orderly manner, and with as little disruption as possible on each side. We want to make sure that Europe remains strong and prosperous and is capable of projecting its values, leading in the world, and defending itself from security threats. We want the United Kingdom, through a new deep and special partnership with a strong European Union, to play its full part in achieving these goals. We therefore believe it is necessary to agree the terms of our future partnership alongside those of our withdrawal from the European Union.

The Government wants to approach our discussions with ambition, giving citizens and businesses in the United Kingdom and the European Union—and indeed from third countries around the world—as much certainty as possible, as early as possible.

I would like to propose some principles that may help to shape our coming discussions, but before I do so, I should update you on the process we will be undertaking at home, in the United Kingdom.

THE PROCESS IN THE UNITED KINGDOM

As I have announced already, the Government will bring forward legislation that will repeal the Act of Parliament—the European Communities Act 1972—that gives effect to EU law in our country. This legislation will, wherever practical and appropriate, in effect convert the body of existing European Union law (the "acquis") into UK law. This means there will be certainty for UK citizens and for anybody from the European Union who does business in the United Kingdom. The Government will consult on how we design and implement this legislation, and we will publish a White Paper tomorrow. We also intend to bring forward several other pieces of legislation that address specific issues relating to our departure from the European Union, also with a view to ensuring continuity and certainty, in particular for businesses. We will of course continue to fulfil our responsibilities as a member state while we remain a member of the European Union, and the legislation we propose will not come into effect until we leave.

From the start and throughout the discussions, we will negotiate as one United Kingdom, taking due account of the specific interests of every nation and region of the UK as we do so. When it comes to the return of powers back to the United Kingdom, we will consult fully on which powers should reside in Westminster and which should be devolved to Scotland, Wales and Northern Ireland. But it is the expectation of the Government that the outcome of this process will be a significant increase in the decision-making power of each devolved administration.

NEGOTIATIONS BETWEEN THE UNITED KINGDOM AND THE EUROPEAN UNION

The United Kingdom wants to agree with the European Union a deep and special partnership that takes in both economic and security cooperation. To achieve this, we believe it is necessary to agree the terms of our future partnership alongside those of our withdrawal from the EU.

If, however, we leave the European Union without an agreement the default position is that we would have to trade on World Trade Organisation terms. In security terms a failure to reach agreement would mean our cooperation in the fight against crime and terrorism would be weakened. In this kind of scenario, both the United Kingdom and the European Union would of course cope with the change, but it is not the outcome that either side should seek. We must therefore work hard to avoid that outcome.

It is for these reasons that we want to be able to agree a deep and special partnership, taking in both economic and security cooperation, but it is also because we want to play our part in making sure that Europe remains strong and prosperous and able to lead in the world, projecting its values and defending itself from security threats. And we want the United Kingdom to play its full part in realising that vision for our continent.

PROPOSED PRINCIPLES FOR OUR DISCUSSIONS

Looking ahead to the discussions which we will soon begin, I would like to suggest some principles that we might agree to help make sure that the process is as smooth and successful as possible.

i. We should engage with one another constructively and respectfully, in a spirit of sincere cooperation

Since I became Prime Minister of the United Kingdom I have listened carefully to you, to my fellow EU Heads of Government and the Presidents of the European Commission and Parliament. That is why the United Kingdom does not seek membership of the single market: we understand and respect your position that the four freedoms of the single market are indivisible and there can be no "cherry picking". We also understand that there will be consequences for the UK of leaving the EU: we know that we will lose influence over the rules that affect the European economy. We also know that UK companies will, as they trade within the EU, have to align with rules agreed by institutions of which we are no longer a part—just as UK companies do in other overseas markets.

ii. We should always put our citizens first

There is obvious complexity in the discussions we are about to undertake, but we should remember that at the heart of our talks are the interests of all our citizens. There are, for example, many citizens of the remaining member states living in the United Kingdom, and UK citizens living elsewhere in the European Union, and we should aim to strike an early agreement about their rights.

iii. We should work towards securing a comprehensive agreement

We want to agree a deep and special partnership between the UK and the EU, taking in both economic and security cooperation. We will need to discuss how we determine a fair settlement of the UK's rights and obligations as a departing member state, in accordance with the law and in the spirit of the United Kingdom's continuing partnership with the EU. But we believe it is necessary to agree the terms of our future partnership alongside those of our withdrawal from the EU.

iv. We should work together to minimise disruption and give as much certainty as possible

Investors, businesses and citizens in both the UK and across the remaining 27 member states—and those from third countries around the world—want to be able to plan. In order to avoid any cliff-edge as we move from our current relationship to our future partnership, people and businesses in both the UK and the EU would benefit from implementation periods to adjust in a smooth and orderly way to new arrangements. It would help both sides to minimise unnecessary disruption if we agree this principle early in the process.

v. In particular, we must pay attention to the UK's unique relationship with the Republic of Ireland and the importance of the peace process in Northern Ireland

The Republic of Ireland is the only EU member state with a land border with the United Kingdom. We want to avoid a return to a hard border between our two countries, to be able to maintain the Common Travel Area between us, and to make sure that the UK's withdrawal from the EU does not harm the Republic of Ireland. We also have an important responsibility to make sure that nothing is done to jeopardise the peace process in Northern Ireland, and to continue to uphold the Belfast Agreement.

vi. We should begin technical talks on detailed policy areas as soon as possible, but we should prioritise the biggest challenges

Agreeing a high-level approach to the issues arising from our withdrawal will of course be an early priority. But we also propose a bold and ambitious Free Trade Agreement between the United Kingdom and the European Union. This should be of greater scope and ambition than any such agreement before it so that it covers sectors crucial to our linked economies such as financial services and network industries. This will require detailed technical talks, but as the UK is an existing EU member state, both sides have regulatory frameworks and standards that already match. We should therefore prioritise how we manage the evolution of our regulatory frameworks to maintain a fair and open trading environment, and how we resolve disputes. On the scope of the partnership between us—on both economic and security matters—my officials will put forward detailed proposals for deep, broad and dynamic cooperation.

vii. We should continue to work together to advance and protect our shared European values

Perhaps now more than ever, the world needs the liberal, democratic values of Europe. We want to play our part to ensure that Europe remains strong and prosperous and able to lead in the world, projecting its values and defending itself from security threats.

THE TASK BEFORE US

As I have said, the Government of the United Kingdom wants to agree a deep and special partnership between the UK and the EU, taking in both economic and security cooperation. At a time when the growth of global trade is slowing and there are signs that protectionist instincts are on the rise in many parts of the world, Europe has a responsibility to stand up for free trade in the interest of all our citizens. Likewise, Europe's security is more fragile today than at any time since the end of the Cold War. Weakening our cooperation for the prosperity and protection of our citizens would be a costly mistake.

The United Kingdom's objectives for our future partnership remain those set out in my Lancaster House speech of 17 January and the subsequent White Paper published on 2 February.

We recognise that it will be a challenge to reach such a comprehensive agreement within the two-year period set out for withdrawal discussions in the Treaty. But we believe it is necessary to agree the terms of our future partnership alongside those of our withdrawal from the EU. We start from a unique position in these discussions—close regulatory alignment, trust in one another's institutions, and a spirit of cooperation stretching back decades. It is for these reasons, and because the future partnership between the UK and the EU is of such importance to both sides, that I am sure it can be agreed in the time period set out by the Treaty.

The task before us is momentous but it should not be beyond us. After all, the institutions and the leaders of the European Union have succeeded in bringing together a continent blighted by war into a union of peaceful nations, and supported the transition of dictatorships to democracy. Together, I know we are capable of reaching an agreement about the UK's rights and obligations as a departing member state, while establishing a deep and special partnership that contributes towards the prosperity, security and global power of our continent.

Appendix D

European Council (Art. 50) Guidelines for Brexit Negotiations, 29 April 2017

European Council (Art. 50) guidelines following the United Kingdom's notification under Article 50 TEU.

On 29 March 2017, the European Council received the notification by the United Kingdom of its intention to withdraw from the European Union and Euratom. This allows for the opening of negotiations as foreseen by the Treaty.

European integration has brought peace and prosperity to Europe and allowed for an unprecedented level and scope of cooperation on matters of common interest in a rapidly changing world. Therefore, the Union's overall objective in these negotiations will be to preserve its interests, those of its citizens, its businesses and its Member States.

The United Kingdom's decision to leave the Union creates significant uncertainties that have the potential to cause disruption, in particular in the United Kingdom but also, to a lesser extent, in other Member States. Citizens who have built their lives on the basis of rights flowing from the British membership of the EU face the prospect of losing those rights. Businesses and other stakeholders will lose the predictability and certainty that come with EU law. It will also have an impact on public authorities. With this in mind, we must proceed according to a phased approach giving priority to an orderly withdrawal. National authorities, businesses and other stakeholders should take all necessary steps to prepare for the consequences of the United Kingdom's withdrawal.

Throughout these negotiations the Union will maintain its unity and act as one with the aim of reaching a result that is fair and equitable for all Member States and in the interest of its citizens. It will be constructive and strive to find an agreement. This is in the best interest of both sides. The Union will work hard to achieve that outcome, but it will prepare itself to be able to handle the situation also if the negotiations were to fail.

These guidelines define the framework for negotiations under Article 50 TEU and set out the overall positions and principles that the Union will pursue throughout the negotiation. In this context, the European Council welcomes the resolution of the European Parliament of 5 April 2017. The European

Council will remain permanently seized of the matter, and will update these guidelines in the course of the negotiations as necessary. Negotiating directives will be adjusted accordingly.

I. CORE PRINCIPLES

1. The European Council will continue to base itself on the principles set out in the statement of Heads of State or Government and of the Presidents of the European Council and the European Commission on 29 June 2016. It reiterates its wish to have the United Kingdom as a close partner in the future. It further reiterates that any agreement with the United Kingdom will have to be based on a balance of rights and obligations, and ensure a level playing field. Preserving the integrity of the Single Market excludes participation based on a sector-by-sector approach. A non-member of the Union, that does not live up to the same obligations as a member, cannot have the same rights and enjoy the same benefits as a member. In this context, the European Council welcomes the recognition by the British Government that the four freedoms of the Single Market are indivisible and that there can be no "cherry picking". The Union will preserve its autonomy as regards its decision-making as well as the role of the Court of Justice of the European Union.
2. Negotiations under Article 50 TEU will be conducted in transparency and as a single package. In accordance with the principle that nothing is agreed until everything is agreed, individual items cannot be settled separately. The Union will approach the negotiations with unified positions, and will engage with the United Kingdom exclusively through the channels set out in these guidelines and in the negotiating directives. So as not to undercut the position of the Union, there will be no separate negotiations between individual Member States and the United Kingdom on matters pertaining to the withdrawal of the United Kingdom from the Union.
3. The core principles set out above should apply equally to the negotiations on an orderly withdrawal, to any preliminary and preparatory discussions on the framework for a future relationship, and to any form of transitional arrangements.

II. A PHASED APPROACH TO NEGOTIATIONS

4. On the date of withdrawal, the Treaties will cease to apply to the United Kingdom, to those of its overseas countries and territories currently

associated to the Union, and to territories for whose external relations the United Kingdom is responsible. The main purpose of the negotiations will be to ensure the United Kingdom's orderly withdrawal so as to reduce uncertainty and, to the extent possible, minimise disruption caused by this abrupt change.

To that effect, the first phase of negotiations will aim to:

- provide as much clarity and legal certainty as possible to citizens, businesses, stakeholders and international partners on the immediate effects of the United Kingdom's withdrawal from the Union;
- settle the disentanglement of the United Kingdom from the Union and from all the rights and obligations the United Kingdom derives from commitments undertaken as Member State.

The European Council will monitor progress closely and determine when sufficient progress has been achieved to allow negotiations to proceed to the next phase.

5. While an agreement on a future relationship between the Union and the United Kingdom as such can only be finalised and concluded once the United Kingdom has become a third country, Article 50 TEU requires to take account of the framework for its future relationship with the Union in the arrangements for withdrawal. To this end, an overall understanding on the framework for the future relationship should be identified during a second phase of the negotiations under Article 50 TEU. We stand ready to engage in preliminary and preparatory discussions to this end in the context of negotiations under Article 50 TEU, as soon as the European Council decides that sufficient progress has been made in the first phase towards reaching a satisfactory agreement on the arrangements for an orderly withdrawal.
6. To the extent necessary and legally possible, the negotiations may also seek to determine transitional arrangements which are in the interest of the Union and, as appropriate, to provide for bridges towards the foreseeable framework for the future relationship in the light of the progress made. Any such transitional arrangements must be clearly defined, limited in time, and subject to effective enforcement mechanisms. Should a time-limited prolongation of Union acquis be considered, this would require existing Union regulatory, budgetary, supervisory, judiciary and enforcement instruments and structures to apply.
7. The two year timeframe set out in Article 50 TEU ends on 29 March 2019.

III. AGREEMENT ON ARRANGEMENTS FOR AN ORDERLY WITHDRAWAL

8. The right for every EU citizen, and of his or her family members, to live, to work or to study in any EU Member State is a fundamental aspect of the European Union. Along with other rights provided under EU law, it has shaped the lives and choices of millions of people. Agreeing reciprocal guarantees to safeguard the status and rights derived from EU law at the date of withdrawal of EU and UK citizens, and their families, affected by the United Kingdom's withdrawal from the Union will be the first priority for the negotiations. Such guarantees must be effective, enforceable, non-discriminatory and comprehensive, including the right to acquire permanent residence after a continuous period of five years of legal residence. Citizens should be able to exercise their rights through smooth and simple administrative procedures.
9. Also, the United Kingdom leaving the Union will impact EU businesses trading with and operating in the United Kingdom and UK businesses trading with and operating in the Union. Similarly, it may affect those who have entered into contracts and business arrangements or take part in EU-funded programmes based on the assumption of continued British EU membership. Negotiations should seek to prevent a legal vacuum once the Treaties cease to apply to the United Kingdom and, to the extent possible, address uncertainties.
10. A single financial settlement - including issues resulting from the MFF as well as those related to the European Investment Bank (EIB), the European Development Fund (EDF) and the European Central Bank (ECB) - should ensure that the Union and the United Kingdom both respect the obligations resulting from the whole period of the UK membership in the Union. The settlement should cover all commitments as well as liabilities, including contingent liabilities.
11. The Union has consistently supported the goal of peace and reconciliation enshrined in the Good Friday Agreement in all its parts, and continuing to support and protect the achievements, benefits and commitments of the Peace Process will remain of paramount importance. In view of the unique circumstances on the island of Ireland, flexible and imaginative solutions will be required, including with the aim of avoiding a hard border, while respecting the integrity of the Union legal order. In this context, the Union should also recognise existing bilateral agreements and arrangements between the United Kingdom and Ireland which are compatible with EU law.

12. The Union should agree with the United Kingdom on arrangements as regards the Sovereign Base Areas of the United Kingdom in Cyprus and recognise in that respect bilateral agreements and arrangements between the Republic of Cyprus and the United Kingdom which are compatible with EU law, in particular as regards safeguarding rights and interests of those EU citizens resident or working in the Sovereign Base Areas.
13. Following the withdrawal, the United Kingdom will no longer be covered by agreements concluded by the Union or by Member States acting on its behalf or by the Union and its Member States acting jointly. The Union will continue to have its rights and obligations in relation to international agreements. In this respect, the European Council expects the United Kingdom to honour its share of all international commitments contracted in the context of its EU membership. In such instances, a constructive dialogue with the United Kingdom on a possible common approach towards third country partners, international organisations and conventions concerned should be engaged.
14. The withdrawal agreement would also need to address potential issues arising from the withdrawal in other areas of cooperation, including judicial cooperation, law enforcement and security.
15. While the future location of the seats of EU agencies and facilities located in the United Kingdom is a matter for the 27 Member States to settle rapidly, arrangements should be found to facilitate their transfer.
16. Arrangements ensuring legal certainty and equal treatment should be found for all court procedures pending before the Court of Justice of the European Union upon the date of withdrawal that involve the United Kingdom or natural or legal persons in the United Kingdom. The Court of Justice of the European Union should remain competent to adjudicate in these procedures. Similarly, arrangements should be found for administrative procedures pending before the European Commission and Union agencies upon the date of the withdrawal that involve the United Kingdom or natural or legal persons in the United Kingdom. In addition, arrangements should be foreseen for the possibility of administrative or court proceedings to be initiated post-exit for facts that have occurred before the withdrawal date.
17. The withdrawal agreement should include appropriate dispute settlement and enforcement mechanisms regarding the application and interpretation of the withdrawal agreement, as well as duly circumscribed institutional arrangements allowing for the adoption of measures necessary to deal with situations not foreseen in the withdrawal agreement. This should be done bearing in mind the Union's interest to effectively

protect its autonomy and its legal order, including the role of the Court of Justice of the European Union.

IV. PRELIMINARY AND PREPARATORY DISCUSSIONS ON A FRAMEWORK FOR THE UNION - UNITED KINGDOM FUTURE RELATIONSHIP

18. The European Council welcomes and shares the United Kingdom's desire to establish a close partnership between the Union and the United Kingdom after its departure. While a relationship between the Union and a non Member State cannot offer the same benefits as Union membership, strong and constructive ties will remain in both sides' interest and should encompass more than just trade.
19. The British government has indicated that it will not seek to remain in the Single Market, but would like to pursue an ambitious free trade agreement with the European Union. Based on the Union's interests, the European Council stands ready to initiate work towards an agreement on trade, to be finalised and concluded once the United Kingdom is no longer a Member State.
20. Any free trade agreement should be balanced, ambitious and wide-ranging. It cannot, however, amount to participation in the Single Market or parts thereof, as this would undermine its integrity and proper functioning. It must ensure a level playing field, notably in terms of competition and state aid, and in this regard encompass safeguards against unfair competitive advantages through, inter alia, tax, social, environmental and regulatory measures and practices.
21. Any future framework should safeguard financial stability in the Union and respect its regulatory and supervisory regime and standards and their application.
22. The EU stands ready to establish partnerships in areas unrelated to trade, in particular the fight against terrorism and international crime, as well as security, defence and foreign policy.
23. The future partnership must include appropriate enforcement and dispute settlement mechanisms that do not affect the Union's autonomy, in particular its decision-making procedures.
24. After the United Kingdom leaves the Union, no agreement between the EU and the United Kingdom may apply to the territory of Gibraltar without the agreement between the Kingdom of Spain and the United Kingdom.

V. PRINCIPLE OF SINCERE COOPERATION

25. Until it leaves the Union, the United Kingdom remains a full Member of the European Union, subject to all rights and obligations set out in the Treaties and under EU law, including the principle of sincere cooperation.
26. The European Council recognises the need, in the international context, to take into account the specificities of the United Kingdom as a withdrawing Member State, provided it respects its obligations and remains loyal to the Union's interests while still a Member. Similarly the Union expects the United Kingdom to recognise the need of the 27 Member States to meet and discuss matters related to the situation after the withdrawal of the United Kingdom.
27. While the United Kingdom is still a member, all ongoing EU business must continue to proceed as smoothly as possible at 28. The European Council remains committed to drive forward with ambition the priorities the Union has set itself. Negotiations with the United Kingdom will be kept separate from ongoing Union business, and shall not interfere with its progress.

VI. PROCEDURAL ARRANGEMENTS FOR NEGOTIATIONS UNDER ARTICLE 50

28. The European Council endorses the arrangements set out in the statement of 27 Heads of State or Government on 15 December 2016.

Appendix E

European Council Guidelines, December 2017

1. The European Council welcomes the progress achieved during the first phase of negotiations as reflected in the Communication from the Commission and the Joint Report and decides that it is sufficient to move to the second phase related to transition and the framework for the future relationship. It calls on the Union negotiator and the United Kingdom to complete the work on all withdrawal issues, including those not yet addressed in the first phase, in conformity with the European Council guidelines of 29 April 2017, to consolidate the results obtained, and to start drafting the relevant parts of the Withdrawal Agreement. It underlines that negotiations in the second phase can only progress as long as all commitments undertaken during the first phase are respected in full and translated faithfully into legal terms as quickly as possible.
2. In the negotiations during the second phase addressing transitional arrangements as well as the overall understanding on the framework for the future relationship the European Council guidelines of 29 April 2017 continue to apply in their entirety and must be respected.
3. As regards transition, the European Council notes the proposal put forward by the United Kingdom for a transition period of around two years, and agrees to negotiate a transition period covering the whole of the EU acquis, while the United Kingdom, as a third country, will no longer participate in or nominate or elect members of the EU institutions, nor participate in the decision-making of the Union bodies, offices and agencies.
4. Such transitional arrangements, which will be part of the Withdrawal Agreement, must be in the interest of the Union, clearly defined and precisely limited in time. In order to ensure a level playing field based on the same rules applying throughout the Single Market, changes to the acquis adopted by EU institutions, bodies, offices and agencies will have to apply both in the United Kingdom and the EU. All existing Union regulatory, budgetary, supervisory, judiciary and enforcement instruments and structures will also apply, including the competence of the Court of Justice of the European Union. As the United Kingdom

will continue to participate in the Customs Union and the Single Market (with all four freedoms) during the transition, it will have to continue to comply with EU trade policy, to apply EU customs tariff and collect EU customs duties, and to ensure all EU checks are being performed on the border vis-à-vis other third countries.

5. The European Council calls on the Commission to put forward appropriate recommendations to this effect, and on the Council to adopt additional negotiating directives on transitional arrangements in January 2018.
6. The European Council reconfirms its desire to establish a close partnership between the Union and the United Kingdom. While an agreement on a future relationship can only be finalised and concluded once the United Kingdom has become a third country, the Union will be ready to engage in preliminary and preparatory discussions with the aim of identifying an overall understanding of the framework for the future relationship, once additional guidelines have been adopted to this effect. Such an understanding should be elaborated in a political declaration accompanying and referred to in the Withdrawal Agreement.
7. The Union takes note that the United Kingdom has stated its intention to no longer participate in the Customs Union and the Single Market after the end of the transition period, and the European Council will calibrate its approach as regards trade and economic cooperation in the light of this position so as to ensure a balance of rights and obligations, preserve a level playing field, avoid upsetting existing relations with other third countries, and to respect all other principles set out in its guidelines of 29 April 2017, in particular the need to preserve the integrity and proper functioning of the Single Market.
8. The European Council reconfirms its readiness to establish partnerships in areas unrelated to trade and economic cooperation, in particular the fight against terrorism and international crime, as well as security, defence and foreign policy.
9. The European Council will continue to follow the negotiations closely and will adopt additional guidelines in March 2018, in particular as regards the framework for the future relationship. It calls on the United Kingdom to provide further clarity on its position on the framework for the future relationship. The European Council invites the Council (Art. 50) together with the Union negotiator to continue internal preparatory discussions, including on the scope of the framework for the future relationship.

Appendix F

European Council Guidelines, 23 March 2018

1. The European Council welcomes the agreement reached by the negotiators on parts of the legal text of the Withdrawal Agreement covering citizens' rights, the financial settlement, a number of other withdrawal issues and the transition. The European Council recalls that other issues still require agreement and negotiations can only progress as long as all commitments undertaken so far are respected in full, and welcomes in this respect Prime Minister May's written assurances notably regarding Ireland/Northern Ireland. The European Council calls for intensified efforts on the remaining withdrawal issues as well as issues related to the territorial application of the Withdrawal Agreement, notably as regards Gibraltar, and reiterates that nothing is agreed until everything is agreed.
2. The European Council recalls and reconfirms its guidelines of 29 April and 15 December 2017, which continue to apply in full and whose principles will have to be respected by the future relationship with the UK. The European Council takes note of the European Parliament resolution of 14 March 2018 on the framework of the future EU-UK relationship.
3. The European Council restates the Union's determination to have as close as possible a partnership with the UK in the future. Such a partnership should cover trade and economic cooperation as well as other areas, in particular the fight against terrorism and international crime, as well as security, defence and foreign policy.
4. At the same time, the European Council has to take into account the repeatedly stated positions of the UK, which limit the depth of such a future partnership. Being outside the Customs Union and the Single Market will inevitably lead to frictions in trade. Divergence in external tariffs and internal rules as well as absence of common institutions and a shared legal system, necessitates checks and controls to uphold the integrity of the EU Single Market as well as of the UK market. This unfortunately will have negative economic consequences, in particular in the United Kingdom.
5. Against this background, the European Council sets out the following guidelines with a view to the opening of negotiations on the overall

understanding of the framework for the future relationship, that will be elaborated in a political declaration accompanying and referred to in the Withdrawal Agreement.

6. The approach outlined below reflects the level of rights and obligations compatible with the positions stated by the UK. If these positions were to evolve, the Union will be prepared to reconsider its offer in accordance with the principles stated in the guidelines of 29 April and of 15 December 2017 as well as in the present guidelines.
7. In this context, the European Council reiterates in particular that any agreement with the United Kingdom will have to be based on a balance of rights and obligations, and ensure a level playing field. A non-member of the Union, that does not live up to the same obligations as a member, cannot have the same rights and enjoy the same benefits as a member. The European Council recalls that the four freedoms are indivisible and that there can be no "cherry picking" through participation in the Single Market based on a sector-by-sector approach, which would undermine the integrity and proper functioning of the Single Market. The European Council further reiterates that the Union will preserve its autonomy as regards its decision-making, which excludes participation of the United Kingdom as a third-country in the Union Institutions and participation in the decision-making of the Union bodies, offices and agencies. The role of the Court of Justice of the European Union will also be fully respected.
8. As regards the core of the economic relationship, the European Council confirms its readiness to initiate work towards a balanced, ambitious and wide-ranging free trade agreement (FTA) insofar as there are sufficient guarantees for a level playing field. This agreement will be finalised and concluded once the UK is no longer a Member State. Such an agreement cannot however offer the same benefits as Membership and cannot amount to participation in the Single Market or parts thereof. This agreement would address:
   i) trade in goods, with the aim of covering all sectors and seeking to maintain zero tariffs and no quantitative restrictions with appropriate accompanying rules of origin. In the overall context of the FTA, existing reciprocal access to fishing waters and resources should be maintained;
   ii) appropriate customs cooperation, preserving the regulatory and jurisdictional autonomy of the parties and the integrity of the EU Customs Union;
   iii) disciplines on technical barriers to trade (TBT) and sanitary and phytosanitary (SPS) measures;

iv) a framework for voluntary regulatory cooperation;

v) trade in services, with the aim of allowing market access to provide services under host state rules, including as regards right of establishment for providers, to an extent consistent with the fact that the UK will become a third country and the Union and the UK will no longer share a common regulatory, supervisory, enforcement and judiciary framework;

vi) access to public procurement markets, investments and protection of intellectual property rights, including geographical indications, and other areas of interest to the Union.

9. The future partnership should address global challenges, in particular in the areas of climate change and sustainable development, as well as cross-border pollution, where the Union and the UK should continue close cooperation.

10. The future partnership should include ambitious provisions on movement of natural persons, based on full reciprocity and non-discrimination among Member States, and related areas such as coordination of social security and recognition of professional qualifications. In this context, options for judicial cooperation in matrimonial, parental responsibility and other related matters could be explored, taking into account that the UK will be a third country outside Schengen and that such cooperation would require strong safeguards to ensure full respect of fundamental rights.

11. In terms of socio-economic cooperation, the following could be envisaged:

i) regarding transport services, the aim should be to ensure continued connectivity between the UK and the EU after the UK withdrawal. This could be achieved, inter alia, through an air transport agreement, combined with aviation safety and security agreements, as well as agreements on other modes of transport, while ensuring a strong level playing field in highly competitive sectors;

ii) regarding certain Union programmes, e.g. in the fields of research and innovation and of education and culture, any participation of the UK should be subject to the relevant conditions for the participation of third countries to be established in the corresponding programmes.

12. Given the UK's geographic proximity and economic interdependence with the EU27, the future relationship will only deliver in a mutually satisfactory way if it includes robust guarantees which ensure a level playing field. The aim should be to prevent unfair competitive advantage that the UK could enjoy through undercutting of levels of protection

with respect to, inter alia, competition and state aid, tax, social, environment and regulatory measures and practices. This will require a combination of substantive rules aligned with EU and international standards, adequate mechanisms to ensure effective implementation domestically, enforcement and dispute settlement mechanisms in the agreement as well as Union autonomous remedies, that are all commensurate with the depth and breadth of the EUUK economic connectedness. Any future framework should safeguard financial stability in the Union and respect its regulatory and supervisory regime and standards and their application.

13. In other areas than trade and economic cooperation, where the Union has already signalled its readiness to establish specific partnerships, the European Council considers that:
    i) law enforcement and judicial cooperation in criminal matters should constitute an important element of the future EU-UK relationship in the light of the geographic proximity and shared threats faced by the Union and the UK, taking into account that the UK will be a third country outside Schengen. The future partnership should cover effective exchanges of information, support for operational cooperation between law enforcement authorities and judicial cooperation in criminal matters. Strong safeguards will need to be established that ensure full respect of fundamental rights and effective enforcement and dispute settlement mechanisms;
    ii) in view of our shared values and common challenges, there should be a strong EU-UK cooperation in the fields of foreign, security and defence policy. A future partnership should respect the autonomy of the Union's decision-making, taking into account that the UK will be a third country, and foresee appropriate dialogue, consultation, coordination, exchange of information, and cooperation mechanisms. As a pre-requisite for the exchange of information in the framework of such cooperation a Security of Information Agreement would have to be put in place.
14. In the light of the importance of data flows in several components of the future relationship, it should include rules on data. As regards personal data, protection should be governed by Union rules on adequacy with a view to ensuring a level of protection essentially equivalent to that of the Union.
15. The governance of our future relationship with the UK will have to address management and supervision, dispute settlement and enforcement, including sanctions and cross-retaliation mechanisms. Designing

the overall governance of the future relationship will require to take into account:

i) the content and depth of the future relationship;
ii) the necessity to ensure effectiveness and legal certainty;
iii) the requirements of the autonomy of the EU legal order, including the role of the Court of Justice of the European Union, notably as developed in the jurisprudence.

16. The European Council, with the support of the Council, will continue to follow the negotiations closely, in all their aspects, and will return in particular to the remaining withdrawal issues and to the framework for the future relationship at its June meeting. In the meantime, the European Council calls upon the Commission, the High Representative of the Union for Foreign Affairs and Security Policy and the Member States to continue the work on preparedness at all levels for the consequences of the UK withdrawal, taking into account all possible outcomes.

Appendix G

UK Checkers Plan. Excerpt from Policy Paper—The Future Relationship between the United Kingdom and the European Union, Updated 17 July 2018

....

3. EXECUTIVE SUMMARY

The United Kingdom will **leave the European Union on 29 March 2019** and begin to chart a new course in the world.

The Government will have **delivered on the result of the 2016 referendum**—the biggest democratic exercise in this country's history. And it will have reached a key milestone in its principal mission—to build a country that works for everyone. A country that is stronger, fairer, more united and more outward-looking.

4. A DETAILED VISION

To fulfil that mission, the Government is advancing a detailed proposal for a **principled and practical Brexit**.

This proposal **underpins the vision set out by the Prime Minister at Lancaster House, in Florence, at Mansion House and in Munich**, and in doing so addresses questions raised by the EU in the intervening months—explaining how the relationship would work, what benefits it would deliver for both sides, and why it would respect the sovereignty of the UK as well as the autonomy of the EU.

At its core, it is a package that strikes a **new and fair balance** of rights and obligations.

One that the Government hopes will yield a **redoubling of effort in the negotiations**, as the UK and the EU work together to develop and agree the framework for the future relationship this autumn.

5. A PRINCIPLED BREXIT

A principled Brexit means **respecting the result of the referendum** and the decision of the UK public to take back control of the UK's laws, borders and money—and doing so in a way that supports the Government's wider objectives across five key areas of the UK's national life.

For the **economy**, developing a broad and deep economic relationship with the EU that maximises future prosperity in line with the modern Industrial Strategy and minimises disruption to trade between the UK and the EU, protecting jobs and livelihoods—at the same time making the most of trading opportunities around the world.

For **communities**, addressing specific concerns voiced in the referendum by ending free movement and putting in place a new immigration system, introducing new independent policies to support farming and fishing communities, using the Shared Prosperity Fund to spark a new wave of regeneration in the UK's towns and cities, and keeping citizens safe.

For the **union**, meeting commitments to Northern Ireland by protecting the peace process and avoiding a hard border, safeguarding the constitutional and economic integrity of the UK, and devolving the appropriate powers to Edinburgh, Cardiff and Belfast—while ensuring the deal delivers for the Crown Dependencies, Gibraltar and the other Overseas Territories, noting there will be no change in their long-standing relationships with the UK.

For **democracy**, leaving the EU's institutions and reclaiming the UK's sovereignty, ensuring the laws people live by are passed by those they elect and enforced by UK courts, with clear accountability to the people of the UK.

For the **UK's place in the world**, continuing to promote innovation and new ideas, asserting a fully independent foreign policy, and working alongside the EU to promote and protect shared European values of democracy, openness and liberty.

5.1 A new relationship

Guided by these principles, the Government is determined to build a **new relationship that works for both the UK and the EU**. One which sees the UK leave the Single Market and the Customs Union to seize new opportunities and forge a new role in the world, while protecting jobs, supporting growth and maintaining security cooperation.

The Government believes this new relationship needs to be broader in scope than any other that exists between the EU and a third country. It should **reflect the UK's and the EU's deep history, close ties, and unique starting point**. And it must deliver real and lasting benefits for both sides, supporting shared prosperity and security—which is why the Government is proposing to structure the relationship around an economic partnership and a security partnership.

The future relationship also needs to be informed by both the UK and the EU taking a **responsible approach to avoiding a hard border between Northern Ireland and Ireland**, in a way that respects the constitutional and economic integrity of the UK and the autonomy of the EU.

5.2 Economic partnership

In designing the new trading relationship, the UK and the EU should therefore focus on ensuring continued **frictionless access at the border to each other's markets for goods**.

To deliver this goal, the Government is proposing the establishment of **a free trade area for goods**.

This free trade area would **protect the uniquely integrated supply chains and 'just-in-time' processes** that have developed across the UK and the EU over the last 40 years, and the jobs and livelihoods dependent on them, ensuring businesses on both sides can continue operating through their current value and supply chains. It would avoid the need for customs and regulatory checks at the border, and mean that businesses would not need to complete costly customs declarations. And it would enable products to only undergo one set of approvals and authorisations in either market, before being sold in both.

As a result, the free trade area for goods would see the UK and the EU **meet their shared commitments to Northern Ireland and Ireland** through the overall future relationship. It would avoid the need for a hard border between Northern Ireland and Ireland, without harming the internal market of the UK—doing so in a way that fully respects the integrity of the EU's Single Market, Customs Union, and its rules-based framework.

These **close arrangements on goods should sit alongside new ones for services and digital**, giving the UK the freedom to chart its own path in the areas that matter most for its economy. The Government wants to minimise new barriers to trade between the UK and the EU, and hopes that both sides will work together to reduce them further over time—but acknowledges that there will be more barriers to the UK's access to the EU market than is the case today.

Finally, a relationship this deep will need to be supported by provisions giving both sides confidence that **the trade that it facilitates will be both open and fair.** So the Government is proposing reciprocal commitments that would ensure UK businesses could carry on competing fairly in EU markets, and EU businesses operating in the UK could do the same.

On this basis, the Government's vision is for an **economic partnership** that includes:

- a common rulebook for **goods including agri-food**, covering only those rules necessary to provide for frictionless trade at the border—meaning that the UK would make an upfront choice to commit by treaty to ongoing harmonisation with the relevant EU rules, with all those rules legislated for by Parliament or the devolved legislatures;
- participation by the UK in those EU **agencies that provide authorisations for goods** in highly regulated sectors—namely the European Chemicals Agency, the European Aviation Safety Agency, and the European Medicines Agency—accepting the rules of these agencies and contributing to their costs, under new arrangements that recognise the UK will not be a Member State;
- the phased introduction of a new **Facilitated Customs Arrangement** that would remove the need for customs checks and controls between the UK and the EU as if they were a combined customs territory, which would enable the UK to control its own tariffs for trade with the rest of the world and ensure businesses paid the right or no tariff, becoming operational in stages as both sides complete the necessary preparations;
- in combination with **no tariffs on any goods**, these arrangements would avoid any new friction at the border, and protect the integrated supply chains that span the UK and the EU, safeguarding the jobs and livelihoods they support;
- new arrangements on **services and digital**, providing regulatory freedom where it matters most for the UK's services-based economy, and so ensuring the UK is best placed to capitalise on the industries of the future in line with the modern Industrial Strategy, while recognising that the UK and the EU will not have current levels of access to each other's markets;
- new economic and regulatory arrangements for **financial services**, preserving the mutual benefits of integrated markets and protecting financial stability while respecting the right of the UK and the EU to control access to their own markets—noting that these arrangements will not replicate the EU's passporting regimes;
- continued cooperation on **energy and transport**—preserving the Single Electricity Market in Northern Ireland and Ireland, seeking broad cooperation on energy, developing an air transport agreement, and exploring reciprocal arrangements for road hauliers and passenger transport operators;

- a **new framework** that respects the UK's control of its borders and enables UK and EU citizens to continue to travel to each other's countries, and businesses and professionals to provide services—in line with the arrangements that the UK might want to offer to other close trading partners in the future; and
- in light of the depth of this partnership, binding provisions that guarantee an **open and fair trading environment**—committing to apply a common rulebook for state aid, establishing cooperative arrangements between regulators on competition, and agreeing to maintain high standards through non-regression provisions in areas including the environment and employment rules, in keeping with the UK's strong domestic commitments.

Taken together, such a partnership would see the UK and the EU **meet their commitments to Northern Ireland and Ireland through the overall future relationship** : preserving the constitutional and economic integrity of the UK; honouring the letter and the spirit of the Belfast ('Good Friday') Agreement; and ensuring that the operational legal text the UK will agree with the EU on the 'backstop' solution as part of the Withdrawal Agreement will not have to be used.

And while what the Government is proposing is ambitious in its breadth and depth, it is also workable and delivers on the referendum result—**fully respecting the sovereignty of the UK, just as it respects the autonomy of the EU**—with Parliament having the right to decide which legislation it adopts in the future, recognising there could be proportionate implications for the operation of the future relationship where the UK and the EU had a common rulebook.

In short, this proposal represents a **fair and pragmatic balance** for the future trading relationship between the UK and the EU—one that would protect jobs and livelihoods, and deliver an outcome that is truly in the interests of both sides.

. . . .

Appendix H

Summary of November 2018 Withdrawal Agreement Excerpts from European Commission Press Release on Withdrawal Agreement

BREXIT NEGOTIATIONS: WHAT IS IN THE WITHDRAWAL AGREEMENT

Brussels, 14 November 2018

QUESTIONS & ANSWERS

What has been agreed today?

The European Commission and the United Kingdom's negotiators have reached an agreement on the entirety of the Withdrawal Agreement of the United Kingdom of Great Britain and Northern Ireland from the European Union and the European Atomic Energy Community, as provided for under Article 50 of the Treaty on European Union.

The Withdrawal Agreement establishes the terms of the UK's withdrawal from the EU. It ensures that the withdrawal will happen in an orderly manner, and offers legal certainty once the Treaties and EU law will cease to apply to the UK.

The Withdrawal Agreement covers the following areas:

- **Common provisions**, setting out standard clauses for the proper understanding and operation of the Withdrawal Agreement.
- **Citizens' rights**, protecting the life choices of over 3 million EU citizens in the UK, and over 1 million UK nationals in EU countries, safeguarding their right to stay and ensuring that they can continue to contribute to their communities.
- **Separation issues,** ensuring a smooth winding-down of current arrangements and providing for an orderly withdrawal (for example, to allow for goods placed on the market before the end of the transition to continue to their destination, for the protection of existing intellectual property rights including geographical indications, the winding down

of ongoing police and judicial cooperation in criminal matters and other administrative and judicial procedures, the use of data and information exchanged before the end of the transition period, issues related to Euratom, and other matters).

- A **transition period,** during which the EU will treat the UK as if it were a Member State, with the exception of participation in the EU institutions and governance structures. The transition period will help in particular administrations, businesses and citizens to adapt to the withdrawal of the United Kingdom.
- The **financial settlement**, ensuring that the UK and the EU will honour all financial obligations undertaken while the UK was a member of the Union.
- The overall **governance structure** of the Withdrawal Agreement, ensuring the effective management, implementation and enforcement of the agreement, including appropriate dispute settlement mechanisms.
- The terms of a **legally operational backstop** to ensure that there will be no hard border between **Ireland and Northern Ireland**. The protocol on Ireland/Northern Ireland also contains UK commitments not to diminish rights set out in the Good Friday (Belfast) Agreement 1998, and to protect North-South cooperation. It provides for the possibility to continue the Common Travel Area arrangements between Ireland and the UK, and preserves the Single Electricity Market on the island of Ireland.
- A protocol on the Sovereign Base Areas (SBA) in **Cyprus**, protecting the interests of Cypriots who live and work in the Sovereign Base Areas following the UK's withdrawal from the Union.
- A Protocol on **Gibraltar**, which provides for close cooperation between Spain and the UK in respect of Gibraltar on the implementation of citizens' rights provisions of the Withdrawal Agreement, and concerns administrative cooperation between competent authorities in a number of policy areas.

....

I. What is included in the Common Provisions of the Withdrawal Agreement?

This part sets out the necessary clauses to ensure the correct understanding, operation and interpretation of the Withdrawal Agreement. They provide the basis for the correct application of the Agreement. From the outset of the negotiations, the EU has attached great importance to the fact that the provisions of the Withdrawal Agreement must clearly have **the same legal effects** in the UK as in the EU and its Member States.

The Agreement explicitly includes such a requirement, meaning that both Parties should ensure in their respective legal orders primacy and direct effect, as well as consistent interpretation with the case law of the Court of Justice of the European Union (CJEU) handed down until the end of the transition. Direct effect is mentioned explicitly with reference to all provisions of the Withdrawal Agreement which meet the conditions of direct effect under Union law. This basically means that concerned parties can invoke the Withdrawal Agreement directly before national courts both in the UK, as well as in the EU Member States.

It is also mandatory for the purposes of interpreting the Agreement to use the methods and general principles of interpretation applicable within the EU. This covers, for instance, the obligation to interpret the concepts or provisions of Union law referred to in the Withdrawal Agreement in a manner consistent with the Charter of Fundamental Rights.

Furthermore, UK courts must abide by the principle of consistent interpretation with the CJEU case law handed down until the end of the transition period and pay due regard to CJEU case law handed down after that date.

The Agreement specifically requires the UK to ensure compliance with the above through primary domestic legislation, specifically empowering UK judicial and administrative authorities to disapply inconsistent or incompatible national law.

This section also makes clear that references to Union law in the Withdrawal Agreement shall be understood as including amendments made until the last day of the transition period. Few exceptions are foreseen, notably for specific financial settlement provisions, to avoid imposing additional obligations on the UK, and for the transition period, during which Union law will continue to apply dynamically to and in the UK. They shall be understood also as including the acts supplementing or implementing referenced provisions.

Finally, the Agreement provides that the UK shall be disconnected at the end of the transition period from all EU databases and networks, unless specifically provided otherwise.

II. What has been agreed on citizens' rights?

The right for every EU citizen and their family members to live, work or study in any EU Member State is one of the foundations of the European

Union. Many EU and UK citizens have made their life choices based on rights related to free movement under Union law. **Protecting the life choices of those citizens and their family members** has been the first priority from the beginning of the negotiation.

The Withdrawal Agreement safeguards the right to stay and continue their current activities for over 3 million EU citizens in the UK, and over 1 million UK nationals in EU countries.

Who is protected by the Withdrawal Agreement?

The Withdrawal Agreement protects those EU citizens who were residing in the UK and UK nationals who were residing in one of the 27 EU Member States at the end of the transition period, where such residence is in accordance with EU law on free movement.

The Withdrawal Agreement also protects the family members that are granted rights under EU law (current **spouses and registered partners, parents, grandparents, children, grandchildren and a person in an existing durable relationship**), who do not yet live in the same host state as the Union citizen or the UK national, to join them in the future.

Children will be protected by the Withdrawal Agreement, wherever they are born before or after the UK's withdrawal, or whether they are born inside or outside the host state where the EU citizen or the UK national resides. The only exception foreseen concerns children born after the UK's withdrawal and for which a parent not covered by the Withdrawal Agreement has sole custody under the applicable family law.

Which rights are protected?

The Withdrawal Agreement enables both EU citizens and UK nationals, as well as their respective family members, to continue to exercise their rights derived from Union law in each other's territories, for the rest of their lives, where those rights are based on life choices made before the end of the transition period.

Union citizens and UK nationals, as well as their respective family members can **continue to live, work or study** as they currently do under the same substantive conditions as under Union law, benefiting in full from the application of the prohibition of any discrimination on grounds of nationality and of the right to equal treatment compared to host state nationals. The only restrictions which apply are those derived from Union law or as provided for under the Agreement. The Withdrawal Agreement does not prevent the UK or Member States from deciding to grant more generous rights.

Residence rights

The substantive conditions of residence are and will remain the same as those under current EU law on free movement. In the case where the host states opted for a mandatory registration system, decisions for granting the new residence status under the Withdrawal Agreement will be made based on objective criteria *(i.e. no discretion)*, and on the basis of the exact same conditions set out in the Free Movement Directive (Directive 2004/38/EC): Articles 6 and 7 confer a right of residence for up to five years on those who work or have sufficient financial resources and sickness insurance, Articles 16—18 confer a right of permanent residence on those who have resided legally for five years.

In essence, EU citizens and UK nationals meet these conditions if they are: workers or self-employed; or have sufficient resources and sickness insurance; or are family members of some other person who meets these conditions; or have already acquired the right of permanent residence and are therefore no longer subject to any conditions.

The Withdrawal Agreement does not require physical presence in the host state at the end of the transition period— temporary absences that do not affect the right of residence and longer absences that do not affect the right of permanent residence are accepted.

Those protected by the Withdrawal Agreement who have not yet acquired permanent residence rights—if they have not lived in the host state for at least five years—will be fully protected by the Withdrawal Agreement, and will be able to continue residing in the host state and acquire permanent residence rights also after the UK's withdrawal.

EU citizens and UK nationals arriving in the host state during the transition period will enjoy exactly the same rights and obligations under the Withdrawal Agreement as those who arrived in the host state before 30 March 2019. Their rights will be subject to the same restrictions and limitations, too. The persons concerned will no longer be beneficiaries of the Withdrawal Agreement if they are absent from their host state for more than five years.

Rights of workers and self-employed persons, and recognition of professional qualifications

The persons covered by the Withdrawal Agreement will have the right to take up **employment** or to carry out an economic activity as a **self-employed** person. They will also keep all their workers' rights based on Union law. For example, they will maintain the right not to be discriminated against on ground of nationality as regards employment, remuneration and other conditions of work and employment; the right to take up and pursue an activity in accordance with the rules applicable to the nationals of the host state, the right to employment assistance under the same conditions as the nationals of the host state, the right to equal treatment in respect of conditions of employment and work, the right to social and tax advantages, collective rights, and the right for their children to access education.

The Withdrawal Agreement will also protect the rights of frontier workers or frontier self-employed persons in the countries where they work.

Additionally, when a person covered by the Withdrawal Agreement who had his or her **professional qualifications** recognised in the country (an EU Member State or the UK) where he or she currently resides or, for frontier workers, where he or she works, will be able to continue to rely on the recognition decision there for the purpose of carrying out the professional activities linked to the use of those professional qualifications. If he or she has already applied for the recognition of his or her professional qualifications before the end of the transition period, his or her application will be processed domestically in accordance with the EU rules applicable when the application was made.

Social security

The Withdrawal Agreement provides for rules on social security coordination in relation to the beneficiaries of the citizens' part of the Withdrawal Agreement, and to other persons who at the end of the transition period are in a situation involving both the United Kingdom and a Member State from the social security cooperation perspective.

Those persons will maintain their **right to healthcare, pensions and other social security benefits**, and if they are entitled to a cash benefit from one country, they may be able to receive it even if they decide to live in another country.

The social security provisions of the Withdrawal Agreement will address the rights of EU citizens and UK nationals in social security cross-border situations involving the UK and (at least) one Member State at the end of the transition period.

Those provisions can be extended to cover "triangular" social security situations involving a Member State (or several Member States), the UK and an EFTA country (Iceland, Liechtenstein, Norway and Switzerland). This will allow the rights of EU citizens, UK nationals as well as EFTA country citizens who are in that type of triangular situations to be protected.

For this to be operational, three different agreements need to be applicable: an article in the Withdrawal Agreement protecting EFTA nationals, provisions protecting EU citizens in corresponding agreements between the UK and the EFTA countries, and provisions protecting UK nationals in corresponding agreements between the EU and the EFTA countries.

Only if the two latter agreements are concluded and applicable, the article in the Withdrawal Agreement protecting EFTA nationals will be applicable as well. The decision on the applicability of this article will be taken by the Joint Committee created by the Withdrawal Agreement.

III. What has been agreed on separation issues?

In agreement with the European Council (Article 50) guidelines, the Withdrawal Agreement, where needed, seeks to ensure an orderly withdrawal and provides the detailed provisions that are needed for the winding down of ongoing processes and arrangements in a number of policy areas.

Goods placed on the market

The Withdrawal Agreement provides that goods lawfully placed on the market in the EU or the UK before the end of the transition period may continue to freely circulate in and between these two markets, until they reach their end-users, without any need for product modifications or re-labelling.

This means that goods that will still be in the distribution chain at the end of the transition period can reach their end-users in the EU or the UK without having to comply with any additional product requirements. Such goods may also be put into service (where provided in the applicable provisions of Union law), and will be subject to continued oversight by the market surveillance authorities of the Member States and the UK.

By way of exception, the movement of live animals and animal products between the Union market and the UK's market will, as from the end of the transition period, be subject to the applicable rules of the Parties on imports and sanitary controls at the border, regardless of whether they were placed on the market before the end of the transition period.

This is necessary in view of the high sanitary risks associated with such products, and the need for effective veterinary controls when these products, as well as live animals, enter the Union market or the UK market.

(….)

IV. What has been agreed regarding the transition period?

The Withdrawal Agreement provides for a transition period until the end of 2020. The continued application of EU law during this period will give time to national administrations and businesses to prepare for the new relationship. It will also provide the EU and the UK with time to negotiate the future relationship.

The transition period is set to **end on 31 December 2020**, taking into account the initial request from the UK for a transition period of around two years, and making it coincide with the end of the current long-term EU budget (the Multiannual Financial Framework 2014-2020).

During this period, the entire Union acquis will continue to apply to and in the UK as if it were a Member State. This means that the UK will continue to participate in the EU Customs Union and the Single Market (with all four freedoms) and all Union policies. Any changes to the Union acquis will automatically apply to and in the UK. The direct effect and primacy of Union law will be preserved. All existing Union regulatory, budgetary, supervisory, judiciary and enforcement instruments and structures will apply, including the competence of the Court of Justice of the European Union.

During this transition period, the UK will have to comply with the EU's trade policy and will continue to be bound by the Union's exclusive competence, in particular in respect of the Common Commercial Policy.

The UK will remain bound during the transition period by the obligations stemming from all EU international agreements. In the area of trade, this means that third countries keep the same UK market access. During this period, the UK cannot become bound by new agreements on its own in areas of Union exclusive competence unless authorised to do so by the EU.

As of the withdrawal date (i.e. including during the transition period), the UK, having left the EU, will no longer be part of **EU decision-making**. It will no longer be represented in the EU institutions, agencies and bodies, and persons appointed, nominated, or representing the UK, and persons elected in the UK, will no longer take part in the EU institutions, agencies, and bodies.

Subject to exceptions, the UK will no longer participate in meetings of Member State groups. The UK cannot, during the transition period, act as a "rapporteur" for European authorities (such as conducting a risk assessment for the EU Chemicals Agency) or for Member States (such as assessing the safety and efficacy of a medicine).

The transition period also offers clarity and predictability to interested parties, including international partners, on **fisheries**, as it extends the applicability of the Common Fisheries Policy (and terms of relevant international agreements) to the UK throughout the transition. The UK shall be bound by the decisions on fishing opportunities until the end of the transition period. It will be consulted at various stages of the annual decision-making process in respect of its fishing opportunities. Upon invitation by the Union and to the extent permitted by the particular forum, the UK may attend international consultations and negotiations in view of preparing its future membership in relevant international fora.

Possible extension of the transition period

The Withdrawal Agreement includes the possibility for the Joint Committee to extend the transition period. This possibility can only be used once and must be decided by the Joint Committee before 1 July 2020.

This provision also offers the opportunity for the UK to request additional time to make sure that a future agreement, including provisions for avoiding a hard border in Ireland, may be reached before the end of the transition period.

The extension can only be done by mutual agreement of the Union and the UK. All other terms agreed in March in respect of the transition will remain applicable. To recall, this means, in short, full application of Union law to the UK and full powers of the Union institutions, including the Court of Justice.

However, during a possible extension of the transition period, the UK will be treated as a third country for the purposes of the future Multiannual Financial Framework as of 2021. For that framework, the UK will be able to participate in EU programmes based on the legal bases for third countries that will be agreed in EU regulations.

Extending the transition period will require a fair financial contribution from the UK to the EU budget, which will have to be decided by the Joint Committee established by the Withdrawal Agreement.

UK's participation in European foreign and defence policies during the transition period

The Common Foreign and Security Policy will apply to the United Kingdom during the transition period. In particular, the UK will have to implement the Union's restrictive measures in place or decided during the transition period, or to support EU statements and positions in third countries and international organisations.

The UK will have the possibility to participate in EU military operations and civilian missions established under the Common and Security Defence Policy (CSDP), yet without any leading capacity. For example, the Operation Headquarters of the EU operation fighting piracy, Atalanta, is transferred from Northwood to Rota in Spain.

The UK will have the possibility to participate in projects of Common Foreign and Security Policy Agencies, including the European Defence Agency, but without having any decision-making role.

UK's participation in Justice and Home Affairs during the transition period

All elements of the Justice and Home Affairs policy will continue to apply to the United Kingdom during the transition period, and the UK will remain bound by EU acts applicable to it upon its withdrawal. It may choose to exercise its right to opt-in/opt-out with regard to measures amending, replacing or building upon those acts.

However, during the transition period the UK will not have the right to opt-in to completely new measures. The EU may nevertheless invite the UK to cooperate in relation to such new measures, under the conditions set out for cooperation with third countries.

....

V. What has been agreed regarding the financial settlement?

The European Council guidelines of 29 April 2017 requested a single financial settlement covering the EU budget, the termination of the United Kingdom's membership of all bodies or institutions established by the Treaties and the participation of the UK in specific funds and facilities related to the Union policies. The financial settlement agreed covers all these points and settles the accounts.

According to the Withdrawal Agreement, the **UK will honour its share of financing all the obligations undertaken while it was a member of the Union**, in relation to the EU budget (and in particular the Multi-annual Financial Framework 2014-2020, including for the payments that will happen after the end of the transition period in relation to the closure of the programmes), the European Investment Bank, the European Central Bank, the Facility for Refugees in Turkey, EU Trust Funds, Council agencies and also the European Development Fund.

Against this backdrop, the Commission and the UK negotiators have agreed on a fair methodology to calculate the UK's obligations in the context of its withdrawal.

The principles underlying the agreed methodology are that:

- no Member State should pay more or receive less because of the United Kingdom's withdrawal from the Union;
- the United Kingdom should pay its share of the commitments taken during its membership; and
- the United Kingdom should neither pay more nor earlier than if it had remained a Member State. This implies in particular that the United Kingdom should pay based on the actual outcome of the budget, i.e. adjusted to implementation.

How much will the UK pay?

The objective of the negotiations was to settle all obligations that will exist on the date of the UK's withdrawal from the European Union. Therefore, the agreement is not about the amount of the UK's financial obligation, but about **the methodology for calculating** it.

Both sides agreed on an objective methodology which allows honouring all joint commitments vis-à-vis the Union budget (2014-2020), including outstanding commitments at the end of 2020 ("Reste à liquider") and liabilities which are not matched by assets.

The UK will also continue to guarantee the loans made by the Union before its withdrawal and will receive back its share of any unused guarantees and subsequent recoveries following the triggering of the guarantees for such loans.

In addition, the UK agreed to honour all outstanding commitments of the EU Trust Funds and the Facility for Refugees in Turkey. The UK will remain party to the European Development Fund and will continue to contribute to the payments necessary to honour all commitments related to the current 11th EDF as well as the previous Funds.

The UK's paid-in capital in **the European Central Bank** will be reimbursed to the Bank of England and the UK will cease to be a member of the ECB. In relation to **the European Investment Bank**, the UK paid-in capital will be reimbursed between 2019 and 2030 in annual instalments but will be replaced by a (additional) callable guarantee. The UK will maintain a guarantee of the stock of outstanding EIB's operations from the date of withdrawal until the end of their amortisation.

The UK will also maintain the EIB privileges and immunities (protocol 5 and 7 of the Treaty) for the stock of operations existing at the date of withdrawal.

(….)

VI. What has been agreed on the governance of the Withdrawal Agreement?

The Withdrawal Agreement includes the institutional arrangements to ensure the effective management, implementation and enforcement of the agreement, including appropriate dispute settlement mechanisms.

The EU and the UK have agreed on the **direct effect and the supremacy of the entire Withdrawal Agreement** under the same conditions as those applicable in Union law, as well as the fact that the **Court of Justice of the European Union** (CJEU) is the ultimate arbiter for matters related to EU law or Union law concepts. This is a necessary guarantee to make sure that Union law is applied in a consistent manner.

Important parts of the Withdrawal Agreement are built on Union law, which is used to make sure that the withdrawal happens in an orderly manner. Therefore, it is all the more important that the same legal effects, methods and principles of interpretation as for Union law apply.

In the event of a dispute on the interpretation of the Withdrawal Agreement, an initial political consultation would take place in a **Joint Committee**. If no solution is found, either party can refer the dispute to binding arbitration. In those cases where the dispute involves a question of EU law, the arbitration panel has an obligation to refer the question to the CJEU for a binding ruling. In addition, each party may request that the panel refers a question to the CJEU. In such cases, the arbitration panel must refer the question to the CJEU, unless it considers that the dispute in reality does not touch on EU law. It must give the reasons for its assessment and the parties may ask for a review of its assessment.

The decision of the arbitration panel will be binding on the Union and the UK. In case of non-compliance, the arbitration panel may impose a lump sum or penalty payment to be paid to the aggrieved party.

Finally, if compliance is still not restored, the Agreement allows parties to suspend proportionately the application of the Withdrawal Agreement itself, except for citizens' rights, or parts of other agreements between the Union and the UK. Such suspension is subject to review by the arbitration panel.

Appendix I

Excerpts from Revised Protocol on Ireland/Northern Ireland, 17 October 2019

(....)

ARTICLE 4

Customs territory of the United Kingdom

Northern Ireland is part of the customs territory of the United Kingdom. Accordingly, nothing in this Protocol shall prevent the United Kingdom from including Northern Ireland in the territorial scope of any agreements it may conclude with third countries, provided that those agreements do not prejudice the application of this Protocol. In particular, nothing in this Protocol shall prevent the United Kingdom from concluding agreements with a third country that grant goods produced in Northern Ireland preferential access to that country's market on the same terms as goods produced in other parts of the United Kingdom. Nothing in this Protocol shall prevent the United Kingdom from including Northern Ireland in the territorial scope of its Schedules of Concessions annexed to the General Agreement on Tariffs and Trade 1994.

ARTICLE 5

Customs, movement of goods

1. No customs duties shall be payable for a good brought into Northern Ireland from another part of the United Kingdom by direct transport, notwithstanding paragraph 3, unless that good is at risk of subsequently being moved into the Union, whether by itself or forming part of another good following processing. The customs duties in respect of a good being moved by direct transport to Northern Ireland other than from the Union or from another part of the United Kingdom shall be the duties applicable in the United Kingdom, notwithstanding paragraph 3, unless

that good is at risk of subsequently being moved into the Union, whether by itself or forming part of another good following processing. No duties shall be payable by, as relief shall be granted to, residents of the United Kingdom for personal property, as defined in point (c) of Article 2(1) of Council Regulation 1186/20091, brought into Northern Ireland from another part of the United Kingdom.

2. For the purposes of the first and second subparagraph of paragraph 1, a good brought into Northern Ireland from outside the Union shall be considered to be at risk of subsequently being moved into the Union unless it is established that that good: (a) will not be subject to commercial processing in Northern Ireland; and (b) fulfils the criteria established by the Joint Committee in accordance with the fourth subparagraph of this paragraph. For the purposes of this paragraph, 'processing' means any alteration of goods, any transformation of goods in any way, or any subjecting of goods to operations other than for 1 Council Regulation (EC) No 1186/2009 of 16 November 2009 setting up a Community system of reliefs from customs duty (OJ L 324, 10.12.2009, p. 23). the purpose of preserving them in good condition or for adding or affixing marks, labels, seals or any other documentation to ensure compliance with any specific requirements. Before the end of the transition period, the Joint Committee shall by decision establish the conditions under which processing is to be considered not to fall within point (a) of the first subparagraph, taking into account in particular the nature, scale and result of the processing. Before the end of the transition period, the Joint Committee shall by decision establish the criteria for considering that a good brought into Northern Ireland from outside the Union is not at risk of subsequently being moved into the Union. The Joint Committee shall take into consideration, inter alia: (a) the final destination and use of the good; (b) the nature and value of the good; (c) the nature of the movement; and (d) the incentive for undeclared onward-movement into the Union, in particular incentives resulting from the duties payable pursuant to paragraph 1. The Joint Committee may amend at any time its decisions adopted pursuant to this paragraph. In taking any decision pursuant to this paragraph, the Joint Committee shall have regard to the specific circumstances in Northern Ireland.
3. Legislation as defined in point (2) of Article 5 of Regulation (EU) No 952/2013 shall apply to and in the United Kingdom in respect of Northern Ireland (not including the territorial waters of the United Kingdom). However, the Joint Committee shall establish the conditions, including in quantitative terms, under which certain fishery and aquaculture products, as set out in Annex I to Regulation (EU) 1379/2013 of the

European Parliament and of the Council2 , brought into the customs territory of the Union defined in Article 4 of Regulation (EU) No 952/2013 by vessels flying the flag of the United Kingdom and having their port of registration in Northern Ireland are exempted from duties.

4. The provisions of Union law listed in Annex 2 to this Protocol shall also apply, under the conditions set out in that Annex, to and in the United Kingdom in respect of Northern Ireland.
5. Articles 30 and 110 TFEU shall apply to and in the United Kingdom in respect of Northern Ireland. Quantitative restrictions on exports and imports shall be prohibited between the Union and Northern Ireland.
6. Customs duties levied by the United Kingdom in accordance with paragraph 3 are not remitted to the Union. Subject to Article 10, the United Kingdom may in particular: 2 Regulation (EU) No 1379/2013 of the European Parliament and of the Council of 11 December 2013 on the common organisation of the markets in fishery and aquaculture products amending Council Regulations (EC) No 1184/2006 and (EC) No 1224/2009 and repealing Council Regulation (EC) No 104/2000 (OJ L 354, 28.12.2013, p. 1). (a) reimburse duties levied pursuant to the provisions of Union law made applicable by paragraph 3 in respect of goods brought into Northern Ireland; (b) provide for circumstances in which a customs debt which has arisen is to be waived in respect of goods brought into Northern Ireland; (c) provide for circumstances in which customs duties are to be reimbursed in respect of goods that can be shown not to have entered the Union; and (d) compensate undertakings to offset the impact of the application of paragraph 3. In taking decisions under Article 10, the European Commission shall take the circumstances in Northern Ireland into account as appropriate.
7. No duties shall be payable on consignments of negligible value, on consignments sent by one individual to another or on goods contained in travellers' personal baggage, under the conditions set out in the legislation referred to in paragraph 3.

(....)

Bibliography

CONTENTS

INTRODUCTION

The purpose of this introduction to the bibliography is to give an overview of the literature on Britain's exit (Brexit) from the European Union (EU) and thus guide the reader who may want to go deeper into the subject matter.

When you start studying the EU's relations with a state, be it a member state or a third country, or one moving from the first to the second category as the United Kingdom (UK) chose to do by referendum in 2016 and accomplished on Brexit Day, the 31 January 2020, with some delay, there will be official documents that ideally should be consulted, but which will most often be written in an esoteric technical, legalistic language, which can be difficult to read for the layman, not to say journalists and social scientists. Sometimes the parties will issue press releases that can help us understand what it is all about.

The news media, the written press, radio and TV, and various online media will try to keep citizens informed about what is going on and offer various interpretations and explanations.

Historians will eventually give their accounts. Social scientists, political scientists in particular, will offer their explanations, applying various conceptual frameworks and theories to put order in all the "facts."

As a contemporary event, many readers who may get hold of this book, will have had the chance to follow much of the Brexit drama, especially Prime Minister Theresa May's battle with the UK Parliament in the first part of 2019 to get her Withdrawal Agreement with the EU approved and ratified. Many will remember how the Speaker John Bercow would shout "order" again and again so that the debate could continue. For observers who are used to follow parliaments on the European continents the House of Commons seems rather noisy.

The cutoff date used in this book is 31 December 2020, the day the UK officially left the EU. The UK had become a "third country"—a non-member state. A transition period started during which the idea is to negotiate the future relations. It may well be that another drama lies ahead. And maybe extensions of the transition period will be needed. Or worst case: no final deal.

This bibliography lists the most important official documents. Then there are sections on EU politics (a relatively short list), UK politics, the UK's relations with the European integration process, and the Brexit negotiations.

The Brexit negotiations had barely started before books started appearing. Now that the Brexit negotiations have concluded, arguably some of those books are becoming dated. They necessarily included elements of speculation. A more definitive, preferably theory-guided, account of these negotiations remains to be written. The information, apart from what can be learned from official documents, largely stems from the media. The full list of that literature is of course not possible. This study relied much on the media *Euractiv* published online daily in Brussels. This bibliography therefore has a rather extensive list of Brexit-related articles published in that medium.

OFFICIAL DOCUMENTS

Joint EU-UK Official Documents

"Joint Report from the Negotiators of the European Union and the United Kingdom Government on Progress During Phase 1 of Negotiations under

Article 50 TEU on the United Kingdom's Orderly Withdrawal from the European Union," 8 December 2017, https://ec.europa.eu/commission/sites/beta-political/files/joint_report.pdf.

"Draft Agreement on the Withdrawal of the United Kingdom of Great Britain and Northern Ireland from the European Union and the European Atomic Energy Community Highlighting the Progress Made (Coloured Version) in the Negotiation Round with the UK of 16–19 March 2018," https://ec.europa.eu/commission/sites/beta-political/files/draft_agreement_coloured.pdf.

"Withdrawal Agreement and Political Declaration on the Future Relationship between the UK and the EU as Endorsed by Leaders at a Special Meeting of the European Council on 25 November 2018," https://www.gov.uk/government/publications/withdrawal-agreement-and-political-declaration.

"Revised Protocol on Ireland and Northern Ireland Included in the Withdrawal Agreement," 17 October 2019, https://ec.europa.eu/commission/publications/revised-protocol-ireland-and-northern-ireland-included-withdrawal-agreement_en.

Official EU Documents

"European Commission, White Paper on the Future of Europe: Reflections and Scenarios for EU27 by 2025," 1 March 2017, https://ec.europa.eu/commission/sites/beta-political/files/white_paper_on_the_future_of_europe_en.pdf.

"European Council (Art. 50) Guidelines for Brexit Negotiations," 29 March 2017, https://www.consilium.europa.eu/en/press/press-releases/2017/04/29/euco-brexit-guidelines/.

"European Parliament, Resolution of 5 April 2017 on Negotiations with the United Kingdom Following its Notification that it Intends to Withdraw from the European Union (2017/2593(RSP))," http://www.europarl.europa.eu/doceo/document/TA-8-2017-0102_EN.html?redirect.

"European Parliament Resolution of 3 October 2017 on the State of Play of Negotiations with the United Kingdom (2017/2847(RSP))," http://www.europarl.europa.eu/doceo/document/TA-8-2017-0361_EN.html.

"European Parliament Resolution of 13 December 2017 on the State of Play of Negotiations with the United Kingdom (2017/2964(RSP))," http://www.europarl.europa.eu/doceo/document/TA-8-2017-0490_EN.html.

"European Council Guidelines December 2017," https://www.consilium.europa.eu/media/32236/15-euco-art50-guidelines-en.pdf.

"European Parliament Resolution of 14 March 2018 on the Framework of the Future EU-UK Relationship (2018/2573(RSP))," http://www.europarl.europa.eu/doceo/document/TA-8-2018-0069_EN.html.

"EU Guidelines," 23 March 2018, https://www.consilium.europa.eu/media/33458/23-euco-art50-guidelines.pdf.

"European Parliament, European Parliamentary Research Service, The EU-UK Withdrawal Agreement: Progress to Date and Remaining Difficulties," July 2018, http://www.europarl.europa.eu/RegData/etudes/IDAN/2018/625110/EPRS_IDA(2018)625110_EN.pdf.

"European Commission Fact Sheet, Brexit Negotiations: What is in the Withdrawal Agreement," 14 November 2018, http://europa.eu/rapid/press-release_MEMO-18-6422_en.htm.

"Revised Protocol on Ireland and Northern Ireland Included in the Withdrawal Agreement," https://ec.europa.eu/commission/publications/revised-protocol-ireland-and-northern-ireland-included-withdrawal-agreement_en.

Official UK Documents

"The Government's Negotiating Objectives for Exiting the EU: PM Speech [Theresa May's Lancaster House Speech 17 January 2017]," https://www.gov.uk/government/speeches/the-governments-negotiating-objectives-for-exiting-the-eu-pm-speech.

"The United Kingdom's Exit from and New Partnership with the European Union White Paper," 2 February 2017, https://www.gov.uk/government/publications/the-united-kingdoms-exit-from-and-new-partnership-with-the-european-union-white-paper.

"Full Text: Theresa May's Article 50 Letter," 29 March 2017, https://assets.publishing.service.gov.uk/government/uploads/system/uploads/attachment_data/file/604079/Prime_Ministers_letter_to_European_Council_President_Donald_Tusk.pdf.

"Policy Paper. The United Kingdom's Exit from, and New Partnership with, the European Union White Paper," Updated 15 May 2017, https://www.gov.uk/government/publications/the-united-kingdoms-exit-from-and-new-partnership-with-the-european-union-white-paper/the-united-kingdoms-exit-from-and-new-partnership-with-the-european-union--2.

"PM's Florence Speech: A New Era of Cooperation and Partnership between the UK and the EU," 22 September 2017, https://www.gov.uk/government/speeches/pms-florence-speech-a-new-era-of-cooperation-and-partnership-between-the-uk-and-the-eu.

"House of Commons Exiting the European Union Committee, EU Exit Analysis Cross Whitehall Briefing," January 2018, https://www.parliament.uk/documents/commons-committees/Exiting-the-European-Union/17-19/Cross-Whitehall-briefing/EU-Exit-Analysis-Cross-Whitehall-Briefing.pdf.

"The Future Relationship between the United Kingdom and the European Union [Checkers Plan]," 17 July 2018, https://www.gov.uk/govern

ment/publications/the-future-relationship-between-the-united-kingdom-and-the-european-union/the-future-relationship-between-the-united-kingdom-and-the-european-union-html-version#contents.

"European Union (Withdrawal Agreement) Bill, 2019," https://publications.parliament.uk/pa/bills/cbill/2019-2019/0007/20007.pdf.

"New Withdrawal Agreement," https://assets.publishing.service.gov.uk/government/uploads/system/uploads/attachment_data/file/840655/Agreement_on_the_withdrawal_of_the_United_Kingdom_of_Great_Britain_and_Northern_Ireland_from_the_European_Union_and_the_European_Atomic_Energy_Community.pdf.

"New Political Declaration," https://assets.publishing.service.gov.uk/government/uploads/system/uploads/attachment_data/file/840656/Political_Declaration_setting_out_the_framework_for_the_future_relationship_between_the_European_Union_and_the_United_Kingdom.pdf.

"Protocol of Ireland/Northern Ireland," https://assets.publishing.service.gov.uk/government/uploads/system/uploads/attachment_data/file/840230/Revised_Protocol_to_the_Withdrawal_Agreement.pdf.

"Declaration on Consent in Northern Ireland," https://assets.publishing.service.gov.uk/government/uploads/system/uploads/attachment_data/file/840657/Declaration_by_Her_Majesty_s_Government_of_the_United_Kingdom_of_Great_Britain_and_Northern_Ireland_concerning_the_operation_of_the__Democratic_consent_in_Northern_Ireland__provision_of_the_Protocol_on_Ireland_Northern_Ireland.pdf.

"Statement that Political Agreement Has Been Reached," https://assets.publishing.service.gov.uk/government/uploads/system/uploads/attachment_data/file/840658/Statement_that_political_agreement_has_been_reached_and_that_the_United_Kingdom_has_concluded_an_agreement_with_the_European_Union_under_Article_50_2__of_the_Treaty_on_European_Union.pdf.

"House of Commons Library, The October 2019 EU-UK Withdrawal Agreement," *Briefing Paper, No. CBP 8713*, 17 October 2019, https://commonslibrary.parliament.uk/research-briefings/cbp-8713/.

OUTSIDE PUBLICATIONS

European Union Politics

Bitsch, Marie-Thérèse, *Histoire de la construction européenne*. Brussels: Éditions Complexe, 1999.

Dinan, Desmond, *Ever Closer Union: An Introduction to European Integration*, 4th edition. Basingstoke: Palgrave Macmillan, 2010.

Gerbet, Pierre, *La construction de l'Europe*, 4th edition. Paris: Armand Colin, 2007.

Hix, Simon and Bjørn Høyland, *The Political System of the European Union*, 3rd edition. Basingstoke: Palgrave Macmillan, 2011.

Laursen, Finn, ed., *Designing the European Union: From Paris to Lisbon.* Basingstoke: Palgrave Macmillan, 2012.

———, *Historical Dictionary of the European Union.* Lanham, MD: Rowman & Littlefield, 2016.

Lindberg, Leon N. and Stuart A. Scheingold, *Europe's Would-Be Polity.* Englewood Cliffs, NJ: Prentice-Hall, 1970.

Loth, Wilfried, *Building Europe: A History of European Unification.* Oldenbourg: De Gruyter, 2015.

Moravcsik, Andrew, *The Choice for Europe: Social Purpose and State Power from Messina to Maastricht.* Ithaca, NY: Cornell University Press, 1998.

Parsons, Craig, *A Certain Idea of Europe.* Ithaca, NY and London: Cornell University Press, 2003.

Patel, Kiran Klaus, *Project Europe: A History.* Cambridge: Cambridge University Press, 2020.

Piris, Jean-Claude, *The Lisbon Treaty: A Legal and Political Analysis.* Cambridge: Cambridge University Press, 2010.

Webber, Douglas, *European Disintegration? The Politics of Crisis in the European Union.* London: Macmillan International and Red Globe Press, 2019.

British Politics

Blackburn, Robert, "Britain's Unwritten Constitution," *British Library*, 13 Match 2015, https://www.bl.uk/magna-carta/articles/britains-unwritten-constitution.

Blair, Tony, *A Journey.* London: Arrow Books, 2011.

Breay, Claire and Julian Harrison, "Magna Carta: An Introduction," *British Library*, 28 July 2014, https://www.bl.uk/magna-carta/articles/magna-carta-an-introduction.

Cameron, D., *For the Record.* London: William Collins, 2013.

Gimson, Andrew, *Boris: The Adventure of Boris Johnson.* London: Simon & Schuster, 2016.

Griffiths, Simon and Robert Leach, *British Politics*, 3rd edition. London: Palgrave, 2018.

Heath, Edward, *The Course of My Life: My Autobiography.* London: Hodder & Stoughton, 1998.

Jones, Bill, *British Politics: The Basics.* Abingdon: Routledge, 2016.

Knight, Julian, *British Politics for Dummies*, 2nd edition. Chichester: John Wiley & Sons, Ltd., 2015.

Major, J., *The Autobiography.* London: Harper Collins, 1999.

Naughtie, J., *The Accidental American: Tony Blair and the Presidency.* Basingstoke: Macmillan, 2004.

Richards, Steve, *The Prime Ministers; Reflections on Leadership from Wilson to May.* London: Atlantic Books, 2019.

Seldon, Anthony and Peter Snowdon, *Cameron at 10: The Verdict.* London: William Collins, 2016.
Seldon, Anthony and Raymond Newelll, *May at 10.* London: Biteback Publishing Ltd., 2019.
Thatcher, Margaret, *The Downing Street Years.* London: Harper Collins, 1993.
Wright, Tony, *British Politics: A Very Short Introduction.* Oxford: Oxford University Press, 2013.

Britain in Europe

Bailey, Richard, *The European Connection: Implications of EEC Membership.* Oxford: Pergamon Press, 1983.
Beddington-Behrens, Edward, *Is there any Choice? Britain must Join Europe.* Harmondsworth: Penguin Books, 1966.
Best, Edward, "The United Kingdom and the Ratification of the Maastricht Treaty," in Finn Laursen and Sophie Vanhoonacker, eds., *The Ratification of the Maastricht Treaty.* Dordrecht: Martinus Nijhoff, 1994, pp. 245–278.
———, "The United Kingdom: From Isolation Towards Influence?," in Finn Laursen, ed., *The Amsterdam Treaty: National Preference Formation, Interstate Bargaining and Outcome.* Odense: Odense University Press, 2002, pp. 359–378.
Bidwell, Charles, *Maastricht and the UK.* Oxford: Public Affairs Consultants Europe Limited, 1993.
Butler, David and Uwe Kitzinger, *The 1975 Referendum*, 2nd edition. London: Macmillan Press, 1996.
Blair, Alasdair, "Britain and the European Union: A Laggard Leader?," in Derek Beach and Colette Mazzucelli, eds., *Leadership in the Big Bangs of European Integration.* Basingstoke: Palgrave Macmillan, 2007, pp. 178–200.
———, "The United Kingdom and the Constitutional Treaty: Leading from Within?," in Finn Laursen, ed., *The Rise and Fall of the EU's Constitutional Treaty.* Leiden: Martinus Nijhoff, 2008, pp. 201–223.
———, *The European Union since 1945*, 2nd edition. London: Longman, 2010.
———, "Britain and the Negotiation of the Lisbon Treaty," in Finn Laursen, ed., *The Making of the EU's Lisbon Treaty.* Brussels: P. I. E. Peter Lang, 2012, pp. 97–122.
———, "The United Kingdom and the European Union," *Oxford Research Encyclopedia of Politics*, 2020 (online).
Camps, Miriam, *Britain and the European Community 1955–1963.* Princeton, NJ: Princeton University Press; London: Oxford University Press, 1964.
Davidson, Ian, *Britain and the Making of Europe.* London: Macdonald, 1971.
De La Serre, Françoise, *La Grade-Bretagne et la Communauté européenne.* Paris: Presses Universitaires de France, 1987.
Franklin, Michael and Marc Wilke, *Britain's Future in Europe.* London: The Royal Institute of International Affairs/Pinter Publishers, 1990.
Geddes, Andrew, *Britain and the European Union.* London: Palgrave Macmillan, 2013.

George, Stephen, *An Awkward Partner: Britain in the European Community*, 3rd edition. Oxford: Oxford University Press, 1998.

Grob-Fitzgibbon, Benjamin, *Continental Drift: Britain and Europe from the End of Empire to the Rise of Euroscepticism.* Cambridge: Cambridge University Press, 2016.

Jenkins, Roy, *Britain and the EEC.* London: The Macmillan Press, 1983.

King, Anthony, *Britain Says Yes: The 1975 Referendum on the Common Market.* Washington, DC: American Enterprise Institute for Public Policy Research, 1977.

Kitzinger, U. W., *Diplomacy and Persuasion: How Britain Joined the Common Market.* London: Thames and Hudson, 1973.

Larsen, Henrik, "United Kingdom: New Approach and New Influence?," in Finn Laursen, ed., *The Treaty of Nice: Actor Preferences, Bargaining and Institutional Choice.* Leiden: Martinus Nijhoff Publishers, 2006, pp. 307–321.

Liddle, R., *The European Dilemma: Britain and the Drama of EU Integration.* London: I. B. Tauris, 2014.

May, Alex, *Britain and Europe since 1945.* London and New York, NY: Routledge, 1999.

Uri, Pierre, ed., *From Common Wealth to Common Market.* Harmondsworth: Penguin Books, 1968.

Wester, Robert, "The United Kingdom and European Political Union," in Finn Laursen and Sophie Vanhoonacker, eds., *The Intergovernmental Conference on Political Union.* Dordrecht: Martinus Nijhoff Publishers, 1992, pp. 189–201.

Wall, Stephen, *A Stranger in Europe: Britain and the EU from Thatcher to Blair.* Oxford: Oxford University Press, 2008.

Young, J. W., *Britain, France and the Unity of Europe, 1945–51.* Leicester: Leicester University Press, 1984.

———, *Britain and European Unity*, 2nd edition. Basingstoke: Palgrave Macmillan, 2000.

Brexit

Books

Ani, Peace E., *Brexit: The Benefit of Hindsight.* Kibworth Beauchamp: Matador, 2019.

Armour, John and Horst Eidenmüller, *Negotiating Brexit.* Munich: C. H. Beck, 2017.

Armstrong, Kenneth A., *Brexit Time: Leaving the EU—Why, How and When?* Cambridge: Cambridge University Press, 2017.

Ashcroft, Michael and Kevin Culwick, *Well, you did ask: Why the UK voted to leave the EU.* London: Biteback Publishing Ltd., 2016.

Banks, Arron, *The Bad Boys of Brexit Tales of Mischief, Mayhem and Guerrilla Warfare in the EU Referendum Campaign.* London: Biteback Publishing Ltd., Fully Updated, 2017.

Barnet, Anthony, *The Lure of Greatness: England's Brexit & America's Trump.* London: Unbound, 2017.

Bennett, Owen, *The Brexit Club; The Inside Story of the Leave Campaign's Shock Victory*. London: Biteback Publishing, 2016.

Bootle, Roger, *Making a Success of Brexit and Reforming the EU. The Brexit Edition of the Trouble with Europe*, 4th edition. London: Nicholas Brealey Publishing, 2017.

Clarke, Harold D., Mathew Goodwin, and Paul Whiteley, *Brexit: Why Britain Voted to Leave the European Union*. Cambridge: Cambridge University Press, 2017.

Clegg, Nick, *How To Stop Brexit (And Make Britain Great Again)*. London: The Bodley Head, 2017.

Cowley, Philip and Dannis Kavanagh, eds., *The British General Election of 2017*. Cham, CH: Palgrave Macmillan/Springer Nature, 2018.

Desmet, Lode and Edward Stourton, *Blind Man's Brexit: How the EU Took Control of Brexit*. London: Simon & Schuster, 2019.

Diamond, P., P. Nedergaard, and B. Rosamond, eds., *Routledge Handbook of the Politics of Brexit*. London: Routledge, 2018.

Dunt, Ian, *Brexit: What the Hell Happens Now?* Kingston upon Thames: Canbury Press, 2016.

Emerson, Michael, ed., *Britain's Future in Europe: The Known Plan A to Remain or the Unknown Plan B to Leave*, 2nd edition. Brussels: Centre for European Policy Studies; London: Rowman and Littlefield International, 2016.

Evans, Geoffrey and Anand Menon, *Brexit and British Politics*. Cambridge: Polity, 2017.

Fabrini, F., ed., *The Law and Politics of Brexit*. Oxford: Oxford University Press, 2017.

Fossum, John Erik and Hans Petter Graver, *Squaring the Circle of Brexit: Could the Norway Model Work?* Bristol: Bristol University Press, 2018.

Gibbon, Gary, *Breaking Point: The UK Referendum on the EU and its Aftermath*. London: Haue Publishing, 2016.

Hannan, Daniel, *How to get the Best from Brexit: What Next*. London: Head of Zeus, Ltd., 2016.

Hillman, Jennifer A. and Gary Horlick, eds., *Legal Aspects of the United Kingdom's Decision to Withdraw from the European Union*. Washington, DC: Institute of International Economic Law, 2017.

MacShane, Denis, *Brexit: How Britain Left Europe*. London: E. B. Taurus, 2016.

Martill, Benjamin and Uta Staiger, eds., *Brexit and Beyond: Rethinking the Futures of Europe*. London: UCL Press, 2018.

Merrit, Giles, *Slippery Slope: Brexit and Europe's Troubled Future*. Oxford: Oxford University Press, 2016.

Oliver, Craig, *Unleashing Demons: The Bestselling Inside Story of Brexit*. London: Hodder & Stoughton Ltd., Updated with new material, 2017.

Oliver, Tim, *Europe's Brexit: EU Perspectives on Britain's Vote to Leave*. Newcastle upon Tyne: Agenda Publishing, 2018.

O'Rourke, Kevin, *A Short History of Brexit: Brom Brentry to Backstop*. UK: Pelican Books, Penguin Random House, 2018.

Ross, Tim and Tom McTague, *Betting the House: The Inside Story of the 2017 Election.* London: Biteback Publishing, 2017.

Schnapper, Pauline and Emanuelle Avril, *Où va le Royaume-Uni? Le Brexit et après.* Paris: Odile Jacob, 2019.

Shipman, Tim, *All Out War: The Full Story of Brexit.* London: William Collins. Revised and updated, 2017.

Taylor, Graham, *Understanding Brexit: Why Britain Voted to Leave the European Union.* Bingley: Emerald Publishing, 2017.

Wallwork, Nicholas, *Brexit for Dummies.* Hoboken, NJ: John Wiley & Sons, Inc., 2019.

Whyman, Philip B. and Alina I. Petrescu, *The Economics of Brexit: A Cost-Benefit Analysis of the UK's Economic Relationship with the EU.* London: Palgrave Macmillan, 2017.

Book chapters on Brexit

Baker, Andrew and Scott Lavery, "Brexit and the Future Model of British Capitalism," in P. Diamond, P. Nedergaard, and B. Rosamond, eds., *Routledge Handbook of the Politics of Brexit.* London: Routledge, 2018, pp. 66–79.

Bellamy, Richard, "Losing Control: Brexit and the Demoi-Cratic Disconnect," in Benjamin Martill and Uta Staiger, eds., *Brexit and Beyond: Rethinking the Futures of Europe.* London: UCL Press, 2018, pp. 222–228.

Bickerton, Chris, "The Brexit Iceberg," in Benjamin Martill and Uta Staiger, eds., *Brexit and Beyond: Rethinking the Futures of Europe.* London: UCL Press, 2018, pp. 132–137.

Cini, Michelle and Amy Verdun, "The implications of Brexit for the future of Europe," in Benjamin Martill and Uta Staiger, eds., *Brexit and Beyond: Rethinking the Futures of Europe.* London: UCL Press, 2018, pp. 63–71.

Cini, Michelle and Nieves Pérez-Solórzano-Borragán, "Brexit," in Cini, Michelle and Nieves Pérez-Solórzano-Borragán, eds., *European Union Politics*, 6th edition. Oxford: Oxford University Press, 2019, pp. 406–424.

Corbett, Anne and Claire Gordon, "Brexit and Higher Education Research," in P. Diamond, P. Nedergaard, and B. Rosamond, eds., *Routledge Handbook of the Politics of Brexit.* London: Routledge, 2018, pp. 103–117.

Curtin, Deirdre, "The Ties that Bind: Securing Information-Sharing after Brexit," in Benjamin Martill and Uta Staiger, eds., *Brexit and Beyond: Rethinking the Futures of Europe.* London: UCL Press, 2018, pp. 148–155.

Daddow, Oliver, "Brexit and Britain's Role in the World," in P. Diamond, P. Nedergaard, and B. Rosamond, eds., *Routledge Handbook of the Politics of Brexit.* London: Routledge, 2018, pp. 208–222.

De Búrca, Gráinne, "How British was the Brexit Vote?" in Benjamin Martill and Uta Staiger, eds., *Brexit and Beyond: Rethinking the Futures of Europe.* London: UCL Press, 2018, pp. 46–52.

Diamond, Patrick, "Brexit and the Labour Party: Euro-Caution vs. Euro-Fanaticism? The Labour Party's 'Constructive Ambiguity' on Brexit and the European Union," in P. Diamond, P. Nedergaard, and B. Rosamond, eds., *Routledge Handbook of the Politics of Brexit.* London: Routledge, 2018, pp. 167–178.

Drake, Helen, "France, Britain and Brexit," in Benjamin Martill and Uta Staiger, eds., *Brexit and Beyond: Rethinking the Futures of Europe.* London: UCL Press, 2018, pp. 97–104.

Eeckhout, Piet, "The Emperor has No Clothes: Brexit and the UK Constitution," in Benjamin Martill and Uta Staiger, eds., *Brexit and Beyond: Rethinking the Futures of Europe.* London: UCL Press, 2018, pp. 165–172.

Favell, Adrian and Roxana Barbulescu, "Brexit, 'Immigration' and Anti-Discrimination," in P. Diamond, P. Nedergaard, and B. Rosamond, eds., *Routledge Handbook of the Politics of Brexit.* London: Routledge, 2018, pp. 118–133.

Flinders, Mathew, "The (Anti-)Politics of Brexit," in P. Diamond, P. Nedergaard, and B. Rosamond, eds., *Routledge Handbook of the Politics of Brexit.* London: Routledge, 2018, pp. 179–193.

Fossum, John Erik, "Brexit and the EU's Affiliated Non-Members," in P. Diamond, P. Nedergaard, and B. Rosamond, eds., *Routledge Handbook of the Politics of Brexit.* London: Routledge, 2018, pp. 278–289.

Gillingham, John R., "A Speculation on the Future of Europe," in Benjamin Martill and Uta Staiger, eds., *Brexit and Beyond: Rethinking the Futures of Europe.* London: UCL Press, 2018, pp. 193–201.

Glencross, Andrew, "Cameron's European Legacy: How Brexit Demonstrates the Flawed Politics of Simple Solutions," in Benjamin Martill and Uta Staiger, eds., *Brexit and Beyond: Rethinking the Futures of Europe.* London: UCL Press, 2018, pp. 22–27.

Glynn, Jack and Anand Menon, "Brexit," in Philip Cowley and Dannis Kavanagh, eds., *The British General Election of 2017.* Cham, CH: Palgrave Macmillan/Springer Nature, 2018, pp. 21–40.

Grant, Wyn, "Brexit and Agriculture," in P. Diamond, P. Nedergaard, and B. Rosamond, eds., *Routledge Handbook of the Politics of Brexit.* London: Routledge, 2018, pp. 92–102.

Hadfield, Amelia, "Britain against the World? Foreign and Security Policy in the 'Age of Brexit'," in Benjamin Martill and Uta Staiger, eds., *Brexit and Beyond: Rethinking the Futures of Europe.* London: UCL Press, 2018, pp. 174–182.

Hayton, Richard, "Brexit and the Conservative Party," in P. Diamond, P. Nedergaard, and B. Rosamond, eds., *Routledge Handbook of the Politics of Brexit.* London: Routledge, 2018, pp. 157–166.

Hill, Christopher, "Turning Back the Clock: The Illusion of a Global Political Role for Britain," in Benjamin Martill and Uta Staiger, eds., *Brexit and Beyond: Rethinking the Futures of Europe.* London: UCL Press, 2018, pp. 183–192.

Hix, Simon, "Decentralised Federalism: A New Model for the EU," in Benjamin Martill and Uta Staiger, eds., *Brexit and Beyond: Rethinking the Futures of Europe.* London: UCL Press, 2018, pp. 72–80.

Innes, Abby, "The New Crisis of Ungovernability," in Benjamin Martill and Uta Staiger, eds., *Brexit and Beyond: Rethinking the Futures of Europe*. London: UCL Press, 2018, pp. 138–145.

Isiksel, Turkuler, "Square Peg, Round Hole: Why the EU Can't Fix Identity Politics," in Benjamin Martill and Uta Staiger, eds., *Brexit and Beyond: Rethinking the Futures of Europe*. London: UCL Press, 2018, pp. 239–250.

James, S. and K. Oppermann, "Britain and the European Union," in T. Casey, ed., *The Blair Legacy: Policy, Governance and Foreign Affairs*. Basingstoke: Palgrave Macmillan, 2009, pp. 285–298.

Jensen, Mads Dagnis and Holly Snaith, "Brexit and the European Union: Hanging in the Balance?" in P. Diamond, P. Nedergaard, and B. Rosamond, eds., *Routledge Handbook of the Politics of Brexit*. London: Routledge, 2018, pp. 254–265.

Keating, Michael, "Brexit and Scotland," in P. Diamond, P. Nedergaard, and B. Rosamond, eds., *Routledge Handbook of the Politics of Brexit*. London: Routledge, 2018, pp. 40–48.

Larsen, Henrik, "Brexit and the EU as an International Actor," in P. Diamond, P. Nedergaard, and B. Rosamond, eds., *Routledge Handbook of the Politics of Brexit*. London: Routledge, 2018, pp. 223–231.

Lequesne, Christian, "Brexit and the Future of EU Theory," in P. Diamond, P. Nedergaard, and B. Rosamond, eds., *Routledge Handbook of the Politics of Brexit*. London: Routledge, 2018, pp. 290–297.

Morgan, Glyn, "Is the EU 'a Crap 1950s Idea'?" in Benjamin Martill and Uta Staiger, eds., *Brexit and Beyond: Rethinking the Futures of Europe*. London: UCL Press, 2018, pp. 37–45.

Murphy, Mary C., "Brexit and the Irish Case," in P. Diamond, P. Nedergaard, and B. Rosamond, eds., *Routledge Handbook of the Politics of Brexit*. London: Routledge, 2018, pp. 27–39.

Murray-Evans, Peg, "Brexit and the Commonwealth: Fantasy Meets Reality," in P. Diamond, P. Nedergaard, and B. Rosamond, eds., *Routledge Handbook of the Politics of Brexit*. London: Routledge, 2018, pp. 197–207.

Nedergaard, Peter and Maja Friis Henriksen, "Brexit and British Exceptionalism," in P. Diamond, P. Nedergaard, and B. Rosamond, eds., *Routledge Handbook of the Politics of Brexit*. London: Routledge, 2018, pp. 134–146.

Nicolaïdis, Kalypso, "Sustainable Integration in a Demoicratic Polity: A New (Or Not So New) Ambition for the EU after Brexit," in Benjamin Martill and Uta Staiger, eds., *Brexit and Beyond: Rethinking the Futures of Europe*. London: UCL Press, 2018, pp. 212–221.

Nugent, Neill, "Brexit: Yet Another Crisis for the EU," in Benjamin Martill and Uta Staiger, eds., *Brexit and Beyond: Rethinking the Futures of Europe*. London: UCL Press, 2018, pp. 54–62.

Odermatt, Jed, "Brexit and British Trade Policy," in P. Diamond, P. Nedergaard, and B. Rosamond, eds., *Routledge Handbook of the Politics of Brexit*. London: Routledge, 2018, pp. 80–91.

Patel, Kiran Klaus, "Something New Under the Sun? The Lessons of Alegria and Greenland," in Benjamin Martill and Uta Staiger, eds., *Brexit and Beyond: Rethinking the Futures of Europe*. London: UCL Press, 2018, pp. 114–120.

Paterson, William E., "Britain's Singular Other: Germany and the Brexit Crisis," in Benjamin Martill and Uta Staiger, eds., *Brexit and Beyond: Rethinking the Futures of Europe*. London: UCL Press, 2018, pp. 88–96.

Quaglia, Lucia, "Brexit and EU Financial Regulation," in P. Diamond, P. Nedergaard, and B. Rosamond, eds., *Routledge Handbook of the Politics of Brexit*. London: Routledge, 2018, pp. 244–253.

Rasmussen, Mikkel Vedby, "Brexit and European Defence: Why More Defence Does Not Equal More Integration," in P. Diamond, P. Nedergaard, and B. Rosamond, eds., *Routledge Handbook of the Politics of Brexit*. London: Routledge, 2018, pp. 233–243.

Schelkle, Weltraud, "What Impact Will Brexit Have On the Euro Area," in Benjamin Martill and Uta Staiger, eds., *Brexit and Beyond: Rethinking the Futures of Europe*. London: UCL Press, 2018, pp. 124–131.

Shackleton, Michael, "Wither the 27?," in Benjamin Martill and Uta Staiger, eds., *Brexit and Beyond: Rethinking the Futures of Europe*. London: UCL Press, 2018, pp. 204–211.

Shaw, Jo, "Citizenship and Free Movement in a Changing EU: Navigating and Archipelago of Contradictions," in Benjamin Martill and Uta Staiger, eds., *Brexit and Beyond: Rethinking the Futures of Europe*. London: UCL Press, 2018, pp. 156–164.

Staiger, Uta, "The Heart of the Matter: Emotional Politics in the New Europe," in Benjamin Martill and Uta Staiger, eds., *Brexit and Beyond: Rethinking the Futures of Europe*. London: UCL Press, 2018, pp. 230–238.

Staiger, Uta and Benjamin Martill, "Rethinking the Futures of Europe," in Benjamin Martill and Uta Staiger, eds., *Brexit and Beyond: Rethinking the Futures of Europe*. London: UCL Press, 2018, pp. 260–265.

Talani, Leila Simona, "Brexit and the City of London: The Revenge of the Ultraliberals?" in P. Diamond, P. Nedergaard, and B. Rosamond, eds., *Routledge Handbook of the Politics of Brexit*. London: Routledge, 2018, pp. 49–65.

Van Middelaar, Luuk, "Seven Brexit Propositions: Towards a Union that Protects," in Benjamin Martill and Uta Staiger, eds., *Brexit and Beyond: Rethinking the Futures of Europe*. London: UCL Press, 2018, pp. 81–86.

Van Parijs, Philippe, "Fair Brexit for a Just Europe," in Benjamin Martill and Uta Staiger, eds., *Brexit and Beyond: Rethinking the Futures of Europe*. London: UCL Press, 2018, pp. 251–258.

Weale, Albert, "Brexit and the Improvised Constitution," in Benjamin Martill and Uta Staiger, eds., *Brexit and Beyond: Rethinking the Futures of Europe*. London: UCL Press, 2018, pp. 28–36.

Wincott, Daniel, "Brexit and the State of the United Kingdom," in P. Diamond, P. Nedergaard, and B. Rosamond, eds., *Routledge Handbook of the Politics of Brexit*. London: Routledge, 2018, pp. 15–26.

Wivel, Anders and Baldur Thorhallsson, "Brexit and Small Stetes in Europe. Hedging, Hiding or Seeking Shelter?" in P. Diamond, P. Nedergaard, and B. Rosamond, eds., *Routledge Handbook of the Politics of Brexit.* London: Routledge, 2018, pp. 266–277.

Wright, Nicholas, "Brexit and Ireland: Collateral Damage?" in Benjamin Martill and Uta Staiger, eds., *Brexit and Beyond: Rethinking the Futures of Europe.* London: UCL Press, 2018, pp. 105–113.

Journal articles of Brexit

Bulmer, Simon and Lucia Quaglia, "The Politics and Economics of Brexit," *Journal of European Public Policy* 25, no. 8 (2018): 1089–1098.

Curtice, J., "Why Leave Won the UK's Referendum," *Journal of Common Market Studies* 55 (Annual Review, 2017): 19–37.

Glencross, A., "Why a British Referendum on EU Membership Will Not Solve the Europe Question," *International Affairs* 91, no. 2 (2015): 303–317.

Hix, Simon, "Brexit: Where is the EU-UK Relationship Heading?" *Journal of Common Market Studies* 56 (Annual Review, 2018): 11–27.

Hobolt, Sara B., "The Brexit Vote: A Divided Nation, a Divided Continent," *Journal of European Public Policy* 23, no. 9 (2016): 1259–1277.

Menon, A. and J. P. Salter, "Brexit: Initial Reflections," *International Affairs* 92, no. 6 (2016): 1297–1318.

O'Donald, C. M. and R. G. Whitman, "European Policy under Gordon Brown: Perspectives on a Future Prime Minister," *International Affairs* 83, no. 1 (2007): 277–296.

Ott, Ursula F. and Pervez N. Ghauri, "Brexit Negotiations: From Negotiation Space to Agreement Zones," *Journal of International Business Studies* 50 (2019): 137–149.

Schimmelfennig, Frank, "Brexit: Differentiated Disintegration in the European Union," *Journal of European Public Policy* 25, no. 8 (2018): 1154–1173.

Smith, J., "The 1975 Referendum," *Journal of European Integration History* 5, no. 1 (1999): 41–56.

Smith, J., "A Missed Opportunity? New Labour's European Policy 1997–2005," *International Affairs* 81, no. 4 (2005): 703–721.

Taggart, Paul and Aleks Szczerbiak, "Putting Brexit into Perspective: The Effect of the Eurozone and Migration Crises and Brexit on Euroscepticism in European States," *Journal of European Public Policy* 25, no. 8 (2018): 1194–1214.

Wallace, H., "At Odds with Europe," *Political Studies* 45, no. 4 (1997): 677–688.

Selected articles from news media and think tanks

Arnholz, Jack, "Brexit Saga's Key Players: A Guide to the Central Political Figures," https://abcnews.go.com/International/guide-biggest-political-players-ongoing-brexit-saga/story?id=65428846.

Blair, Tony, "Brexit—What We Now Know," *Institute for Global Change*, January 2018, https://institute.global/tony-blair/tony-blair-brexit-what-we-now-know.

"Brexit: Jargon-Busting Guide to the Key Terms," https://www.bbc.com/news/uk-43470987.

"Brexit: The Key Players," https://www.rte.ie/news/brexit/2018/0329/950824-brexit-five-key-players/.

"Brexit: The People Who Are Negotiating," https://www.bbc.com/news/world-europe-39236683.

"Brexit Report 23 June 2018 by DCU Scholars," http://dcubrexitinstitute.eu/2018/06/brexit-report-23-june-2018-by-dcu-scholars/.

Busch, Berthold, et al., "Brexit and Europe's Future: A Game Theoretical Approach," *German Economic Institute (IW) Policy Paper No. 18/2016*, https://www.econstor.eu/bitstream/10419/148940/1/875856403.pdf.

Colvile, Robert, "12 People Who Brought About Brexit," https://www.politico.eu/article/12-people-who-brought-about-brexit-leave-remain-referendum-campaign-euroskeptics-tension/.

Dean, Alex, "Rules of Origin: The Biggest Brexit Problem You Didn't Know About," April 2018, https://www.prospectmagazine.co.uk/economics-and-finance/rules-of-origin-the-biggest-brexit-problem-you-didnt-know-about%E2%80%A8%E2%80%A8.

Dehousse, Franklin, "Brexit Will Not Be 'the Greatest Negotiation of All Times'," *Egmont*, December 2016, http://www.egmontinstitute.be/brexit-will-not-be-the-greatest-negotiation-of-all-times/.

———, "Why the Future Role of the European Court of Justice is a Tricky Topic for Brexit," *Egmont*, June 2017, http://www.egmontinstitute.be/why-the-future-role-of-the-european-court-of-justice-is-a-tricky-topic-for-brexit/.

Duff, Andrew, "What Now? Options for Brexit—And a Cry for Help," *Federal Trust*, June 2017, https://fedtrust.co.uk/what-now-options-for-brexit-and-a-cry-for-help/.

———, "Brexit: No Ordinary Third Country," *European Policy Centre Discussion Paper*, July 2017, https://europe-solidarity.eu/documents/brexitnoordinarythirdcountry.pdf.

———, "Brexit: What Theresa May's White Paper Must Do," *European Policy Centre Discussion Paper*, May 2018, https://vip.politicsmeanspolitics.com/2018/05/16/brexit-what-theresa-mays-white-paper-must-do/.

———, "Brexit: Last Call," *European Policy Centre Discussion Paper*, July 2018, http://www.epc.eu/en/Publications/Brexit-Last-call~203424.

Grant, Charles, "Deal or No Deal? Five Questions on Johnson's Brexit Negotiation," *Centre for European Reform*, 20 September 2019, https://www.cer.eu/sites/default/files/insight_CG_20.9.19.pdf.

Hayward, Katy, Maurice Campbell, and Rob Murphy, "The Irish Border as Customs Frontier after Brexit," July 2017, https://www.ceps.eu/ceps-publications/irish-border-customs-frontier-after-brexit/.

Institute for Government, "Brexit Brief: Options for the UK's Future Trade Relationship with the EU," https://www.instituteforgovernment.org.uk/sites/default/files/publications/Brexit%20Options%20A3%20November%20update.pdf.

———, "Brexit Deal: Political Declaration on the Future UK-EU Relationship," https://www.instituteforgovernment.org.uk/printpdf/7395.

———, "Euratom," https://www.instituteforgovernment.org.uk/printpdf/5181.

———, "Frictionless Trade? What Brexit Means for Cross-Border Trade in Goods," https://www.instituteforgovernment.org.uk/sites/default/files/publications/5704%20IFG%20-%20Frictionless%20Trade%20Web.pdf.

———, "Parliament's 'Meaningful Vote' on Brexit," https://www.instituteforgovernment.org.uk/explainers/parliament-meaningful-vote-brexit.

———, "The Options for the UK's Trading Relationship with the EU," (June 2017), https://www.instituteforgovernment.org.uk/explainers/options-uk-trading-relationship-eu.

———, "UK-EU Future Relationship: Association Agreements," https://www.instituteforgovernment.org.uk/explainers/future-relationship-association-agreements.

———, "UK-EU Future Relationship: UK and EU Mandates," https://www.instituteforgovernment.org.uk/explainers/future-relationship-uk-eu-mandates.

Kennedy, Simon, "Brexit Timeline: From the Referendum to Article 50," https://www.bloomberg.com/news/features/2017-03-20/brexit-timeline-from-eu-referendum-to-theresa-may-and-article-50.

Kreilinger, Valentin, Sophia Becker, and Laura Maria Wolfstädter, "Brexit. Negotiation Phases and Scenarios of a Drama in Three Acts," *Policy Paper 182*, 25 January 2017, Jacques Delors Institut Berlin, https://www.researchgate.net/publication/315831425_BREXIT_NEGOTIATION_PHASES_AND_SCENARIOS_OF_A_DRAMA_IN_THREE_ACTS.

Liberto, Daniel, "The Key Players in Brexit," https://www.investopedia.com/key-players-of-brexit-4584676.

Martill, Benjamoin and Uta Staiger, "Cultures of Negotiation: Explaining Britain's Hard Bargaining in the Brexit Negotiations," *Dahrendorf Forum, Working Paper No. 04*, 14 September 2018, http://www.lse.ac.uk/ideas/Assets/Documents/Dahrendorf/Cultures-of-Negotiation.pdf.

McClean, Paul, "Brexit Timeline: Key Dates in UK's Divorce with EU," https://www.ft.com/content/64e7f218-4ad4-11e7-919a-1e14ce4af89b.

Montera-Marinez, Camino and Christian Odendahl, "What Free Movement Means to Europe and Why It Matters For Britain," *Centre for European Reform*, January 2017, https://www.cer.eu/publications/archive/policy-brief/2017/what-free-movement-means-europe-and-why-it-matters-britain.

Moravcsik, Andrew, "Brexit: Welcome, Britain, to the Hotel California," *Princeton Alumni Weekly*, September, 2016, https://paw.princeton.edu/article/brexit-welcome-britain-hotel-california.

———, "One Year after the Brexit Vote, Britain's Relationship with the E.U. is Unlikely to Change Much. Here's Why," *Washington Post*, June 26, 2017, https://www.princeton.edu/~amoravcs/library/Washington%20Post%20FINAL.pdf.

Piris, Jean-Claude, "Brexit: The Transition Period," *Fondation Robert Schuman Policy Paper*, February 2018, https://www.robert-schuman.eu/en/european-issues/0461-brexit-the-transition-period.

Politics@Surrey, "More Negotiation Theory in Article 50," 12 October 2017, https://blogs.surrey.ac.uk/politics/2017/10/12/more-negotiation-theory-in-article-50/.

———, "The Impact of UK MEPs on the European Parliament," May 2019, https://blogs.surrey.ac.uk/politics/2019/05/09/the-impact-of-uk-meps-on-the-european-parliament/.

Politics@Surrey and Simon Usherwood, "Phase II of Article 50: From Leaning in to Falling Out?" 2 November 2017, https://politicsatsurrey.ideasoneurope.eu/2017/11/02/phase-ii-article-50-leaning-falling/.

———, "The Negative-Sum Game of Brexit," 9 November 2017, https://politicsatsurrey.ideasoneurope.eu/2017/11/09/negative-sum-game-brexit/.

Rediker, Douglas A., "Oder from Chaos: The Brexit Options, Explained," January 2018, https://www.brookings.edu/blog/order-from-chaos/2018/01/05/the-brexit-options-explained/.

Sandford, Alasdair, "Brexit Timeline 2016–2020: Key Events in the UK's Path from Referendum to EU Exit," https://www.euronews.com/2020/01/30/brexit-timeline-2016-2020-key-events-in-the-uk-s-path-from-referendum-to-eu-exit (Accessed 17 March 2020).

"Theresa May's Florence Speech: Key Points," https://www.theguardian.com/politics/2017/sep/22/theresa-mays-florence-speech-key-points.

Tilford, Simon, "The Limits to Labour's 'Constructive Ambiguity' Over Brexit," *Centre for European Reform*, July 2017, https://www.cer.eu/publications/archive/policy-brief/2017/what-free-movement-means-europe-and-why-it-matters-britain.

Usherwood, Simon, "What Negotiation Theory Tells Us About How the EU has Handled Article 50," June 2018, https://www.academia.edu/36631085/What_negotiation_theory_tells_us_about_how_the_EU_has_handled_Article_50.

———, "Could the EU Really Be Convinced to Budge on the Backstop?" 11 February 2019, https://theconversation.com/brexit-could-the-eu-really-be-convinced-to-budge-on-the-backstop-111515.

———, "The EU View on the Article 50 Endgame," 5 March 2019, https://ukandeu.ac.uk/the-eu-view-on-the-article-50-endgame/.

———, "Theresa May's Failure to Lead," 13 March 2019, https://ukandeu.ac.uk/theresa-mays-failure-to-lead/.

———, "Three Simple Reasons why the EU Won't Give Any More to the UK on the Backstop," 15 March 2019, https://ukandeu.ac.uk/three-simple-reasons-why-the-eu-wont-give-any-more-to-the-uk-on-the-backstop/.

———, "The Millwallisation of May's Brexit Strategy," 21 March 2019, https://ukandeu.ac.uk/the-millwallisation-of-mays-brexit-strategy/.

———, "Looking Back at the Brexit Negotiations," April 2019, https://ukandeu.ac.uk/looking-back-at-the-brexit-negotiations/.

———, "The TV Debate Bear-Trap," June 2019, https://ukandeu.ac.uk/the-tv-debate-bear-trap/.

———, "Brexit: It's No Just Where Britain's Going that Matters, But How It Gets There," July 2019, https://theconversation.com/brexit-its-not-just-where-britains-going-that-matters-but-how-it-gets-there-120127.

———, "Supreme Court Case: Not the Best Way To Go About Things," September 2019, https://ukandeu.ac.uk/supreme-court-case-not-the-best-way-to-go-about-things/.

———, "Boris Johnson's Brexit Deal: What is in It and How is It Different to Theresa May's Version?" October 2019, https://theconversation.com/boris-johnsons-brexit-deal-whats-in-it-and-how-is-it-different-to-theresa-mays-version-125446.

———, "The EU's Mandate for the Future Partnership," 26 February 2020, https://ukandeu.ac.uk/the-eus-mandate-for-the-future-partnership/.

———, "Negotiation Theory and Extending Transition," 29 April 2020, https://ukandeu.ac.uk/negotiation-theory-and-extending-transition/.

Von Ondarza, Nicolai, "The Trouble with Transition: No Off-the-Shelf Arrangement for the UK after Brexit," *SWP Comments*, December 2017, https://www.swp-berlin.org/fileadmin/contents/products/comments/2017C54_orz.pdf.

Von Ondarza, Nicolai and Camille Borrett, "Brexit and EU Agencies: What the Agencies' Existing Third Country Relations Can Teach Us About the Future EU-UK Relationship," *SWP Working Paper*, April 2018, https://www.swp-berlin.org/fileadmin/contents/products/arbeitspapiere/Brexit_and_EU_agencies.pdf.

"What Will the EU27 Governments and the EP Actually Want from Brexit?" *VoteWatch Europe*, June 2017, https://www.votewatch.eu/blog/what-will-the-eu27-governments-and-the-ep-actually-want-from-brexit/.

"Who's Who in Brexit?" https://www.dw.com/en/whos-who-in-brexit/g-42888417.

Zalan, Eszter, "UK and EU Stuck on 'Philosophy' of Brexit Bill," https://euobserver.com/uk-referendum/138641.

———, "Brexit Timeline—'The Clock is Ticking'," *EUobserver*, 29 December 2017, https://euobserver.com/europe-in-review/139787.

Articles in EURACTIV

23-01-2013: "Cameron Takes Gamble with In/Out EU Referendum Pledge," https://www.euractiv.com/section/uk-europe/news/cameron-takes-gamble-with-in-out-eu-referendum-pledge/.

16-03-2015: "Tusk Calls Cameron's EU Reform Plans 'Mission Impossible'," https://www.euractiv.com/section/uk-europe/news/tusk-calls-cameron-s-eu-reform-plans-mission-impossible/.

16-03-2015: "Voting on Brexit: The EU Issues Shaping the UK Election," https://www.euractiv.com/section/uk-europe/linksdossier/voting-on-brexit-the-eu-issues-shaping-the-uk-election/.

03-05-2015: "The UK's EU Referendum: On the Path to Brexit?" https://www.euractiv.com/section/uk-europe/linksdossier/voting-on-brexit-the-eu-issues-shaping-the-uk-election/.

18-12-2015: "Cameron Drops Big 2016 Hint for Brexit Referendum Date," https://www.euractiv.com/section/uk-europe/news/cameron-drops-big-2016-hint-for-brexit-referendum-date/.

09-05-2016: "Juncker Says Brexit Would Have 'Unforeseeable Consequences'," https://www.euractiv.com/section/uk-europe/news/juncker-says-brexit-would-have-unforeseeable-consequences/.

13-06-2016: "Tusk and Juncker see Brexit as Threat to Western Civilisation," https://www.euractiv.com/section/uk-europe/news/tusk-and-junker-see-brexit-as-threat-to-western-civilisation/.

16-06-2016: "Juncker: Brexit Won't be the Death of the EU," https://www.euractiv.com/section/uk-europe/news/juncker-brexit-wont-be-the-death-of-the-eu/.

20-06-2016: "Tusk Begs Brits to Vote Remain in Brexit Referendum," https://www.euractiv.com/section/uk-europe/news/tusk-begs-brits-to-vote-remain-in-brexit-referendum/.

24-96-2016: "Scotland, Northern Ireland and Gibraltar Eye Turbulent Future," https://www.euractiv.com/section/uk-europe/news/scotland-northern-ireland-and-gibraltar-eye-turbulent-future/.

27-06-2016: "Archived: Britain Votes to Leave the European Union," https://www.euractiv.com/section/uk-europe/news/juncker-says-brexit-would-have-unforeseeable-consequences/.

27-06-2016: "Scotland Seeks 'Immediate Discussions' to Stay in EU," https://www.euractiv.com/section/enlargement/news/scotland-seeks-immediate-discussions-to-stay-in-eu/.

29-06-2016: "Gibraltar and Scotland Discuss Staying in EU," https://www.euractiv.com/section/enlargement/news/scotland-and-gibraltar-discuss-staying-in-eu/.

14-07-2016: "Who's Who in the Brexit Government?" https://www.euractiv.com/section/uk-europe/news/whos-who-in-the-brexit-government/.

27-07-2016: Barnier, Battler of British Bankers, is Commission's New Brexit Boss," https://www.euractiv.com/section/uk-europe/news/barnier-battler-of-british-bankers-is-commissions-new-brexit-boss/.

21-07-2016: "EU's Barnier Builds Brexit Negotiation Team, Plans European Tour," https://www.euractiv.com/section/uk-europe/news/eus-barnier-builds-brexit-negotiation-team-plans-european-tour/.

13-09-2016: "Germany and France Seeks Stronger EU Defence after Brexit," https://www.euractiv.com/section/security/news/germany-and-france-seek-stronger-eu-defence-after-brexit/.

15-09-2016: "Sabine Weyand joins Barnier to Lead Brexit Negotiations," https://www.euractiv.com/section/uk-europe/news/sabine-weyand-joins-barnier-to-lead-brexit-negotiations/.

16-09-2016: "Tusk in Bratislava: Maybe the EU will be Stronger after Brexit," https://www.euractiv.com/section/uk-europe/news/tusk-in-bratislava-maybe-eu-will-be-stronger-after-brexit/.

19-09-2016: "UK Banks to Lose EU 'Passport' Post-Brexit, Warns ECB Boss," https://www.euractiv.com/section/uk-europe/news/uk-banks-to-lose-eu-passport-post-brexit-warns-ecb-boss/.

05-10-2016: "Spain Steps Up Efforts to Share Control of Gibraltar after Brexit," https://www.euractiv.com/section/uk-europe/news/spain-steps-up-efforts-to-share-control-of-gibraltar-after-brexit/.

15-11-2016: "Leaked Memo: UK Government has No Brexit Strategy," https://www.euractiv.com/section/uk-europe/news/leaked-memo-uk-government-has-no-brexit-strategy/.

25-11-2016: "Barnier Steps Up Brexit Talk Preparations," https://www.euractiv.com/section/uk-europe/news/barnier-steps-up-brexit-talk-preparations/.

30-11-2016: "Tusk Rebuffs Call to Start Brexit Talks on Expat Rights," https://www.euractiv.com/section/uk-europe/news/tusk-rebuffs-call-to-start-brexit-talks-on-expat-rights/.

03-01-2017: "UK Ambassador in Brussels Quits on Eve of Brexit Negotiations," https://www.euractiv.com/section/uk-europe/news/report-uk-ambassador-in-brussels-quits-on-eve-of-brexit-negotiations/.

04-01-2017: "UK Ambassador's Damning Final Email: 'Speak Truth to Power'," https://www.euractiv.com/section/uk-europe/news/uk-ambassadors-damning-final-email-speak-truth-to-power/.

24-01-2017: "UK Parliament Must Approve Triggering Article 50, Supreme Court Rules," https://www.euractiv.com/section/uk-europe/news/uk-parliament-must-approve-triggering-article-50-supreme-court-rules/.

02-02-2017: "UK Unveils Brexit Blueprint," https://www.euractiv.com/section/uk-europe/news/uk-unveils-brexit-blueprint/.

02-02-2017: "Brexit Bill Clears First Hurdle in UK Parliament," https://www.euractiv.com/section/uk-europe/news/brexit-bill-clears-first-hurdle-in-uk-parliament/.

02-02-2017: "Gibraltar Urges MEPs to Work Towards 'Sensible' Brexit," https://www.euractiv.com/section/uk-europe/news/gibraltar-urges-meps-to-work-towards-sensible-brexit/.

10-02-2017: "Ireland Tells EU Brexit Bosses, We Are Firmly on Your Side," https://www.euractiv.com/section/future-eu/news/ireland-tells-eu-brexit-bosses-we-are-firmly-on-your-side/.

06-03-2017: "Juncker Will Fight For 'More Europe' in Post-Brexit EU," https://www.euractiv.com/section/future-eu/news/juncker-will-fight-for-more-europe-in-post-brexit-eu/.

20-03-2017: "Part-Brexit 'Member States Will Fall in Love with Each Other Again', Insists Junker," https://www.euractiv.com/section/future-eu/news/post-brexit-member-states-will-fall-in-love-with-each-other-again-insists-juncker/.

20-03-2017: "May to Trigger Article 50 on 29 March," https://www.euractiv.com/section/politics/news/may-to-trigger-article-50-on-29-march/.

21-03-2017: "EU to Hold Special Brexit Summit on 29 April," https://www.euractiv.com/section/politics/news/eu-to-hold-special-brexit-summit-on-29-april/.

22-03-2017: "EU Brexit Boss Warns of 'Serious Repercussions' If Divorce Talks Fail," https://www.euractiv.com/section/politics/news/eu-brexit-boss-warns-of-serious-repercussions-if-brexit-talks-fail/.

27-03-2017: "UK Manufacturers Urge May to Drop Threat of No Brexit Deal," https://www.euractiv.com/section/uk-europe/news/uk-manufacturers-urge-may-to-drop-threat-of-no-brexit-deal/.

31-03-2017: EU Offers Brexit Trade Talks, Sets Tough Transition Terms," https://www.euractiv.com/section/uk-europe/news/eu-offers-brexit-trade-talks-sets-tough-transition-terms/.

24-04-2017: "Brexit Talks Place Citizens' Rights in Limbo," https://www.euractiv.com/section/uk-europe/news/brexit-sr-brexit-negotiators-face-extraordinarily-complex-talks-over-eu-rights/.

27-04-2017: "Europe's Car Industry Appeals for Tariff Free Trade Deal Ahead of Brexit Summit," https://www.euractiv.com/section/transport/news/europes-car-industry-appeals-for-tariff-free-trade-deal-ahead-of-brexit-summit/.

29-04-2017: "Leaders Call for Discipline to Maintain Fragile Unity in Brexit Talks," https://www.euractiv.com/section/uk-europe/news/leaders-call-for-discipline-to-maintain-fragile-unity-in-brexit-talks/.

02-05-2017: "'Sceptical' Juncker Fears Theresa May is Living 'in Another Galaxy'," https://www.euractiv.com/section/uk-europe/news/sceptical-juncker-fears-theresa-may-is-living-in-another-galaxy/.

02-05-2017: "EU Says United Ireland Would Be Automatic Full Member," https://www.euractiv.com/section/uk-europe/news/eu-says-united-ireland-would-be-automatic-full-member/.

01-06-207: "Brexit GDP Losses to Dwarf Britain's EU Budget Contributions," https://www.euractiv.com/section/uk-europe/news/brexit-gdp-losses-to-dwarf-britains-eu-budget-contributions/.

12-06-2017: "'Brexit' Election Results in Alliance with DUP Anti-Abortionists," https://www.euractiv.com/section/freedom-of-thought/news/brexit-election-results-in-alliance-with-dup-anti-abortionists/.

13-06-2017: "EU Seeks Post-Brexit Powers over London Euro Clearing," https://www.euractiv.com/section/banking-union/news/eu-seeks-post-brexit-powers-over-london-euro-clearing/.

15-06-2017: "UK Imports and Exports will Suffer from Brexit Isolation," https://www.euractiv.com/section/economy-jobs/news/uk-imports-and-exports-will-suffer-from-brexit-isolation/.

19-06-2017: "Brexit Talks Start with Smiles, Focus on Tough Issues," https://www.euractiv.com/section/uk-europe/news/brexit-talks-start-with-smiles-focus-on-tough-issues/.

23-06-2017: "Merkel Calls UK Offer on Citizens' Rights a 'Good Start'," https://www.euractiv.com/section/uk-europe/news/merkel-calls-uk-offer-on-citizens-rights-a-good-start/.

26-06-2017: "Britain's Offer to EU Nationals after Brexit," https://www.euractiv.com/section/uk-europe/news/britains-offer-to-eu-nationals-after-brexit/.

27-06-2017: "German Industry Warns 'Both Sides Underestimating' Brexit Talks," https://www.euractiv.com/section/uk-europe/news/german-industry-warns-both-sides-underestimating-brexit-talks/.

28-06-2017: "Irish PM Warns Turning Goodwill into Border Solution Looks 'Extremely Difficult'," https://www.euractiv.com/section/uk-europe/news/irish-pm-warns-turning-goodwill-into-border-solution-looks-extremely-difficult/.

03-07-2017: "Britain Moves to 'Take Back Control' Over Fishing in Its Waters," https://www.euractiv.com/section/uk-europe/news/britain-moves-to-take-back-control-over-fishing-in-its-waters/.

12-07-2017: "Barnier Tells Britain 'Trust Needed to Build New Relationship'," https://www.euractiv.com/section/uk-europe/news/barnier-tells-britain-trust-needed-to-build-new-relationship/.

19-07-2017: "UK Challenges Obligations to Every EU Programme," https://www.euractiv.com/section/uk-europe/news/uk-challenges-obligations-to-every-eu-programme/.

20-07-2017: "No Solution in Sight for Brexit's Controversial Issues," https://www.euractiv.com/section/uk-europe/news/no-solution-in-sight-for-brexit-controversial-issues/.

04-08-2017: "EU Fishing Boats can Operate in UK Waters after Brexit, Says Gove," https://www.euractiv.com/section/uk-europe/news/eu-fishing-boats-can-operate-in-uk-waters-after-brexit-says-gove/.

16-08-2017: "UK Links Trade to Post-Brexit Irish Border Plans," https://www.euractiv.com/section/economy-jobs/news/uk-links-trade-to-post-brexit-irish-border-plans/.

17-08-2017: "Britain Confident of Making Progress in Brexit Talks by October," https://www.euractiv.com/section/uk-europe/news/britain-confident-of-making-progress-in-brexit-talks-by-october/.

21-08-2017: "How the Post-Brexit Trade Deal Will Affect British Farmers," https://www.euractiv.com/section/agriculture-food/news/how-the-post-brexit-trade-deal-will-affect-british-farmers/.

22-09-2017: "May Asks for Two-Year Transition Deal after Brexit," https://www.euractiv.com/section/uk-europe/news/may-asks-2-year-transition-deal-after-brexit/.

22-09-2017: "Italians Approve of May's Speech Venue, But Not Content," https://www.euractiv.com/section/uk-europe/news/italians-approve-of-mays-speech-venue-but-not-by-content/.

03-10-2017: "Juncker Warns May Not to 'Go Over Barnier's Head'," https://www.euractiv.com/section/uk-europe/news/juncker-warns-may-not-to-go-over-michel-barniers-head/.

12-10-2017: "Brexit Talks Hit Cash Impasse, Barnier Worried About 'Thousands of Projects'," https://www.euractiv.com/section/uk-europe/news/brexit-talks-hit-cash-impasse-barnier-worried-about-thousands-of-projects/.

13-10-2017: "EU Summit to Offer May Hope of Talks on Post-Brexit Relationships," https://www.euractiv.com/section/uk-europe/news/eu-summit-to-offer-may-hope-of-talks-on-post-brexit-relationship/.

16-10-2017: "Guess Who's Coming for Dinner? Theresa May in Brussels Today," https://www.euractiv.com/section/uk-europe/news/guess-whos-coming-for-dinner-theresa-may-in-brussels-today/.

18-10-2017: "Firms Must Prepare for Hard Brexit, Irish Central Bank Says," https://www.euractiv.com/section/uk-europe/news/firms-must-prepare-for-hard-brexit-irish-central-bank-says/.

20-10-2017: "May Pleads for Brexit Deal She Can Sell at Home," https://www.euractiv.com/section/uk-europe/news/may-pleads-for-brexit-deal-she-can-sell-at-home/.

03-11-2017: "Livestock Farmers Warn MPs of Bleak Future After Hard Brexit," https://www.euractiv.com/section/agriculture-food/news/livestock-farmers-warn-mps-of-bleak-future-after-hard-brexit/.

06-11-2017: "Most EU Firms Plan Retreat from UK Suppliers," https://www.euractiv.com/section/uk-europe/news/most-eu-firms-plan-retreat-from-uk-suppliers/.

07-11-2017: "EU Finance Chiefs Thrash Out Post-Brexit Future," https://www.euractiv.com/section/economic-governance/news/eu-finance-chiefs-thrash-out-post-brexit-future/.

08-11-2017: "EU Ambassadors 'Brainstorm' Post-Brexit Ties," https://www.euractiv.com/section/future-eu/news/eu-ambassadors-brainstorm-post-brexit-ties/.

08-11-2017: "Denmark Warns of 'Severe' Brexit Impact on Fishermen," https://www.euractiv.com/section/uk-europe/news/denmark-warns-of-severe-brexit-impact-on-fishermen/.

08-11-2017: "Irish PM Sees Brexit Talks Moving to Next Stage in December," https://www.euractiv.com/section/uk-europe/news/irish-pm-sees-brexit-talks-moving-to-next-stage-in-december/.

09-11-2017: "Brexit Talks Resume, Slow Progress Set to Cause Delays in Roadmap," https://www.euractiv.com/section/uk-europe/news/brexit-talks-resume-slow-progress-set-to-cause-delays-in-roadmap/.

10-11-2017: "EU Concerned About Slow-Moving Brexit Talks," https://www.euractiv.com/section/uk-europe/news/eu-concerned-about-slow-moving-brexit-talks/.

13-11-2017: "UK No Closer to Revealing Brexit Bill Offer," https://www.euractiv.com/section/uk-europe/news/uk-no-closer-to-revealing-brexit-bill-offer/.

27-11-2017: "Liam Fox: No Irish Border Deal Before EU Trade Agreement," https://www.euractiv.com/section/uk-europe/news/liam-fox-no-irish-border-deal-before-eu-trade-agreement/.

04-12-2017: "Ireland 'Disappointed' Following Theresa May's Brussels Talks," https://www.euractiv.com/section/uk-europe/news/ireland-disappointed-following-theresa-mays-brussels-talks/.

07-12-2017: "Davis: Britain Has Not Formally Assessed Impact of Brexit on Economy," https://www.euractiv.com/section/uk-europe/news/davis-britain-has-not-formally-assessed-impact-of-brexit-on-economy/.

08-12-2017: "Brexit Breakthrough as Commission Says 'Sufficient Progress' Made," https://www.euractiv.com/section/uk-europe/news/may-in-brussels-amid-talk-of-brexit-breakthrough/.

13-12-2017: "EU Readies 'David Davis-Proof' Brexit Summit," https://www.euractiv.com/section/uk-europe/news/eu-readies-david-davis-proof-brexit-summit/.

20-12-2017: "Post-Brexit 'Free Trade' Talks with UK to Start in January, EU Says," https://www.euractiv.com/section/uk-europe/news/post-brexit-free-trade-talks-with-uk-to-start-in-january-eu-says/.

04-01-2018: "Tony Blair Warns British Voters: Time is Running Out to Stop Brexit Folly," https://www.euractiv.com/section/uk-europe/news/tony-blair-warns-british-voters-time-is-running-out-to-stop-brexit-folly/.

08-01-2018: "May to Appoint a 'No Deal' Brexit Minister in Cabinet Reshuffle," https://www.euractiv.com/section/uk-europe/news/may-to-appoint-a-no-deal-brexit-minister-in-cabinet-reshuffle/.

09-01-2018: "Bemused Commission Defends Planning for 'No Deal' Brexit," https://www.euractiv.com/section/uk-europe/news/bemused-commission-defends-planning-for-no-deal-brexit/.

11-01-2018: "UK Ministers Make Brexit Pitch to Germany Over Barnier's Head," https://www.euractiv.com/section/uk-europe/news/uk-ministers-make-brexit-pitch-to-germany-over-barniers-head/.

12-01-2018: "UK Won't Pay to Access Single Market Post-Brexit," https://www.euractiv.com/section/uk-europe/news/uk-wont-pay-to-access-single-market-post-brexit/.

09-02-2018: "Irish Border Checks 'Unavoidable' If UK Leaves Single Market, Warns Barnier," https://www.euractiv.com/section/uk-europe/news/irish-border-checks-unavoidable-if-uk-leaves-single-market-warns-barnier/.

16-02-2018: "Employers Suggest Turkish-Style UK-EU Customs Union to Solve Brexit Impasse," https://www.euractiv.com/section/uk-europe/news/employers-suggest-turkish-style-uk-eu-customs-union-to-solve-brexit-impasse/.

21-02-2018: "'It's Absolute Shambles'—UK Manufacturers Demand Clarity on Brexit," https://www.euractiv.com/section/uk-europe/news/its-an-absolute-shambles-uk-manufacturers-demand-clarity-on-brexit/.

28-03-2018: "Brexit Financial Services Deal Will Be Difficult," https://www.euractiv.com/section/uk-europe/opinion/brexit-financial-services-deal-will-be-difficult/.

11-04-2018: "Brexit: 'Most Difficult Part is Still to Come', Warns Barnier," https://www.euractiv.com/section/uk-europe/interview/brexit-most-difficult-part-is-still-to-come-warns-barnier/.

19-04-2018: "Theresa May Suffers Embossing Brexit Defeat in Parliament's Upper House," https://www.euractiv.com/section/uk-europe/news/theresa-may-suffers-embarrassing-brexit-defeat-in-parliaments-upper-house/.

24-04-2018: "Commission Defends 'Equivalence' with UK for Financial Services," https://www.euractiv.com/section/uk-europe/news/commission-defends-equivalence-with-uk-for-financial-services/.

26-04-2018: "Customs Union: The Least Bad Brexit Compromise that Nobody Wants," https://www.euractiv.com/section/uk-europe/news/customs-union-the-least-bad-brexit-compromise-that-nobody-wants/.

30-04-2018: "Barnier Warns Brexit Deal at Risk over Irish Border," https://www.euractiv.com/section/uk-europe/news/barnier-warns-brexit-deal-at-risk-over-irish-border/.

14-05-2018: "France Says June is 'Ultimate Deadline' for Brexit Progress on Irish Border," https://www.euractiv.com/section/uk-europe/news/france-says-june-is-ultimate-deadline-for-brexit-progress-on-irish-border/.

15-05-2018: "'The Clock is Ticking'—EU Warns Britain of Poor Brexit Progress," https://www.euractiv.com/section/uk-europe/news/the-clock-is-ticking-eu-warns-britain-of-poor-brexit-progress/.

05-07-2018: "Carmaker Jaguar Says 'Bad Brexit' Would Mean it Could Not Stay in UK," https://www.euractiv.com/section/uk-europe/news/carmaker-jaguar-says-bad-brexit-would-mean-it-could-not-stay-in-uk/.

08-07-2018: "Key Points of Britain's Post-Brexit Trade Plan," https://www.euractiv.com/section/all/news/key-points-of-britains-post-brexit-trade-plan/.

09-07-2018: "Brexit Minister Davis Steps Down in Big Blow to May," https://www.euractiv.com/section/uk-europe/news/brexit-minister-davis-steps-down-in-big-blow-to-may/.

12-07-2018: "UK Brexit Paper Backs Ukraine-Style Association Pact," https://www.euractiv.com/section/uk-europe/news/uk-brexit-paper-backs-ukraine-style-association-pact/.

13-07-2018: "May's Brexit Blueprint Faces Backlash after Sacrificing Services," https://www.euractiv.com/section/uk-europe/news/mays-brexit-blueprint-faces-backlash-after-sacrificing-services/.

19-07-2018: "European Economy to Lose 1.5% of GDP with 'No-Deal' Brexit," https://www.euractiv.com/section/uk-europe/news/european-economy-to-lose-1-5-of-gdp-with-no-deal-brexit/.

19-07-2018: "EU Commission: Keep Calm and Brace for Hard Brexit," https://www.euractiv.com/section/uk-europe/news/eu-commission-keep-calm-and-brace-for-hard-brexit/.

20-07-2018: "UK to Warn Public Every Week Over 'No-Deal Brexit'," https://www.euractiv.com/section/uk-europe/news/uk-to-warn-public-every-week-over-no-deal-brexit/.

23-07-2018: "Irish PM Tours EU Capitals as Fears of Hard Brexit Grow," https://www.euractiv.com/section/uk-europe/news/irish-pm-tours-eu-capitals-as-fears-of-hard-brexit-grow/.

25-07-2018: "Theresa May Takes Control of Brexit Talks," https://www.euractiv.com/section/uk-europe/news/theresa-may-takes-control-of-brexit-talks-raab-to-focus-on-domestic-preparation/.

27-07-2018: "U Rejects Britain's Key Elements of Special Customs Plan after Brexit," https://www.euractiv.com/section/uk-europe/news/eu-rejects-britains-key-elements-of-special-customs-plan-after-brexit/.

31-07-2018: "Hard Brexit Not an Option, Britain's Car Industry Warns," https://www.euractiv.com/section/uk-europe/news/hard-brexit-not-an-option-britains-car-industry-warns/.

31-07-2018: "MPs Lambast May Government's 'Failure' To Set Out Post-Brexit Migration Rules," https://www.euractiv.com/section/uk-europe/news/mps-lambast-may-governments-failure-to-set-out-post-brexit-migration-rules/.

02-08-2018: "Ambitious EU-UK Trade Deal Possible after Brexit, Need Ireland Solution First," https://www.euractiv.com/section/uk-europe/news/ambitious-eu-uk-trade-deal-possible-after-brexit-need-ireland-solution-first/.

20-08-2018: "UK Warns of Damage to EU without Special Deal on Financial Services," https://www.euractiv.com/section/uk-europe/news/uk-warns-of-damage-to-eu-without-special-deal-on-financial-services/.

21-08-2018: "Brexit Talks 'Continuous', Say Negotiators As They Vow to Ramp Up Talks," https://www.euractiv.com/section/uk-europe/news/brexit-talks-continuous-say-negotiators-as-they-vow-to-ramp-up-talks/.

11-09-2018: "EU Leaders Brace for Emergency Brexit Summit in Mid-November," https://www.euractiv.com/section/uk-europe/news/eu-leaders-brace-for-emergency-brexit-summit-in-mid-november/.

18-09-2018: "UK Should End Special Access for EU Migrants after Brexit—Report," https://www.euractiv.com/section/uk-europe/news/uk-should-end-special-access-for-eu-migrants-after-brexit-report/.

20-09-2018: "EU Leaders 'Nice' to May Buy No Sign of Brexit Deal," https://www.euractiv.com/section/uk-europe/news/eu-leaders-nice-to-may-but-no-sign-of-brexit-deal/.

20-09-2018: "Malta PM Claims EU Leaders 'Almost Unanimous' for Second Brexit Vote," https://www.euractiv.com/section/uk-europe/news/malta-pm-claims-eu-leaders-almost-unanimous-for-second-brexit-vote/.

21-09-2018: "EU Targets October Brexit Agreement, Ready for 'No Deal'," https://www.euractiv.com/section/uk-europe/news/eu-targets-october-brexit-agreement-ready-for-no-deal/.

21-09-2018: "May Blames EU for Brexit 'Impasse' as 'No Deal' Prospects Soar," https://www.euractiv.com/section/uk-europe/news/may-blames-eu-for-brexit-impasse-as-no-deal-prospects-soar/.

24-09-2018: "Labour Late-Night Meeting Strikes Decision on Second Brexit Referendum Stance," https://www.euractiv.com/section/uk-europe/news/labour-late-night-meeting-strikes-decision-on-second-brexit-referendum-stance/.

02-10-2018: "May Confirms EU Immigration Restrictions after Brexit," https://www.euractiv.com/section/uk-europe/news/may-confirms-eu-immigration-restrictions-after-brexit/.

03-10-2018: "Back Me or Risk Collapse of Brexit, Mat Warns Warring Tories," https://www.euractiv.com/section/uk-europe/news/back-me-or-risk-collapse-of-brexit-may-warns-warring-tories/.

03-10-2018: "Rhetoric, Boris and Alternate Brexit Realities in Birmingham," https://www.euractiv.com/section/uk-europe/news/rhetoric-boris-and-alternate-brexit-realities-in-birmingham/.

05-10-2018: "Tusk Slams UK Slurs on EU, Urges 'Canada+++' Brexit Deal," https://www.euractiv.com/section/uk-europe/news/tusk-slams-uk-slurs-on-eu-urges-canada-brexit-deal/.

15-10-2018: "Brexit Deal is Close. May Tells Fractious MPs," https://www.euractiv.com/section/uk-europe/news/brexit-deal-is-close-may-tells-fractious-mps/.

16-10-2018: "The Ulster Question: Taking 'the Union' Out of the Brexit Debate," https://www.euractiv.com/section/uk-europe/opinion/the-ulster-question-taking-the-union-out-of-the-brexit-debate/.

17-10-2018: "War on all Fronts as May Faces Puzzle of Brexit Rubik's Cube," https://www.euractiv.com/section/uk-europe/news/war-on-all-fronts-as-may-faces-puzzle-of-brexit-rubiks-cube/.

18-10-2018: "May and EU Consider Extending Transition to Break Brexit Impasse," https://www.euractiv.com/section/uk-europe/news/may-and-eu-consider-extending-transition-to-break-brexit-impasse/.

19-10-2018: "EU's Barnier Says 'Yes', Irish Border Issue Could Sink Brexit Deal," https://www.euractiv.com/section/uk-europe/news/eus-barnier-says-yes-irish-border-issue-could-sink-brexit-deal/.

08-11-2018: "EU Hopes Fade for November Summit to Seal Brexit Deal," https://www.euractiv.com/section/uk-europe/news/eu-hopes-fade-for-november-summit-to-seal-brexit-deal/.

13-11-2018: "EU, UK Reach Draft Brexit Deal but Details Remain Shrouded," https://www.euractiv.com/section/uk-europe/news/eu-uk-reach-draft-brexit-deal-but-details-remain-shrouded/.

15-11-2018: "EU Prepares Brexit War Plan for Weeks Ahead as Uncertainty Grows," https://www.euractiv.com/section/uk-europe/news/eu-prepares-brexit-war-plan-for-weeks-ahead-as-uncertainty-grows/.

15-11-2018: "The 585-Page Draft Brexit Agreement in a Nutshell," https://www.euractiv.com/section/uk-europe/news/the-585-page-draft-brexit-agreement-in-a-nutshell/.

15-11.2018: "May Wins Narrow Cabinet Backing for Brexit Deal," https://www.euractiv.com/section/uk-europe/news/may-wins-narrow-cabinet-backing-for-brexit-deal/.

16-11-2018: "UK Cabinet Chaos as May Tries to Steady the Ship," https://www.euractiv.com/section/uk-europe/news/uk-cabinet-chaos-as-may-tries-to-steady-the-ship/.

19-11-2018: "Brexit: Gibraltar Article Came 'Out of Nowhere,' Spain Says," https://www.euractiv.com/section/uk-europe/news/brexit-gibraltar-article-came-out-of-nowhere-spain-says/.

20-11-2018: "Brexit vs No Brexit at All: Government Agrees to Publish Forecasts," https://www.euractiv.com/section/uk-europe/news/brexit-vs-no-brexit-at-all-government-agrees-to-publish-forecasts/.

21-11-2018: "Days from EU Summit, May Takes Brexit Battle to Brussels," https://www.euractiv.com/section/uk-europe/news/days-from-eu-summit-may-takes-brexit-battle-to-brussels/.

25-11-2018: "Sadness the Flavour of the Day as EU27 Approve Brexit Deal," https://www.euractiv.com/section/uk-europe/news/sadness-the-flavour-of-the-day-as-eu27-approve-brexit-deal/.

10-12-2018: "May Presses on with Brexit Vote as MPs Demand Better Deal," https://www.euractiv.com/section/uk-europe/news/may-presses-on-with-brexit-vote-as-mps-demand-better-deal/.

10-12-2018: "EU Court Offers Brexit Way Out as May Moves to Delay Crunch Vote," https://www.euractiv.com/section/uk-europe/news/eu court-offers-brexit-way-out/.

10-12-2018: "Theresa May Buys One Last Chance after Shelving Brexit Vote," https://www.euractiv.com/section/uk-europe/news/theresa-may-buys-one-last-chance-after-shelving-brexit-vote/.

11-12-2018: "Juncker Warns May: 'No Room' to Renegotiate Brexit Deal," https://www.euractiv.com/section/uk-europe/news/juncker-warns-may-no-room-to-renegotiate-brexit-deal/.

12-12-2018: "May's Premiership Hangs by a Thread Ahead of EU Summit," https://www.euractiv.com/section/uk-europe/news/mays-premiership-hangs-by-a-thread-ahead-of-eu-summit/.

14-12-2018: "Warm Words but No Brexit Concessions, as May Leaves Brussels Empty-Handed," https://www.euractiv.com/section/uk-europe/news/warm-words-but-no-brexit-concessions-as-may-leaves-brussels-empty-handed/.

08-01-2019: "EU Looks at Help for May, But Will Not Rework Brexit Deal," https://www.euractiv.com/section/uk-europe/news/eu-looks-at-help-for-may-but-will-not-rework-brexit-deal/.

09-01-2019: "MPs Defeat May, Urge Her to Rule Out 'No Deal' Brexit," https://www.euractiv.com/section/uk-europe/news/mps-defeat-may-urge-her-to-rule-out-no-deal-brexit/.

09-01-2019: "EU Open to Brexit Delay, But Asks: 'What For?'," https://www.euractiv.com/section/uk-europe/news/eu-open-but-wary-on-british-interest-in-brexit-delay/.

15-01-2019: "May to Face Confidence Vote after Brexit Deal Suffers Crushing Defeat," https://www.euractiv.com/section/uk-europe/news/may-to-face-confidence-vote-after-brexit-deal-suffers-crushing-defeat/.

16-01-2019: "Tusk Hints at Cancellation, as UK Government Faces Crisis," https://www.euractiv.com/section/uk-europe/news/tusk-hints-at-brexit-cancellation-as-uk-government-faces-crisis/.

16-01-2019: "May Offers Cross-Party Talks after Surviving Confidence Vote," https://www.euractiv.com/section/uk-europe/news/may-offers-cross-party-brexit-talks-after-surviving-confidence-vote/.

29-01-2019: "Tear Up Irish Backstop, MPs Tell May in New Brexit Twist," https://www.euractiv.com/section/uk-europe/news/tear-up-irish-backstop-mps-tell-may-in-new-brexit-twist/.

04-02-2019: "May Will Seek 'Pragmatic' Solution to Brexit Deal in Brussels," https://www.euractiv.com/section/uk-europe/news/may-will-seek-pragmatic-solution-to-brexit-deal-in-brussels/.

04-02-2019: "Merkel Drops Hint of a 'Creative' Brexit Irish Backstop Compromise," https://www.euractiv.com/section/uk-europe/news/merkel-drops-hint-of-a-creative-brexit-irish-backstop-compromise/.

07-02-2019: "No Clarity on Post-Brexit Trade, Concedes UK Trade Minister," https://www.euractiv.com/section/uk-europe/news/no-clarity-on-post-brexit-trade-concedes-uk-trade-minister/.

12-02-2019: "'Something Has To Give,' Barnier Tells Brexit Britain," https://www.euractiv.com/section/uk-europe/news/something-has-to-give-barnier-tells-brexit-britain/.

25-02-2019: "Brexit Will Be Painful for the EU27 Too. This is Where It Will Hit Hardest," https://www.euractiv.com/section/economy-jobs/news/brexit-will-be-painful-for-the-eu27-too-this-is-where-it-will-hit-hardest/.

26-02-2019: "Diabetics Stock Up on Insulin Over Brexit Fears," https://www.euractiv.com/section/uk-europe/news/diabetics-stock-up-on-insulin-over-brexit-fears/.

26-02-2019: "May Offers MPs Three Month Extension to Brexit Talks," https://www.euractiv.com/section/uk-europe/news/may-offers-mps-three-month-extension-to-brexit-talks/.

05-03-2019: "May's Team Confident as Crunch Brexit Vote Looms," https://www.euractiv.com/section/uk-europe/news/mays-team-confident-as-crunch-brexit-vote-looms/.

11-03-2019: "Britain Braces for Decisive Week of Brexit Votes," https://www.euractiv.com/section/uk-europe/news/britain-braces-for-decisive-week-of-brexit-votes/.

12-03-2019: "May Gets 'Legally Binding' Assurances on Backstop from Last-Ditch Strasbourg Trip," https://www.euractiv.com/section/uk-europe/news/may-gets-legally-binding-assurances-on-backstop-from-last-ditch-strasbourg-trip/.

12-03-2019: "UK Set to Demand Brexit Extension after MPs Hand Heavy Defeat to May," https://www.euractiv.com/section/uk-europe/news/uk-set-to-demand-brexit-extension-after-mps-hand-heavy-defeat-to-may/.

13-03-2019: "EU to Ponder Brexit Delay Amid Calls for 'Credible Justification,'" https://www.euractiv.com/section/uk-europe/news/eu-to-ponder-brexit-delay-amid-calls-for-credible-justification/.

13-03-2019: "UK May Have to Hold Elections, May Warns after MPs Rule Out 'No Deal' Brexit," https://www.euractiv.com/section/uk-europe/news/uk-may-have-to-hold-eu-elections-may-warns-after-mps-rule-out-no-deal-brexit/.

14-03-2019: "May to Request Brexit Delay after MPs Back Extension," https://www.euractiv.com/section/uk-europe/news/may-to-request-brexit-delay-after-mps-back-extension/.

27-03-2019: "EU Lawmakers Urge UK to Adopt Alternative Brexit Plan," https://www.euractiv.com/section/uk-europe/news/eu-lawmakers-urge-uk-to-agree-on-alternative-brexit-plan/.

28-03-2019: "May's Offer to Quit Fails to Clean the Brexit Mess," https://www.euractiv.com/section/uk-europe/news/mays-offer-to-quit-fails-to-clean-the-brexit-mess/.

29-03-2019: "Pivotal Vote on 29 March: The Brexit Day that Wasn't," https://www.euractiv.com/section/uk-europe/news/pivotal-vote-on-29-march-the-brexit-day-that-wasnt/.

03-04-2019: "May Offers Cross-Party Talks, Increasing Hopes of Sift Brexit," https://www.euractiv.com/section/uk-europe/news/may-offers-cross-party-talks-increasing-hopes-of-soft-brexit/.

04-04-2019: "Leave Vote Softens but UK Still Split Down the Middle on Brexit, Says Polling Guru," https://www.euractiv.com/section/uk-europe/interview/leave-vote-softens-but-uk-still-split-down-the-middle-on-brexit-says-polling-guru/.

04-04-2019: "Common Vote 313 to 312 to Seek Brexit Extension," https://www.euractiv.com/section/uk-europe/news/commons-vote-313 to 312-to-seek-brexit-extension/.

05-04-2019: "On the Quiet, UK Prepares for 'Zombie' European Elections," https://www.euractiv.com/section/eu-elections-2019/news/on-the-quiet-uk-prepares-for-zombie-european-elections/.

08-04-2019: "May Urges 'Both Sides' to Compromise in Cross-Party Brexit Talks," https://www.euractiv.com/section/uk-europe/news/may-urges-both-sides-to-compromise-in-cross-party-brexit-talks/.

09-04-2019: "UK Almost Certain to Contest EU Elections as May Prepares to Make New Concessions," https://www.euractiv.com/section/uk-europe/news/uk-almost-certain-to-contest-eu-elections-as-may-prepares-to-make-new-concessions/.

11-04-2019: "Poll: Tories Facing Crushing Defeat If UK Holds EU Elections," https://www.euractiv.com/section/eu-elections-2019/news/poll-tories-facing-crushing-defeat-if-uk-holds-eu-elections/.

11-04-2019: "Trick or Treat for May as EU Leaders Agree on Halloween Brexit Date," https://www.euractiv.com/section/uk-europe/news/trick-or-treat-for-may-as-eu-leaders-agree-on-halloween-brexit-date/.

22-05-2019: "Theresa May's 'New Brexit Deal' Set for Rejection, Again," https://www.euractiv.com/section/uk-europe/news/theresa-mays-new-brexit-deal-set-for-rejection-again/.

24-05-2019: "May Expected to Announce Date of her Departure," https://www.euractiv.com/section/elections/news/may-expected-to-announce-date-of-her-departure/.

29-05-2019: "UK PM Frontrunner Boris Johnson Summoned to Court for Brexit 'Lies'," https://www.euractiv.com/section/uk-europe/news/uk-pm-frontrunner-boris-johnson-summoned-to-court-for-brexit-lies/.

03-06-2019: "Trump Brings Brexit Advice on State Visit to Troubled UK," https://www.euractiv.com/section/uk-europe/news/trump-brings-brexit-advice-on-state-visit-to-troubled-uk/.

04-06-2018: "Trump Offers UK 'Phenomenal' Post-Brexit Trade Deal," https://www.euractiv.com/section/economy-jobs/news/trump-offers-uk-phenomenal-post-brexit-trade-deal/.

11-06-2019: "Deal or No Deal? Britain's PM Hopefuls Divided Over Brexit," https://www.euractiv.com/section/uk-europe/news/deal-or-no-deal-britains-pm-hopefuls-divided-over-brexit/.

12-06-2019: "Johnson Vows to Re-Negotiate Brexit Deal as He Launches PM Bid," https://www.euractiv.com/section/uk-europe/news/johnson-vows-to-re-negotiate-brexit-deal-as-he-launches-pm-bid/.

11-07-2019: "New EU Chief Nominee Says Brexit Could Be Delayed Again," https://www.euractiv.com/section/uk-europe/news/new-eu-chief-nominee-says-brexit-could-be-delayed-again/.

25-07-2019: "Johnson Purges the No Deal Non-Believers," https://www.euractiv.com/section/uk-europe/news/pm-johnson-purges-the-no-deal-non-believers/.

26-07-2019: "EU Rebuffs Boris Johnson's Call to Rework Brexit Deal," https://www.euractiv.com/section/uk-europe/news/eu-rebuffs-boris-johnsons-call-to-rework-brexit-deal/.

30-08-2019: "UK, EU Brexit Teams to Meet Twice-Weekly in September," https://www.euractiv.com/section/uk-europe/news/uk-eu-brexit-teams-to-meet-twice-weekly-in-september/.

02-09-2019: "Johnson Mulls Snap Election as MPs Seek to Block No-Deal Brexit," https://www.euractiv.com/section/uk-europe/news/johnson-mulls-snap-election-as-mps-seek-to-block-no-deal-brexit/.

05-09-2019: "Johnson to Hold New Vote on Snap Election, as Brother Quits Over Brexit Strategy," https://www.euractiv.com/section/uk-europe/news/johnson-to-hold-new-vote-on-snap-election-as-brother-quits-over-brexit-strategy/.

19-09-2019: "Table Brexit Plans by September 30 or Talks are 'Over', Johnson Warned," https://www.euractiv.com/section/uk-europe/news/table-brexit-plans-by-september-30-or-talks-are-over-johnson-warned/.

24-09-2019: "No Brexit Breakthrough as Tusk, Johnson Meet in New York," https://www.euractiv.com/section/uk-europe/news/no-brexit-breakthrough-as-tusk-johnson-meet-in-new-york/.

01-10-2019: "Ireland Dismisses Reported UK Brexit Border Proposal," https://www.euractiv.com/section/uk-europe/news/ireland-dismisses-reported-uk-brexit-border-proposal/.

08-10-2019: "Tusk Tells British PM Johnson to Stop Playing 'Stupid' Brexit Blame Game," https://www.euractiv.com/section/uk-europe/news/tusk-tells-british-pm-johnson-to-stop-playing-stupid-brexit-blame-game/.

09-10-2019: "Britain's Brexit Talks with EU on Verge of Collapse," https://www.euractiv.com/section/uk-europe/news/britains-brexit-talks-with-eu-on-verge-of-collapse/.

11-10-2019: "New Brexit Hopes after Johnson and Varadkar Say 'Pathway to Deal' Exists," https://www.euractiv.com/section/uk-europe/news/new-brexit-hopes-after-johnson-and-varadkar-say-pathway-to-deal-exists/.

14-10-2019: "Britain, EU Enter Make-Or-Break Brexit Week," https://www.euractiv.com/section/uk-europe/news/britain-eu-enter-make-or-break-brexit-week/.

17-10-2019: "DUP Blocking Brexit Deal, Pound Plummets on Summit Day," https://www.euractiv.com/section/uk-europe/news/dup-blocking-brexit-deal-as-pound-plummets-on-summit-day/.

17-10-2019: "EU and UK on Brink of a Brexit Deal Despite Unionist Concerns," https://www.euractiv.com/section/uk-europe/news/eu-and-uk-on-brink-of-a-brexit-deal-despite-unionist-concerns/.

17-10-2019: "Johnson Gets His Deal and Plaudits, Now Eyes Shift to Westminster," https://www.euractiv.com/section/uk-europe/news/johnson-gets-his-deal-and-plaudits-now-eyes-shift-to-westminster/.

22-10-2019: "Explainer: As Johnson Pushes Ahead with Brexit, What Happens Now in UK's Parliament?" https://www.euractiv.com/section/uk-europe/news/explainer-as-johnson-pushes-ahead-with-brexit-what-happens-now-in-uks-parliament/.

22-10-2019: "UK Government to Abandon Brexit Bill If MPs Fail to Back Timetable," https://www.euractiv.com/section/uk-europe/news/breaking-uk-government-to-abandon-brexit-bill-if-mps-fail-to-back-timetable/.

22-10-2019: "Johnson's Deal Secures Majority but Parliament Pushes for Ratification Delay," https://www.euractiv.com/section/uk-europe/news/johnsons-deal-secures-majority-but-parliament-pushes-for-ratification-delay/.

24-10-2019: "Johnson Demands December Election, Abandons 'Do or Die' Brexit Promise," https://www.euractiv.com/section/uk-europe/news/johnson-demands-december-election-abandons-do-or-die-brexit-promise/.

28-10-2019: "EU Approves Brexit 'Flextension' Until 31 January," https://www.euractiv.com/section/uk-europe/news/eu-approves-brexit-flextension-until-31-january/.

29-10-2019: "Johnson Gets His Election as UK Lawmakers Finally Agree December Poll," https://www.euractiv.com/section/uk-europe/news/johnson-gets-his-election-as-uk-lawmakers-finally-agree-december-poll/.

13-12-2019: "Brexit Confirmed as Johnson Secures Decisive Win," https://www.euractiv.com/section/uk-europe/news/brexit-confirmed-as-johnson-secures-decisive-election-win/.

13-12-2019: "Brexit Battle Over: New Battles Begin," https://www.euractiv.com/section/uk-europe/news/brexit-battle-over-new-battles-begin/.

13-12-2019: "EU Leaders Prepare for Brexit after Johnson Win," https://www.euractiv.com/section/uk-europe/news/eu-leaders-prepare-for-brexit-after-johnson-win/.

30-12-2019: "Johnson Takes Control but Charts a Bumpy Brexit Course," https://www.euractiv.com/section/uk-europe/news/boris-takes-control-but-charts-a-bumpy-brexit-course/.

10-01-2020: "British Lawmakers Finally Approve Historic Brexit Deal," https://www.euractiv.com/section/uk-europe/news/british-lawmakers-finally-approve-historic-brexit-deal/.

24-01-2020: "EU Chiefs Sign Brexit Deal Ahead of Parliament Vote," https://www.euractiv.com/section/uk-europe/news/eu-chiefs-sign-brexit-deal-ahead-of-parliamentary-vote/.

31-01-2020: "'New Dawn' or 'Biggest Gamble'? UK Headlines on Brexit Day," https://www.euractiv.com/section/uk-europe/news/new-dawn-or-biggest-gamble-uk-headlines-on-brexit-day/.

About the Author

Finn Laursen (Cand. scient. pol. Aarhus University, Denmark, 1974; PhD in Political Science, University of Pennsylvania, Philadelphia, United States, 1980) holds a Jean Monnet Chair *ad personam* since 2007 and is an honorary professor at the University of Southern Denmark, Odense, where he was also Velux visiting professor March 2015–January 2017. He held the Canada Research Chair in European Union Studies at the Dalhousie University, Halifax, NS, Canada, 2006–2013, where he further directed the EU Centre of Excellence (EUCE). He was a researcher at the European University Institute (EUI) in Florence, 1977–1980, and a John Parker Compton visiting fellow at Princeton University, 1980–1981. Teaching positions include being a lecturer at the London School of Economics (LSE) (1985–1988); professor at the European Institute of Public Administration (EIPA), Maastricht, the Netherlands (1988–1995); professor and director, the Thorkil Kristensen Institute for East-West Studies at South Jutland University Centre, Esbjerg, Denmark (1995–1998); foreign professor, Tsukuba University, Japan (1998–1999); and professor of International Politics, University of Southern Denmark (1999–2006). He has published extensively. He has authored and edited or coedited about 25 books and published about 100 journal articles or book chapters. His articles have appeared in leading international journals, such as *World Politics, Ocean Development and International Law, Journal of Common Market Studies, Futures, Annals of the American Academy of Political and Social Science, International Review of Administrative Sciences, International Journal, Nordic Journal of International Law, Cooperation and Conflict, Journal of Legislative Studies,* and *l'Europe en formation.* Recent edited books include *The Rise and Fall of the Constitutional Treaty* (Nijhoff, 2008), *The EU in the Global Political Economy* (P.I.E. Peter Lang, 2009), *The EU as a Foreign and Security Policy Actor* (Republic of Letters Publishing, 2009), *Comparative Regional Integration: Europe and Beyond* (Ashgate, 2010), *The Making of the EU's Lisbon Treaty: the Role of the Member States* (P.I.E. Peter Lang, 2012), *The Lisbon Treaty: Institutional Choices and Implementation* (Ashgate, 2012), *The EU, Security and Transatlantic*

Relations (P.I.E. Peter Lang, 2012), *The EU and the Political Economy of Transatlantic Relations* (P.I.E. Peter Lang, 2012), *Designing the European Union: From Paris to Lisbon* (Palgrave Macmillan, 2012), *The EU and the Eurozone Crisis* (Ashgate 2013), and *EU Enlargement: Current Challenges and Strategic Choices* (P.I.E. Peter Lang, 2013). Recent fully authored books include *Historical Dictionary of the European Union* (Rowman & Littlefield, 2016), and *The Development of the EU as a Sea-Policy Actor: Fish, Ships and Navies* (Edward Elgar, 2020).

Since January 2015 Finn Laursen has also been a senior editor of *Oxford Research Encyclopedia of Politics* (OREP), and from March 2017 he has been editor-in-chief of the *Oxford Encyclopedia of European Union Politics*, which is due to be published in a multivolume print edition in early 2021.

CPSIA information can be obtained
at www.ICGtesting.com
Printed in the USA
LVHW091655010921
696699LV00001B/14

9 781538 113608